THE GOVERNANCE OF FEMALE DRUG USERS
Women's experiences of drug policy

Natasha Du Rose

First published in Great Britain in 2015 by

Policy Press   North America office:
University of Bristol   Policy Press
1-9 Old Park Hill   c/o The University of Chicago Press
Bristol   1427 East 60th Street
BS2 8BB   Chicago, IL 60637, USA
UK   t: +1 773 702 7700
t: +44 (0)117 954 5940   f: +1 773 702 9756
pp-info@bristol.ac.uk   sales@press.uchicago.edu
www.policypress.co.uk   www.press.uchicago.edu

© Policy Press 2015

British Library Cataloguing in Publication Data
A catalogue record for this book is available from the British Library

Library of Congress Cataloging-in-Publication Data
A catalog record for this book has been requested

ISBN 978 1 84742 672 7 hardcover

The right of Natasha Du Rose to be identified as author of this work has been asserted by her in accordance with the Copyright, Designs and Patents Act 1988.

All rights reserved: no part of this publication may be reproduced, stored in a retrieval system, or transmitted in any form or by any means, electronic, mechanical, photocopying, recording, or otherwise without the prior permission of Policy Press.

The statements and opinions contained within this publication are solely those of the author and not of the University of Bristol or Policy Press. The University of Bristol and Policy Press disclaim responsibility for any injury to persons or property resulting from any material published in this publication.

Policy Press works to counter discrimination on grounds of gender, race, disability, age and sexuality.

Cover design by Policy Press
Front cover image: Vassiliki Koutsothanasi
Printed and bound in Great Britain by CPI Group (UK) Ltd, Croydon, CR0 4YY
Policy Press uses environmentally responsible print partners

Contents

Acknowledgements		iv
About the author		v
Introduction		1
Part One		**15**
one	Research context	17
two	Political context	43
Part Two		**61**
three	Prohibition	67
four	Medicalisation	91
five	Welfarisation	117
Part Three		**137**
six	Psychosocial accounts	151
seven	Social stories	203
Conclusion		269
Appendix: Research methods		277
Bibliography		279
Index		341

Acknowledgements

I would like to thank all my family and friends who have supported me over the years, with a special thanks to my husband, Matthew John Tan. This book is dedicated to all the women interviewed for this study, and all women who have taken drugs and suffered at the hands of 'the authorities'. The book is also dedicated to my baby boy, Byron Melvin Tan.

About the author

Natasha Du Rose is a senior lecturer in criminology at the University of Roehampton. She has extensive research experience in drug use and policy and has also conducted research on restorative justice and self-injury. Before receiving her PhD at the University of Bath in 2006, Natasha worked in women's therapy and crisis centres for seven years, co-ordinating and training helpline volunteers and training professionals on women's mental health.

Introduction

This book is about the ways in which the governance of illicit drug use shapes female users' lives. It examines how women drug users' subjectivities, and hence their experiences, are shaped and regulated by drug policies. The construction of female users' subjectivities in policy discourse and the impact the characteristics ascribed to them has on these women's experiences are explored. The insights are based on in-depth accounts from the perspectives of women users themselves. It is argued that in the regulation of illicit drug-using women, particular subjectivities are constructed which, in themselves, become part of the narrative sustaining women in their problematic drug use. It is suggested that women users experience drug policy as something that exacerbates their social and economic marginalisation, and contributes to their lives being plunged into further poverty, social and economic marginalisation.

At the same time, the book analyses the contradictory choices, adaptations and resistances of female users. Although women users internalise many of the negative constructions of themselves found in policy discourse, they also find ways to resist them. Their resistances are explored through an examination of the pleasurable and painful aspects of the women's drug use; drug use as a means of escape from oppressive social circumstances; the social inclusion and 'belonging' found in marginalisation; the agency, rationality and control wielded in the face of 'chaos'; and the women's responses to the negative impacts of the treatment, welfare and criminal justice systems. In this process, I subvert popular misconceptions of women users that condition oppressive interventions, and hope to contribute to the formulation of drug policies based on empowerment, gender equity and social justice.

The rest of this chapter discusses the main theoretical schools of thought informing the arguments in the book, including feminist sociological perspectives, the work of Foucault on government, power and the subject, criminological and sociological theories of drug use, drug policy and the social order. Finally, it provides an outline of the book's contents.

Governing mentalities

The main concepts and arguments in this book draw on the theoretical works of Foucault and the concept of governmentality, in particular, the 'art of government' (Foucault, 2002 [1978], p 201). This refers to the mentalities, techniques and procedures for managing the habits of subjects. Governmentality is concerned with ways of thinking ('rationalities') and ways of doing ('technologies'). These governing mentalities and tactics are deployed not only by the state, but also by a whole variety of authorities, including the individual subject, in practices of self-regulation. The adoption of a governmentality approach is thus a fruitful way of opening up the terrain and experience of policy for analysis.

The concept of governmentality is used not only as a critical tool, but also as a way of seeing and understanding how women's illicit drug use has been governed. It facilitates an understanding of government not simply as the management of a given set of social issues, but as a process through which particular phenomena come to be identified as social problems and targeted for intervention. It allows questions to be asked concerning how women users are governed, or more specifically, how female users as objects of government are constructed, and what rationalities condition these constructions. In this respect, the 'problem' of women's illicit drug use is understood as a realm brought into existence by government itself. The governmentality approach is compatible with critical strands in the drug debate, within which the 'war on drugs' is viewed as not actually founded in scientific knowledge about the dangerousness of drugs. Rather, it is viewed as originating in colonialism, imperialism, the control of 'immigrants', Christian morality and the moral regulation of female sexuality (Boyd, 2004). The 'problem' of women's drug use within this framework can be seen as not to do with individual, pathological behaviour, but as rooted in a war that has been waged on them. This framework can also, of course, be used to understand men's illicit drug use (see 'A feminist sociological perspective', p 7-8).

Political power is not understood as emanating simply from the actions of the state and its agencies (Rose and Miller, 1992, Rose, 1996). The state is just one instrument of government (Carrington, 1993, p xv). The governmentality approach draws attention to the diversity of forces that, in heterogeneous ways, seek to shape, guide, correct and modify the behaviour of female illicit drug users. The art of government involves non-state agencies such as the family, the school and the workplace, as well as state agencies such as the criminal justice system and the medical profession. It is not concentrated in the state apparatus, but is dispersed through a multitude of locales and authorities (Garland, 1999). These include:

- State agencies such as the criminal justice system, the medical profession and social services.
- Non-state agencies such as the family, drugs subcultures and voluntary organisations.
- Institutions, including hospitals, prisons, courtrooms, hostels and rehabilitation centres.
- Rationalities such as freedom, equality, welfare, justice and economic growth.
- Technologies, including the ascription of characteristics, normalisation and responsibilisation.
- Norms – 'technologies which have been internalized to the extent that they are not recognized as technologies at all' (Worrall, 1990, p 9).
- Practices such as incarceration, methadone maintenance, needle exchanges and drugs counselling.
- Individuals such as drugs workers, doctors, nurses, midwives, housing officers, counsellors, boyfriends, friends and family members.

This approach enables a form of investigation into the social control and regulation of female drug users that moves beyond the idea of governmental power as a centralised, top-down process. It allows for the consideration of the diversity of forces that bring the thoughts, actions, choices and aspirations of women who use illicit drugs into alignment with the objectives of government.

Governmentality is often referred to as 'government at a distance' as it refers to a set of techniques or technologies of governance where members play an active role in their own self-governance (Miller and Rose, 1990; Rose 1996). Foucault argues that a population's government is a highly 'personal' matter involving reflections on modes of living, on choices of existence, on the way to regulate one's behaviour, and the attachment of oneself to certain ends and means (Foucault, 2000 [1982], p 89). Within this mode of governance individuals are constituted as free, choice-making, entrepreneurs of themselves, and through this freedom of choice are obliged to maximise their lives (Rose et al, 2006).

Governmental power is not imposed on subjects but is transmitted by and through them. Relations of power involve the assumption of a 'free subject'. This doesn't mean an individual who enjoys a space of freedom, but 'one whose subjection is consistent with forms of choice' (Dean, 1994, p 178). As Foucault argues:

> Power is exercised only over free subjects, and only insofar as they are "free." By this we mean individual or collective subjects who are faced with a field of possibilities in which several kinds of conduct, several modes of behaviour are available. (2002 [1982], p 342)

Governmental power thus presupposes and requires the agency of those it seeks to govern. Agency here refers not to the intentions of an individual, but to their capability of exerting power or producing an effect. Foucault also argues that 'where there is power, there is resistance' (1990 [1976], p 95). Agency and the possibility of resistance to power are thus always present in power relations. Hence, even when technologies of domination are in operation, they only constitute one side of a system through which individuals are governed (Burchell, 1996). Foucault's notion of governmentality thus enables the avoidance of an analysis through which women are either constituted as the passive victims of men and/or drugs or as rational, 'free' agents in a world devoid of power structures and systems of domination. It opens up the space for an investigation into the governmental subjection of female illicit drug users that takes account of their freedom, agency and choice.

The project of the self as a desiring, consuming, enterprising, self-making entity is at the same time a technique of government whereby individuals feel obliged to self-govern. Social control is thus individualised and internalised (Reith, 2004). This has been described as the move from act to identity-based governance, where individuals are governed through who they are rather then what they do (Valverde, 1997; Rose, 1999; Reith, 2004). Governance involves 'the shaping of particular kinds of subjectivity' (Reith, 2004, p 294). The subject is not conceived of as a given entity or substance, but as a changing form that is organised, shaped and dislocated within various discursive fields and relations of power. Therefore, the government of women's illicit drug use doesn't just simply involve the external regulation of the women's actions and behaviours; it involves the self-regulating capacities of the women themselves, their internal thoughts, feelings and desires. As Rose (1990, p 1) argues:

> Our personalities, subjectivities, and "relationships" are not private matters.... On the contrary they are intensively governed.... Thoughts, feelings and actions may appear as the very fabric and constitution of the intimate self, but they are socially organised and managed in minute particulars.

This book examines how the subjectivities of women's illicit drug use are 'intensively governed' (Rose, 1990, p 1). It does so by examining the operation of various technologies of power that operate in the lives of 40 female users. It explores how women users make sense of their drug taking, and how their problematic illicit drug use is shaped and sustained by the regulation of their drug-using identities through the technologies of power analysed.

Expertise

Crucial to governing at a distance is the authoritative knowledge of 'experts' who promote individual self-advancement. According to Foucault, over the late 19th and early 20th century the rise of the modern professions such as medicine, psychiatry and law, the language of expertise and the authority attached to them involved 'a radical extension of the capacity to govern' (Johnson, 1993, p 142). The authority of expertise became inextricably linked to the formal political apparatus of rule (Rose, 1996). 'Truths' were produced and disseminated by the positive sciences of economics, statistics, sociology, medicine, biology, psychology and psychiatry. The rise of 'expert' figures involved the exercise of 'authority and the deployment of a range of scientific and technical knowledges' (Rose, 1996, p 39). Consequently, more aspects of the self became amenable to governmental control and surveillance.

The 'psy' sciences in particular, such as psychology, psychiatry, social work, counselling and therapy, have been identified as effective tools in achieving the desired objectives of government (Rose, 1999). Rose (1999) argues that in modern liberal societies, various 'experts' or 'engineers of the soul' provide authority and guidance on the management of every aspect of inner life including consumption. He observes:

> In compelling, persuading and inciting subjects to disclose themselves, finer and more intimate regions of personal and interpersonal life come under surveillance and are opened

up for expert judgment, and normative evaluation, for classification and correction. (Rose, 1990, p 240)

Women's susceptibility to the control and surveillance of the 'psy' sciences and the medical profession is gendered. Women outnumber men as patients of depression, anxiety and somatic symptoms, are more likely to seek help from and disclose mental health problems to their primary healthcare physician, and to be prescribed psychotropic drugs (WHO, 2009). Women also visit doctors more often as the sole users of birth control products, due to their reproductive needs and as the caretakers of their families' health (Boyd, 2004). Global estimates and national estimates in the UK and US indicate that a third of illicit drug users are female (Simpson and McNulty, 2008). A recent study by the National Treatment Agency (NTA) (2010) in the UK found that contrary to in the past, women users are '"well represented" in drug treatment services' (NTA, 2010, p 5). However, the key issues are (a) historically expert knowledge has designed interventions and treatments predominantly aimed at male users, and (b) many interventions and treatments specific to female users situate them as pathological or unfit mothers.

Technologies of power

The control and surveillance of female (and male) illicit drug users is administered through various governmental technologies of power. This book investigates the dominant governmental technologies of power from which the key constructions of women as problematic drug users emanate. Technologies of power are the ways of acting or the programmes, techniques, tactics, procedures and apparatuses through which authorities seek to give effect to governmental objectives (Foucault, 2000 [1982], p 225). Prohibition and punishment, medicalisation and welfarisation are the key governmental techniques of power through which female users are governed. They are viewed as 'technologies of domination' (Foucault, 2000 [1982], p 225), that is, practices of power that constrain and limit in order to shape conduct. The technology of prohibition is the practice of prohibiting the manufacture, transportation, import, export, sale and consumption of certain drugs by law. Medicalisation is a technology through which non-medical problems come to be defined and treated as if they are medical issues. Welfarisation is the process that constructs individuals or groups as needing social support, or constitutes them as unworthy of it.

The book also explores how female users are governed and govern themselves through 'technologies of the self' (Foucault 2000 [1982], p 225). These are 'the means by which individuals determine their identity, maintain it or transform it' (Foucault, 2000 [1969], p 87). The technologies of the self examined are the ascription of characteristics, normalisation and responsibilisation. The ascription of characteristics is the process through which subjects come to embody particular identities or subjectivities. It is the means by which women are defined, categorised and differentiated from others within various discursive fields and relations of power. Normalisation is the process through which deviant subjects are brought into conformity with a constructed norm (Foucault, 1991 [1975], pp 183-4). Technologies of normalisation operate by identifying norms of conduct and setting up techniques for distinguishing and correcting individuals deviating from these norms (Foucault, 1991 [1975], pp 183-4). Finally, the technology of responsibilisation establishes techniques that constitute individuals and non-state agencies as responsible for meeting the objectives of central government. All these technologies are understood as operating as gendered forms of control and regulation, and are discussed in more detail in Parts Two and Three of the book.

A feminist sociological perspective

Although the focus of this study is on the ways female illicit drug users are governed, the governmental technologies of power discussed shape and regulate the experiences of male *and* female users. Male users are subject to the same governmental forces, and therefore many of the arguments presented in this book also apply to them. However, this book explores the specific and particular ways in which women experience drug policy and the impact it has on their lives. The critical orientation of this book is guided by feminist sociological perspectives and feminist research and theorising about women's drug use. This approach begins from the assumption that women experience social situations differently, and need different facilities from men. Gaining an understanding of women's lives therefore requires separate investigation. Although this book does not focus on men's illicit drug use, it is acknowledged that interventions aimed at men are not gender-free, and men also receive gendered forms of intervention in accordance with the social construction of masculinity that require separate analysis. Female illicit drug users face gendered forms of intervention, treatment, control and surveillance not experienced by men who use illicit drugs, including during pregnancy, as mothers, and generally, in relation to their sexual behaviour.

A comparative approach

The book takes a comparative approach to the analysis of drug policy, and evaluates the evidence regarding its impact on female users in the UK, US and Canada. It explores how drug policy has an impact on the lives of drug-using and offending women in the UK, and compares and contrasts this with impacts experienced by women users and offenders in other Western neoliberal states. The UK, US and Canada are all subject to the same global prohibition approach established by the United Nations (UN) Single Convention of 1961, the same approach which applies to a greater or lesser extent to countries all over the world. The US is of comparative interest as it has led the world in instigating and leading global drug prohibition, and continues to be seen as one of the most punitive Western countries in terms of drug law enforcement and the incarceration of its drug offenders. It provides an illustration of some of the harshest impacts of governmental technologies on female and male illicit drug users in the Western world. At one time the UK was seen as one of the leading countries in the world for its treatment rather than criminal justice and punishment-focused approach to drug law enforcement. In recent decades, however, it seems to have moved towards a more criminal justice-oriented US regulatory model, as have other Western countries, such as Sweden, although it is acknowledged that there are other Western countries, including the Netherlands, Belgium, Portugal and the Czech Republic, and some US states such as Colorado, Washington and California, that have moved in the other direction.

As a comparative country, Canada sits somewhere between the US and the UK in terms of its emphasis on punishment and treatment respectively. Regardless of the emphasis placed on criminal justice, treatment or welfare, the UK, US and Canada all provide a good illustration of the regulatory powers of the 'helping' professions, and how treatment, welfare and punitive forces can combine to create a complex and efficient form of governmental control, surveillance and regulation in the lives of female (and male) drug users. The book does not provide a comprehensive review of all the evidence available for the three countries; rather, it provides an analysis of the impact of the operation of governmental technologies of power on the lives of female drug users. Selected substantive examples from the three countries are used to illustrate specific points of analysis. The approach is considered a useful one in that it avoids isolationism and can provide reflections on similarities and differences that can potentially stimulate points of action. It is informed by some empirical work involving qualitative interviews with a sample of 40 female drug users in three English cities in the UK. The interview data provides an in-depth case study of how UK drug policy has an impact on female illicit drug users' lives based on the perspectives of the women themselves, and allows for an analysis of the range of governmental techniques that govern their subjectivities.

Outline of the book

The book is divided into three parts. Part One consists of two chapters; Chapter One provides an overview of the research context in which contemporary drug policy has emerged by examining early constructions of female drug users in academic discourse, for instance, as pathological or as bad mothers. It is argued that academic or 'expert' discourses help to identify women's drug use as a problem to be governed and contribute to the formation of social policies. Feminist challenges to traditional work on female users and the contribution this book will make is also discussed.

Chapter Two discusses the political context in which the research was undertaken. It provides an insight into the 'mentalities', 'governmental rationalities' or 'political rationalities' embedded in governmental approaches to female illicit drug use. The historical basis of prohibition, the illegal/legal drug divide created by prohibition, and how it operates as a gendered, 'race' and class-based form of governance is explored. How prohibition and the 'war on drugs' is wielded within the political climate of neoliberalism is examined, and how this is linked to the ascendancy of the 'risk' approach to governing illicit drug use and the process of 'othering' it sustains is also examined. The aim of this chapter is therefore to provide a general picture of the political domain in which specific drug policies in the UK, US and Canada have emerged. The discussion also aims to provide a framework for the ensuing chapters that focus more closely on the specific governmental techniques and procedures used in the control and regulation of women's illicit drug use.

Part Two provides a cross-national analysis of women's drug policy, not in terms of particular legislation and policies, but in terms of the key techniques of power deployed. Contemporary drug policy in the UK, US and Canada is constituted by discourses of prohibition and punishment, public health and social welfare. This part of the book investigates the rationalities of these discourses and the technologies of power underpinning them, including prohibition, medicalisation and welfarisation in the lives of female drug users. Chapter Three focuses on the impact of the technology of prohibition. It examines how the war on drugs is a war on women. The research evidence on the impact of drug policy on the lives of women users is discussed. How drug policy discourses in the UK, US and Canada construct the problem to be governed, including in terms of harm to the individual female user, to the community, children and foetuses, is explored. The chapter then outlines the proposed solutions to the 'problem' of women's drug use. Not all women are treated equally in the war on drugs, and some are responsibilised more than others, including black, poor and vulnerable women. Arguably, the war on drugs causes more harm to women than the drugs themselves. This idea is explored through research evidence on women in prison, the criminalisation of pregnancy and drug-using women's punishment and medicalisation as both offenders and victims of crime.

Chapter Four is concerned with the public health strand of drug policy discourse and the technology of medicalisation underpinning it. Medicalisation operates as a form of control and regulation whereby social structural issues such as poverty and social inequalities are individualised and deflected into the realm of disease. This chapter discusses the disease model of addiction, the construction of drug users and drug-using women in particular as pathological. How female users are situated in contemporary drug policy, as, on the one hand, irresponsible, bad choice makers, and on the other, as responsible for their predicament and for coming off drugs, are explored. Harm minimisation and recovery discourse, coercive policies and the marginalisation of women in treatment is discussed. It is argued that medicalisation has been deployed in part to facilitate and reinforce punishment regimes, widening the net of social control, and failing to address the social problems female users face.

Chapter Five discusses the social welfare strand of drug policy discourse and the technology of welfarisation. Welfarisation constructs individuals or groups as needing social support, or constitutes them as unworthy of it. How female drug users are targeted for welfarisation or 'soft policing' through formal and informal social control mechanisms is explored. Interventions in the lives of female users presented as policies and practices of welfare (concerned with their wellbeing) are often experienced as intrusive, coercive and punitive. This chapter investigates the surveillance and regulation of drug-using women through welfare and social work policies and practices. Some contextual background is provided, including neoliberal policies focusing on risk and responsibility rather than needs and rights. How welfarisation policies such as the denial of social security benefits and social work interventions have an impact on female users and their children is discussed.

Part Three is an analysis of the impact drug policy has on the lives of 40 female drug users. The impact of governmental technologies of power is explored through an examination of detailed life historical interviews that focus on how 40 female illicit drug users see themselves. The stories the women tell about their drug use, with a particular focus on the subject positions the women adopt for themselves, is examined. It takes into account the techniques of power discussed in Part Two, but also focuses on how authoritative discourses shape women drug users' identities by examining the key techniques of the self women users themselves deploy in the management of their drug-using identities. These include the ascription of characteristics, normalisation and responsibilisation. This part examines how female users are made visible, defined and categorised through the characteristics ascribed to them through 'authoritative' discourses. It also examines the normalisation and responsibilisation they experience at the hands of the 'authorities'. At the same time, it argues that female users do not passively internalise the characteristics ascribed to them, and nor do they simply accept attempts to normalise and responsibilise them, and their identities can also be seen as sites of resistance.

Chapter Six investigates the most dominant stories the women told: psychosocial stories in which they relate their experiences of drug use and the social conditions in which it occurs, to their psychological wellbeing. It explores how the psychosocial accounts provided by the women reflect the wider sociopolitical context in which their accounts occur, wherein illicit drug use is both psychologised and individualised. It examines how the women viewed themselves in various paradoxical ways that rendered them responsible for their own predicament. They saw themselves as chemically driven addicts, immoral criminals, bad mothers, self-medicating victims of abuse, and a waste of time and resources. At the same time, they saw themselves as 'normal' rational, free agents who wanted to be counselled, saved, educated and employed. The chapter also explores how within the women's psychosocial accounts there were traces of alternative subjectivities to those ascribed to them by 'the authorities'.

Chapter Seven demonstrates that although the psychosocial accounts the women provided were dominant, they also told other more social stories that relocate their lives in particular social and economic contexts. These accounts are tales of gender, poverty and regulation that undermine dominant and official understandings of the women. The women users saw themselves as rational choice makers in the context of economic and social disadvantage. They faced initially reduced options due to poverty, a disrupted education and limited job prospects. While in the discourse of 'the authorities' women drug users' maladaptive thinking rather than their social circumstance is seen as the cause of their drug dependence, the women did not see themselves as maladaptive or pathological. Instead, they interpreted their behaviour as adaptive, normal and understandable, given the poverty and marginalisation that characterised their lives.

Focusing on the intervention of social services, the treatment system and the criminal justice system, this chapter examines how the women experienced the very control mechanisms brought into place to deal with the perceived chaos in their lives, as plunging them into being out of control and in chaos. The very mechanisms used to 'help' the women, that is, treatment and social services, were often experienced as punitive. The criminal justice system not only punished the women by taking away their freedom, but also damaged their relationships with their children, destroyed their careers and/or job prospects and caused them to become homeless. The chapter examines how most of the women were punished through the criminal justice system for committing crimes to get money for drugs. At the same time, they had been victims of crimes of violence and abuse, the perpetrators of which had never been punished.

The women in this study expressed a desire to be 'normal', that is, to have a stable home, a job and/or a family. In the discourse of current drug policy, women drug users are constructed as socially marginalised but as saveable, programmable and changeable through the provision of education and/or employment. The women described a range of difficulties in overcoming social marginalisation and stopping drug use, including a lack of services to fit their needs, unsatisfactory services, exposure to others who were still using drugs, disillusionment about what a life without drugs could offer them, and being unable to imagine a life without drugs. Their accounts suggest that drug users are hindered by various issues when trying to get off heroin and/or crack that cannot be reduced to problems with access to education and/or employment. The women did not see themselves as immoral criminals, deserving of punishment or as programmable victims, but as normal, rational, adaptive women in the face of poverty, marginalisation, violence and victimisation. While personal motivation was seen as important in stopping drug use, most other factors seen as significant were social, concerning their social situation, relationships with helpers, partners and peers.

The final concluding chapter summarises the main arguments contained in the previous chapters, and explores some of the implications for policy. The research has shown that the contradictory basis of drug policy has real objective effects in the lives of female illicit drug users. It argues that the dichotomous programmable victim versus punishable criminal approach to drug policy is, to a large extent, fruitless. It is suggested that what is needed is a more integrated approach to drug policy that does not criminalise drug-using women or see them as maladaptive individuals who can or need to be reprogrammed. The chapter concludes that the contradictory axis on which drug policy is constituted means that a more holistic approach to dealing with drug users is not an option. As long as drug policy is based on a contradiction, too many dependent, female, drug users are likely to continue to feel their lives are hopeless, and drug policy itself will remain a hopeless cause.

Part One

Part One of the book begins from the premise that objects of government are discursively constructed. The meaning of female illicit drug use is not self-evident or an objective entity but is constructed in different discourses (e.g. prohibition, medical or welfare) and takes different forms. Drawing on Foucault's concepts of discourse and governmentality, the 'problem' of women's illicit drug use is understood as a realm brought into existence by government itself. As Foucault (1972) [1969] argues, discourses are formed by 'systems of dispersion' or 'forms of division' (Foucault 1972, [1969] p. 37) which 'systematically form the objects of which they speak' (Foucault 1972, p. 49). It is assumed that in order to gain an understanding of how women who use illicit drugs are governed, it is necessary to examine the discourses that define, categorise and differentiate them from others. It is these discourses that help to identify women's illicit drug use as a 'social problem' and make women who use illicit drugs amenable to governmental intervention and regulation.

This approach permits an analysis of illicit drug use and female (and male) illicit drug users that does not presume a chronological development of ideas advancing closer to the truth. Rather, it is one that allows for the exploration of the underlying points of differentiation, exclusion and contradiction in constructions of drug use and female users, as well as some of the material effects of these structuring principles. The accuracy and validity of particular constructions of drug taking and female drug users is not questioned. Rather, the underlying demarcations that condition the different constructions of drug use and women drug users are located. In this process, the space is revealed for alternative understandings of drug use and women's constructions of resistant identities.

Part One is comprised of two chapters investigating 'authoritative discourse' on female illicit drug use. Academic and drug policy discourses are understood as 'authoritative discourses' which construct and situate female drug users identities in particular ways. These discourses produce a particular network of material relations which involve the production of various material effects on the lives of female illicit drug users (i.e. their subjection to various forms of state intervention).

Chapter One analyses the various constructions of women drug users in academic discourse. It does not call into question the validity or accuracy of previous explanations of women's illicit drug use. Instead the different ways their illicit drug use has been made sense of and the different subject positions made available to them within academic discourse are traced. Academic discourse is understood as an authoritative discourse comprised of 'experts' with 'scientific' knowledge who help to inform and shape current drug policy. The assumption is that 'scientific' data is often used as a framework for social policies, and therefore how questions are framed within academic research has social consequences. An examination of early constructions of women drug users in academic discourse, for instance, as pathological and as bad mothers, is important as such constructions prevail in the formation of policy and in the governance of female drug use.

Chapter Two provides an overview of the key 'political rationalities' or 'government mentalities' underpinning contemporary drug policies in the UK, US and Canada. It investigates the political context conditioning the various techniques and procedures shaping and regulating female drug users. Prohibition, neoliberalism and risk-management are identified as central rationalities guiding contemporary drug policies and their impact on the ways female drug users are governed is considered.

ONE

Research context

This chapter discusses the research context in which this book is located, including the traditional inclination to view women's drug use as peripheral or pathological. It examines feminist work on female drug use and how this has challenged traditional understandings of female users. It concludes with a discussion of the contribution this book will make. This chapter investigates the various ways female illicit drug use has been made sense of and the different ways female users have been constructed within academic discourse. It explores how different explanations of women's illicit drug use have shaped the meaning of it in different ways and how the subject position of a female illicit drug user is continuously being modified and transformed as new and different explanations emerge in the chain of knowledge about it.

Traditionally, research on illicit drug use focused on male users, and women were ignored or seen as peripheral to predominantly male worlds of drug usage (File, 1976; Marsh, 1982; Jeffries, 1983; Gomberg, 1986). When the issue of female illicit drug use was focused on, the bulk of the research was concerned with women's deviation from traditional gender roles, pregnancy and motherhood (Rosenbaum, 1997). Early studies that did include women were predominantly medical, psychiatric and psychological, and based on women in treatment (Rosenbaum, 1981). Women were considered as a subset of a larger male population or compared with male users (Taylor, 1993). Within this literature female users were constructed as more deviant, 'sicker', passive and emotionally and psychologically disordered than male users and 'normal' women (Rosenbaum, 1981 1997; Taylor, 1993). By the 1970s a growing body of research, mostly from the US, began to appear on the physiological effects of women's illicit drug use on the foetus and newborn, and the 'management' of the pregnant user.

Baby vessels and bad mothers

The effect of women's illicit drug use on reproduction and childrearing largely dominated academic discourse on female illicit drug use in the 1960s and 1970s, and still continues to thrive, emerging from the clinical fields of obstetrics (see, for example, Naeye et al, 1973, 1976; Fraser, 1976; Kandall et al, 1976; Wilson et al, 1979; Lutiger et al, 1991; Mathias, 1992; Hepburn, 1993) and psychiatry and psychology (see, for example, Densen-Gerber et al, 1972; Carr et al, 1975; Pagliaro and Pagliaro, 1999). Within such studies, women users were considered predominantly in terms of their biology as bearers of children or as mothers. Female users were regarded as the 'independent variable', as the source of the problem under investigation. Constructed as 'baby vessels' and 'bad mothers', female users were positioned as irresponsible, selfish, indifferent to the needs of their foetuses and children, and incapable of bringing healthy children into society.

In early obstetrics studies on pregnant drug-using women, the needs of the woman and foetus were assumed to be in conflict. The analysis tended to be largely asocial, with no reference to confounding influences on foetal outcomes such as the mother's socioeconomic status, nutrition, health, alcohol and tobacco use, mental health, support networks, work stress or presence of an abusive relationship (see, for example, Kandall et al, 1976; Philips, 1986; Mathias, 1992; Hepburn, 1993). For example, an early UK study conducted by Fraser (1976) reports on 32 pregnancies in 29 women addicted to heroin or methadone over eight years in one obstetric department. The focus of the article is the effect of the mother's drug use on the unborn foetus. Fraser states that the women were all under 30, white and British, and that most of them had drug-addicted partners. The only other information provided about the women is on the medical complications of their pregnancies and their attendance at the antenatal clinic. Typically, they are characterised as antagonistic and uncooperative. Fraser (1976, pp 897-8) reports:

> Regrettably, the drug addict is notoriously uncooperative. Only 9 patients consented to admission and some of these discharged themselves.... Considerable tolerance is required towards these patients, who are antagonistic to society, who all too readily ignore advice, and who encourage potentially disastrous consequences for themselves and their children.

The 'bad' behaviour of the pregnant drug user is attributed to her craving for her drug of choice. Mothering becomes a matter of alternating 'love and indifference' for female illicit drug users, due to their 'ever increasing urge for drug relief' (Fraser, 1976, p 899). In such studies, sole responsibility for foetal wellbeing and children was seen as with pregnant or female drug users (that is, not with fathers or wider society).

In 1985 a case study by Ira Chasnoff in the US, which reported the damaging effects of cocaine use during pregnancy, set off a massive media response and a subsequent moral panic about an epidemic of 'crack babies' in the US (Coffin, 1996; Rosenbaum, 1997). By the late 1980s the government had stepped in, with nearly half the states in the US hoping to solve the 'problem' of drug use in pregnancy through prosecution (Rosenbaum, 1997). Due to the 'criminalisation of pregnancy', research on female drug use in the 1980s and 1990s in the US continued to be dominated by a concern with pregnancy and motherhood, particularly in relation to crack use. In contrast, in the UK and Canada in the 1980s, there was no corresponding moral panic, and pregnant female illicit drug users did not face the threat of prosecution for using drugs while pregnant. However, the US literature served as a source of scientific knowledge and a reference frame for practitioners in the UK and Canada, and pregnant female users were subjected to increased intervention into their lives (Waldby, 1988; Klee, 2002). Many heroin and/or crack-using women lost custody of their children as they were viewed as 'unfit mothers' (Klee, 2002).

In the discourse on women's drug use, taking drugs prescribed by the doctor to control the 'condition' of pregnancy or postnatal depression is constructed as responsible and a sign of a 'normal' woman. However, taking or 'self-prescribing' drugs while pregnant or when mothering is taken as a sign of irresponsible, uncaring behaviour and abnormality. Furthermore, since many pregnancies are unplanned, it is likely that women will have taken drugs before knowing they were pregnant, but the same attention is not given to pregnant women who have taken medication for chronic illnesses such as anticonvulsants or antidepressants (Boyd, 2004). As Siney (1995) argues, in discourse on pregnant drug users, if a woman is dependent on illicit drugs, her physical and psychological dependence is viewed as a matter of choice, and if she does not stop taking these drugs, then apparently she thinks the wellbeing of her baby is less important than her own.

The US Office of National Drug Control Policy (ONDCP) (2014) cite the National Institute on Drug Abuse (NIDA) for the official line on the prenatal effects of illicit drugs. NIDA list premature delivery, low birth weight, smaller head circumference and shorter length as some of the effects of prenatal cocaine use (NIDA, 2011). Also according to NIDA, heroin use during pregnancy is associated with low birth weight; methamphetamines with premature delivery, placental abruption, fetal growth retardation, and heart and brain abnormalities; and marijuana with altered responses to visual stimuli, increased tremulousness and a high pitched cry (NIDA, 2005). NIDA concede that although these effects are documented by numerous scientific studies, it is difficult to establish the specific harms caused by any one drug due to the many confounding factors, especially the use of other drugs, that have an impact on maternal, fetal and child outcomes (NIDA, 2011). Furthermore, alcohol and tobacco, which are legal drugs, arguably put the foetus at a greater risk than illegal drugs.

Existing research shows that while using illicit drugs cannot be seen as 'safe', no scientific basis exists for concluding that exposure will inevitably cause harm. A foetus may be exposed to a particular drug in utero, but this does not mean it will be harmed by the exposure (NAPW, 2010). The response to pregnant illegal drug users is guided not by toxicity, on scientific accuracy, but by the social meaning of the drugs. Recent research highlights the multiple determinants of poor maternal outcomes, including the amount and number of all drugs used, poverty, poor nutrition, homelessness, lack of prenatal care, domestic violence and other health conditions (NIDA, 2011, 2012). These can all interact to have an impact on birth outcomes. To isolate the impact of exposure to any one drug from the combined effects of all confounding variables is not easily achieved. Controlling for the effects of other substances used during pregnancy is nearly impossible as subjects typically use other illegal and legal drugs during pregnancy (Singer et al, 2002a).

It is now acknowledged that concerns that crack babies would never function in society and become a 'biological underclass' (Hopkins, 1989) were unfounded (Leshner, 1999), and that there is no actual condition, syndrome or disorder that can be termed 'crack baby' (Arendt et al, 2004). However, assumptions about the pregnant female illicit drug user and the supposed effects of illicit drug use on the foetus continue to underpin the criminalisation of pregnancy in the US, and to have an impact on the treatment of pregnant female users in Canada and the UK. The behaviour of female users is viewed as posing a threat to public health and as evidence for the justification of various punitive forms of state intervention, including mandatory 'treatment', the loss of child custody, and incarceration (Boyd, 2004)

(This issue is discussed in detail in Part Two of this book. See Chapter Three, pp 81–86 and Chapter Five, pp 131–136).

A closely related strand of academic discourse is concerned with the effects of women's illicit drug use on mothering and childrearing, and comes from the fields of psychiatry and psychology. The focus is on the children of drug-using women, and the women feature as the source of the problem under investigation (see, for example, Cregler and Mark, 1986; Deren, 1986; Regan et al, 1987; Famularo et al, 1989; Bays, 1990; Staples, 1990; Kelley, 1992; Krutilla, 1993; Leifer et al, 1993; Muller et al, 1994; Egami et al, 1996; Pagliaro and Pagliaro, 1999). Maternal drug use is constructed as causing psychological deprivation, separation, loss and abandonment, physical abuse and neglect, murder, academic failure and pain and suffering for the next generation. Female users are situated as 'unfit' mothers and therefore 'abnormal' women. For example, in *Substance use among women*, Pagliaro and Pagliaro (1999, p 87) state:

> If ... substance abuse kills the heart and murders the soul, it is no more apparent than in the context of the effects of substance use upon mothering and child rearing.

They then cite a number of studies, seeking to provide evidence that drug-using mothers are incapable, indifferent, neglectful and selfish. The following is an excerpt from a life history conducted with a 28-year-old crack cocaine-using woman:

> As she got more addicted to crack, she developed an attitude about her kids that she describes as "hey, get the fuck out of here." She wanted them away from her. She said, "Drugs keep you from loving the people who you love, you only love the drugs...." (Woodhouse, 1992, quoted in Pagliaro and Pagliaro, 1999, p 87)

Issues of separation, loss and abandonment, physical abuse and neglect of children are all attributed to maternal drug use (see, for example, Famularo et al, 1989; Bays, 1990; Kelley, 1992; Leifer et al, 1993; Muller et al, 1994; Egami et al, 1996; Pagliaro and Pagliaro, 1999). Female users are judged 'inadequate' mothers, so dependent on their drug of choice that they are incapable of thinking or caring about anything else. Brooks et al (1994, p 204) assert, 'Addiction prevents a mother from responding to her infant's needs; her primary focus is on her drug of choice, not on her child.' Carr (1975, p 70) argues, 'although the mother may be physically present, she remains a distant, non-nurturing figure to the child psychologically.' Female users are deemed incapable of establishing a 'normal' maternal infant bond with their newborns (see, for example, Densen-Gerber et al, 1972). This is often explained as due to the likelihood of having psychological problems and having received bad mothering in their childhoods (see, for example, Carr, 1975).

Concern was raised about the long-term psychological, developmental and behavioural effects that drug use could have on the children of drug-using mothers, who, it was argued, were destined to become the 'problem individuals' of the next generation (Fontana, 1971). Densen-Gerber et al (1972) asserted that psychopathology and sociopathy would be passed to the next generation. Carr (1975, p 66) stated:

> ... those children whose mothers are drug dependent ... represent an extremely "high-risk" group in terms of developmental, behavioural and psychological problems ... these children will be disproportionately represented in future groups of addicts, criminals, the mentally retarded and persons requiring the aid of mental health or other social services.

Pagliaro and Pagliaro (1999) argue that a mother's substance use may lead to the pain and suffering of their children, depression and suicide for those children in adulthood, and even give rise to another generation of substance users. Furthermore, they propose, maternal drug use could have long-term negative effects on the cognitive and academic performance of children.

Female users were not only constituted as threatening the wellbeing of individual children, there was also concern about how this may lead to a threat to public health. Thus, for example, Carr (1975, pp 73-4) argued:

> ... in terms of long term cost to the individual and to society, children raised by drug-dependent mothers may be a more serious social and public health hazard than leukaemia or poliomyelitis.

To prevent this problem from reaching 'epidemic proportions' (Carr, 1975, p 77), it was claimed that coercive state intervention was required in the form of mandatory treatment or removal of the child from the mother's custody (Densen-Gerber et al, 1972; Densen-Gerber and Rohrs, 1973; Carr, 1975; Kelley, 1992).

The findings of these clinical works were translated into policies that have resulted in millions of illicit drug-dependent women losing their children. It was assumed that women who consume illicit drugs are 'bad', 'unnatural' mothers, and are solely responsible for the wellbeing of their foetuses and children. They are constructed as victims of the addictive properties of drugs, over-determined by a compulsive dependence. This compulsion is supposedly so powerful that a mother will have no concern for her foetus or love for her child. Feminist studies have challenged claims made in traditional research about female users as 'unfit mothers', and claimed that many drug-using women show themselves to be loving mothers with parenting skills paralleling those of non-drug-using women, and many more are able to thrive as mothers with appropriate support (see, for example, Colten, 1980, 1982; Boyd, 1999; Baker and Carson, 1999; Campbell, 1999; Klee, 2002).

Psychopathological and emotionally disturbed women

Traditional research focusing on women's illicit drug use, other than in terms of their reproduction and social roles as mothers, has been primarily psychiatric or psychological in orientation. Since the 1960s, both in Europe and the US, medical and sociological discourse constituted women who use illicit drugs as psychopathological and/ or neurotic (see, for example, Chein et al, 1964; Ellinwood et al, 1966; D'Orban, 1970; Densen-Gerber et al, 1972; de Leon, 1974; Levy and Doyle, 1974; Polit et al, 1976; Colten, 1977; Christmas, 1978; Cuskey, 1982; Gossop, 1986; *Women 2000*, 1987). Personality or character disorders were a common diagnosis for female users, followed by neurosis, psychosis and sociopathy (see, for example, Chein et al, 1964; Ellinwood et al, 1966; Hall, 1968; D'Orban, 1970; Cuskey, 1972; Densen-Gerber et al, 1972; Ross and Berzins, 1974).

In early studies of female drug users, the psychopathology attributed to them was frequently constructed as a response to a disturbed and abnormal family background (see, for example, Chein et al, 1964; Ellinwood et al, 1966; D'Orban, 1970; Carr, 1975; Cuskey, 1982) or a broken home (see, for example, Chambers et al, 1970; D'Orban, 1970; Barr et al, 1973; Binion, 1977). Chein et al (1964, p 313) asserted that female addicts develop their 'psychopathology and difficulties through immersion in a malignant family environment.' Female users' psychopathology was also often constituted as a response to an inability to adjust to various social institutions including school, work and marriage. D'Orban (1970) asserted that educational failure, premature school leaving, an inability to hold down jobs and 'unstable drifting' were all prominent features in the lives of the women in his study. However, the co-occurrence of family issues, psychological problems and drug use doesn't necessarily indicate that the drug use or psychological issues were caused by family problems; rather, a range of wider social factors are likely to have contributed to both. Furthermore, the co-occurrence of drug use and a lack of engagement with social institutions, such as education and work, may indicate a lifestyle choice rather than psychopathology.

The subjects chosen for the studies discussed in the early literature were women in treatment. However, women in treatment are likely to comprise of a very specific group of illicit drug-using women, with a range of needs, who do not represent the wider population of female drug users (Taylor, 1993). Reports of female illicit drug users as pathological and emotionally disturbed do not address the positive functions drug taking may serve in their lives (for example, for pleasure or for blocking out pain), or consider the wider social contexts in which women move and make choices. Such accounts therefore served to provide a skewed view of female users.

Early academic discourse on illicit drug use generally constructed women as more pathological and emotionally disturbed than their male counterparts (see, for example, D'Orban, 1970; Densen-Gerber et al, 1972; de Leon, 1974; Christmas, 1978; Cuskey, 1982; Gossop, 1986). Discourse on female illicit drug use is replete with observations that women who use illicit drugs are more emotional, dependent, demanding, needy, anxious and depressed than male users (see, for example, Chein et al, 1964; Ellinwood et al, 1966; Colten, 1977). For instance, in *Women 2000* (1987), a report on an international conference on women and drug abuse, it is asserted that 'drug-abusing' women are likely to have higher levels of depression and anxiety and lower levels of self-esteem than male drug users. However, culturally, women have tended to be viewed as sicker, more emotional, excessively dependent, more depressed and needy than men. What is appropriate 'feminine' behaviour for women is close to a number of 'neurotic illnesses' often called the 'worried well', for which legal drugs are readily prescribed. Hence, it might be argued that the only thing distinguishing the construction of female illicit drug users from non-using 'normal' women is that they take illegal drugs. Drugs prescribed by those with the medical authority to serve a normalising function are constructed as socially necessary, but are constructed as signalling a lack of normality when self-administered.

Explanations for female illicit drug users' greater propensity for psychological and emotional disturbance are diverse, but basically fall into two categories. One constitutes the problem as inherent in the women themselves. For example, as women's use of illicit drugs represents a greater departure from traditional sex roles than men's, the female drug user is 'sicker' than the male (see, for example, Margulies, 1972; Kaufman, 1984). The other argues that women receive greater maltreatment from society, and consequently have more about which to complain (see, for example, Colten, 1977; Mondanaro, 1989; Ettorre, 1992). Maltreated, victimised and abused women are believed to use illicit drugs as a coping mechanism for emotional trauma and/ or impaired self-esteem (see, for example, Suffet and Brotman, 1976; Hser et al, 1987a, 1987b; Mondanaro, 1989; Reed, 1991; Russel and Wilsnack, 1991). This thesis is known as the drug use as 'self-medication' hypothesis.

In terms of women's drug use involving a departure from gender roles, in traditional research female users were more likely than males to be constructed as '*sexually* maladjusted' (Chein et al, 1964; Ellinwood et al, 1966; D'Orban, 1970; Barr et al, 1973). 'Normal' psychological adjustment meant behaving within prescribed gender norms. High incidence of out-of wedlock pregnancies, never married, homosexual, separated or divorced women were noted (Chein et al, 1964; Ellinwood et al, 1966; D'Orban, 1970; Barr et al, 1973). Female users were generally thought to have problems with sexual identity (Cuskey, 1982). Feminists thus argue that traditional drug theory constructs female drug use as a deviation from 'normal' femininity (see, for example, Ettorre, 1992; Rosenbaum, 1981, 1997). For example, Rosenbaum (1997, p 1) argues:

> Historically women's drug use has been defined as problematic when their traditional gender roles were violated or abandoned, therefore jeopardised.

While feminists have challenged the construction of female illicit drug users as psychologically disordered (see, for example, Rosenbaum, 1981; Taylor, 1993), the notion of women illicit drug users as neurotic is still very much alive in relation to the drug use as 'self-medication' hypothesis. The proponents of this hypothesis, including some feminists, assert that illicit drug use serves as a coping mechanism for women experiencing psychological and emotional problems and/or situational stresses (see, for example, Mondanaro, 1989; Russel and Wilsnack, 1991). Feminist versions of this discourse draw attention to the ways in which factors such as low esteem and depression 'relate to the general lot of women in society' (Maher, 1997, p 5). For example, Mondanaro (1989, pp 2-3) argues:

> The legacy of growing up female in a society that undervalues and denigrates the role of women is a low sense of self-esteem, high levels of depression and anxiety, and a sense of powerlessness. Learned helplessness is another result of the daily confrontation with the dominant culture.... All these characteristics act in concert to immobilize many chemically dependent women.

Research indicates a disproportionate number of female dependent drug users have experiences of sexual abuse, rape and trauma (see, for example, Najavits et al, 1997; Welle et al, 1998; Hawke et al, 2000; Pettinati et al, 2000; Gilbert et al, 2001; Neaigus, 2001; Becker and Duffy, 2002; Agrawal et al, 2005; Brady and Ashley, 2005). Research also shows a high incidence of sexual abuse histories in illicit drug or alcohol-using women in treatment (see, for example, Miller et al, 1987; Russell, 1983; Harrison, 1989; Mondanaro, 1989; Hurley, 1991; Reed, 1991). Some studies have suggested that as many as 75 per cent of women in treatment for alcohol or drug problems have histories of childhood sexual abuse or incest (see, for example, Miller et al, 1987; Mondanaro, 1989; Reed, 1991).

Studies investigating the relationship between childhood sexual abuse and drug use have suggested that substance use may serve the purpose of enabling sexual abuse survivors to cope with the symptoms of post-traumatic stress syndrome (Root, 1989), numb emotional pain and/or block out flashbacks (Blume, 1990b), create a sense of aliveness when survivors feel dead inside (Blume, 1990b), socialise with minimal interpersonal closeness (Singer et al, 1989) and enhance feelings of self-esteem (Russell and Wilsnack, 1991). In most studies, drug use thus serves as 'self-medication' for the symptoms of abuse, the negative effects of which are preferable to the symptoms of abuse such as depression, anxiety or post-traumatic stress syndrome (see, for example, Root, 1989; Blume, 1990b). However, Russell and Wilsnack (1991) offer a more complex 'vicious cycle causation' model, more specific to the use of crack cocaine, according to which the negative experiences of childhood abuse are thought to impair self-esteem, which is enhanced with the use of crack.

Female users have been constituted as more pathological and emotionally disturbed than men, and more recently as victimised and abused women who use illicit drugs as a coping mechanism for emotional trauma and/or impaired self-esteem. Both constructions give authority to policies and practices that responsibilise female users for their drug problems and situate them as a special case requiring special treatment and as intractable, difficult service users (See Chapter Four, pp 109–116). While there may be some female dependent users with psychological and emotional issues, the majority will not see themselves as psychologically disordered. Furthermore, those who do may not view this or even their drug use as the most pressing problem in their lives. While it has been estimated that at least one in three females (as opposed to one in six males) will have survived some form of sexual abuse before reaching the age of 18 (Black et al, 2011), this would indicate that the prevalence of drug use has been seriously under-estimated (Maher, 1997). While there is some evidence from research drawing from the accounts of female users themselves that illicit drug use is used to block out memories of childhood abuse, such studies typically fail to explore the contribution that other factors such as socioeconomic status, peer groups, proximity to drug cultures and social relationships may have. Finally, constructions of female users as victims of abuse or the pharmacology of drugs fail to take account of women's agency.

Polluted and polluting women

Another strand of academic discourse on women's illicit drug use emerged in response to the advent of the HIV/AIDS pandemic of the 1980s. In the 1980s illicit drug users became the target of a number of 'moral panics' (McGrath, 1993, p 158). Drug users, intravenous drug users in particular, were identified by the media, politicians and medical professionals as among one of the main groups of individuals defined as at 'high risk' of contracting and infecting others with HIV/AIDS. Female drug users were targeted as a result not only of their drug use, but also their sexual behaviour. They were constituted as immoral, diseased women and/or prostitutes who threatened to contaminate and pollute the general populace. One strand of this discourse emerging from the US focused on crack, and constructed female users as capable of doing anything to feed their addiction. Female users were also situated as primarily responsible for the sexual health and moral standards of communities.

In the light of the HIV/AIDS and crack epidemics in the 1980s and 1990s, numerous studies were conducted documenting the risky sexual behaviours of female illicit drug users (see, for example, Mondanaro, 1987; Kinnel, 1989; Plant et al, 1989; Worth, 1989; Corby et al, 1991; Inciardi et al, 1993; Gossop et al, 1995). Women who use illicit drugs were frequently conflated with prostitutes – another group deemed as 'high risk'. In the US researchers began to focus on 'sex for crack' exchanges and the impact of crack on sexual behaviour (see, for example, Siegal et al, 1992; Edlin et al, 1994; Inciardi, 1995; Jones et al, 1998). With the rise of crack use in the UK and other European countries, this association migrated (see, for example, Mondanaro, 1987; Cohen et al, 1989; Worth, 1989; Feucht et al, 1990; Lewis and Watters, 1991; Schilling et al, 1991; McKeganey et al, 1992; Klee, 1993, 1996; Brown and Weissman, 1994; Rhodes et al, 1994; Gossop et al, 1995; Fortenberry et al, 1997; Stevens et al, 1998). Female users were constituted as 'polluted' and 'polluting', as carriers of medical and moral disease, posing a threat to the moral fabric and public health of the majority.

In the UK concern about the HIV/AIDs pandemic led to female illicit drug users becoming the focus for research into risky sexual behaviour and unsafe injecting practices, as well as various harm reduction strategies including needle exchange and condom distribution programmes. Female intravenous drug users were constructed as more likely to engage in high drug-related HIV risk behaviours than men (see, for example, Stevens et al, 1998; Metsch et al, 1999). Women who use drugs intravenously were generally believed to share needles more frequently than men (Dwyer et al, 1994; Wechsberg et al, 1995), to be more likely to have sexual partners who were also intravenous drug users (Dwyer et al, 1994), and to inject after the man in a drug injection episode (Metsch et al, 1999). The idea that women are more likely to engage in high drug-related HIV risk behaviours than men was usually attributed to the unequal power relationships between male and female users (see, for example, Murphy and Rosenbaum, 1987; Wayment et al, 1993; Brown and Weissman, 1994; Amato, 1995; Metsch et al, 1999). For instance, it was found that women were more likely to acquire drugs through a male partner who often controlled the amount of drugs they had access to (Murphy and Rosenbaum, 1987; Wayment et al, 1993).

The responsibility for safer sex practices to prevent the spread of HIV/AIDs was predominantly placed on female drug users whose sexual behaviour was seen as a threat to public health (Henderson, 1990; Ettorre, 1992). Various authors explored how during the 1980s and early 1990s prostitutes and female illicit drug users were constituted in the media as reservoirs of sexual disease and scapegoated as 'polluting' the general public with HIV/AIDS (see, for example, Maher, 1997; Phoenix, 1999; Malloch, 2000). Phoenix (1999) argued that in this context strategic use was made of the 'junkie-whore' stereotype – the drug-dependent woman who sells sex to fund her habit. Since the early 1990s discourse on women's illicit drug use, prostitution and HIV/AIDS became increasingly intertwined with a flourish of research scrutinising the sexual behaviour of female illicit drug users, particularly those trading sex for money or drugs (see, for example, Kinnel, 1989; Plant et al, 1989; Plant, 1990; Corby et al, 1991; Dorfman et al, 1992; McKeganey et al, 1992; Inciardi et al, 1993; Gossop et al, 1995).

For example, in *AIDS, drugs, and prostitution* (Plant, 1990), a range of authors from Europe, North America, Australia and Africa explore the interrelations between prostitution or 'sex work', HIV/AIDS and the use of psychoactive drugs and opiates. The title of the collection in itself illustrates how discourse on illicit drug use, prostitution and HIV/AIDS, had become interconnected. Most of the studies in the collection are attempts to gauge the extent of the HIV/AIDS risk behaviours of female sex workers who use illicit drugs. In the concluding chapter of the book, Plant (1990, p 200) argues:

> Prostitute women and their clients are clearly at risk of HIV infection. This is because most prostitutes and many of their clients have multiple sexual partners and because intravenous drug use is fairly commonplace among prostitutes in many areas ... prostitution may well be a means for accelerating the spread of HIV infection.

The prostitute female drug user was assumed unlikely to follow 'safer sex' guidelines. Rather, she was assumed likely to contract or transmit HIV through sex with clients rather than, for instance, while having sex with a regular sexual partner who may be an intravenous drug user.

Women's use of crack cocaine in particular was associated with sex-related HIV/AIDS risk behaviours in relation to the phenomena of sex-for-crack exchanges. For example, in *Women and crack cocaine*, an ethnographic analysis of the Miami crack scene, Inciardi et al (1993) assert that crack users are 'high-risk' individuals for the spread of HIV due to their sexual behaviour. They describe the sexual behaviours of female crack users:

> Many crack-addicted women engage in any manner of sexual activity, under *any* circumstances, in private or in public, and with multiple partners of either sex (or both sexes simultaneously). Indeed, the tendency of crack users to engage in high-frequency sex with numerous anonymous partners is a feature of crack dependence and crack house life in a myriad of locales. (Inciardi et al, 1993, pp 95-6)

Female crack users were thus portrayed as capable of doing anything under any circumstance to feed their addiction, including engaging in unsafe sex. This behaviour is explained by the disinhibiting effects of crack and/or craving and compulsion. Plant (1990, p 199) states:

> Very often both the prostitute and the client are under the influence of legal or illicit psycho-active drugs.... Individuals are clearly less likely to implement "safer sex" guidelines when disinhibition from such substances is combined with the even stronger disinhibition of sexual arousal.

The pharmacological properties of illicit drugs, it is argued, create an 'overpowering' force driving women's behaviour. The explanation for women's willingness to obtain crack 'through any means' and to engage in 'any manner of sexual activity' relies heavily on the idea of female users as victims of cracks pharmacology. According to Inciardi et al (1993), addicted women's crack acquisition becomes more important than their family, work, social responsibility, health, values, modesty, morality or self-respect (Inciardi et al, 1993, p 97).

Such constructions of female users' behaviour do not take account of other factors that may influence safer sex practices, including unequal gender dynamics, cultural beliefs about the disinhibiting effects of illegal drugs or women's agency and power (Anderson, 1990). The research literature on HIV/AIDS prevention has recently drawn attention to the issue of gender inequalities in negotiating safe sex practices (see, for example, Worth, 1989; Amato, 1995; Farmer et al, 1996; Gomez and van Oss, 1996; O'Leary, 2000). According to this literature, worldwide, men's power and privilege is embedded in heterosexual relationships and encounters. Women's experiences of gender-based violence and unequal power in relationships can make negotiating safe sex practices very difficult (Higgins et al, 2009). At the same time, not practising safe sex may also be an issue of a woman's choice and agency, and be a matter of their pleasure or preference (Jolly and Cornwall, 2006;

Randolph et al, 2007; Higgins et al, 2009). However, women in general and drug-using and sex-working women in particular became the targets of prevention strategies, while heterosexual men, the clients of sex workers or the male partners of drug users, were seen as outwith the prevention domain.

In the UK, the perceived threat that women who use illicit drugs (along with prostitutes) pose to public health led to them becoming the focus for harm reduction strategies (such as medical examinations, needle exchange and condom distribution programmes) and a potential priority for services (Malloch, 2000). Most significantly, they were given the major responsibility for the prevention of the spread of AIDS in the heterosexual community, and were allocated the role of safer sex educators (Henderson, 1990; Ettorre, 1992). As Henderson (1990, p 14) suggests:

> Much of the public health education on HIV/AIDS geared to heterosexuals has placed the responsibility for promoting safer sex, as birth control, upon women.

According to Patton (1985), this is a responsibility that women have always held. In a political context in which the promotion of the 'family' was central, the HIV/AIDS pandemic appeared as an ideal opportunity for the state control, intervention and containment of female sexuality (Malloch, 2000). Women were expected to take responsibility for the spread of HIV/AIDS by insisting on safe sex practices. The assumption was that only women are interested in HIV/AIDS prevention, and men are inherently incapable or uninterested in it (Higgins et al, 2009). Women's sexual pleasure and preferences were not considered, and instead it was conjectured that women were motivated to prevent HIV (Higgins et al, 2009). Furthermore, it was supposed, in line with traditional notions of masculinity, that men's sexual behaviour was unchangeable and uncontrollable (Higgins et al, 2009).

Passive dependents or emancipated lawbreakers?

A less prominent strand of discourse on women's illicit drug use seeks to explain their drug-related criminal activities. In its more traditional configuration, this discourse posits women who use illicit drugs as 'victims' or passive dependents, devoid of agency, choice and accountability. Women users' criminality is constituted as a result of their experiences as victims of males, the chemical properties of drugs or of abuse. More recently an alternative strand of this discourse has emerged in which women are situated as emancipated individuals, rational agents taking advantage of the opportunities presented to them.

The construction of women as passive and dependent victims of males has been prevalent in academic discourse. In the literature on initiation, women frequently feature as the victims of more experienced, sometimes 'evil', males, who lead them into drug taking (see, for example, Waldorf, 1973; File, 1976; Rosenbaum, 1981; Hser et al, 1987b; Parker et al, 1988; Blom and van den Berg, 1989). In line with this notion is the idea that women's drug-related criminal activity is also a result of them being led astray by a more dominant male (see, for example, Covington, 1985; Pettiway, 1987). A common conception is that of an innocent, vulnerable young woman who begins her career in the 'underworld' by being coerced or coaxed into prostitution by a pimp, dealer or partner (Maher, 1997). Anderson (1990, p 88) describes the phenomenon of the 'drug-dealer-as-pimp':

> In behaving as a type of pimp, the dealer may get the young woman to try the highly addictive crack, then encourage her to prostitute herself to get more, sending her out on the streets in this manner.

A similar figuration is that of the woman who is led into committing crimes such as shoplifting, burglary, robbery or drug dealing by a criminal boyfriend or husband. For instance, Covington (1985, p 348) argues that women are initiated into crime by men:

> [F]emales passively acquiesce and follow males into crime rather than launching their careers independently in female-dominated peer groups.

Pettiway (1987) attributes women illicit drug users' involvement in criminal activities to their 'domestic arrangements'. According to Pettiway (1987), married or co-habiting women are more likely to become involved in crime partnerships and commit 'male-type' crimes such as burglary, robbery or assault. Female users are thus situated as impressionable victims who do not initiate their own criminal activities but are led into crime by men.

Female illicit drug users have been viewed as parasites, unable to support their consumption without a man (see, for example, Sutter, 1966; File et al, 1974; Fiddle, 1976; Smithberg and Westermeyer, 1985; Miller, 1986; Hser et al, 1987b; Morningstar and Chitwood, 1987). Miller (1986) argues that young women who have been introduced to the use of narcotics by their boyfriends would not normally become involved in hustling to support their own use unless their boyfriends left them, they overdosed or were arrested. Female users have also been characterised as passive accomplices to their partners in drug-related criminal activity (see, for example, File, 1976; Fiddle, 1976; Covington, 1985; Pettiway, 1987). According to various writers, women may carry illicit drugs, conceal stolen goods, gain access to targets of crime, or act as lookouts (see, for example, Fiddle, 1976; File, 1976; Covington, 1985; Pettiway, 1987). Covington asserts that it is the more traditional females who end up becoming accomplices. They attach themselves to males in personal relationships 'in hopes of learning the necessary skills and inheriting the business (for example, drug dealing)' (Covington, 1985, p 331).

Women are thought to take on the role of accomplice for several reasons. One is that women lack criminal opportunities in the same way as men due to male resistance to their participation in crime organisations. Women are thought to lack the strength, muscle and skill required for many criminal acts, or (Steffensmeier, 1983; Covington, 1985) it is viewed by men as too dangerous, degrading and unfeminine for women (Steffensmeier, 1983). Consequently, according to this thesis, men prefer to work, associate and do business with other men in the world of crime (Steffensmeier, 1983). Characteristics constructed as 'typically' male are reinforced within criminal subcultures, while those considered 'typically' female are shunned (Steffensmeier, 1983; Covington, 1985). As Covington asserts (1985, p 348):

> [T]here is no female subculture that supports and reinforces crime among women in a manner parallel to male cultures.

Women are also socialised to be submissive and dependent (Steffensmeier, 1983; Covington, 1985). The only women illicit drug users who are not dependent on males and successfully 'go it alone' in the world of crime are prostitutes (see, for example, Steffensmeier, 1983; Covington, 1985; Pettiway, 1987), 'masculine' females (see, for example, Colten, 1977; Shover and Norland, 1978; Cullen et al, 1979), or lesbians (see, for example, Fiddle, 1976; File, 1976). Women are purported to prostitute themselves not only for money, but to be independent (Miller, 1986; Pettiway, 1987).

Female users' participation in crime is thus constituted as peripheral to predominantly male-dominated crime networks. They are situated as lacking agency, self-determination and independence, as parasitic accomplices to males, or otherwise as sex workers. Only through their sexuality are women conceptualised as able to achieve some level of independence. Feminist authors have challenged these constructions of female users, highlighting their agency and self-determination. They have demonstrated how women in their studies have instigated their own drug-using and criminal careers, and have supported their drug habits through a range of strategies other than sex work, including shoplifting and dealing (see, for example, Rosenbaum, 1981; Taylor, 1993; Maher, 1997; Anderson, 2008; Caputo, 2008).

In a more recent strand of discourse on women's illicit drug use, female lawbreakers have been constructed as emancipated women, active, rational agents, maximising criminal opportunities (see, for example, Bourgois, 1989, 1995; Baskin et al, 1993; Bourgois and Dunlap, 1993; Taylor, 1993; Wilson, 1993; Fagan, 1994, 1995; Mieczkowski, 1994). They are constituted as members of a new generation of women who are shedding their traditional constraints and limited roles as housewives and mothers, and demanding equality in the public sphere. There are two main explanations for the 'emancipation' of female lawbreakers. The first asserts that the emancipation of women in the wider society has somehow filtered on to the streets and had an impact on women as crack users and drug market participants (see, for example, Bourgois, 1989, 1995; Bourgois and Dunlap, 1993; Taylor, 1993; Wilson, 1993). The second argues that the expansion of the drug economy and shifts in the structure of drug markets have led to increased opportunities for women (see, for example, Baskin et al, 1993; Taylor, 1993; Fagan, 1994, 1995; Mieczkowski, 1994).

The female lawbreaker as 'emancipated' thesis is a recent addition to the drug use literature. However, as Maher (1997) has pointed out, this idea is not a new one, and is renowned among criminologists as the 'emancipation' or 'opportunity' thesis (see, for example, Adler, 1975; Simon, 1975). In the mid-1970s, Adler (1975) attributed the increase in the number of women arrested to the feminist movement. Since then, the 'emancipation' thesis has been largely discredited within criminological discourse (see, for example, Crites, 1976; Smart, 1976, 1979; Chapman, 1980; Steffensmeier, 1980, 1983; Box and Hale, 1983; Chesney-Lind and Rodriguez, 1983; Messerschmidt, 1986; Naffine, 1987). In particular, the notion of there being a direct causal link between women's crime and women's emancipation has been deemed problematic (see Carlen, 1988).

In the discourse on women's illicit drug use, the construction of female lawbreakers as emancipated has found new expression. Bourgois (1989, p 643) argues that the increase in women's involvement in crack in the US is a reflection of women's emancipation 'throughout all aspects of inner-city life, culture and economy.' Apparently, the fact that more women are pursuing careers in the underground economy mirrors increased female participation in the legal labour market:

> Women – especially the emerging generation, which is most at risk for crack addiction – are no longer obliged to stay at home and maintain the family as they were a generation ago. They no longer so readily sacrifice public life or forgo independent opportunities to generate personally disposable income. (Bourgois, 1989, pp 643-5)

Underlying this claim is Bourgois' (1989, p 644) assertion that women constitute a large proportion of the population of crack dependents, and 'are the fastest-growing segment of the population being arrested for street crimes.' In a similar vein, Taylor (1993, pp 198-9) argues:

> In the streets, in the crack houses, in the bars, and in the correctional facilities, women are beginning to demand to be respected and acknowledged.... Acquisition for women in a minority culture is a reflection of what women in the larger society seek.

A variation of this argument can be found in the work of Wilson (1993, p 190), who asserts that a new criminal opportunity for women as crack cocaine dealers has occurred, and that 'gendered patterns of crime mirror the patterns of straight world economic activity.' Wilson (1993) contends that traditional gender relations condition women's access to 'equal opportunity' crime. According to Wilson (1993), the traditional gendered division of labour, with men taking care of business and women in the home caring for children, is reproduced in drug distribution networks. Women's participation in these networks is underpinned by their domesticity and complements male participation:

> The mesh between women's provision of a home base and their lack of mobility and men's lack of a home base but high mobility may be a combination that works well for a sexually integrated drug network. (Wilson, 1993, p 188)

Again, underpinning this argument is the idea that patterns of men and women's drug use and crime are converging, and that this convergence is evidence of women's emancipation. Wilson argues, 'women's astonishing increase in drug arrests may reflect an equal opportunity crime' (1993, p 188).

Another strand of the 'emancipation' thesis holds that changes in drugs and drug markets largely due to the advent of crack have enabled women to participate in drug taking and selling (see, for example, Baskin et al, 1993; Fagan, 1994). The new opportunities available to women in the drug economy are attributed to the weakening of male-dominated street networks in the inner city. A high incidence of incarceration and homicide among young, inner-city, minority males, as a result of their participation in the drug trade, has diminished their 'gatekeeper' and mediating roles. This has provided an 'opportunity structure for female entry into the informal economy' (Baskin et al, 1993, pp 410-11). Another influence has been the decline of the prestige and authority of 'female old-heads' who promoted hard work and family values, and served as pillars of informal social control in poor communities (Anderson, 1990; Baskin et al, 1993; Fagan, 1994). These were replaced with new female role models who 'displayed the "high life," buying fancy clothes, jewellery, drugs and alcohol' (Fagan, 1994, p 185). According to Fagan (1994, p 210), signs of the changing status of women in the drug economy is evident in the 'relatively high incomes some achieve, and the relatively insignificant role of prostitution in generating income.'

The assumption uniting these approaches is that the expansion of crack markets has been accompanied by increased opportunities for women. However, there are many instances in which the expansion of markets for legal and illegal products has not meant increased opportunities for women (Maher, 1997). In addition, despite expanding markets, male kinship and ethnic ties may continue to perform important gatekeeping functions within drug markets (see Waterston, 1993; Maher and Daly, 1996). In the research by Maher and Daly (1996) there was little evidence of increased female participation or a breakdown in the hegemonic masculinity of drug markets (Maher, 1997). Some research continues to suggest that when women are represented in drug distribution populations, they tend to be active at a low level of distribution (see, for example, Dunlap et al, 1997).

Some commentators have argued that while crack has prompted shifts in the composition of street networks, these have not necessarily been beneficial to or strengthened the position of women (see Austin, 1992; Maher and Curtis, 1992; Maher and Daly, 1996). It has been noted by several writers that more women, particularly black women, are breaking the law and being incarcerated; more are becoming involved in prostitution, receiving less remuneration for their services, and are experiencing increased levels of violence and exploitation within the crack economy (see, for example, Austin 1992).

Rational agents

In 1981, Rosenbaum's *Women on heroin* in the US was the first major in-depth study to focus on the 'career' of the female drug user. The notion of 'career' was successfully applied in ethnographic works by male scholars in the US and UK, and explored the drug use of men from the viewpoint of the male users themselves (see, for example, Sutter, 1966; Feldman, 1968; Agar, 1973; Fiddle, 1976; Auld et al, 1986; Pearson et al, 1986; Pearson, 1987; Unell, 1987; Gilman, 1988; Williams, 1989). In this work, the male drug user was:

> ... characterised as a purposeful, resourceful person responding in a rational manner to particular sets of social circumstances. (Taylor, 1993a, p 6)

Women's drug use was not analysed through the lens of the concept of 'career' until Rosenbaum's (1981) study. Rosenbaum described women's heroin use as a career of 'narrowing options', whereby conventional ways of living become increasingly closed off to them. However, this work stood in 'splendid isolation' (Pearson, 1999, p 482). It was not for another decade, in the 1990s, that women's illicit drug use really began to receive attention from feminist researchers (see, for example, Perry, 1991; Ettorre, 1992; Taylor, 1993a; Maher, 1997; Boyd, 1999; Henderson, 1999). These studies began to challenge prevailing views of female users. They questioned and subverted the stereotypes that had been perpetuated in previous research which constituted women as deviant, pathological, promiscuous, passive, and as unfit to mother. Instead they attempted to provide empowering accounts of women's illicit drug use. For instance, Taylor (1993a) showed that female users were not passive victims, and illustrated their drug-using 'careers' involve active agency, independence and autonomy. The women, rather than pathological deviants, were portrayed as rational decision-makers, making choices according to the 'contingencies of their drug using careers and their roles and status in society' (Taylor, 1993a, p 8). Boyd's (1999) *Mothers and illicit drugs* aimed to transcend many of the myths surrounding women and substance use in pregnancy, and challenged the conventional ideology of motherhood and the idea that women users were categorically 'unfit to parent'. Like these ground-breaking works, this book examines the agency of women within their drug-using careers, and disputes the view of them as unfit to parent.

Feminist scholars began to show how an understanding of female illicit drug use can only be gained in the context of the social construction of women's gender role, within the 'ideology of femininity' and the 'ideology of reproduction' (Ettorre, 1992, cited in Harding, 2008). Feminist researchers on illicit drug use have continued to focus on the importance of gender as a regulatory regime. Malloch (2000) argued that female illicit drug use defies 'normal' womanhood in contrast to male illicit drug use that can be seen as a culturally appropriate expression of masculinity. Women's illicit drug use is therefore seen as 'doubly deviant' – not only have female users broken the law, but they have also transgressed appropriate female behaviour in selfish, hedonistic, pleasure-seeking behaviour. Feminist criminologists had used the term 'doubly deviant' over a decade earlier to refer to the social construction of women's crime more generally (Heidensohn, 1985).

The study of the pursuit of pleasure provided a starting point for feminist researchers examining women's illicit drug use in the context of the dance scene of the 1990s. For instance, Henderson (1999) studied recreational Ecstasy use within dance cultures. She found that while drug use may be a source of risk, it may also embody a type of sensual pleasure and personal agency for women. Her study revealed that gender roles vary between drug cultures, as Ecstasy use is viewed as acceptable risk-taking behaviour for both men and women within the dance scene. Henderson (1999) argues that feminist researchers should aim to examine different cultures of women's drug use as opposed to a 'one size fits all approach'. While not advocating drug use, Ettorre (1992) underlines the importance of asking why and how women experience their substance use as pleasurable, and whether it can contribute to a woman's sense of autonomy, empowerment and wellbeing. More recently, Ettorre (2004, p 48) has suggested 'illegal pleasures may become escapes from powerlessness and domination in everyday life.' While the research field has until recently focused on the risk, pain and danger involved in drug use rather than pleasure, Ettorre (2004, p 10) argues that women who use illicit drugs 'can be seen to enact pleasure side by side with negative emotions and "displeasure".' This book addresses the pleasure and pain experienced by female drug users.

From the 1990s onwards, feminist work emphasised the importance of providing a structural analysis of women's illicit drug use. Several studies have emerged highlighting how as well as gender, poverty, racism, social and economic marginalisation structure the lives of female users of heroin and crack (Maher, 1997; Campbell, 2000; Malloch, 2000; Boyd, 2004; Bush-Baskette, 2010). This work has analysed the political, social and cultural forces shaping women's drug use and the policy response to it. It has also focused on the way the war on drugs shapes and sustains structural inequalities. For instance, Boyd (2004) explores how race, class and gender inequalities inform drug law and policy. She examines how the war on drugs reinforces these inequalities and has an impact on women's daily lives. These laws and policies, she argues, are underpinned historically by white Western Christian beliefs about sobriety, the family and motherhood. In *Misguided justice*, Bush-Baskette (2010) investigates the affect of the war on drugs on the incarceration of women and black people in general, and on how it has an impact on black women specifically. This work examines the political, social and cultural forces shaping women's drug use, and highlights the social and economic marginalisation structuring their lives.

Another key concern of feminist scholars in the last few decades has been women users' agency and capacity for resistance despite oppressive social structures, laws and policies. For instance, Maher's (1997) concern is to resist the tendency to characterise women users as victims of social structures, pharmacology or relationships, or to over endow them with criminal agency and free will. Drawing on accounts from women in the street-level drug economy in *Sexed work*, Maher (1997, p 201) examines the 'active, creative and often contradictory choices, adaptations and resistances that constitute women's agency' in the context of the poverty, racism, violence, and enduring marginality that characterise their lives. As in Maher's research, this book resists the tendency to characterise women users as victims, or to over-endow them with criminal agency. It examines the contradictory choices and adaptations that shape women's lives in the context of political, social and cultural forces that marginalise, stigmatise and impoverish them.

Feminist studies attempted to provide empowering accounts of women's drug use. Malloch (2000) argued that the issue of empowerment is crucial, as a discourse dominated by images of criminality and disease make women users more vulnerable to adverse legal intervention. Ettorre (2004) outlines two paradigms of research practice on drugs: the 'classical' that pathologises and the 'postmodern' that empowers. The classical paradigm concentrates on addiction as a disease, analysing the 'sick' individual. Drug use is viewed as undermining individual health and community, causing anti-social behaviour and crime. The post-modern paradigm, which is the approach adopted in this research, is concerned with consumption cultures and rituals, and the cultural shaping of the drug problem as a social issue. It is concerned with how social exclusion shapes the transgression of users, ethics and the human rights of users, and acknowledges inequalities of race, class and gender.

In sum, this book continues the work of early feminist studies of female drug users in its aim to subvert popular misconceptions of them. This is important, as it is these misconceptions that condition oppressive forms of governance. It also continues the work of studies that have provided a structural analysis of female drug use, and explores the poverty, social and economic marginalisation shaping female users' lives. Few studies have explored how laws and policies have reinforced women's poverty, social and economic marginalisation, but this book continues this work. It advances the work of feminists concerned with female users' agency and capacity for resistance. It examines their adaptations, agency and resistance, not only to oppressive circumstances, but also to negative forms of governance administered through the criminal justice, treatment and welfare systems. So, while other works have studied women's drug use from the perspectives of the women themselves, examined oppressive structural forces that shape and sustain their marginalisation, how drug policy has an impact on their lives and their agency and capacity for resistance, this book explores and links all these elements of women's drug use together.

The purpose of this chapter was not simply to provide a review of the literature, but to draw on a Foucauldian framework to illustrate how academic discourse defines, categorises and differentiates female illicit drug users as a problem to be governed. While feminist research has helped to challenge conventional constructions, traditional academic understandings continue to inform and shape punitive and pathologising drug policies and practices. Research is restricted, by and large, to what governments define as important or has the capacity to contribute to the solution of pre-defined social problems. The selection of which 'findings' to include in scientific journals is decided by what counts as 'serious scholarship', and government-sanctioned and funded research is typically regarded as such. The publication of research findings is a political act. As Rosenbaum (1995) argues:

> Most [researchers] have a covert investment in the status quo, the preservation of traditional values (including gender roles), and prevailing (prohibitionist) policy toward drugs.

At the same time, feminist research and awareness of how gender conditions forms of governance has contributed to some positive changes in policy and practice around female drug users. For example, women's-only services addressing the specific needs of female users offering supportive care in pregnancy, services offering childcare, and addressing issues affecting women such as domestic violence and sexual abuse have increasingly appeared in the UK, US and Canada (see, for example, UNODC, 2004). Despite there being some pockets of good practice, there is still considerable work to be done at the policy level, however. The following chapter explores the political context in which women's illicit drug use is governed in the UK, US and Canada.

TWO

Political context

This chapter discusses the political context in which the research was undertaken. It provides an insight into the 'mentalities', 'governmental rationalities' or 'political rationalities' embedded in governmental approaches to female illicit drug use. The history of prohibition, the 'war on drugs', and how this is wielded within the political climate of neoliberalism is explored. This is linked to the ascendancy of the 'risk' approach to governing illicit drug use, responsibilisation and the process of 'othering' these modes of governing sustain. The aim of this chapter is therefore to provide a general picture of the political domain in which specific drug policies in the UK, US and Canada have emerged. The discussion also aims to provide a framework for the ensuing chapters that focus more closely on the specific governmental techniques and procedures used in the control and regulation of women's illicit drug use.

History of prohibition

Prohibition is the practice of formally forbidding the manufacture, transportation, import, export, sale and consumption of certain drugs by law. Although less than 100 years old, it is widely regarded as necessary and/or inevitable (Shiner, 2009). However, the intentional use of mind-altering or psychoactive drugs has a very long history. Every past society has used and explored drugs as part of its cultural practice and social life, which indicates that drugs are an integral part of human nature – humans have been using psychoactive drugs since ancient times (Sullivan and Hagan, 2002; UNODC, 2008). In the 19th century in Europe and North America many elixirs, medicines and cough mixtures contained narcotics, cocaine or marijuana. Most women could not afford to see a doctor, and so self-medicated (Boyd, 2004). Opiates were used for many ailments considered specific to women, including menstruation pains, menopause and childbirth (Berridge and Edwards, 1981). Upper-class women visited opium dens, and opium eating and smoking were considered aristocratic vices (Brecher et al, 1972). Women were treated with cocaine for a range of nervous conditions, reproductive problems and illnesses (Kandall, 1999). Marijuana was prescribed to women for menstrual pain as well as migraines, asthma and depression.

While the late 19th century saw an increased public concern with drug use and dependency, it was not considered a major social problem. This situation changed radically in the first two decades of the 20th century, however, and 'by the middle of the 1920s opiates were prohibited, users were seen as "dope fiends" and a criminal subculture emerged' (Conrad and Schneider, 1992, p 121). Harry Anslinger, Commissioner of Narcotics in the US from 1930 to 1962, played a fundamental role in the making of international drug prohibition. He took an exaggerated view of drugs such as opium and cocaine, and developed a hatred for marijuana, which he contended was a source of crime, especially murder, as well as insanity and suicide. He single-handedly set the tone for 20th-century attitudes towards drugs in the US that later developed into a global approach. Anslinger's technique was to draw on fears about foreign 'others', both inside and outside national boundaries, and he exaggerated the dangers caused first by opium and cocaine, and then marijuana. He went to great lengths, using extensive propaganda, to ensure that drugs played into US citizens' racist fears and were associated with Chinese, black and Mexican immigrants. Anslinger also drew on existing concerns about national security during the Cold War, tapping into xenophobic fears about the spread of communism around the world to further the cause of prohibition (Kinder and Walker, 1986). Throughout the 1950s Anslinger accused a number of communist nations of trading in narcotics (Kinder and Walker, 1986). Using this tactic he was able to persuade his peers in government to adopt stricter drug control legislation and to promote anti-narcotics agreements internationally (Kinder and Walker, 1986).

Commentators have traced how historically, the drugs targeted for prohibition have been those used by immigrant groups, the poor and black people deemed a 'threat' to the social order (see, for example, Chomsky, 1998; Boyd, 2004; Guy, 2009).[1] These groups, also sometimes referred to as the 'dangerous classes', have been viewed as not subscribing to the norms and values of white Christian society, or as superfluous in the capitalist drive to make profit and create wealth (Chomsky, 1998; Boyd, 2004; Guy, 2009). Drugs such as opium, marijuana and cocaine associated with the 'dangerous classes' have therefore been targeted for control, while other harmful drugs have not. This has led some to argue that the war on drugs is a war on the poor and minority ethnic groups (Chomsky, 1998).

Female sexuality as well as race has been cited as a key variable in the drive for prohibitive measures. The relationship between female sexual morality and racist fears about its contamination by immigrants has been discussed by various commentators as key to understanding the origins of the war on drugs (see, for example, Boyd, 2004; Guy, 2009). As traditional expectations of women in Western societies have located them as the guardians of moral virtue, the control of women's sexuality has been pivotal in the historical construction of the 'drug problem'. Fears in the US, which then spread to Canada and the UK, about Chinese opium smokers contaminating the morality of white women fuelled drug prohibition (Boyd, 2004; Guy, 2009). Prior to prohibition, opium dens were considered to be places of evil, where white women could be seduced by immigrants. The association between recreational drug use and interracial sexual activity served to provide legitimacy to the prohibition movement as part of 'a felt need to protect citizens from unscrupulous foreign criminals' who, it was thought, would 'corrupt our nation's people, undermine its moral values and degrade its national stock' (Guy, 2009).

Guy (2009) describes how variations of this discourse around the deviant black man seducing the innocent white woman have reoccurred at various points in history. In the 1950s in the UK, fears about the sexuality of African and African-Caribbean men defiling white women were expressed through concerns that innocent young women may be enticed into hemp smoking. Newspaper coverage of cocaine use before and after the First World War drew on the same themes in this instance to argue against women's emancipation (Guy, 2009). Commentators have thus concluded that the status of a substance as illegal is not simply a reflection of its actual dangerousness or capacity to cause harm, but of the political agendas of governments to control certain populations (Berridge, 1984; Kohn, 1992; Kohn and Gootenberg, 1999; Chomsky, 1998; Boyd, 2004; McKormack, 2007; Guy, 2009). Furthermore, legislative moves have been intrinsically bound up with concerns about (white) women's sexuality, morality and independence (Kohn, 1992; Kohn and Gootenberg, 1999; Boyd, 2004; Guy, 2009).

Boyd (2004) argues that prohibition as it relates to women in particular can be traced back to the witch-hunts and condemnation of women's knowledge of natural medicine. Women healers and midwives were among those accused of being witches, and their knowledge of various plants to relieve pain and suffering was suppressed. As a result, up to the present day women have lost control of their own sexuality, reproduction and independence (Boyd, 2004). While all drugs have risks, the prohibition of drugs such as heroin and crack creates a situation in which women who use these drugs are exposed to all kinds of dangers that they would otherwise not encounter (Boyd, 2004), such as homelessness, violence from other users and dealers, sex work and risk of overdose. The illegal/legal divide also has an impact on the lives of poor women more than other women. Poor women buying small amounts of an illicit drug at one time are more likely to end up being subject to fluctuation in the potency and quality of the drug, and thus find themselves at an increased risk of overdose (Boyd, 2004). They are also more likely to be exposed to violence, arrest and criminalisation (Boyd, 2004). These issues are discussed in more detail in Chapters Seven and Eight, in an analysis of the accounts of 40 female drug users.

Punitive regulation

A punitive political climate has underpinned drug policy in the US, UK and Canada to greater or lesser degrees for the last quarter-century. This is reflected in the rise of each of their prison populations for drug offences since the 1980s (see Chapter Three), and corresponds with the reduction of state welfare provision and investment in law and order, characteristic of neoliberal states (Wacquant, 2010). Most women in the UK, US and Canada are arrested for drug possession rather than dealing or trafficking, and mostly for marijuana rather than heroin, crack or amphetamines (Boyd, 2004). Due to media distortions, it is often thought that all or most drug users engage in criminal activity to fund their drug use, but this constitutes a small minority of users who tend to engage in non-violent, low-level crimes, such as shoplifting, dealing or fraud.

The US has led the international approach of prohibition and punishment, and has had a huge influence on its spread and popularity around the world. In 1961, under the direction of Harry Anslinger and the Federal Bureau of Narcotics (FBN), the US instigated the United Nations (UN) drug convention (United Nations, 2013), resulting in an international treaty to prohibit the production and supply of specific drugs. This has resulted in global drug prohibition that no country can withdraw from without breaking the terms of the treaty and risking severe political and economic consequences. As Andreas (1999, p 127) has argued:

> Open defection ... would place the defecting country in the category of a pariah "narcostate," generate material repercussions in the form of economic sanctions and aid cutoffs, and damage the country's moral standing in the international community.

Since 1971 the prohibitive approach of drug policy in the US has been known as the 'war on drugs' as declared by President Nixon, and prohibition acquired further momentum. Successive governments in the US have found the demonisation of drugs and anti-drug crusades to be rhetorically, financially and politically useful, as have other countries around the world (Levine, 2001). Governments have found that the expansion of military and police powers and resources mobilised in the name of prohibition served to encompass broader national security concerns (Kinder and Walker, 1986), and can be used for non-drug-related means such as wars against political opponents and surveillance (Levine, 2001; Scott, 2003, 2010; Seiler, 2008). Drug dependence can be used as a scapegoat for numerous social ills such as poverty, crime, delinquency, unemployment, urban decay, violence and mental illness (Levine, 2001; Scott, 2003, 2010; Seiler, 2008). In the US, drug policy continues to be shaped around the idea that drugs cause crime and drug use can be reduced through enforcement, the punishment of drug possession and drug-related behaviours. People who use drugs and possess relatively small quantities are likely to receive criminal sanctions and even a prison sentence, as drug use is predominantly viewed as a criminal rather than a public health or social problem – the US has mandatory sentencing for the possession of small amounts of illegal substances. These laws were introduced in the 1980s, and largely apply to the possession of crack cocaine.

The punitive approach found in the US associating drug use and crime increasingly dominates British drug policy. However, drug use is meant to be reduced through a public health approach by steering users into treatment. Possession of small quantities of drugs would not usually result in a prison sentence, while drug offences such as dealing or production may receive harsh punitive sanctions, although not as harsh as in the US. Drug trafficking is subject to a mandatory minimum sentence, as in the US. Up until the 1960s the UK was known for its tolerant public health approach to drug-dependent users. Between 1916 and the 1960s the UK separated the treatment of dependent drug users from the punishment of unregulated users and suppliers (Reuter and Stevens, 2007). This was known as the 'British system', whereby doctors had the power to prescribe and slowly reduce dependent users with heroin and cocaine. The 'British system' was established as a result of the Rolleston Committee report of 1926 (Departmental Committee Report, 1926), which concluded that as addiction at the time was a problem for a relatively small number of people and a primarily middle-class phenomenon, criminal sanctions were unnecessary (Reuter and Stevens, 2007). This lasted for 40 years, in the context of the development and establishment of a strong national healthcare system. However, the 'British System' lost precedence as recreational drug use became more widespread and came to be associated with a politically subversive youth culture in the 1960s and working-class, male heroin addicts in the 1980s (Reuter and Stevens, 2007). Doctors lost their powers to prescribe heroin and cocaine and the legal control of these and other drugs increased.

In recent decades in the UK, alongside the ascendance of neoliberalism and the gradual demise of a well-established welfare state, the treatment system has increasingly become intertwined with the criminal justice system as crime prevention concerns have gained ascendance. This has led one theorist to describe recent trends in the UK as 'the criminalisation of British drug policy' (Seddon, 2008a, p 1). Drug-related offenders are likely to be sentenced to coercive treatment through the criminal justice system, a modality which some argue impedes recovery. However, a key difference between US policy and other countries is that of voluntary access to affordable treatment. In the UK government-funded or subsidised treatment is available. In contrast, in the US treatment is only available privately to those with health insurance or through the criminal justice system.

Canadian drug policy, as in the UK and US, is situated within a punitive, neoliberal political climate corresponding with welfare state dismantling and benefit cutbacks since the 1990s. In Canada, as in the UK, drug use is meant to be reduced through a public health approach by steering users into treatment. Possession of small quantities of drugs would not usually result in a prison sentence, while drug offences such as dealing, production or trafficking is subject to harsh punitive sanctions, although not as harsh as in the US. As in the UK, funded or subsidised treatment is available, although Boyd (2004) argues that the situation is similar to that in the US in that voluntary treatment is in short supply and funding is inadequate.

The aim of prohibition has been to stifle and eventually eradicate the supply of illegal drugs and to protect citizens from drug-related harms (IDPC, 2010). In 1998 the UN held a declared goal of eventually creating 'a drug-free world' through global prohibition. The rationale behind prohibition and the war on drugs is that unlawful drugs are dangerous to the health of the individual. The 'danger' of certain drugs is constituted as residing in their individual properties, and the physical, psychological and social harm they are constructed as causing is what must be prevented. However, an Independent Inquiry in the UK into the harmfulness of the drugs prohibited and classified according to the Misuse of Drugs Act 1991 concluded that most controlled substances are no more harmful than alcohol or tobacco, and cannabis is less harmful than both of them (UKDPC, 2008b; Shiner, 2009). The harmfulness of many legal and prescribed drugs is widely recognised. Although one may assume that drug policy is based on 'expert' scientific knowledge about the harmfulness of illicit drugs, the legal/illegal distinction between drugs such as cannabis, tobacco, alcohol and heroin in terms of the harm caused or potential for dependence has no scientific legitimacy. Political forces rather than the pharmacological properties of drugs determine their illegal status.

There has been global acceptance of prohibition by countries throughout the world. Governments and institutions have found prohibition to be politically and ideologically advantageous in numerous ways. The war on drugs has become an international multi-billion dollar industry, creating thousands of jobs and flourishing companies (Davis, 1999; Zeese, 2001; DPA, 2010). The extensive economic, political and military power and influence of the US is only a partial explanation (Levine, 2001). Aside from the benefits already discussed, romantic ideologies about state power to protect its citizens from harm and police various aspects of life for the common good in the 20th century aided the spread of prohibition (Levine, 2001). Political leaders of all stripes could compete among each other nationally and unite cross-nationally to win the war on drugs (Levine, 2001). The UN provided prohibition with legitimacy and authority for it to be extended (Levine, 2001).

Despite the efforts of penal systems and enforcement agencies over the past few decades, drug usage has continued to increase in most countries in Europe and the US (Ramsay et al, 2001; Reuter and Trautmann, 2009). It has proved impossible to reduce significantly and sustainably the overall scale of illegal drug markets (SEU, 2003; IDPC, 2010). Consequently, illegal drugs are cheaper and more available than ever before (Transform, 2006). This has led many to conclude that the war on drugs has been lost (Chambliss, 1995; Bertram, 1996; Zeese and Lewin, 1999; Gray, 2001; Huggins, 2005; Rowe, 2006; *The Economist*, 2009).

Opponents of the war on drugs argue that it has not only failed to protect citizens from harm, but is at the root of most ills typically attributed to drugs. The effects of the criminalisation and marginalisation of drug users have contributed to a growth in drug-related health problems such as the spread of HIV/AIDS, hepatitis and other blood-borne diseases (Ball et al, 1998; Miron, 2004; WHO et al, 2009). Seizures by enforcement agencies are linked to increases in the impurities found in illicit drugs, placing the health of users in greater danger (SEU, 2003). Some dependent users may be deterred from seeking drug treatment for fear of being added to a government registry of addicts, and consequently losing employment or custody of their children (IDPC, 2010).

The war on drugs increases profits and the reach of organised criminals who are also routinely involved in murder, violence, illegal arms trading, terrorism, corruption, fraud and money laundering (Miron, 2004; Transform, 2006). Successful operations against a dealing network can increase violence as gangs may fight over the vacant turf (Roberts et al, 2004; ICSDP, 2010; IDPC, 2010). Prohibition creates the conditions for increased acquisitive crime such as theft or burglary as low-income users need to raise money to cover the inflated cost (Miron, 2004; Transform, 2006). Despite substantial enforcement, millions of people continue to sell, purchase and consume drugs (Miron, 2004). Prohibition criminalises and marginalises whole sections of the population in countries all over the world.

Despite these issues, the current political climate is predominantly unfavourable to the decriminalisation of drugs (Husak, 1992; Bean, 2010), although moves to liberalise drugs in various countries around the world seems to be growing. Governments frequently claim that legalisation would result in increased drug use, and produce a dramatic rise in related health and behavioural problems (Bean 2010). However, in view of the harms produced by prohibition, the International Drug Policy Consortium (IDPC) (2010) suggest that a paradigm shift is needed in the design and implementation of national drug control policies where human rights law is recognised as a core element. The UN system has drawn attention to the fundamental human rights and freedoms that have been breached in pursuit of drug control objectives (IDPC, 2010). For instance, attention has been paid to the use of the death penalty for drug offences, the compulsory detention of drug users in drug treatment, the restricted access to essential medicines, HIV prevention, treatment, care and support, and the discriminatory application of drug control laws (IDPC, 2010).

Husak (1992) argues that the war on drugs is a misnomer, and it is actually 'a war on drug users'. Increases in arrest rates and incarceration since the 1970s have been explained with reference to the war on drugs (see, for example, Tonry, 1995). Focus has been placed on how, in keeping with its historical roots, the war on drugs has disproportionately and specifically targeted and had an impact on poor and low-level users and dealers, women, black and minority ethnic groups (Tonry, 1995; Human Rights Watch, 2000, 2008; Boyd, 2004; Beatty et al, 2007; King, 2008; Guy, 2009; Wacquant, 2009). Some writers, focusing on the ways the war on drugs has had an impact on the lives of women, have taken Husak's statement further, and suggested that the war on drugs is a war on women (see, for example, Bloom et al, 1994; Feinman, 1994; Chesney-Lind, 1995, 1997; Owen, 1998, 2000; Bush-Baskette, 1999, 2004, 2010; Szalavitz, 1999; Bloom and Chesney-Lind, 2000; Belknap, 2001; Tyler, 2010), and in particular, a war on black women (Bush-Baskette, 1998, 2004, 2010).

Dramatic increases in female arrest and incarceration rates in the US, Canada and the UK since the 1970s have prompted various debates about women, crime and punishment. In the 1970s a moral panic ensued about women's crime, suggesting that the apparent increases were caused by women's emancipation, and that a new, more violent, breed of female criminal was emerging (see, for example, Adler, 1975; Simon, 1975). Adler (1975) and Simon (1975) linked increases in the numbers of women arrested to women's desire for social and economic equality. Although this thesis received wide public acceptance, a closer analysis of arrest data found little to support this notion (see, for example, Steffensmeier, 1980). Instead it was argued that there was no discernable change in women's criminal behaviour; rather, the harsher treatment of women within the criminal justice system was occurring, especially for women and girls who do not comply with conventional female stereotypes (see, for example, Carlen, 1983; Heidensohn, 1985; Worrall, 1990).

More recently it has been suggested that the increase in women's arrest and imprisonment rates since the 1970s is largely attributable to stricter enforcement against women for drug law violations (Feinman, 1994; Chesney-Lind, 1995; Mann, 1995; Bush-Baskette, 1998, 2004, 2010; Kruttschnitt and Gartner, 2003; Boyd, 2004). The increases in the rates of female incarceration in general, and for drug offences in particular, far exceed the increases in the rates of men's (Kruttschnitt, 2010). Although overall there are more men behind bars for drug offences, the war on drugs has had a more severe impact on women incarcerated than men (Kruttschnitt, 2010).

Neoliberalism, freedom and disordered production

Increased punitiveness towards women and men's drug use has occurred precisely when neoliberal modes of governance and the championing of consumer freedom have been paramount. Neoliberalism is a rationality of government that emerged in the 1980s and continues to the present (Braithwaite, 2000; Rose et al, 2006; Seddon, 2010). It was constituted out of critiques of welfare liberalism and the view that the interventionist state generated a culture of dependency, rather than activity and independence (O'Malley, 2008, p 13). This mode of governance privileges market forces, deregulation of business, global economic trade, enterprise and individualism. There has been a shift from Income Support to welfare to work, limiting of eligibility, increased privatisation of services, cuts to healthcare, childcare, social services, mental health services, a loss of workers' rights, longer, flexible and fragmented working hours, corporate welfare over people welfare, and rising inequalities.

Researchers have attempted to make sense of how punitive drug laws operate within the political context of neoliberalism (see, for example, Reith, 2004; O'Malley, 2008; Bean, 2010; Seddon, 2010). They have asked how punitive, interventionist approaches to drug consumption are reconciled with neoliberal modes of governance, emphasising consumer freedom and choice. A key characteristic of neoliberalism is the assumption of a 'free' subject, an autonomous, enterprising individual with choices, rights and the freedom to realise their desires. In such forms of government the regulation of citizens' conduct becomes a matter of their desire to pursue their own civility, wellbeing and advancement. Governmental power presupposes the freedom of its subjects in that they are understood as having a range of choices available.

> Power is exercised only over free subjects, and only insofar as they are "free." By this we mean individual or collective subjects who are faced with a field of possibilities in which several kind of conduct, several modes of behaviour are available. (Foucault, 2002 [1982], p 342)

In a neoliberal climate, where having the freedom to choose is of paramount importance, one would assume that individuals would have the right and freedom to alter their consciousness and consume their drug/s of choice. However, stricter enforcement against drug users and offenders in the UK, US and Canada has accompanied the rise of neoliberalism.

Drawing on the work of Braithwaite (2008), Seddon (2010) argues that the key to understanding the persistence of prohibition, in spite of neoliberalist concerns with non-interventionism and the rolling back of the state, is recognition of the 'myth of deregulation' (Braithwaite, 2008). Despite the idea that neoliberalism involves a move away from interventionism, it 'has been accompanied by an extension and expansion of regulation' (Seddon, 2010, p 134). While governments profess the importance of non-interventionism in the lives of citizens, they have increased involvement in the punitive regulation of the poor and marginalised with suspicion, risk assessments, surveillance and control techniques across criminal justice, medical and welfare settings. The demise of welfarism involved a reduction in social provision but not of social regulation. Interventionism, as found in the continuation of punitive drug laws, mass incarceration, immigration control, the expansion of police powers and the prison industrial complex, is, in fact, alive and well. Only certain freedoms are compatible with and accepted in neoliberal states – one has freedoms only in as much as they are compatible with free market capitalism.

As an individual in a neoliberal state one is expected to act as a functioning economic unit, working, earning, spending and consuming. One's behaviour is shaped and interpreted along economic lines, and 'everyone is defined by his or her consumption' (Bauman, 1988, p 93). In order to function effectively as an economic unit it is assumed that at the same time as expressing one's desires, one will behave responsibly, rationally, be hardworking, self-sufficient, pursue a healthy lifestyle, practice self-discipline, self-control, self-denial and demonstrate morals compatible with capitalism and a consumer lifestyle (Rose, 1999). Drug use, but particularly illicit and excessive drug use, is seen as obstructing an individual from fulfilling his or her role as a fully functioning citizen. The addict is rendered 'blameworthy' for this predicament as addiction is constituted as self-induced. Users have voluntarily started taking drugs in the first place (Stein, 1985), and exhibit a lack of self-control and will. The addict has abdicated his or her freedom to consume responsibly. As a result, dependent users transgress the boundary that keeps production and consumption in balance, as 'disordered consumption also implies disordered production' (Reith, 2004, p 289). They thus represent a 'surplus population' (Wacquant, 2001), embodying 'the antithesis of the Protestant work ethic' (Reith, 2004, p 289).

The responsibility attributed or 'blameworthiness' of a drug user is conditioned by class. It has frequently been asserted that the policing and punishment of the poor and working classes dominate criminal justice preoccupations (see, for example, Rusche and Kirchheimer, 1939; UN, 1976; Reiman, 1979; Box and Hale, 1985; Box, 1987; Cook, 1988; Carlen and Cook, 1989; Gordon, 1994; Wacquant, 2009). This has also been said of the policing and punishment of low-income illicit drug users, dealers and traffickers (Christie, 1993; Gordon, 1994; Western, 2010). In the political terrain of neoliberalism, the disproportionate punishment given to the drug use, dealing and trafficking of the poor can be seen as an attempt to ensure that those who do not conform to their role as functioning, disciplined workers in the licit economy are held to account. As Gordon (1994, p 127) argues:

> ... the sins of the latest dangerous classes as they are exemplified in the "drug problem" go beyond the immorality of promoting or participating in habits of self-destruction and harm to others. They are also challenges to values of hard work and initiative or, in the case of dealers, perverters of the dream of free enterprise. Cultural and economic threats merge, as the dangerous classes are seen as responsible for declines in national productivity as well as moral righteousness.

O'Malley (2008, p 3) argues that the most striking development in criminal justice of the 1970s and 1980s during the emergence of neoliberalism in the UK, US and Australia was the shift towards:

> ... rational choice models of the offender and punitive/deterrence approaches that emphasised the moral and rational foundations of criminal responsibility.

The same discourses that construct particular notions of the addicted subject also attempt to control, regulate and restore them to 'normality'. The addict's refusal to exercise self-discipline is frowned upon within neoliberal modes of governance, and gives rise to the appearance of its 'hidden despotism' (Valverde, 1998). Within this political climate, those who appear not to possess the attributes required for freedom become party to 'various forms of intervention and discipline or are even denied freedom altogether' (Reith, 2004, p 296). The war on drugs thus reinforces neoliberal regimes of power. The drug addict represents a disobedient subject who refuses to be 'free to choose', and is to be punished for this affront.

The neoliberal welfare state, risk and responsibility

The rise of neoliberalism has not only had an impact on the governance of drug users and offenders in terms of drug law enforcement. The restructuring of the welfare state and continued cuts to welfare assistance in the UK, US and Canada over the past 40 years or more has made female drug users more vulnerable to governmental control, surveillance and regulation in other ways. Processes of neoliberalism have greatly diminished social provisions for and the rights of citizens in the UK, US and Canada, and particularly those of low-income people and disadvantaged groups such as immigrants, racial minorities, single mothers and drug users. Welfare, health and social service provision have been reconfigured with a focus on risk thinking and individual responsibility, and this has affected the way male and female users are constructed as a problem to be governed.

Spending on social provisions has been reduced in the UK, US and Canada, while punitive laws and policies have been pursued. In the UK, welfare spending on housing, education, healthcare, social security and personal social services was 'rolled back' from the beginning of the Thatcher administration. The aim was to create a free market economy to promote individual initiative and to end welfare dependency. This has been continued by successive Conservative and Labour governments (Bashevkin, 2002). Blair emphasised responsibility and helping people to help themselves (Blair, 2002). He prompted all benefit recipients, including single mothers, people with disabilities and older people, to find work rather than remain on benefits (Blair, 2002). The coalition government claimed to have inherited a welfare system that 'trapped people in poverty and encouraged irresponsibility', and has vowed to end 'the culture of entitlement' (Cameron, 2012). The 2010 UK Drug Strategy (Home Office, 2010) denounces the heroin and crack users it states claim benefits, and asserts plans to sanction users who do not enter treatment by making treatment a condition of benefits.

In the US, former President Bill Clinton stated that he 'would end welfare as we know it', and proceeded to dismantle the welfare state. His introduction of the Personal Responsibility and Work Opportunity Reconciliation Act (PRWORA) of 1996 limited welfare assistance to five years in one lifetime, instituting Temporary Assistance for Needy Families (TANF). Other changes included tighter conditions for the eligibility of food stamps, reductions in immigrant welfare assistance, and work requirements for claimants. The Act includes a strong workfare component, and was thus proclaimed a 'reassertion of America's work ethic' by the US Chamber of Commerce. The US imposes a lifetime welfare ban on food stamps and cash assistance for drug offenders, including those found in possession of a small quantity (Smith, 2007).

Since the 1990s, the control of welfare policy has shifted to provincial governments in Canada, and conservative governments in these provinces have devastated the welfare state by cutting welfare benefits, social spending and reducing eligibility criteria (Boyd, 2004). The introduction of the Canada Health and Social Transfer in 1996 saw an end to national standards, and workfare and employment programmes were no longer banned (Boyd, 2004). Provinces such as Ontario, Alberta and British Columbia have created their own criteria for financial aid, and these are not based on financial need (Boyd, 2004). In Ontario, former Premier Harris claimed that women on welfare were drug users (Boyd, 2004). He asserted that welfare claimants should abstain from drugs, be subject to mandatory drug testing, and those who did not comply would risk losing their benefits (Boyd, 2004).

In neoliberal political discourse, the immorality of women on welfare was central to arguments for eradicating the dependency cultures that were believed to have developed in the UK, US and Canada. Women with children entitled to welfare benefits were constructed as idle and unwilling to work. Single mothers in particular, in political rhetoric and tabloid media discourse, were constructed as the scourge of society. Domestic and mothering responsibilities regarded as predominantly 'women's work' are not seen as forms of work that contribute to or count in society. Neoliberal discourse responsibilises poor women who care for children, older people or people with disabilities for their poverty, and requires them to enter into low-paid, unskilled work in the public sphere, and leave the care of their children or relatives to other, often low-paid, workers. The obstacles women face in finding work offering childcare and/or flexible working demands have not changed, and are not considered in neoliberal discourses that construct women who do not work, especially single mothers, as idle, immoral, irresponsible, welfare dependents. Poor drug-using women, and especially those with children dependent on welfare, are seen as the epitome of immorality and irresponsibility.

Welfare policy, social service and health provision play as much a role in the regulation and social control of poor drug-using women as prohibition and criminal law. Risk discourse, the identification and management of risks, is a key feature of neoliberal modes of governance (see, for example, O'Malley, 1992, 1996, 1999; Rose, 2000; Reith, 2004; Pollack, 2010). It has become a standard way of managing social exclusion, and poor and marginalised populations, such as offenders, single mothers, immigrants, the homeless and drug users, as a post-welfare strategy of control (see, for example, O'Malley, 1992, 1996, 1999; Rose, 2000; Reith, 2004; Pollack, 2010). Risk management practices span criminal justice, welfare, medicine, mental health and child protection services, and are mobilised by professionals such as social workers, prison officers, probation workers, doctors and psychologists, who have become administrators of neoliberal agendas or 'translators of state power' (Pollack, 2010, p 1275).

Neoliberalism is also a mode of governing, which places emphasis on individual responsibility, the responsibility of families and communities in their own self-governance (O'Malley, 2008, p 3). The self-governing approaches of neoliberalism are encapsulated within harm reduction strategies. Within the harm reduction discourse there is some recognition that drug use is relatively widespread and thus 'normal', and the free choice of drug users as consumers is tolerated to some extent, provided their use does not interfere with the social order. The assumption is that if provided with appropriate information, the rational, responsible citizen will avoid experimenting with illicit drugs altogether, or at least avoid the risks of the potential harms caused by drugs (O'Malley, 1992, 2008). The drug 'addict' has thus failed to effectively govern, avoid risk and take responsibility for his or her drug consumption.

Risk discourse is partially dependent on the creation of 'others' who are unable or unwilling to effectively self-govern and behave responsibly (O'Malley, 1992, 2008). This incites risk aversion and obedience to 'norms' (that is, governmental objectives). The 'drug addict' is situated as interfering with the social order by engaging in risky behaviours that run completely counter to all those so highly valued in neoliberal states, and failing to manage the risks (Reith, 2004). He or she represents the antithesis of the functional, self-governing, hardworking, disciplined, economic, neoliberal subject. The 'addict' is situated as a lazy, undisciplined, unemployed, criminal parasite, the embodiment of ill health, lack of self-control and discipline. He or she is configured as a waster, a welfare scrounger who does not want to work.

Risk avoidance and responsibility are embodied by men and women in different ways. Social constructions of gender mean that women are expected to avoid certain risk behaviours more than men. Illegal drug use is a criminal, risky activity consistent with the expression of masculinity. Women who adopt risky, drug-using identities interfere with the social order and the 'gender order'. Stricter enforcement against women for drug use violations in the US, Canada and the UK is testimony to the greater responsibility for risk avoidance female drug users have to bear. Within drug policy, categories of risk constitute women illicit drug users as more likely to engage in risky sexual behaviour and injecting practices than men, to risk the health and wellbeing of the foetus in pregnancy and their children, and place communities at risk of moral contamination (Tardiff et al, 1997; Ettorre, 2007). Women's illicit drug use is frequently constructed as signalling sexual promiscuity and associated with prostitution (see, for example, Inciardi et al, 1993). As Ettorre (1992, p 78) argues:

> Whether or not a woman heroin addict has ever exchanged her body for drugs or money for her habit, she is characterized as an impure woman, an evil slut or a loose female.

Women users' bodies are thus inscribed with risk more so than men's. As Boyd (2004, p 105) observes:

> Risk categories, appearing neutral and scientific, deflect attention away from how they are used as gendered, class-based, and racialized measurements.

Poor, vulnerable, black and minority ethnic women are more likely to be located within categories of risk and constructed as a problem to be governed (Boyd, 2004).

Hannah-Moffatt (2000) argues that neoliberal states provide a political context in which the 'needs' of poor, drug-dependent men and women are relegated to their 'risk' management. Drugs such as cannabis, cocaine, heroin and amphetamines, and the people who use them, are predominantly constructed as potentially 'dangerous' rather than vulnerable individuals in need of social support.

The female addict is situated across all these spheres as the most abhorrent of all, flouting all social expectations of women as guardians of morality, the family unit and family values. She fails to conform to notions of the nuclear family which she is meant to uphold, and has broken the 'class deal' and the 'gender deal' (Carlen, 1988). The dependent drug-using woman is constituted as an unfit mother, a useless, defunct, non-woman – 'surplus population' in a double sense, for failing to be a functional economic unit in the public and private spheres.

This is the political terrain in which the governance of women's illicit drug use in the UK, US and Canada is currently carried out. In the punitive climate of the war on drugs, female users are stigmatised, blamed and viewed as immoral non-women for disordered, irrational and irresponsible consumption. This book explores how female users resist these negative constructions of themselves, and attempt to shape a positive identity for themselves.

Note

[1] The prohibition of drugs has also been linked to colonial practices and the suppression of the spiritual and religious practices of indigenous populations (Boyd, 2004).

Part Two

The next three chapters draw on Foucault's concepts of governmentality and technologies of power to provide an analysis of the specific governmental techniques and procedures adopted in contemporary drug policy. They examine three key technologies of power through which women users are governed: prohibition, medicalisation and welfarisation. Foucault describes governmentality or the 'art of government' as 'the encounter between technologies of the domination of others and those of the self' (Foucault, 2000 [1982], p 225). Prohibition, medicalisation and welfarisation may be seen as technologies of domination. These are practices of power that 'determine the conduct of individuals and submit them to certain ends' (p 225). Through these technologies relations of power become 'firmly set and congealed', and the freedom of the individual becomes 'extremely constrained and limited' (Foucault, 2000 [1984], p 283). Prohibition, medicalisation and welfarisation can also be seen as:

> ... technologies imbued with aspirations for the shaping of conduct [behaviour] in the hope of producing certain desired effects and averting certain undesired ones. (Rose, 1999, p 52)

In the governance of illicit drug use prohibition, medicalisation and welfarisation form a curious meld as the criminal justice system, medical treatment establishment and welfare regimes intersect in the regulation of illicit drug use.

The technology of prohibition is the practice of prohibiting the manufacture, transportation, import, export, sale and consumption of certain drugs by law. The rationale underpinning prohibition is that unlawful drugs are dangerous to the health of the individual. Prohibition is enforced through the technology of punishment. Punishment as exercised by the state in law involves matching fair consequence to crimes to achieve justice. A fundamental element of punishment is the process of criminalisation, which, in modern neoliberal societies, is a tactic of government that endures after sentencing due to the criminal records system.

The medicalisation of drug use is based on the 'disease' model of addiction, and the distinction between 'normal' and 'out-of-control' behaviour. Historically, women, the poor, the working class and immigrants are assumed to be more at risk of the disease of addiction or the 'disease of the will'. However, the medicalisation of women's illicit drug use is arguably an inconsistent aspect of drug policy when the over-prescribing of legal drugs to women and their dependence on them is taken into account. Legal drugs are prescribed to women by 'experts' with medical authority to serve a normalising function as 'coping mechanisms', but are constructed as deviant and immoral when self-administered. Women who use illegal drugs are considered irresponsible, irrational and selfish. However, once they comply with their drug use being administered through the medical profession within the treatment or criminal justice systems, regardless of the relative addictiveness or harmfulness of the drugs prescribed, their normality, rationality and responsibility is considered to be restorable.

Welfarisation is the process individuals encounter when benefit, social work or other agents construct them as needing social support. The same process may constitute the individual as unworthy of support, or may provide the rationale for an unwanted intervention. Policies of welfare also operate as mechanisms of control and surveillance over the lives of marginalised groups and individuals. Penal and welfare regimes can be seen as closely intertwined in the governance of female illicit drug use. The ascendance of risk management as a technique of governance consolidates their relationship. A key governmental rationality embedded within the technology of welfarisation is the distinction between the deserving and undeserving poor. By virtue of having chosen to use drugs, women and men dependent on drugs are automatically regarded as culpable members of the 'undeserving poor'.

Drug use as a medical-moral-legal hybrid

Conrad (1992) argues that some behaviours such as illicit drug use have come to be seen as medical-moral-legal hybrids. The continued medicalisation of illicit drug use means drug dependency is still widely seen as a disease or illness, although it has not been fully medicalised. At the same time, it is seen as deviant and immoral, and remains a criminal, punishable offence. Illicit drug use is considered a legal problem for the criminal justice system, and at the same time a medical problem requiring treatment. The intersection of the criminal justice system and treatment establishment is evident in many aspects of the governance of illicit drug users, such as mandatory drug treatment, drug treatment within prison, drug testing on arrest and punitive approaches in treatment settings (see Seddon, 2008a).

There is a somewhat 'muddy relationship' between the legal and medical aspects of drug use, and because of this it is unclear when a drug problem should be considered a moral or legal problem or a medical one (Murphy, 2007, pp 1-2). Some argue that it is none of these, but rather, 'in a free market economy ... addiction is primarily a political, social and economic problem' (Alexander, 2001, p 19). Nevertheless, due to the blurring of the boundaries between the legal and medical aspects of drug use, illicit drug users may receive mixed messages. They may believe, on the one hand, that they are not to blame for their dependency as they have a medical problem, but on the other, find they are still to be legally punished for 'the illness' (Murphy 2007).

As drug use is only partially medicalised (Conrad, 1992), users are not granted absolution for their 'wrong doing' and are not freed from taking responsibility for their drug abuse. As discussed previously (see pp 53–4), drug taking becomes a form of disordered consumption whereby users have made the wrong choices (Reith, 2004). The war on drugs and the management of illicit drug use as a medical-moral-legal hybrid (Conrad, 1992) makes dependent users responsible for their wrong choices and their disease of mind. The 'disease' is seen as brought on by dependent users themselves. Individuals who are seen to have flouted their duties as morally responsible citizens, by allowing themselves to become addicted to an illicit drug, are considered responsible for getting 'clean', and if they fail to do so, are deemed appropriate subjects for punishment. This form of governance, whereby drug users are constituted as responsible for their own predicament, is responsibilisation. This is discussed in detail in Part Three as a technology of the self.

More recently there has been a shift in the responsibilisation of dependent users, and the way they are expected to manage their 'disease'. Recovery discourse has placed the welfarisation of drug users centre stage, with an emphasis on the need for users to have access to welfare services such as support with employment, housing and parenting programmes alongside medical or psychotherapeutic treatments. This, at least in part, is underpinned by moralistic views of dependent drug users as criminals, benefit scroungers and unfit parents in need of reform. In addition, female dependent users have been responsibilised through welfarisation, subject to the interventions of child welfare services, for decades. Welfarisation thus intersects with and is increasingly intertwined with the criminal justice and treatment establishments, and completes the medical-moral-legal hybrid definition of drug use, creating a three-pronged 'carceral continuum'.

This three-pronged mechanism of surveillance and control has to be negotiated within all contexts at the organisational level and by users themselves (Murphy, 2007). One would not simply subscribe to one aspect of the medical-moral-legal hybrid definition of drug use in one setting and another component when the user entered another setting. Users will inevitably have to make sense of seemingly contradictory subjectivities that are ascribed to them by the authorities. Although the medical-moral-legal hybrid status of drug use is likely to be a difficult negotiation for illicit drug users themselves, it may be considered beneficial from the perspective of those working with illicit drug users. Using interview data from workers in both criminal justice and treatment settings, Murphy (2007) illustrates how workers viewed the institutions as complementing each other's work and providing mutual benefits. She shows how 'both settings articulate the importance of the other' (p 19), and hence serve to reinforce each other in the governance of illicit drug use. In other words, the powers of medicalisation and prohibition and punishment combine, producing a heterosis, a technology of power with hybrid vigour and increased functionality in the governance of female users. Murphy (2007) suggests that consequently, the current mix of moral, criminal and medical methods of labelling and managing substance abuse is likely to continue indefinitely. Part Three of this book focuses on how this hybrid mode of governing female drug users is experienced by women users themselves. It examines how they make sense of and negotiate the contradictory subjectivities that are ascribed to them, and how they both internalise and resist them (see Chapters Six and Seven).

A concept that can be seen as useful here is that of Wacquant's 'deadly symbiosis'. While it is used in a very specific sense by Wacquant to describe the affinity between the prison and the ghetto in the US, the relationship between the criminal justice system, treatment and welfare services in the UK, US and Canada can be described as forming a 'deadly symbiosis' in the governance of dependent illicit drug users. As subjects of government, illicit drug users are not constructed as simply immoral, thus justifying their treatment, medicalisation and welfarisation, and nor are they simply viewed as diseased, hence justifying their punishment. The realms of governance have become interdependent. Through the technologies of punishment, medicalisation and welfarisation, treatment, welfare and prison systems 'meet and mesh', reinforcing each other to assure the exclusion of dependent illicit drug users from general society (Wacquant 2001, 2009). This idea is explored further in the ensuing chapters of the book.

Alexander (2001, p 19) argues that debates concerning whether drug use and dependency are best understood as a medical or criminal issue is erroneous, but rather 'in a free market economy ... addiction is primarily a political, social and economic problem.' He argues that addictions are not necessarily good or bad, as coffee, reading or heroin may not harm a person. In contrast, negative addiction refers to destructive types of behaviour, 'where in the absence of achievable, healthy possibilities ... lifestyles are built around ... violence and excess' (Alexander, 1998, p 29). However, it is not even negative drug use that is the problem, as this is part of a larger pattern of social response to prolonged dislocation. This is defined as poverty of the spirit which is 'the absence of that essential integration & identification with family, community, society & spiritual values that makes "straight" life bearable most of the time & joyful at its peaks' (Alexander, 1998, p 29). Drug use is only one type of response to dislocation. Dislocation occurs in global market-driven societies where traditional cultures, economies and social relationships are destroyed. Free market economies thus contribute to self-destructive behaviours. This suggests that political, social and economic solutions should be sought for the problem of addiction.

The following three chapters examine how through technologies of power female users have been and continue to be constructed as a problem to be governed. The chapters also begin to discuss the impact of these technologies of power on the lives of female users. These technologies are examined at the level of policy and the discourses that constitute it.

Drug policy discourse

Drug policy discourses are comprised of various, distinct strands, including that of punishment and prohibition, medicalisation and welfarism. Although the emphasis on the respective strands vary cross-nationally, each of the discursive strands comprise an important aspect of overall governmental responses. The discourses of drug policy, including punishment and prohibition, medicalisation and welfarism, are ultimately all concerned with three key harms: harm to the individual, to communities and to children. Over the last three or four decades the UK, US and Canada have invariably constructed illicit drugs as:

- socially, physically and psychologically harmful to individual users, with an emphasis on 'problematic' drug users and young people;
- harmful to communities due to drug-related crime, fear of crime and anti-social behaviour; as a waste of resources due to the cost of punishing, policing and treating users and suppliers; and as a waste of human resources in terms of the unfulfilled potential of individuals. They are also harmful to farming communities in supply countries;
- harmful to families including children and foetuses.

While it may seem that each of the various strands of drug policy is concerned with distinct constructions and controls of harm (for example, public health discourse with the health and 'treatment' of problematic drug users), these discourses are not mutually exclusive but interweave, overlap and combine in different ways to produce a complex nexus. For example, UK, US and Canadian drug strategies emphasise the control of drug-related crime through 'treatment' within or instigated by the criminal justice system, such as through drug courts, drug abstinence orders, Drug Rehabilitation Orders (DROs), arrest referral schemes or drug treatment programmes in prison. Public health and punishment discourses thus combine as the prevention of crime is sought in the treatment of drug users, and medicalisation is integrated into the criminal justice system.

The discourses constituting drug policy construct the problem of female drug use and ultimately female users in particular ways. The ways female users' subjectivities are constructed in policy has real objective effects on their lives and on those around them. It is therefore important for these discourses to be investigated and challenged. The various strands of the discourse comprising contemporary drug policies and the technologies of power are now discussed in turn. The construction of the harm 'caused' by illicit drugs, the solutions that have been offered, and the impact they have had on women's lives are explored.

THREE

Prohibition

This chapter examines the role of the technology of prohibition in the governance of female drug use. It investigates the operation of this technology by exploring the prohibition and punishment strand of drug policy discourse, how female dependent users, dealers and traffickers are situated within it, and the impact the criminal justice system has on their lives. The rationale embedded within the technology of prohibition is that drugs are dangerous. The 'danger' of certain drugs is constituted as residing in their individual properties, and the physical, psychological and social harm they are constructed as causing is what must be prevented. As outlined in the introduction, the technology of prohibition and punishment is one of the regulatory techniques of government that is used to shape female drug users' and offenders' behaviour through the construction of particular problematic 'identities', for example, an unfit mother. While male drug users and offenders are also subject to this technology of power, this chapter investigates the particular ways it operates as a gendered form of control, for example, through the criminalisation of pregnancy and the gendered iniquity of the criminal justice system.

The proclaimed aim of the drug strategies in the UK, US and Canada is to protect young people, families and communities from the harm caused by illicit drugs. The idea is to do this by preventing, stopping, disrupting and reducing both the supply and demand for drugs. The idea within government rhetoric is that strong enforcement and harsh sanctions at international borders as well as within nation states, including the threat of incarceration, will deter potential users, dealers and traffickers from becoming involved in the illegal drugs market. While the sentences for drug offences vary in the respective countries, a consequence of these criminal sanctions in all of them has been an increase in the number of women and men moving through the criminal justice system for drug offences.

A cross-national analysis in the UK, US and Canada shows that as law and order advocates proclaim the importance of saving the family and upholding family values, they seem intent on destroying them. A consequence of the need to protect young people and families from the harms of illicit drugs has been to incarcerate increasing numbers of women who are mothers, and to separate them from their children. The impact of these strategies is disproportionately experienced by poor women and their families, and in particular, black and minority ethnic women, children and communities.

Furthermore, although drug policy discourse upholds and aims to protect family values, 'families', young people and 'communities', for many women and girls who become dependent on illicit drugs, families and communities are often a source of violence, abuse and poverty. This is a situation that makes women vulnerable to dependence and drug offending in the first place. However, this is not recognised in official discourses of drug policy. Women drug users in prison are often the victims of very serious crimes, notably male violence in its many forms (see, for example, Boyd, 1994; Scottish Executive, 2002; Ramsay, 2003; Malloch, 2004a). However, as a result of their perceived lifestyles, women drug users are denied 'victimhood' as subjects of government, and are consequently rendered punishable. Historically, violent perpetrators of rape, sexual abuse and domestic violence go unpunished, are under-represented in the criminal justice system, or receive more lenient sentences due to the supposed character and demeanour of their victims. In contrast, poor, victimised and black drug-using women, whose lives are shaped and framed by such crimes, are disproportionately locked up.

Construction of the problem for government: protecting families, young people and communities

In the prohibition strand of policy discourses in the UK, US and Canada, a major problem is conceptualised as the continued availability and demand for drugs. The availability of illicit drugs presumably means that more people will potentially initiate illegal drug use, and current users will continue. In the UK particularly, and to some extent in the US drug strategy, the emphasis is on the demand for illegal drugs by young people. Although controlled, recreational drug use is the norm, and the idea that young people need to be protected from harm is the official position. In the UK, US and Canada, illicit drug use is more common among young people. In the UK, the Drug Strategy 2010 (Home Office, 2010) states that resources will be put into protecting young people from the dangers of illegal drug use. Illicit drugs are constituted as having the power to 'impact on young people's education, their health, their families' (Home Office, 2010, p 7) and destroy their 'ambition and potential' (Home Office, 2010, p 3). According to the US *National Drug Control Strategy 2013* (Executive Office of the President of the United States, 2013), Americans apparently witness the 'childhoods [drugs] interrupt' (p 5), and drug use is linked to the 'academic failure' of young people (p 9). Young people are the focus of the preventative action plan of the Canadian *National Anti-Drug Strategy 2013* (Government of Canada, 2013). Drugs and those who distribute them 'endanger youth'. The aim is to target young people at risk of drug involvement, to prevent 'substance abuse', 'increasing youth crime', and the impact on communities.

Families of drug 'misusers' are also situated as in need of protection from harm in drug policy discourse in the UK, US and Canada. In the UK Drug Strategy 2010 illicit drugs are imbued with the capacity to 'destroy families' (Home Office, 2010, p 2) and to 'force families apart' (p 3). Drugs are constituted as causing families pain, having the capacity to destroy relationships and to 'shatter dreams' in the US strategy (2013, p 5). Families are not mentioned in the Canadian *National Anti-Drug Strategy 2013*. However, Rona Ambrose, Minister of Health, is quoted in a Health Canada 2013 News Release as stating: 'Our government understands that dangerous drugs like heroin have a horrible impact on families and communities' (Health Canada, 2013).

Protecting communities from crime is another key problem identified in the prohibition strand of drug policy discourse. In the US *National Drug Control Strategy 2013*, drugs are constructed as having the ability to 'divide' and 'disrupt' communities 'in long-lasting ways' (Executive Office of the President of the United States, 2013, pp 49-50). Drugs are said to 'undermine' communities in the UK strategy. The problem of crime is identified as caused by a minority of heroin and crack addicts who commit acquisitive crime to fund their habits while claiming benefits. In the Canadian strategy, drugs and the 'organised criminals and others who profit from them' apparently 'endanger' communities. Young people who 'abuse' drugs who are increasingly involved in crime are also thought to have a negative impact on communities.

The solution to the problem of protecting families, young people and communities found within prohibition discourse is to prevent, stop, disrupt and reduce both the supply and demand for drugs. As stated above, the idea within government rhetoric is that strong enforcement and harsh sanctions at international borders as well as within nation states will deter potential users, dealers and traffickers from becoming involved in the illegal drugs market. Despite evidence of high levels of recidivism among drug offenders and drug-using offenders, however, imprisonment continues to be used to lock up non-violent, low-level users and dealers (Howard League, 2011).

Unprecedented increase in the female prison population

One of the consequences of attempts to protect families, young people and communities from harm has been disproportionate numbers of men and women, but especially poor, black and minority ethnic women, being incarcerated. Through the technology of prohibition and punishment, poor, marginalised female drug users and offenders are situated as 'bad', 'immoral' 'dangerous' women, who need locking up to protect the public from harm. Since the 1970s there have been dramatic rises in the women's prison population in countries throughout the world. The steepest rise has been in the US, but disproportionate increases in women's prison populations have also occurred in the UK and most European countries, Canada, Australia, New Zealand and Japan (see, for example, Sudbury, 2005a; Sheenhan et al, 2007; Sabol and West, 2008; DCPC, 2010; Prison Reform Trust, 2010; Berman, 2012).

In the US, there has been an eight-fold increase (11,212 to 105,500) in the female prison population over the past 30 years, between 1977-2007 (Bowie, 1982; Sabol and West, 2008; West and Sabol, 2009; Women's Prison Association [WPA], 2009). This compares to a four-fold increase in the male prison population over the same period (WPA, 2009; Sabol and West, 2008; Bowie, 1982). In the last 30-40 years in England and Wales, there has been a three-fold increase in the female prison population, exceeding the rate of increase in the male prison population (Prison Reform Trust, 2010; Berman, 2012). Only 988 women were imprisoned in 1970, compared with 4,161 in 2010. There has also been a three-fold increase in the female prison population in Canada since 1970 (Hannah-Moffat and Shaw, 2000; Statistics Canada, 2000; Boyd, 2004, 2006), despite the overall prison population remaining fairly steady (Webster and Doob, 2007; Gartner et al, 2009).

These unprecedented increases in the female prison populations in the UK, US and Canada are often justified in policy discourse, along with increases in men's prison numbers, as due to an increase in offending (Ministry of Justice, 2013). In fact, governments have planned and continue to plan for prison expansion and growth in the private prison industry to stem the tide of 'immoral', 'bad', 'dangerous' women (and men) who need to be locked up (Lockyer, 2013). However, women are predominantly imprisoned for non-violent crimes such as property crimes and drug offences (Makkai and MacGregor, 2002).

One of the main reasons often provided for the increase in women's imprisonment is the rise in drug and drug-related offending among women (European Monitoring Centre for Drugs and Drug Addiction [EMCDDA], 2000; Malloch, 2004c; Merlo and Pollock, 2006; Drugs and Crime Prevention Committee [DCPC], 2010; Mauer et al, 2013; Ministry of Justice, 2013). However, female drug users and offenders in the UK, US and Canada do not tend to fit the profile of the dangerous, violent user, dealer, trafficker or organised criminal responsible for destroying families and communities and endangering young people.

In the US, drug offences account for much of the rise in the female prison population (Mauer et al, 1999; Boyd, 2004; Bush-Baskette, 2010). For instance, in the years immediately following the Anti-Drug Abuse Acts of 1986 and 1988, the number of women imprisoned for drug offences increased by 888 per cent compared to a rise of 129 per cent in the imprisonment rate for all other offences (Mauer et al, 1999). These policies subjected more women to the greater probability of incarceration for low-level drug offences. An analysis over a 25-year period shows drug offences became the most dominant category of offence for which women were imprisoned (with the figure of 62 per cent in 2006 more than doubling the figure for 1981 at 26 per cent) (Bush-Baskette, 2010).

In the UK, although drug laws against drug offences are not as harsh as they are in the US, the war on drugs has had a significant impact on the women's prison population. Between 1992 and 2002, the number of women sentenced to imprisonment after a drug conviction increased by 414 per cent (Chads and Simes, 2002; Home Office, 2002a). Over half of the increase in the 1990s was the result of increased convictions for drug offences (Boyd, 2004). For instance, in 1996, drug convictions accounted for 68 per cent of the increases (Wedderburn, 2000; Boyd, 2004). In 2002, of the women in prison in the UK, the largest proportion was convicted for drug offences (Chads and Simes, 2002; Boyd, 2004). In Canada, as in the UK, drug laws and sentencing are not as harsh as in the US. However, research indicates a 20 per cent increase in the number of women serving federal drug-related sentences between 1997 and 2002 (Correctional Service Canada, 2002-03; Boyd, 2006).

In the UK, US and Canada, although more men are serving time for drug offences, the proportion of drug offenders in the women's prison population is higher than the men's (Bewley-Taylor et al, 2009). In the

US, women's incarceration for drug offences has increased at a faster rate than men's (Amnesty International, 1999; Boyd, 2004), and a larger proportion of women in prison are drug offenders compared to men in prison (for example, in 2003, 67 per cent of women versus 56 per cent of men) (Boyd, 2004; Bush-Baskette, 2010). In Canada in 2004, around 30 per cent of women were serving time for drug offences compared to 18 per cent of men (Boyd, 2006). The incarceration rate is higher for women than men despite the fact that men serving time in prison for drug-related offences, such as trafficking and importation, are likely to have more extensive criminal histories than women (Boyd, 2006). In the UK, the proportion of drug offenders in the women's prison population is higher than the men's (Bewley-Taylor et al, 2009). In all three countries, as men are more likely to use illicit drugs than women, women are over-represented in prison for drug offences (Boyd, 2004).

Locking up the 'dangerous underclass'

The war on poor women

The prime targets of the technology of prohibition and punishment have been poor and racially marginalised women. Most of the women in prison for drug offences are poor, and there are a disproportionate number of black and minority ethnic women incarcerated (Mauer and Huling, 1995; Tyler, 2010; Boyd, 2004; Lapidus et al, 2005; Bush-Baskette, 2010). Poor and minority ethnic female users and offenders are thus situated as part of a 'dangerous underclass' (Morris, 1994), constructed and scapegoated as the 'carriers of a plague of drug abuse' (Gordon, 1994, p 119). Davis (1998) argues that poor, disenfranchised and racially marginalised populations of women (and men) are disproportionately incarcerated to 'disappear from public view' social problems such as drug addiction, homelessness, unemployment, illiteracy and mental illness, and this has become 'big business' in the prison industrial complex. Furthermore, cuts in welfare provision correspond with prison expansion (Davis, 1998). A study by the Justice Policy Institute in the US found countries with the highest levels of poverty, unemployment and black and minority ethnicities were also those that sentenced their drug offenders to prison at higher rates (Beatty et al, 2007; Bewley-Taylor et al, 2009).

As women are likely to be poorer than men, they may be tempted to get involved in the drug economy to supplement their incomes (Boyd, 2004). Evidence shows that female illicit drug users, dealers and traffickers who have been incarcerated are likely to have experienced higher levels of economic hardship than their male equivalents (Willis and Rushforth, 2003). Poor women who do get involved with drugs are more likely to come into contact with the law than middle-class or upper-class women through police profiling and drug laws focusing on low-level drug dealers and traffickers (Boyd, 2004; Bush-Baskette, 2010). Street-level drug users and dealers are more visible and are more likely to be targeted by law enforcement agents (Gordon, 1994; Waquant, 2009; Bush-Baskette, 2010). For instance, in 1995 in the US, 55 per cent of all female federal drug defendants were classified as low-level offenders, such as street dealers or 'mules', with only 11 per cent of them classified as high-level dealers (Drug Policy Alliance, 2009). The prime police target for drug offences has been poor people and minority ethnic groups (Boyd, 2006; Waquant, 2009). Bush-Baskette (2010) argues that in the US, women have had a greater role to play in the distribution of crack cocaine compared to other drugs. However, as Maher (1997) found, the drug market is not an 'equal opportunity employer', and women do not tend to benefit financially in the same way as men.

Women in prison charged with drug or drug-related offences as well as those entering drug treatment tend to be economically and educationally disadvantaged (Owen, 2000; Covington, 1998), more so than their male counterparts (Green et al, 2002; Hser et al, 2003). Incarcerated women, many of whom, if not the vast majority, will be imprisoned for drug or drug-related offences, are more likely than non-incarcerated women to have lower educational attainment (Canadian Human Rights Commission, 2003; Ramsay, 2003; DCPC, 2010), to be unemployed prior to admission (Allard, 2002; Canadian Human Rights Commission, 2003; Ramsay, 2003; DCPC, 2010), or to work in low-paid jobs working long hours (Allard, 2002; DCPC, 2010), lack access to affordable secure housing, or to have experienced homelessness (DCPC, 2010), to be in debt (DCPC, 2010), or have grown up in single-parent households or the care system (DCPC, 2010). They are likely to return to broken family relationships, homelessness, poverty, unemployment, or limited job prospects (Ramsay, 2003; Willis and Makkai, 2008). Any poverty that female drug offenders and drug-related offenders experience may be compounded through being the primary or sole carers of children (Ramsay, 2003; DCPC, 2010).

Incarcerating poor drug-using and offending women exacerbates their economic hardship and social marginalisation. They are typically caught up in a revolving door phenomenon (Boyd, 2004; DrugScope, 2005; Anderson, 2008; Howard League, 2011). Prohibition and punishment technologies reinforce and compound the economic hardship and social marginalisation of male and female users and drug offenders. Meanwhile, drugs and those involved with them can be blamed as a scourge in society, and the social problems such as poverty, unemployment and homelessness that emerge alongside them can be disregarded or even constructed as caused by the drug 'problem'.

Most women and men who use and sell illicit drugs are not poor or from minority disenfranchised populations. Nor do they necessarily live in inner-city communities (Morgan and Joe, 1997). Drug trafficking is not limited to poor women and black or minority ethnic groups. Nevertheless, the war on drugs has had a disproportionate impact on these groups, especially poor, black and minority ethnic women (Davis, 1998; Boyd, 2004). Rather than protect communities, the investment in the war on drugs and the prison industrial complex deprives communities of resources for education, healthcare and the potential for economic development. It reinforces institutionalised racism and social and economic marginalisation with its disproportionate impact. While the drug strategies in the UK, US and Canada claim to aim to protect families and communities from drug harms, families and communities have been and continue to be a source of poverty for women who become dependent on illicit drugs. This is a situation that makes women vulnerable to dependence and drug offending in the first place, which is not recognised in official discourses of drug policy. This is no more apparent than in the harsh punishments given out to low-level female traffickers or drug 'mules'.

Tough sentencing for trafficking has had a disproportionate impact on poor women. The majority of female drug traffickers arrested are poor, low-level, minor participants in the international drugs trade involving organised criminal gangs who largely 'hire' them (Allen et al, 2003). They are usually vulnerable due to poverty, and targeted for profit as 'pawns in a much bigger game' (Allen et al, 2003). However, they will be subject to the same harsh sentencing policies used to punish high-level traffickers such as mandatory minimum sentences in the US. In the UK, women caught importing drugs into the country may receive one of the longest prison sentences handed down by the courts (Allen et al, 2003). The maximum sentence for importing a Class A drug is life imprisonment, but sentences of 10 years are set down in sentencing guidelines for people convicted of importing 500 grams. This is the average amount that can be swallowed by a drug courier. Such sentences are typically longer than those given out for violent offences or even murder (Bush-Baskette, 2010).

Many women agree to transport drugs across borders because they are poor and are struggling to make ends meet (Huling, 1995;

P Green, 1996; Carlen, 1998; Allen et al, 2003). Drug offences for such women are, in essence, a product of poverty (DCPC, 2010). They tend to come from economically impoverished areas in parts of the world such as the Caribbean, Nigeria, Ghana, South Africa and Eastern Europe, with limited social welfare provision (Allen et al, 2003). Poor women charged with drug offences are less likely to be able to hire costly investigators, and will be less able to defend themselves in court (Boyd, 2004). As they are often at the bottom of a hierarchical network of high-level traffickers, they are unlikely to possess the information required by prosecutors to earn them a reduced sentence. Consequently, as low-level drug 'mules', women are likely to be penalised more harshly then high-level traffickers (Boyd, 2004).

Foreign national women who end up being incarcerated great distances away from their children are likely to find themselves in a position in which they will have no opportunity to see their children for five or more years. And they may not be able to get in touch with a relative in their home country to find out whether their children are being looked after:

> Often these women do not make childcare provisions in the hope or belief that they will be back within a week or so. They are told by drug barons that if caught they will be put on the next plane home. When they are sent to prison their children are left on their own with provisions for a week or so, or with relatives or friends who are told that the mother "will be returning shortly". The relatives or friends may find it difficult to help the children financially for three or five years and the children have been known to die from lack of care and starvation. (Chigwada-Bailey, 2003, p 126)

In the name of protecting young people, families and communities in the West, the children and families of women from poor countries suffer.

The war on black and minority ethnic women

Prohibition and punishment has a disproportionate impact on black and minority ethnic women (Boyd, 2004; Tyler, 2010; Lapidus et al, 2005; Bush-Baskette, 2010). The number of black women who were incarcerated in state prisons for drug offences increased by 828 per cent between 1986 and 1991, and this increase was approximately twice that of males imprisoned for drug offences (429 per cent), and about three times that of white women (241 per cent) (Mauer and Huling, 1995). Although the figures have fluctuated since 1980, black women have continued to be over-represented in the US prison population, particularly for drug offences (Bush-Baskette, 2010).

Black women and men are discriminated against at every stage of the criminal justice system. Indeed, it is assumed by the police, judges and prosecutors that drug dealing is an illegal activity solely carried out by black people (Gordon, 1994; Chigwada-Bailey, 2003; Boyd, 2004). However, the over-representation of black people in arrest, prosecution and imprisonment rates is not reflected in their use of illegal drugs or involvement in their distribution (DPA, 2013). In the US white youth sell and use drugs at the same or higher rates than black people (DPA, 2013), but face disparate treatment within the criminal justice process. For instance, while half of all drug arrests involving white youth result in formal processing, 75 per cent of drug arrests involving black youth are prosecuted (Snyder et al, 1999). This pattern is replicated in the UK and Canada.

Bush-Baskette (2010) conducted an analysis of the dramatic rise in and over-representation of black women in prisons in the US. Between 1981 and 2006, black women were particularly over-represented among women convicted of drug offences involving crack cocaine. This is a disparity that cannot be explained by black women's presence in the general population, or their use of crack cocaine (Bush-Baskette, 2010). Black women were more likely to receive longer mandatory sentences (that is, five or ten years) than white and Hispanic women for relatively small amounts of crack cocaine (that is, less than 5 grams). Bush-Baskette (2010) suggests that this is partially a result of the 100 to 1 sentencing ratio for crack cocaine versus powdered cocaine offences. It is also the result of the association of black women with crack cocaine that was promoted in the media in the 1980s and 1990s, in the imagination of the white middle-class American public, and ultimately among police officers, judges and prosecutors. Bush-Baskette (2010) states that the disproportionate impact on black women for the possession of small amounts of crack cocaine does not follow from the stated intention of American policy makers to target drug 'kingpins'.

Racial disparities in the proportion of women entering prison for drug offences can also be found in the UK. In 2005, 57 per cent of black and minority ethnic women were imprisoned for drug offences, compared with 27 per cent of white prisoners (HM Inspectorate of Prisons, 2009). The proportion of black British women imprisoned for drug offences (42 per cent) was almost twice the proportion of white British women (25 per cent) (HM Inspectorate of Prisons, 2009). Again, these disparities in rates of imprisonment do not reflect the figures for black women's involvement in the use or sale of drugs (Fellner and Vinck, 2008); Lapidus et al, 2005). Similar to the US, in the UK the tabloid press has promoted the association between black people, dealing and crack (Chigwada-Bailey, 2003). There has also been a dramatic rise in the number of foreign national women incarcerated in UK jails on drug trafficking charges. Eight out of ten foreign national women in prison are held for drug offences (Prison Reform Trust, 2004). Many of these are arrested at ports and other locations and convicted of importing drugs. In Canada, First Nations and black women are over-represented in federal prisons (Hannah-Moffat and Shaw, 2000; Statistics Canada, 2000). In 1986/87, for example, white women were the majority admitted to the Vanier Centre for Women (a correctional facility), but by 1992/93, most admitted were black. There was a fifty-fold increase for black women compared to a six-fold increase for white women (Commission on Systematic Racism in the Ontario Justice System, 1995; Boyd, 2006).

There is evidence that black women receive discriminatory treatment by customs agents who believe that these women fit the profile of drug traffickers. The Drug Enforcement Agency (DEA) in the US has claimed that drug couriers are often black women. In US airports black people are more likely to be searched by customs agents than white people (Boyd, 2004). In one study of the practices of the US Customs Service black women were more likely to be strip-searched and were subject to more intrusive personal searches than all other women and men (Ekstrand and Blume, 2000). However, it was found that women, especially black women, were less likely to have illegal contraband on them (Boyd, 2004) – in fact, black women were half as likely as white women to be carrying illegal contraband (Ekstrand and Blume, 2000).

Protection of young people and families through the incarceration of 'unfit' mothers: the impact on children

The negative impact of the policy of prohibition and punishment on the children of incarcerated women is undeniable. While governments claim their aim is to protect children from the harm of illicit drugs, millions of children have been harmed through the incarceration of their mothers and fathers because of prohibition and punishment. As the female prison population has risen dramatically in the UK, US and Canada since the 1970s, with more women serving time for drug charges or for drug-related offences, so has the number of children separated from their families. A consequence of the need to protect young people, families and communities from the harms of illicit drugs has thus been to incarcerate mothers and to separate them from their children. Most women in prison are mothers, and incarcerated mothers are more likely than men to have primary responsibility for their children (Cunningham and Baker, 2004).

Nearly two-thirds of incarcerated women in the US are mothers of around 200,000 young children (Levy-Pounds, 2006). Since 1991, the number of children with a mother in prison in the US has more than doubled, up 131 per cent. In 2007 it was estimated that 1,706,600 minor children have a parent in prison, accounting for 2.3 per cent of the US resident population under the age of 18 (Glaze and Maruschak, 2010). In 2007, black children were seven-and-a-half times more likely than white children to have a parent in prison, and Hispanic children more than two-and-a-half times more likely (Glaze and Maruschak, 2010). In the UK, at least 17,000 children are separated from their mothers when they go to prison (Wilks-Wilfen, 2011). It is likely that the number may be higher, as many women are reluctant to reveal they have children to state authorities for fear of losing them (Boyd, 2004). Eighty-five per cent of women have never been separated from their children for a long period of time prior to their imprisonment. In comparison, only 35 per cent of males in prison lived with their children before their incarceration (Wolfe, 1999). In Canada, around two-thirds of federally sentenced women are mothers of approximately 25,000 children each year (Cunningham and Baker, 2004).

When a mother is sent to prison, children may be sent to live with relatives, forced to live with strangers, to navigate the foster care system or are placed in a children's home (Levy-Pounds, 2006). They are most often at the mercy of family courts and foster care systems to make arrangements for their care, and are likely to be separated from their siblings (Levy-Pounds, 2006). When a single mother is sent to prison, this is even more likely (Levy-Pounds, 2006). A study on the impact of foster care children at Stanford University in the US found that removing children from their parents can cause serious psychological damage – damage more serious than the harm intervention is supposed to prevent (Wald, 1976). Child welfare services may struggle to find suitable homes for children who have been removed from their mothers. Such children may then be subject to living conditions that pose a greater threat to their wellbeing than the ones they were removed from (Paone and Alperen, 1998). While the majority of foster care parents will provide loving homes for the children of incarcerated mothers, there is considerable evidence that children in care may experience psychological, physical or sexual abuse by their foster carers or from other children in care homes (Boyd, 2004; Thoma, 2005; Levy-Pounds, 2006).

When a man goes to prison, mothers can usually be relied on to provide the primary care for their children. In contrast, when a woman is incarcerated, the children are most often cared for by grandparents, or have to enter the foster care system (Boyd, 2004; Glaze and Maruschak, 2010; Levy-Pounds, 2006). In a report by the US Department of Justice, only 37 per cent of mothers said that the father of their child was their primary care giver while they were in prison, compared to 85 per cent of fathers (Glaze and Maruschak, 2010). In a study in the UK it was found that only 5 per cent of incarcerated mothers could rely on the children's fathers to care for the children while they were in prison (Wolfe, 1999).

Children with mothers in prison are likely to experience the kind of grief and loss felt by children suffering the death of a parent (Bloom and Steinhart, 1993). A mother who was imprisoned for a drug offence told Human Rights Watch that she believed her children were punished for her crime as much as she was (Human Rights Watch, 2002). Although it is often assumed that 'criminal' women or women dependent on illicit drugs such as crack and heroin do not really care about their children or are incapable of providing loving homes for them, nonetheless, they may be 'a source of love, care and stability' (Tyler, 2010, p 2). As Tyler (2010, p 2) argues:

> In many cases, community-based substance treatment would address the addicted parents' needs and the public interest, as well as benefit the children far more than incarceration.

Forced separation may cause children anxiety, sadness, perpetual grieving, depression, insecurity, anger, stress, insomnia, shame and low self-esteem. They may resort to withdrawal, aggression, alcohol, drug use or sexual intimacy to mask the trauma of separation (Levy-Pounds, 2006).

While drug policy discourse legitimises harsh sanctions for drug offenders in order to protect young people and families, incarcerated women and men find that prisons and prison policy are constructed so that families are torn apart (Dodge and Pogrebin, 2001). As Boyd (2004, p 251) argues, 'the criminal justice system fosters alienation rather than family unity.' The location of prisons and the techniques and procedures used within the prison system to govern offenders and monitor their visitors make relationships between mothers and their children hard to sustain. It is extremely difficult for mothers to stay in contact with their children when incarcerated (Chigwada-Bailey, 2003). Studies in the US and the UK have found only around half the women who lived with or were in contact with their children prior to their incarceration had ever been visited by them while they were in jail (Allard, 2002; Human Rights Watch, 2002). The longer a woman's sentence, the more likely that she will lose contact with her family (Farrant, 2001). In the US in 1997, in an attempt to limit the amount of time children spent in foster care homes, the Adoption and Safe Families Act was passed. It was an attempt to encourage the permanent adoption of children in care for more than 15 months. Many women who are serving time for drug offences are likely to be serving longer than this, and are therefore unable to regain custody of their children when they are released.

Most women in prison are located long distances away from their families and children, often in remote areas. In Canada, an incarcerated mother may be up to 1,000 miles away from her children, or in the US, 500 miles away (Human Rights Watch, 2002; Boyd, 2004). The transportation costs involved in children seeing their mothers in prison are often expensive, and may be well beyond the means of the children or their carers (Human Rights Watch, 2002; Boyd, 2004; Levy-Pounds, 2006). Visits are also restricted, and phone and mail communication censored. In the US phone calls are exorbitant (Human Rights Watch, 2002; Boyd, 2004; Levy-Pounds, 2006). Punitive prison practices mean that even when children are able to visit their mothers, the trauma involved is too much for them. They may be subjected to body searches or strip-searching, and young children may not comprehend why they cannot stay with their mothers when it comes to the end of a visit (Human Rights Watch, 2002; Boyd, 2004). Children may feel intimidated, humiliated and emotionally distressed at the surveillance practices and coercive displays of power meted out by prison officers (Boyd, 2004).

Mothers who are in prison for drug-related offences, who are known to be drug-dependent or who have received a court order to attend treatment, are especially likely to have difficulty keeping custody of their children. Not only do the courts see them as 'unfit to parent', but as Boyd (2004, p 253) argues, it is also wrongly 'assumed that their compulsion to use drugs is stronger than their commitment to their children.'

Government prohibition and punishment techniques thus constitute a war on the children of poor, marginalised and black and minority ethnic women. The incarceration of mothers (as well as fathers) has 'far-reaching effects' (Bush-Baskette, 2010) that have an impact on future generations. It fractures families, destroying the life chances of already economically disadvantaged young people. While official policy discourses claim to be intent on protecting the young from the harm caused by illicit drugs, as well as helping families, instead, drug policy damages the lives of many women and children. Arguably the impacts of the technology of prohibition and punishment discussed so far can also be applied, to a greater or lesser extent, to male drug users and offenders as well as females. However, there are some gender-specific impacts of this technology that are only experienced by female users and offenders. One of these is the criminalisation of drug-using mothers during pregnancy.

Irresponsible, unfit mothers: the criminalisation of pregnancy

Another strand of prohibition particular to the US that aims to protect with paradoxically harmful consequences are foetal protection policies that criminalise pregnant drug-using women. In the 1980s in the US, the 'crack baby' came to represent the selfishness and immorality of the addicted crack-using woman. Policy makers drew from numerous studies to justify increasingly punitive policies in which 'crack babies' were observed to suffer a variety of abnormalities, including low birth weight, congenital malformations, withdrawal, problems with memory, auditory functioning, attention, hyperactivity, behavioural disturbances, lethargy, non-responsiveness, frenetic movements, low pain thresholds, problems relating to care givers and absence of normal playfulness (Chasnoff et al, 1985, 1987, 1989; Leshner, 1999; Berger et al, 1990). As discussed in the literature review (see Chapter One, p 17), it is now recognised that concerns about 'crack babies' were exaggerated, and there is no such scientific condition (Hopkins, 1989; Leshner, 1999; Arendt et al, 2004). However, the actual harms caused by crack cocaine and other illicit substances remain highly controversial.

Despite the fact that the harms caused by prenatal illicit drug exposure are acknowledged to be uncertain and inconclusive, in official US, Canadian and UK policy, the solution to the perceived harm has been articulated in civil or criminal law proceedings against pregnant women. In the US, pregnant female drug users may undergo criminal prosecution and incarceration due to their prenatal drug use. Currently, pregnant users can be prosecuted for foetal homicide or for exposing the unborn child to chemical endangerment. Women have been prosecuted for crimes such as child endangerment and delivery of a drug to a minor for cocaine use while pregnant. Since the 1980s, over 100 women in the US have been prosecuted for causing harm to their foetuses by using drugs while pregnant (Fentiman, 2008). However, the convictions that occurred during the 1980s and early 1990s during the height of the 'crack baby' scare were ultimately overturned in courts of appeal. Courts recognised that penal laws were being stretched beyond their limits, and that women's constitutional rights were being violated (Paone and Alperen, 1998).

One exception was the case of Cornelia Whitner in South Carolina. The state of South Carolina Supreme Court was the first to uphold a conviction of a woman for child abuse because of prenatal drug use. Whitner received an eight-year sentence for unlawful neglect of a child despite the fact her baby was born healthy. The Supreme Court upheld her conviction under the child endangerment statute, stating that a foetus was a 'child' under the law (Fentiman, 2008). The stretching of these laws depends on the concept of the foetus as a separate entity from the body of the mother who sustains it. Prosecutors have relied on the idea that the foetus should be seen as a legal person, with all the rights that accompany that status (Fentiman, 2008).

In the 1990s more aggressive prosecutions were pursued in various states including South Carolina, Wisconsin, Hawaii, Missouri, Oklahoma and Utah. These states sought to convict women of criminal homicide, including murder, manslaughter, and attempted intentional homicide. Since then, the crusade has intensified and become wider in scope, as numerous states have stretched existing laws to target pregnant users (Fentiman, 2008). Approximately 38 out of 50 states have foetal homicide laws, and at least 21 have foetal homicide laws that apply to the earliest stages of pregnancy (NCSL, 2010). These laws were intended to protect pregnant women and from violent attacks from third parties, usually abusive male partners, but have increasingly been twisted by prosecutors to apply to the women too.

In South Carolina in 1999, Regina McKnight, a homeless African-American woman, addicted to crack cocaine, was convicted of murder (homicide by child abuse) after her child was stillborn (Bhargava, 2000). At 8½ months, McKnight's stillborn daughter was considered a person under state law (Bhargava, 2000). She was sentenced to 20 years in prison. A bare majority South Carolina Supreme Court upheld the conviction in 2003, but it was finally overturned in 2008 (Bhargava, 2000). Other cases in South Carolina, where women were charged with homicide based on their drug use while pregnant when the child died or was stillborn, include that of Jennifer Arrowood, Jamie Lee

Burroughs and Lorraine Patrick. The same charge was also brought against Melissa Rowland in Utah, Theresa Hernandez in Oklahoma and Sheri Lohstein in Missouri. Prosecutors in South Carolina, in particular, have pursued some of the harshest campaigns against pregnant women to date (Schroedel and Fiber, 2013).

Black pregnant women have been disproportionately reported and prosecuted for prenatal drug use. A Florida study found that black women were ten times more likely than white women to be reported to child welfare agencies for prenatal drug use, despite the fact that the rates of urine toxicologies were slightly higher among white women (Chasnoff et al, 1990). In the city of Charleston, South Carolina, in the public hospital, where pregnant women were selectively drug tested and reported to the police if they tested positive, 29 of the 30 women prosecuted were African-American. The only white woman arrested was married to a black man – a fact noted on her medical records (DPA, 2010). Eighty per cent of women prosecuted for giving birth to drug-exposed children were black or Latino even though rates of drug use were similar across races (Paone and Alperen, 1998).

Estimates in the US have suggested that thousands of women have been investigated and lost custody of their children in the civil courts as a result of maternal drug use. While criminal prosecution of the behaviour of women during pregnancy does not occur in the UK or Canada, pregnant users may lose custody of their children and/or be forced into mandatory treatment programmes against their will (Boyd, 1999; Jackson et al, 2002).

The construction of pregnant women who use drugs as murderers, child abusers and unfit mothers is based on the assumption that prenatal drug use causes devastating and irreparable harm to the foetus. The construction is also based on a false separation between foetal interests and maternal autonomy and wellbeing, on a deviant mother versus vulnerable foetus dichotomy. Such a dichotomy is potentially a 'slippery slope' in terms of the potential conflicts of interests that could be construed. As pointed out by the highest court in Maryland in *Kilmon vs State*:

> Everything from becoming (or remaining) pregnant with knowledge that the child likely will have a genetic disorder that may cause serious disability or death, to the continued use of legal drugs that are contraindicated during pregnancy, to consuming alcoholic beverages to excess, to smoking, to not maintaining a proper and sufficient diet, to avoiding proper and available prenatal medical care, to failing to

wear a seat belt while driving, to violating other traffic laws in ways that create a substantial risk of producing or exacerbating personal injury to her child, to exercising too much or too little, indeed to engage in virtually any injury-prone activity that, should injury occur, might reasonably be expected to endanger the life or safety of the child. Such ordinary things as skiing or horseback riding could produce criminal liability. (Wilner, 2015)

In other words, the risk of harm posed by illicit drugs is no greater than risks from other everyday activities, and therefore to focus on a mother's drug use as the only source of foetal and childhood harm is misguided (Fentiman, 2008). Potential harm to the foetus caused by paternal behaviour receives relatively little attention. However, research shows a link between paternal alcoholism, low birth weight and an increased risk of birth defects (Cicero et al, 1998; Passaro et al, 1998; Deng et al, 2013; Jeffery 2014). Studies have also found a connection between paternal smoking and an increased risk of multiple birth defects (Daniels, 2006).

Arguably, criminalising women for prenatal drug use is an approach that fails to take into account the context of these women's lives. The problems many prenatal drug users face include economic disadvantage, abuse, domestic violence and unsupported parenting, and are best dealt with away from the criminal justice system. Rather, social problems caused by inequalities and gender discrimination have been increasingly responded to with punishment and incarceration. Drug use during pregnancy is a health issue that is most appropriately responded to by health professionals rather than law enforcement and criminal justice agents (Stengal and Fleetwood, 2014). A punitive approach allows pregnant users to be demonised and policy makers to 'ignore the underlying social and economic conditions which contribute to drug use' (Paone and Alperen, 1998, p 107).

The construction of pregnant women who use drugs as unfit mothers is also based on an assumption that female users who take drugs are necessarily going to be neglectful parents. However, imprisoning women who use drugs in pregnancy does not serve to protect children. Incarcerating pregnant women who are dependent on illicit drugs can also put the health of the foetus at greater risk. Women may be forced to give birth in substandard, unsanitary conditions with unsatisfactory medical care (Ehrlich, 2008). Pregnant women are sometimes shackled or handcuffed while giving birth, which can endanger foetal and maternal health. This is in violation of the UN standard minimum rules for the treatment of prisoners (Ehrlich, 2008).

It has been suggested that it is not prenatal drug use itself that is being punished, but female behaviours that do not fulfil proscribed gender role expectations. This is because prenatal drug taking 'challenges the sanctity of motherhood' (Paone and Alperen, 1998, p 105).

> Maternal drug users were punished not for their drug use per se, but because they had the audacity to deviate from pre-established gender roles to participate in behaviours which seemed to place their own needs above those of their children, and therefore, did not deserve the privilege of being mothers. (Paone and Alperen, 1998, p 105)

In the US, these punitive responses to poor, marginalised, dependent women are readily adopted in the context of a lack of opportunity for treatment. Punitive measures and coercive policies are apparently pursued with the intention of protecting the foetus. However, rather than intimidating dependent female users to suddenly abstain, such strategies have the effect of compromising the health of the foetus and pregnant woman (Ehrlich, 2008). The threat of criminal prosecution has been found to prevent women from revealing their drug use to healthcare providers (ACOG, 2005). The possibility they could lose their babies or be imprisoned deters them from seeking prenatal care (Ehrlich, 2008; Fentiman, 2008).

A study undertaken in the UK by the specialist drug service CAAAD also found that female drug users were less likely to report abuse, domestic violence or rape to the police for fear that contact with social services may result in their children being placed on the at-risk register (Release, 2010). The idea that the threat of prosecution could act as a deterrent for pregnant women using drugs is questionable (Smith, 2011). The assumption that on becoming pregnant, 'women will be able to immediately overcome addictions that have plagued them for years places an unequal and unnecessary burden on women alone' (Ehrlich, 2008, p 45). Men and women alike struggle to overcome their addictions. As wealthy white men show difficulty in overcoming their addictions, it is unreasonable to expect poor, marginalised women will, just by virtue of them becoming pregnant.

The aim to protect the foetus through the threat of prosecution is confounded by it providing an incentive for abortion. Prosecuting women for continuing a pregnancy to term despite a drug dependency may serve to encourage the termination of a wanted pregnancy to avoid criminal prosecution and loss of child custody (Johnsen, 1992). If intentionally ending a pregnancy through abortion is legal, it is curious that unintentionally causing harm to a foetus through behaviour while pregnant can be illegal (Smith, 2011).

The disciplinary power meted out to female drug users in pregnancy provides a good example of the gendered impact of the technology of punishment and prohibition. Another instance of this is the contrast between the harsh punishment of low-level female drug users and offenders who have often been the victims of male violence, and the historical lack of punishment for male perpetrators of violence against women.

Dangerous criminals and unrecognised victims

Historically, punishment technologies have failed to adequately identify and punish male violence against women in its many forms. Such experiences typically shape and frame the lives of many drug-dependent women who are disproportionately punished as poor, low-level offenders. While the drug strategies in the UK, US and Canada proclaim that they aim to protect families from drug harms, families are often the source of violence and abuse for female users, which can make them vulnerable to dependence and drug offending to begin with.

Women who are dependent on illicit drugs, particularly those who have been incarcerated, seem to have experienced a disproportionate amount of abuse and trauma compared with women in the general population, other prisoners and drug-dependent men in prison (Chesney-Lind, 1997; Carlen, 1988; Becker and Duffy, 2002; Lievore, 2002; Canadian Human Rights Commission, 2003; Johnson, 2006). Research on female drug-dependent populations in prisons, treatment settings and other services for women have highlighted that they have often survived severe forms of emotional, physical and sexual abuse (Russel and Wilsnack, 1991; PRT, 2000; Scottish Executive, 2002; Ramsay, 2003; McKeganey et al, 2005), including rape or sexual assault (Ramsay, 2003) and domestic violence (Ramsay, 2003). They also report experiencing multiple types of abuse (Willis and Rushforth, 2003). Evidence exists to show that male perpetrators of domestic violence may often introduce their partners to alcohol or drug use to increase their dependence on them, and to control their behaviour, and may prevent them from attending treatment (Stella Project, 2004). When outside prison, dependent women also have a high prevalence of domestic violence in a current relationship (Gilbert et al, 2001), and if they are sex workers, they may be exposed to recurrent sexual and physical violence (Sterk and Elifson, 1990; Church et al, 2001; Romero-Daza et al, 2003; Surratt et al, 2004). In other words, female users have often been the victims of serious crime, notably male violence in its many forms (Malloch, 2004a, p 388). This is important because as a result of their perceived lifestyles, women drug users are denied 'victimhood' as an identity (Richardson and May 1999; Malloch, 2004a), and are consequently rendered punishable.

The relationship between women drug-using offenders' experiences, not only as lawbreakers, but also as victims of crime, is important in understanding their offending and the impact of drug policies on their lives. Some criminologists have asserted that this is important in relation to understanding women's crime in general (Kennedy, 1992; Faith, 1993; Edwards, 1996; Carlen, 2002; Malloch, 2004a; White and Habibis, 2005). As discussed in the literature review (see Chapter Two, p 26), there is evidence that some women use drugs as a way of 'coping' with trauma and abuse, to self-medicate and block out negative feelings and emotions (Root, 1989; Blume, 1990b; Russell and Wilsnack, 1991; Du Rose, 2006; Covington et al, 2008). Women from all sections of society may use illegal and legal substances in this way. However, economic deprivation and lack of support inevitably makes some women more vulnerable to becoming viewed as problems to be governed by criminal justice agencies. While upper-class and middle-class women can afford expensive therapies to address their problems, may have access to private healthcare and costly prescribed drugs, the financial resources to leave violent partners and the funds to go to private rehabilitation clinics for their drug and alcohol dependencies, poor, marginalised women have no such options (Boyd, 2004).

> Victims of sexual or physical abuse are more likely to be forced into homelessness and poverty, conditions that frequently precede drug abuse, prostitution and committing economic crimes. Abused women living in poverty are thus more likely to be incarcerated and treated as criminals rather than victims. (Political Research Associates, 2005, p 3)[1]

Historically, violent perpetrators of rape, sexual abuse and domestic violence go unpunished and are under-represented in the criminal justice system. In contrast, poor, victimised and black drug-using women, whose lives are shaped and framed by such crimes, are disproportionately locked up. Perpetrators of rape, sexual abuse and domestic violence receive more lenient sentences or have been seen as worthy of mitigation for their crimes, in relation to the character and demeanour of their female victims. In contrast, women who commit drug or low-level property offences who are shaped and framed by such victimisation, as well as economic hardship and a lack of options, receive no mitigation. A justice system that disproportionately incarcerates female drug-dependent, economically marginalised, victimised, low-level drug and property offenders, while perpetrators of domestic violence, rape and sexual abuse continue to be under-represented, can only be described as a gendered injustice system. As Malloch (2004a, p 387) argues:

> The administration of systems of punishment which penalize women for their poverty and/or lifestyle yet which fail to punish many forms of male violence provides a fundamental indication of the differential impact of disciplinary power.

Furthermore, the identification of victimisation may be interpreted by criminal justice, medical and welfare professionals as suggesting that dependency and any social problems experienced by the female user are a result of individual pathology (Maher, 1997; Carlen, 2002; Tombs, 2004). The focus is shifted from social circumstances and placed on an individual's 'psychological problems' (Maher, 1997; Carlen, 2002; Tombs, 2004). Social problems are depoliticised, medicalised, and the female user blamed and responsibilised to change themselves. Experiences of past trauma and abuse in women are often seen as 'risk' factors for substance abuse, as criminogenic factors that need 'managing'. Although some dependent female drug users describe their use of drugs as a way of 'coping' with trauma and abuse, they do not see themselves as pathological victims. Rather, their actions can be seen as resistant, adaptive responses to abusive and oppressive social conditions (Du Rose, 2006; Geiger, 2006). Thus, being alert to a female dependent drug user's experience of abuse and victimisation enables one to understand 'the context within which that person moves and makes choices' (Chesney-Lind and Pasko, 2004, p 30). This is a theme explored further in Chapters Six and Seven later.

Conclusion

This chapter investigated how the technology of prohibition and punishment shapes and regulates female drug users' subjectivities, and hence their experiences. In the punishment and prohibition strand of drug policy discourse in the UK, US and Canada, economically marginalised, abused, black and minority ethnic, low-level female users, dealers and traffickers are appropriated with particular problematic 'identities'. They are situated as dangerous, criminal women, unfit mothers and child abusers. Young people, families and communities are constructed as in need of protection from harm from drug users, dealers and traffickers, and consequently, disproportionate numbers of these women are locked up.

Prohibition and punishment technologies are counterproductive. While the stated aim of drug policy in the UK, US and Canada is to protect young people, families and communities, many drug-using and offending women who are incarcerated are mothers. The location of prisons and prison policies do not foster family unity, but instead make it difficult for family contact to be maintained, and every year thousands of children are alienated from their mothers and families are torn apart. In many cases this involves permanent separation. As male partners are much less likely to assume the role of primary carer when a woman goes to prison, children are affected much more when mothers rather than fathers are incarcerated. Drug-using mothers in particular are likely to be seen as 'unfit mothers', and are thus more likely to have difficulty keeping custody of their children once they have been sent to prison.

Through incarceration, the technology of punishment and prohibition involves disproportionate impacts on poor, low-level female *and* male users and offenders. Women experience these differently due to their more acute economic disadvantage and primary roles as carers of children. Some impacts of government prohibition and punishment techniques are more unequivocally gendered. For instance, in the US, foetal protection policies mean that the pregnancies of illicit drug-using women are criminalised. Pregnant users have been prosecuted for foetal homicide, chemical endangerment or child abuse, despite the fact that the harms caused by prenatal drug use are acknowledged to be uncertain and inconclusive. Poor, black and minority ethnic women have been those most targeted and affected by these policies. While these coercive and punitive policies aim to protect the health of the foetus, paradoxically, such strategies are likely to place the foetus and pregnant woman at risk.

The technology of prohibition and punishment situates female users and offenders as dangerous criminals who pose a threat to the public. However, they have often been the victims of serious violent crimes such as sexual abuse, rape and domestic violence, the perpetrators of which are under-represented in the criminal justice system. Poor, abused women are disproportionately incarcerated for their lifestyle, poverty, 'race' or even pregnancy, while male violence against them appears to be a low priority for investigation and punishment. This highlights the gendered justice system underpinning drug policies, and the unequal treatment of male and female offenders permeating the operation of the justice system as a whole. Poor, vulnerable and minority ethnic women continue to be routinely abused and exploited all too often, with little consequence, and female behaviours that do not fit proscribed gender roles receive harsh punishment.

What is needed are criminal justice systems and drug policies that are gender-wise, whose overt aims take account of how women users' lives are framed by poverty, family violence and abuse. Instead, poor, abused women are targeted and victimised through drug policies that plunge their lives into further suffering in the name of protecting young people, families and communities. Who is protected? White, middle-class and upper-class families sit safely protected in their homes and communities from the female junkie, the crack whore and everything she represents: an out-of-control, insatiable, female sexuality, an uncontrollable, irresponsible, disordered consumer, and an unfit mother. While poor, abused and black dependent or drug-offending women languish in jails, and their children, families and communities are devastated, the white, middle classes snort their cocaine and drink champagne, drug barons, corrupt officials and the prison industrial complex profit, and governments preach about the importance of family values and consumer freedom in the free market economy.

Note

[1] See also Gilfus 2002.

FOUR

Medicalisation

Medicalisation is a key technology of power through which drug users are governed. It is the process by which non-medical problems come to be defined and treated as if they are medical issues. Another key strand of drug policy discourse in the UK, US and Canada operating alongside prohibition and punishment is that of public health. The technology of medicalisation underpins public health discourse, and compliments prohibition and punishment regimes. Medicalisation operates as a form of social control and regulation whereby social structural issues, such as poverty and social inequalities, are individualised and regarded as symptoms of a disease. It has provided legitimacy to punitive and intrusive policies and practices aimed at drug users. The interdependence of the criminal justice and treatment systems, and the way they reinforce each other in the governance of drug users, can be seen as a 'deadly symbiosis' (Wacquant, 2001).

The technology of medicalisation is grounded in the disease model of addiction. Historically, this was dependent on a distinction between the normal and pathological, and involved a 'stratification of the will', whereby individuals with weak, defective characters were constructed as unable to act freely and responsibly. Constructions of a lack of will on the part of female users are bound up with notions of their mental health, sexuality and maternal role. They are situated as pathological, prone to addiction and weaker-willed than their male counterparts. In its more contemporary configurations, combined with discourses of 'risk', the disease model situates all drug users as rational, free, choice makers. Thus, female and male dependent users are constructed as, on the one hand, irresponsible, irrational, bad choice makers, and on the other, as responsible for their predicament and for coming off drugs. How female users navigate their way through disease and choice discourses and construct their identities is explored in this chapter.

An overview of recent trends in drug treatment policies and practices, how female drug users are situated in relation to these, and the impact they have on their lives in the UK, US and Canada, is provided here. This includes a discussion of the ascendance of harm minimisation in relation to the HIV/AIDS pandemic, methadone maintenance, the current focus on 'recovery' and coerced treatment. Some of the negative impacts of medicalisation on female users, including the way it has been deployed to facilitate and reinforce punishment regimes, the widening of the net of social control, and how it fails to address the social problems female users face, are also explored.

Medicalisation of drug use and mutually reinforcing technologies

Drug use underwent a degree of medicalisation in the 20th century when it became a public health issue, and a discourse of pathology was established. In the process of medicalisation, social life and social problems come to be viewed as 'diseases'. Formerly non-medical conditions such as homosexuality, ageing or drug use are defined as medical problems and come under 'medical dominion, influence and supervision' (Zola, 1983, p 295). While some behaviours have become fully medicalised, for example, alcoholism, some minimally medicalised, for example, sexual addiction, and some demedicalised, for example, homosexuality, illicit drug use has only ever been partially medicalised as it is also viewed as a legal and moral problem (Peyrot, 1984; Conrad, 1992; Appleton, 1995; Murphy, 2007).

Contemporary drug policy in the UK, US and Canada is partially constituted by a discourse of public health and its accompanying technology of power medicalisation. Consequently, drug dependency is still widely seen as a disease or illness. While there are two key strands to public health discourse on drugs – pathology and harm minimisation – the discourse of pathology is the predominant strand. Medicalisation is a complementary governmental technology of power to prohibition and punishment in the governance of illicit drugs. Although prohibition and punishment approaches are often contrasted with public health ones, the protection of public health is the overall goal of prohibitionists. As stated by the Scottish Consortium for Crime and Criminal Justice (SCCCJ):

> [O]ne of the greatest paradoxes of drug policy is that ... we attempt to achieve what are essentially public health goals,

reducing the availability of, and consumption of, dangerous drugs, by means of the criminal law. (SCCCJ, 2002, p 49)

Prohibition is constructed as justified in order to protect citizens from the dangers of illicit drugs through a concern for public health. Illicit drugs are regarded as inherently dangerous and citizens in need of protection.

The lines of the drug debate are thus often drawn as between crime-centred versus health-centred approaches, between law enforcement and the provision of treatment. Many drug researchers argue that illicit drug dependence should be seen primarily as a health problem. This is 'in the hope that drug users might be treated with more dignity, better resources and less judgemental attitudes.... The aim of describing users as ill is to destigmatise them' (Brook and Stringer, 2005, p 3). However, prohibitionists have no problem with adopting the medical understanding of drug use as an addiction. As can be seen in the discourses constituting current drug policy in the UK, US and Canada, the idea that drug dependence is a disease is fully embraced within a largely prohibition and abstention-based framework. For instance, the US National Drug Strategy 2010 states:

> The importance of domestic law enforcement, border control, and international cooperation against drug production and trafficking cannot be overstated. These traditional approaches to the drug problem remain essential, but they cannot by themselves fully address a challenge that is inherently tied to the public health of the American people. Drug addiction is a disease with a biological basis. (Executive Office of the President of the United States, 2013, p 7)

Medical discourse is thus appropriated by prohibitionists who are willing to accept the idea that dependent users are 'victims of a disease' (Brooke and Stringer, 2005).

Social control of pathological users

The term 'medicalisation' emerged in the sociological literature in the 1970s when it was argued by authors such as Conrad, Szasz and Zola that it was a form of social control that should be resisted in the name of liberation (Szasz, 1970; Zola, 1972; Conrad and Schneider, 1992; Conrad, 2007). They contended that medical authorities had always been concerned with social behaviour, and that medicine had begun to take on the role of social regulation traditionally performed by law and religion (Szasz, 1970; Foucault, 2006 [1965]). Marxist authors such as Navarro (1976) linked medicalisation to the oppressive conditions of capitalist societies. According to this thesis, social issues such as poverty and social inequality were deflected into the realm of 'disease', whereby marginalised and oppressed groups were pathologised and treated inappropriately, with medical therapies and drugs. Medicine obscured the underlying causes of 'disease' such as poverty, and instead presented health as an individual issue.

Feminist authors contended that the medical sphere was a largely patriarchal institution which maintained the social inequality of women by using medical constructs of 'disease' to control and regulate women's bodies, particularly through pregnancy and sexual health (see, for example, Ehrenreich and English, 1974). Women's pregnancy and sexual health have been predominant sites of social control in the medicalisation of their illicit drug use. Medical constructions of dependent women who use drugs as sexually immoral, out-of-control carriers of HIV/AIDS, and pregnant women who use drugs as unfit, undeserving mothers in need of surveillance, treatment and/or punishment informed drug policy in the UK, US and Canada. Medical power/knowledge of female users' bodies have provided legitimacy to punitive and intrusive policies and practices such as child apprehension, compulsory treatment, mandatory drug testing, rigid treatment rules and regulations, imprisonment, the denial of welfare benefits, sterilisation as well as the demonisation and stigmatisation of female dependent users in society. Like the technology of punishment and prohibition, medicalisation has a negative and disproportionate impact on the lives of poor, black and vulnerable women. It feeds the drug treatment industry, just as punishment and prohibition fuels the prison industrial complex.

The medicalisation of illicit drug use is grounded in the disease model of addiction, which dominates and continues to shape drug policy in many Western nations today. It emerged in the early 20th century, when addiction came to be seen as a disease caused by mental abnormalities or dysfunction (Seddon, 2007a). In this period, the emerging 'experts' of the 'psy' and criminological sciences applied positivist, determinist principles to human behaviour, undermining classical doctrines of free will and legal responsibility. This involved the move from 'a *philosophy* of freedom to a *psychology* of human behaviour and its determinants' (Garland, 1985, pp 73-91; original emphasis). In the face of addiction the ability to act freely and responsibly is apparently constrained. However, as not all individuals develop an addiction to a particular substance or pattern of behaviour, the emergence of the concept of addiction was dependent on a distinction between 'normal' and pathological behaviour. Individuals with 'weak', defective or malformed 'characters' were unable to act as free and responsible citizens, but were 'pathologically determined by their defective character structures' (Garland, 1985, p 188).

As addiction is seen as a 'disease of the will' (Collins, 1916) that only some individuals are prone to, it is a hybrid concept that still retains elements of the 'moralistic position of classical liberalism' (Seddon, 2007a, p 336). The 'will' is determined by 'character' that is shaped by habit, discipline, genetics and environment (Seddon, 2010). So the assumption of individual responsibility is still retained as part of the moral diagnosis of individuals who have a weak or defective 'character'. The contemporary articulation of this idea is found in the contentious notion of an 'addictive personality' (see Kerr, 1998; Curtiss, 2004; British Library Public Debate, 2013). Consequently, addiction is widely seen as a problem only for certain people, and is thus an individualising and psychologising concept (Boyd, 2004).

Valverde (1998) suggests that during the early 20th century, when the concept of addiction as a 'disease of the will' was established, there emerged a 'stratification of the will' whereby certain groups such as women, poor, working-class people, and immigrants were considered especially weak-willed (Reith, 2004). Historically, women have been constructed as weak, not fully rational and dependent. In this sense, they are constituted as particularly prone to addiction. Furthermore, unlike in the case of males, a lack of 'will' on the part of a woman is bound up with notions of her mental health, maternal role and sexuality. Therefore, women addicts tend to be seen as pathological addicts, unfit mothers, sexually immoral and promiscuous.

The disease model not only pathologises dependency, but also, as O'Malley (2008) argues, strips drug taking of all its pleasurable and social dimensions. O'Malley and Valverde (2004) have demonstrated how pleasure has been silenced in official discourses on illicit drugs. Drug taking is conceived as something that occurs without reason (bestial), as unfree (compulsive), and as thus unpleasant. However, this does not represent the diversity of women's (or men's) experiences of drug use that may be seen by the women themselves as a source of pleasure (Ettorre, 1992, 2007; Hinchcliff, 2001; Hunt et al, 2003; Measham, 2002), a form of pain management (Blume, 1990b; Russel and Wilsnack, 1991; Boyd, 2004; Du Rose, 2006), or both. In other words, drug dependency may not be so much about a lack of will, but instead is continued as it serves a useful or positive function in the lives of users.

The medicalisation of women's illicit drug use is an inconsistent aspect of drug policy when the over-prescribing of legal drugs to women and their dependence on them is taken into account. The use of illegal drugs is perceived as 'dangerous', while pharmaceutical companies profit from drugs prescribed to women with similar effects, the risk of dependency and serious side effects, for example, Valium and Prozac (Haslam, 2004). Legal drugs are prescribed to women by 'experts' with the medical authority to serve a normalising function as 'coping mechanisms', but are constructed as deviant and immoral when self-administered. Women who use illegal drugs are considered irresponsible, irrational, hedonistic and selfish. However, once they comply with their drug use being administered through the medical profession by their GP, within the treatment or criminal justice systems, regardless of the relative addictiveness or harmfulness of the drugs prescribed, their normality, rationality and responsibility is considered to be restorable.

Media coverage has occasionally drawn attention to the contradiction within drug policy comparing prescription drugs with heroin in an attempt to alert the public to the 'dangers'. Headlines have included: 'Drug killing more than heroin' (ITN 2000), 'Prescribed drugs do more harm to babies than heroin' (Hicks, 1999), and 'More addictive than heroin' (MacDonald, 1997). Feminist researchers have focused on the targeting of women for prescribed drugs as pharmaceutical companies target and prescribe more mind-altering drugs to women than men (Boyd, 2004). According to research carried out by Norwich Union Healthcare, GPs do not follow guidelines, and anti-depressants and tranquilizers are too accessible. The prescription of anti-depressants and tranquilizers to women for depression and anxiety is extremely prevalent. In a survey of the prescribing patterns of 250 GPs by Norwich Union Healthcare, 'eight out of 10 said they prescribed more antidepressants for both depression and anxiety than they should do' (Dilner, 2004). Dilner (2004) argues that millions of women in the UK are addicted to 'happy pills'. According to a magazine survey quoted by Dilner (2004), 'more than half of British women have taken anti-depressants'. Female dependent users are thus positioned through medicalisation as immoral, deviant, hedonistic, weak-willed, bad choice makers or the psychopathological clients of 'expert' doctors or nurse prescribers with the medical knowledge/power to 'cure' them.

Harm minimisation and the responsibilisation of dependent users

Female drug users may also be subjected to particular kinds of medicalisation through discourses and practices of harm minimisation. Another key strand of public health discourse constituting drug policy, particularly in countries such as the Netherlands, Portugal, Denmark and Australia, is that of harm minimisation. In the US and Canada, harm minimisation has not gained significant support in official policy. In the UK in the 1980s, harm reduction agendas gained ascendancy in response to the threat to public health from HIV/AIDS. Within this strand of public health discourse, the management of the risks associated with illicit drug use lies in the self-government of their use (O'Malley, 1999). The key premise is that it is not any inherent quality of a drug that makes it harmful, but the consumption choices of individual users. The illicit drug user is thus individualised in a different way from how he or she is within the discourse of pathology or punishment and prohibition. The individual user is situated as a rational, free market consumer. Drug use is not constructed as a medical pathology to be cured through 'treatment' or as a wilful criminal act that should be punished, but is understood in the same way as other 'normal' activities that can be performed in a variety of ways. If drug use can be excessive, it can also be non-excessive; if it can be dependent, it can be non-dependent.

Illicit drug users are constituted as responsible for themselves, and the problem is to equip them with the means to make informed choices about their drug consumption. As O'Malley (1999, p 201) argues:

> The role of state governmental programs is primarily advisory: to establish and broadcast the so called "recommended safe levels of usage", founded on expert evaluations of actuarial data, so that responsible users may moderate their risk-bearing behaviours in line with an officially endorsed risk calculus.

The implication is that drug dependence is a state arising from uninformed or irresponsible behaviour. In this way, drug-dependent users are positioned as uninformed or irresponsible, and disease discourse is re-engaged. At the same time as constituting the drug user as a rational actor, the discourse of harm minimisation thus constitutes a more indirect, liberal mode of governing than punishment and prohibition or pathology. The onus is placed on treatment agencies to properly inform users, and ultimately on individual users to be responsible and make the right choices. The technology of responsibilisation is central to the harm minimisation approach. The emphasis is not on preventing use altogether, but on ensuring that users have the skills, capacities and means to reduce any harm they may cause themselves, for example, informing users about the risks of HIV/AIDS and other infections, and providing them with clean needles.

In harm minimisation discourse, the problem of the control of harm to the individual is constructed in terms of the reduction of various forms of drug-related harm. Harm reduction interventions include needle exchanges, prescribing practices, and the provision of information. Although the forms of harm identified within harm minimisation discourse include social, medical, legal and financial (DH, 1999), the focus has tended to be on the reduction of medical forms of harm, and in particular, on the measurement and prevention of the risk-bearing activities of users (ACMD, 1988, 1989; DH, 1996). Specific harms associated with illicit drug use include HIV infection, hepatitis B and C, thrombosis, abscesses, heart problems, a range of psychiatric and psychological problems and drug-related deaths. As Reith (2004, p 295) argues:

> The language of risk actually reinforces the notion of "addiction" as a realist category, in its postulation of the existence of some state that the individual is actually at risk *from*.

All illicit drug users are given the opportunity to make informed and rational choices about their drug consumption. Paradoxically, this serves to reinforce the perceived *pathology* of dependent users. Drug use is constituted as a risky behaviour that can be avoided through 'choice' rather than an inevitable disease for the weak and pathological (Seddon, 2007a). Addicted users are constituted as individuals who are not capable of managing their 'freedom to consume' (Reith, 2004). They have flouted their duties as morally responsible citizens by allowing themselves to become addicts. Dependent users are constructed as simply needing to make better cognitive behavioural choices. They are considered responsible for getting 'clean', and if they fail to do so are deemed appropriate subjects for punishment (see Part Three, p 148–150). This form of governance, whereby drug users are constituted as responsible for their own predicament, is responsibilisation. The failure to seek and follow treatment renders dependent male and female users irresponsible choice makers (Prochaska and DiClemente,

1992; Grant et al, 2008; Kilty, 2011). As is shown later in Chapter Six, this constituted subject position had a direct impact on the women interviewed in this study. They talked at length about feeling personally responsible for their predicament (see Chapter Six, p 181).

Harm reduction, HIV/AIDS and female drug users

In the UK, the notion of drug use as a pathological disease gave way, in the 1980s, as harm reduction agendas gained ascendancy. With that, drug use began to be conceptualised in new ways. Due to the HIV/AIDS pandemic, government rhetoric and media campaigns began to focus on the relation between illicit drug use and HIV/AIDS. In 1988, the UK Advisory Council on the Misuse of Drugs (ACMD) produced a report stating that HIV/AIDS was a greater risk to public health than illicit drug use. It recommended both harm reduction and multi-agency approaches should be prioritised in order to bring drug users into services and to prevent HIV risk practices (ACMD, 1988). As a result of this report, harm minimisation was adopted and established as a crucial aspect of UK drug policy.

As discussed earlier in Chapter One (see pp 27–31), in media and academic discourse in the UK in the 1980s, illicit drug users and injecting drug users in particular were constructed as likely to engage in HIV/AIDS high-risk behaviours, such as unprotected sex or the sharing of contaminated needles. Female dependent drug users were frequently sexualised, and their out-of-control drug use associated with an out-of-control sexuality (see, for example, Plant, 1990; Inciardi et al, 1993). In drug policy discourse, female users were constructed as a particularly high-risk group, and targeted for intervention. They were constituted as immoral, weak-willed, diseased women and/or prostitutes who threatened to contaminate and pollute the general populace, placing the public health of communities at risk of disease with risky injecting practices and promiscuous and irresponsible sexual behaviour (Malloch, 2000). This perceived threat led to them becoming the focus for harm reduction strategies (such as medical examinations and the distribution of condoms), and a potential priority for services, despite the fact they were under-represented in many, particularly drug, services (Malloch, 2000). Women were given the major responsibility for the prevention of the spread of AIDS in the heterosexual community, and were allocated the role of safer sex educators (Henderson, 1990; Ettorre, 1992). The control of female sexuality and female drug users' sexual behaviour was considered a priority in preventing the spread of HIV/AIDS, while their male equivalents were regarded as of less importance.

This approach distracted from the problem of the sexual behaviour of male users and clients of sex workers, the spread of HIV/AIDS in the general population, as well as the myriad of social problems faced by female drug users.

Rather than supporting female drug users in overcoming poverty, violence and other health risks, instead, the UK government focused on female drug users' sexuality in an effort to prevent the spread of HIV/AIDS. Nevertheless, harm reduction strategies to alleviate the risks from drug use, such as needle exchange programmes in the UK, have been universally acclaimed as effective in reducing the transmission of HIV and hepatitis. Needle exchange programmes have been cited as the reason why the UK has a significantly lower HIV rate among injecting drug users than the majority of other European countries (Stimson, 1995; Reuter and Stevens, 2007; Mathers et al, 2008). The apparent success of these measures has led to them being recommended as universal practice by the World Health Organization (WHO), the United Nations Office on Drugs and Crime (UNODC) and the United Nations Programme on HIV/AIDS (UNAIDS) (Reuter and Stevens, 2007).

In the US, harm reduction programmes such as needle exchanges are still illegal in many states, despite their proven success in reducing the spread of HIV, AIDS and hepatitis C (CDC, 2005). This is because US drug policy has favoured an approach focusing on abstinence. In the US the sexual behaviour of female drug users came under the auspices of the medical professions in a different way, through the criminalisation of pregnancy, as discussed in Chapter Three earlier (see pp 81–86). The medical profession played an important role in identifying pregnant drug-using women for criminalisation. The notion of an out-of-control, sexually promiscuous addict woman exchanging sex for crack was the most prominent configuration of the weak-willed female dependent user (see, for example, Inciardi et al, 1993). The focus on the sexual behaviour and spread of disease by crack-using women distracted from the need for harm minimisation approaches to drug policy. Consequently, HIV, AIDS and hepatitis C rates are relatively high in the US. This has had a negative affect on poor, minority ethnic women in particular. Disproportionate numbers of poor, black women are HIV positive from injecting drugs. In 2004 it was estimated that black and Hispanic women comprised 82 per cent of all women in the US with injection-related AIDS (CDC, 2008). Female drug users were stigmatised as irresponsible, out-of-control, diseased prostitutes, responsible for their predicament and undeserving of protection within public health policy. Their stigmatisation and construction as 'undeserving' allowed for the continuation of the predominance of the disease model and punitive approaches in drug policy.

Notwithstanding the success or failure of these countries to combat HIV/AIDS, it should be noted that the risks from blood-borne diseases are just one risk faced by female dependent drug users. The focus on the risk of HIV/AIDS transmission obscures the broad array of risks female dependent users are subject to. As Maher (2002, p 322) argues, 'the risk of arrest, death, withdrawal, overdose, being attacked, robbed, or ripped off, losing your children, losing a limb and losing your dignity' are interrelated and cumulative problems for dependent female users. The medicalisation of female users' behaviour thus serves to detract from these issues.

Harm reduction as social control: 'state-sponsored' dependent women

Within official discourse on harm minimisation, drug dependence is constructed as a chronic and relapsing condition (NTA, 2012; NIDA, 2014). Substitute prescribing such as methadone maintenance is a practice consistent with this idea, and abstinence is regarded as an unrealistic short-term goal for many dependent users. Methadone maintenance is available to women dependent on heroin in the UK, US and Canada, and emerged in the 1960s (Rosenbaum, 1981; Boyd, 2004,). However, since then it has remained controversial (Boyd, 2004). Programmes in each country involve the service user regularly reporting to a prescribing clinic where they are drug tested. Some programmes administer a gradual (six to nine months) detoxification, whereby the dosage is lowered until the service user is drug-free. Other programmes involve the service user remaining on methadone indefinitely on a stabilised dose. Some service users will remain on methadone for 10, 15 or 20 years (Fernandez and Libby, 2011). Crucially, methadone has a greatly reduced euphoric effect, so it is able to contain the opiate cravings without giving the user so much of a high.

The availability of methadone maintenance in the US and Canada has been in shorter supply and received less funding than in the UK due to the preference for a total abstinence model over medication maintenance. In contrast, in the UK, due to the ascendancy of a harm minimisation approach, methadone prescribing has dominated the treatment field, and some argue that this has been at the expense of the goal of abstinence and sufficient detoxification facilities (Gyngell, 2011; Strang et al, 2012). However, the UK 2010 Drug Strategy's focus on recovery has meant a shift towards abstinence, and concerns have been raised about cuts to funding for methadone prescribing and the pressure for users to achieve abstinence before they are ready to do so (DrugScope, 2010; Release, 2010; SMART Recovery, 2010).

Extensive international evidence supports the use of methadone maintenance and its ability to reduce heroin use (see, for example, WHO et al, 2004; Amato et al, 2005; Strang et al, 2010), reduce crime (Lind et al, 2005; Mattick et al, 2009) increase treatment retention (Mattick et al, 2009), reduce injecting, sex work, HIV infection and transmission (Metzger et al, 1993; Degenhardt et al, 2010), increase health, stability and social functioning (Rosenbaum and Murphy, 1987; Degenhardt et al, 2010), and employment (Powers and Anglin, 1993). However, the use of methadone maintenance has always been more about social control than about the reduction of harm to users (Rosenbaum, 1981; Boyd, 2004). It has been closely tied to a crime reduction agenda (Fernandez and Libby, 2011). Under state supervision and the medical control of doctors, users do not need to resort to crime to fund their drug habits. As Fernandez and Libby (2011, p 105) argue:

> ... the original concept behind methadone maintenance was to use it as a control mechanism.... Richard Nixon's primary concern was crime reduction when methadone maintenance was instituted as federal policy. The political agenda of the day had less to do with relieving the hard lot of heroin addicts than the war on crime.

The focus on this outcome within policy discourse suggests that the primary concern was not the reduction of harm to users, but the protection of the public from them. Although some users may remain dependent on methadone for some time, harm is at least reduced to society. However, it has been argued that there is no real causal link between the amounts spent on methadone treatment, and crime being reduced (Public Accounts Committee, 2010). Some studies have found users continue to commit crime while on methadone (Bloor et al, 2008).

Based on the limited number of studies that have compared heroin and methadone maintenance, there is evidence that heroin prescribing results in better treatment retention, reduced heroin use, criminal activity, mental health and social functioning than methadone maintenance (Hartnoll et al, 1980; McCusker and Davies, 1996; Perneger et al, 1998). Although legal heroin has been prescribed to users on a number of programmes in different countries, this practice has not been adopted on a national basis, despite the fact that users themselves have frequently stated that they would prefer to be prescribed heroin (Boyd, 2004). Methadone is, like heroin, a highly physically addictive drug, and more harmful, according to a number of key indicators. The risk of methadone-related mortality estimates it at around four times that of heroin (Newcombe, 1996). It is also recognised in the research literature and drug-using subcultures that methadone withdrawal is much more severe and longer-lasting than heroin (Gossop and Strang, 1991; Rosenbaum, 1981; Stewart, 1987). It appears that the reason why heroin is not prescribed has less to do with evidence of best practice and scientific knowledge of harmfulness, and more to do with moral attitudes towards heroin addicts. Furthermore, to prescribe heroin as a routine treatment for dependent users would suggest it is somewhat safe to use, and this would undermine its social, political and cultural status as a dangerous, prohibited drug and the drug laws that support it.

Service users in numerous studies have discussed how the inflexible, rigid rules and regulations integral to methadone services are experienced by them as counterproductive, creating obstacles to them leading a 'normal' life, and a way for governments to regulate and control them (see, for example, Rosenbaum, 1981; Rosenbaum and Murphy, 1987; Boyd, 2004; Radcliffe and Stevens, 2008). In the 1974 documentary film, 'Methadone: An American way of dealing', one of methadone's original proponents, Peter Bourne, discusses the advantage of daily methadone prescribing is its ability to control the lives of addicts (cited by Rosenbaum, 1981). Daily appearance at a clinic means heroin users will be gripped in the treatment system, making them, as a population, easier to monitor and control as well as more amenable to other kinds of intervention such as psychological therapy. While there may be obvious advantages to regular, mandatory reporting to a prescribing clinic from the point of view of governments and service providers, this is not necessarily one shared by clients. For instance, one woman in Rosenbaum's book *Women on heroin* stated:

> Methadone scares me. It's a government plot to control people. Once they hook you on it, they never let you go. You can't leave town. They've got records. I'd rather have a $200-a- day habit than go on methadone. (Rosenbaum, 1981, p 117)

Indeed, methadone maintenance is referred to in drug-using subcultures as a 'state-sponsored addiction', and is a view recently expressed in the UK media (see, for example, Reilly, 2010; Gyngell, 2012).

The rigid policies and practices involved in methadone prescribing situate male and female users as difficult, badly behaved, healthcare users who require the control and regulation of the medical profession. In this instance, the technology of medicalisation exerts a disciplinary regime with punitive consequences for non-compliance, such as the termination of a prescription. Nowhere else in the healthcare system is such treatment regarded as acceptable. For instance, patients with lung cancer with histories of tobacco smoking are not subject to the same punitive control and regulation. Illegal drug users are perceived to be immoral, criminal, sick individuals, and moralistic approaches entrench drug policy.

The rigid rules and regulations governing methadone treatment may adversely affect women in particular ways. Rosenbaum (1981) notes that in early methadone programmes in the US, one of the requirements for women to enrol was that they had to be with a man. The idea was that this would attract men to the programme. Although services for female users have improved since then, it is widely acknowledged that they continue to fail to meet the needs of women. Difficulty in staying off drugs is often described by those who have tried to do so as due to the struggle to get away from drug-using peers (Rosenbaum, 1981; Taylor, 1993). Thus, the requirement for methadone clients to attend a clinic on a regular basis, where users meet, can make them vulnerable to relapse. Usually, rules stipulate that methadone clients can only collect a prescription in their place of residence. This means that should a user wish to relocate and extricate themselves from peers or an abusive partner, they would be unable to do so. There is evidence that women are often in relationships with men who are dependent users, and who are sometimes abusive and violent. If a woman is tied to a particular location, it will be more difficult for her to leave an abusive partner (see Chapter Seven, p 263). Finding work with the flexibility to enable a user to pick up a daily prescription may limit job options, especially for women who already have to work around children. The requirement to take prescribed methadone under the supervision of a pharmacist, all in one dose, is experienced as counterproductive, making women feel unwell (See Chapter Seven, p 263.

Recoverable, changeable, transformable women

The goal of recovery is currently one of the most prevalent policy trends within the treatment field. Gender-neutral discourses of choice constitute male and female dependent users as recoverable, changeable and transformable. Recovery theorists, those experiencing recovery, drug treatment professionals and advocates would all concur that recovery 'is an individual, person-centred journey', and 'one that means different things to different people' (Home Office, 2010). The commitment of governments to this principle is, however, questionable. As the disease model of drug use predominates within the treatment field in the US and Canada, recovery from drug dependence has been equated with abstinence. In other words, recovery from drug dependence is understood as becoming drug-free. In the UK, the Drug Strategy 2010 (Home Office 2010) contains a new emphasis on users attaining a 'drug-free life' or a 'full recovery', and the Home Office's (2012) plan, *Putting full recovery first*, for building a new treatment system, aims to 're-orient local treatment provision towards full recovery by offering more abstinence-based support' (p 4). However, this view of recovery is highly contentious. For some, recovery may mean a consistently moderate use of a substance or abstinence supported by prescribed medication (White, 2007; Release, 2010; UKDPC, 2010). This is supported by a growing body of evidence that moderated consumption is a possible resolution for some people with substance dependency, whereby drug dependency and related behaviour are no longer problematic in the individual's life (Dawson, 1996; Larimer and Kilmer, 2000; Miller and Muñoz, 2005; White, 2007). Also, 'for most, the journey of recovery begins with harm reduction and ends with abstinence' (SMART Recovery, 2010, p 2).

That said, official drug policy discourses do offer wider definitions of recovery, although it remains an ambiguous term. In the Home Office's *Putting full recovery first*, recovery is described as a process also involving access to sustained employment, a reduction in offending, accommodation, improved mental and physical health, improved relationships and 'the capacity to be an effective and caring parent' (p 17). In the US, the Substance Abuse and Mental Health Services Administration (SAMHSA) (2012) has come up with a definition of recovery in a year-long consultation with a range of healthcare partners that is meant to capture the common essential experience of those in recovery. They define it as, 'a process of change through which individuals improve their health and wellness, live a self-directed life, and strive to reach their potential.' Abstinence is thereby understood as one of many strategies for achieving recovery, and overall improvements in other dimensions of a user's life, including health, home, purpose, and community, are constructed as equally important.

There is a growing body of literature debating the conceptual parameters of recovery (White, 2000, 2007; Cloud and Granfield, 2008), and thus this will not be discussed any further here. But how recovery is defined and understood shapes the fate of users, and has 'a profound influence on institutional economies and professional careers' (White, 2007, p 239). As women experience drug use differently to men, recovery is likely to mean something different to women and to be experienced differently. For instance, parenting responsibilities may be central to recovery for women (Nelson-Zlupko et al, 1996). Understandings of recovery and treatment practices based on these, that do not take account of the different needs of women, are unlikely to have any lasting positive effect. Whether policy discourses champion recovery, harm minimisation or coercive treatment to prevent crime at any particular time is immaterial, if women's needs in treatment services continue to be marginalised and silenced.

Public health discourse on drug use has two main contradictory strands. One constructs drug use as pathology as a biological disease or mental impairment, and the other as a cognitive choice. How do drug users themselves make sense of these opposing discourses of disease and choice? Kilty (2011) describes how, in her study of 22 former women prisoners in Canada, they invoked both choice and disease discourses of addiction in an effort to manage stigma and their identities as drug users. The women described feeling powerless over their drug use and unable to make 'good' choices. At the same time, when discussing recovery, the women's narratives shifted to a focus on their emerging sobriety as an empowering choice they had made. Kilty found that different selves appeared in tension as the women separated what they saw as their 'true selves' from their 'addict selves' in their narratives about the process of achieving sobriety:

> Participants carried out ... techniques of the self by engaging in a discursive dance between constructing addiction as either a disease or choice; their adoption of these discourses largely depended on their feelings of personal control and empowerment. (Kilty, 2011, p 9)

The women appropriated both addict and non-addict identities for themselves with reference to choice and disease discourses, suggesting that their subjectivities should be seen as 'multivariate and an ongoing negotiation' (Kilty, 2011, pp 11-12). This concurs with McIntosh and McKeganey's (2000) study of service users' narratives of recovery that they found corresponded closely with descriptions of the recovery process in the addictions literature. They suggest that this may result from the fact that the addicts' accounts of recovery may have been constructed in interaction with representatives of drug treatment agencies. In other words, those in recovery appropriate available discourses to manage their identities, and in so doing, internalise and resist different aspects of these discourses as active agents. Kilty (2011) argues that the identities of the women in her study were marked by the stigmas associated with criminalisation, imprisonment and drug addiction, and their 'true selves' did not come out unscathed. At the same time, they rejected the neoliberal construction that they simply needed to make better cognitive behavioural choices, and invoked both choice and disease discourses to manage the stigma of an addict identity.

The women interviewed in this study also invoked disease and choice discourses separating what they saw as their 'true selves' from their 'addict selves' in their accounts of their drug use/recovery. As in Kilty's study, this was an attempt by the women to distance themselves from a deviant and stigmatised 'addict' identity. Similarly, while the women's identities were unavoidably altered by stigmatisation and marginalisation, they continued to resist this by rejecting negative aspects of 'addict identities' (see Chapter Six, pp 187–188 and 215–218). The accounts of the women in this study also problematise the construction of drug users as rational, free agents who are able to avoid dependency and stop using heroin and/or crack simply by getting into treatment.

Responsible and needy women

Women's access to appropriate drug treatment remains problematic due to lack of funding, long waiting lists and services to fit their needs (Rosenbaum, 1995). Drug services continue to be designed for men, are male-dominated, and women have limited access to women-centred treatment (Weissman et al, 1995; Langan and Pelissier, 2001; NTA, 2002; NASADAD, 2008). There is evidence that services for drug users are sexist. For instance, Nelson-Zlupko et al (1996) found sexual harassment was reported by more than half the 24 participants in their study, while talking about previous drug treatment experiences, despite the fact they were not asked about it. Simply providing all-women's groups within conventional services was not helpful to participants who continued to experience negative stereotyping by staff and other clients. Women users in treatment are frequently constructed as more deviant, pathological and 'difficult' than male users (see, for example, Gossop, 1986). There is evidence that they are often treated differently by drug treatment staff, such as being subject to more restrictions (Rhoads, 1983; Friedman and Alicea, 1995; Boyd, 1999; Sterk, 1999). For instance, in Sterk's (1999) study of crack users in Atlanta it was found that women in treatment had a 10pm curfew in order to protect them from the advances of men, while the men were subject to no such curfew.

The failure of treatment services to deliver gender-sensitive treatment to female users in the UK, US and Canada is well documented (Hepburn, 1999; Becker and Duffy, 2002; Simpson and McNulty, 2007; DPA, 2010). Official discourse on drug policy acknowledges that women often have different needs to men, and therefore require different services that are more suited to these (Poole and Dell, 2005; Galvani and Humphreys, 2007; NASADAD, 2008; Brady and Ashley, 2005). There is evidence to support the need for women-only services, services that offer childcare, trauma-based services dealing with issues affecting women such as sexual abuse and domestic violence, and services for sex workers (Nelson-Zlupko et al, 1996; Grella et al, 2000; Marsh et al, 2000; Becker and Duffy, 2002; Poole and Dell, 2005; NASADAD, 2008).

Studies have found that women are more likely to address psychosocial issues key to their recovery in a women-only treatment setting (Nelson-Zlupko et al, 1995; Jannson et al, 1996; Knight et al, 1999; Volpicelli et al, 2000; Greenfield et al, 2007). For example, in a study of 24 women in recovery, Nelson-Zlupko et al (1996) found that conventional treatment programmes and mixed groups failed to provide a forum where women felt they could openly discuss many of the issues they saw as central to their recovery, including childrearing, sexuality and relationships. Participants reported that counsellors and male group members in conventional programmes tended to prompt them to 'focus on their addiction' when they tried to discuss these issues, as if doing so was irrelevant to their recovery. Consequently, the study participants felt that issues most pertinent to their recovery were obscured, minimised and silenced.

Considerable advances are being made in Canada and the US to make treatment systems for women 'trauma-informed' (Harris and Fallot, 2001; Moses et al, 2004; Poole, 2004; Poole and Dell, 2005). Dependent drug use in women is increasingly understood as a symptom of psychological trauma and as a coping mechanism for post-traumatic stress (Poole and Dell, 2005). Women describe different types of triggers compared to men that make them vulnerable to relapse, including severe traumatic stress reactions to early childhood trauma, symptoms of depression and feelings of low self-worth (SAMHSA/CSAT, 2009). While positive treatment services are developing that recognise such issues, there is a danger such moves will bolster the medicalising, psychologising and behavioural emphasis in healthcare, social services and criminal justice. An understanding of the structural and interpersonal contexts of women's lives that looks beyond notions of individual psychology, responsibility and blame is necessary in treatment provision.

In drug policy discourse female users are often constructed as more intractable and pathological, and labelled as treatment failures (Root, 1989). Social problems such as poverty and violence are sidelined, while pathology, individual psychology and chemically driven behaviour are primary concerns. Failure by a woman to 'recover' may be constructed as caused by individual weakness or non-compliance, a sign of pathology and emotional disturbance, rather than a lack of service provision or practical support. This medicalising tendency continues in policy discourse despite the fact that services for female users continue to be understood as inadequate and in need of review and development (Becker and Duffy, 2002; NTA, 2010; Poole and Dell, 2005; Galvani and Humphreys, 2007; NASADAD, 2008). As Malloch argues:

> Services may not be aimed at meeting the needs of women, but any failure to comply will often be perceived – and punished – as individual non-compliance. (Malloch, 2004b, p 304)

While there is recognition that female users have different needs to male users, and there is a lack of services to fit these needs, at the same time, they are constituted as responsible for their predicament. Thus, female users are positioned as both responsible and needy. Their needs are greater than other communities of drug users if only because they have hitherto been neglected. Their needs are extraordinary from those of men's if only because the services already developed do not 'fit'. They are thereby constructed as a 'special case'. Their needs are individualised and psychologised, and the underlying conditions for substance use, such as poverty, violence and trauma, are seen as mental health issues.

In the same way that the structural inequalities and treatment failings affecting dependent women with past experiences of abuse may be recast as mental health issues, social issues faced by pregnant drug-using women have been similarly reconstructed as due to individual weakness. A mind apparently controlled by illicit drugs, combined with a lack of maternal instinct, situates the pregnant female user as the epitome of an irresponsible, bad choice maker. Structural issues such as poverty, violence and inadequate housing may be constructed as symptoms of irresponsible, chemically driven behaviour, and lack of fitness to mother. Failure to attend treatment is less likely to be seen as a lack of adequate treatment, fear of stigma or social service intervention, but as a sign of the disordered thinking, intractability and selfishness of the pregnant drug-using woman in question. This issue is discussed in more detail in the following chapter.

The key obstacle for women going into treatment, whether it is residential, a daily or evening meeting in the community, is lack of childcare (Poole and Isaac, 2001; Boyd, 2004; Galvani and Humphreys, 2007). While abstinence-based treatments, such as in-house detox programmes, are the focus of policy, facilities that enable women to do this are limited because childcare is not provided. Rehabilitation centres requiring women to stay in them for one month to a year are not an option for women with children. While women are often motivated to get clean because of their children, if a treatment programme is unable to take account of their family obligations, it is often unacceptable to them (Rosenbaum, 1981). Women tend to regard their children as their central concern, and are unable to treat drug programmes as their main priority (Boyd, 1999). They are fearful of entering treatment due to the possibility of social services intervention and their drug use being used as evidence of their unfitness to parent (Rosenbaum and Murphy, 1998; Boyd, 1999; Sterk, 1999; Galvani and Humphreys, 2007). Pregnant drug-using women also fear losing custody of their children or, in the US, facing criminal sanctions for drug use during pregnancy, and so are likely to avoid alerting treatment services of their pregnancy (see Chapter Six).

A low priority, but requiring coercion

Drug use has increasingly come to be understood not as a form of potential harm to the self, but as a harm done to others. This has led to an increased focus on crime prevention and use of coercive forms of treatment through the criminal justice system in drug policy. Coercive treatments can be categorised into two types. One is when an offender is ordered by a court to undergo drug treatment. It is compulsory, does not involve informed consent, and the user has no choice. The other is when an offender is given a choice of treatment or prison, referred to as quasi-compulsory treatment. Within drug policy discourse in the UK, US and Canada, dependent users who come into contact with the criminal justice system or, in the case of women perceived to place a foetus or child at risk, are positioned as worthy and deserving of coercive treatment.

In the US, coercive drug policies have a relatively long history, where the idea can be traced back to the 'narcotic farms' of the 1920s (Seddon, 2007b), and where drug courts developed in the 1980s (Franco, 2010). Compulsory treatments were used from the mid-1930s to the 1970s by the US federal government and various states to treat heroin addicts who were forced to enter secure hospitals (Gostin, 1991). In the UK, the shift from a health agenda to a crime prevention one since the late 1990s (Stimson, 2000) has led to the adoption of more coercive approaches in drug policy (Hunt and Stevens, 2004), including Drug Treatment and Testing Orders (DTTOs) and the adoption of drug courts. These quasi-compulsory forms of treatment offer mandatory drug treatment rather than a prison term to some non-violent, drug-using offenders. However, there are many types of coercive treatments that are used at various stages in the criminal justice system (Gostin, 1991; Spooner et al, 2001; Chandler et al, 2009; Hall and Lucke, 2010).

The conceptual parameters of coercion as a mode of treatment have been much debated. It has been argued that there is no simple dichotomy between voluntary and coerced treatment (Bean, 2002), and that coercion is more appropriately viewed as on a continuum (Farabee et al, 1998; Hiller et al, 1998; Longshore et al, 2004). Proponents of quasi-compulsory treatment are keen to emphasise that this type of treatment involves some element of choice, however constrained. Longshore et al (2004) argue that some legally mandated drug users are willing and grateful treatment participants, and are not actually coerced in the sense of being forced against their will. Drug dependent users may experience treatment entry pressures from diverse sources, including financial, family, friends, partners, employers and the state (Longshore et al, 2004). For instance, a drug-using woman with children may 'choose' to enter treatment to avoid the loss of child custody. Therefore, individuals who are referred through the criminal justice system may not necessarily be under greater coercion than those who are not (Longshore et al, 2004). Bean (2004, p 229) points out:

> To talk ... of "coercion" and compare this unfavourably with "voluntary" decisions to enter treatment is to be too optimistic about the nature of many drug users' lives.

However, coercion may not only be experienced at the level of entry. This is significant when considering different treatment modalities that are experienced by women. In other words, there are forms of coercion and control that operate within 'voluntary' treatment that women may experience as controlling and punitive and that may limit their options.

The lives of female users are often characterised by multiple forms of constraint, control and coercion, both in their relationships with others and with the state. Treatments that involve women users thus need to be understood in this context. In an ethnographic study of gender-specific drug treatment options for female offenders in eight correctional facilities and community-based programmes in New York City and Portland, Oregon, Welle et al (1998) found that the women in their sample typically committed crimes to support their own and their male partner's habits, and these relationships were often characterised by abuse and coercion. When these women were arrested for drug-related crimes, they were often put under pressure by their male co-defendants to confess to charges or serve time in prison for crimes they did not commit. Furthermore, male co-defendants threatened to harm women who showed an interest in seeking mandated drug treatment as an alternative to incarceration, and women feared further abuse if they sought mandatory treatment.

Female drug users are subject to coerced forms of treatment that their male equivalents are not. In the US, pregnant female drug users may face mandatory drug treatment. Fathers are not subject to the same requirements in order to retain their legal status and rights as fathers. Furthermore, even where maternal drug use has come to the attention of social services in the UK and Canada, and a child has been placed on an 'at-risk' register, abstinence will be expected of the women or the loss of child custody is a real possibility. In this context, engagement with drug treatment should be considered quasi-compulsory rather than understood as in any sense voluntary. A choice between engagement with treatment or child apprehension cannot realistically be seen as a free choice. The loss of child custody is the 'ultimate sanction', and is likely to be experienced as worse than imprisonment for dependent female drug users (see Chapter Seven, pp 241–243).

Research has demonstrated that voluntary treatment is successful in reducing drug-related harm whereas the evidence on coercive drug treatment is not as clear (Hunt and Stevens, 2004). A cross-national review of quasi-compulsory treatment conducted by Stevens et al (2005) found contradictory evidence for its effectiveness. Boyd (2004) argues that the success of drug courts has been overstated, and the percentage of those unable to complete treatment programmes and sent to prison is high. For instance, Belenko (1998, 2001) found that even though drug court participants are screened before being given access to the programme, about 50 per cent of participants fail to complete and are sent to prison. Drug courts also do little to address 'the impact of poverty, violence against women, drug laws, racial profiling' and 'the structural oppression that shapes their lives' (Boyd, 2004, pp 197-9; see also Anderson, 2000).

Hunt and Stevens (2004) argue that treatments that are increasingly based on coercion are likely to impede treatment effectiveness and reduce the gains treatment may produce. They discuss the ways in which the expansion of coerced treatment undermines voluntary treatment. Coerced clients may have no intention of changing their behaviour, and when placed alongside voluntary clients, may undermine and compromise the intentions of the latter (Hunt and Stevens, 2004; Du Rose and Keene, 2009). Coerced treatments distort how priorities for access to treatment are determined (Hunt and Stevens, 2004; Seddon, 2007b). They prioritise crime prevention over the individual wellbeing of individuals (Hunt and Stevens, 2004). Resources directed to offending drug users means that these resources will not be available for the treatment of other users or for health objectives such as measures to reduce drug-related deaths (Hunt and Stevens, 2004).

Female users are not regarded as a high priority from a criminal justice perspective due to their typically low-level criminal activity, and thus may be 'squeezed out' of treatment (Barton, 1999, cited in Seddon, 2007b), as well as miss out on 'fast-tracked' support. Such priorities may thus serve to further marginalise women from services. Many female (and male) users are likely to benefit from treatment prior to any involvement with the criminal justice system, and to make offending behaviour the qualifying criteria for priority treatment has limited preventative value. Limited access to appropriate treatment in the community in the US and Canada means that 'coerced treatment is problematic when voluntary support is unavailable for most women' (Boyd, 2004, p 196).

Coercive drug policies and practices usually fail to take account of the gendered forms of power and control shaping the choices, decisions and lives of female users. Female users' lives often involve a distinct lack of options, economic hardship, lack of support, primary childcare responsibilities, histories of abuse, violence and coercion in childhood and adult relationships. If voluntary treatment services do not fit women's needs and are insensitive to the social contexts of their lives, to coerce women into such treatment is unethical.

Conclusion

Medicalisation and the various treatment services for drug users that emanate from it are usually seen as a 'benevolent mechanism of emancipation' (Clancey and Howard, 2006). At the same time, as this chapter has demonstrated, it may equally be seen as 'a tool of social control' (Clancey and Howard, 2006) for the poor and marginalised. In league with the criminal justice system, the treatment industry supports and administers its own forms of punitive and coercive interventions into the lives of female users. Vacillating between choice and disease discourses, medicalisation gives authority to pathologising constructions of dependent female drug users that are used to justify their punishment and responsibilisation. Feminist sociologists have argued that the medical sphere is a patriarchal institution that maintains women's social inequality. Medical constructs of disease have been used to control and regulate women's bodies, especially through pregnancy and sexual health. The technology of medicalisation, grounded in the disease model of addiction, provides legitimacy to the punitive and intrusive treatment of female drug users who are constructed as more pathological and weaker-willed than male users. Female dependent users are situated as immoral, hedonistic, selfish, weak-willed, bad choice makers or the psychopathological clients of 'expert' doctors or nurse prescribers with the medical knowledge/power to 'cure' them.

Drug-using women have been subjected to medicalisation through discourses and practices of harm minimisation within which drug use is constructed as a risky behaviour that can be avoided through choice. This serves to reinforce the perceived pathology of dependent users who are constituted as responsible for their situation apparently brought about by them having made the wrong choices. In harm minimisation discourse in the UK, in response to the HIV/AIDS pandemic of the 1980s, female drug users were situated as irresponsible, promiscuous, diseased women, a particularly high-risk group for spreading HIV/AIDS. Consequently, the control of female sexual behaviour was considered a priority in preventing the spread of HIV/AIDS. Female users were targeted for intervention and situated as responsible for the sexual health and moral standards of communities.

In the US during the HIV/AIDS pandemic, the disease model and punitive approaches dominated drug policy. Abstinence-based treatment predominated, and harm reduction programmes remained illegal in many states. Female drug users, particularly crack-using women, were constructed as a danger to public health due to their sexual promiscuity, but undeserving of attention within public health policy. Instead, pregnant drug-using women were medicalised in order to be criminalised, as the medical sphere assisted the criminal justice system in their criminalisation. It has been argued that the lack of a harm minimisation approach was one of the reasons for the disproportionate numbers of poor, black, injecting, drug-using women affected by HIV/AIDS in the US. However, while the prevention of the spread of HIV/AIDS is important, measures to support female dependent users and to address the social marginalisation and other daily risks they experience have not been a priority.

Extensive international evidence supports the use of methadone maintenance to reduce heroin use. However, it has arguably always been more about social control than the reduction of harm to users. This is partly due to the fact it has been closely tied to a crime reduction agenda. Although there is some research evidence that suggests heroin prescribing could result in better treatment outcomes, evidence also suggests it is prescribed for political reasons and due to moral attitudes towards heroin users rather than scientific knowledge of its harmfulness. Service users have described how the inflexible rules and regulations around methadone maintenance are counterproductive to their treatment outcomes. This regulation may adversely affect female users in particular ways, for example, due to their experiences as victims of domestic violence.

A predominant goal in drug policy discourse is to steer drug users into recovery, to change and transform them into functional, working citizens. While it is broadly agreed that recovery is an individual and person-centred goal, the commitment of governments to this principle is questionable. The tendency to equate recovery with drug abstinence in policy discourse is prevalent, but remains highly contentious. Women experience drug use differently to men, and recovery is often likely to mean something different to them. For instance, mothering responsibilities may be a central consideration to them in their recovery. Studies have demonstrated that people appropriate both choice and disease discourses to manage their subjectivities in the recovery process. Female (and male) users are thus able to construct positive identities for themselves by separating their 'true selves' from their 'addict selves'. In so doing, they may somewhat resist stigmatising neoliberal constructions of them as individuals simply needing to make better cognitive choices. The final part of this book explores how female users negotiate their subjectivities, both succumbing to and resisting efforts to control and regulate them.

There is some recognition that female users have different needs to their male equivalents. Some effort is being made to create services more suited to women's needs in the UK, US and Canada. However, there is a danger that some of these moves, such as those focusing on women's psychological and emotional issues, will bolster the medicalising, psychologising emphasis in healthcare, social services and the criminal justice system. Failure by women to 'recover' may be constructed as due to individual weakness rather than a lack of service provision, despite the fact it is acknowledged in drug policy discourse that services for women are in need of review and development. Dependent women are thus situated as psychopathological, marginalised, needy, treatment service users whose needs do not fit existing services. At the same time, they are constituted as responsible for their predicament, for their dependence, and any poverty, violence and psychological trauma they experience.

The responsibilisation of female users serves to somewhat legitimise coercive and punitive policy responses to them. However, there is no straightforward dichotomy between voluntary and coerced treatment, and drug-dependent users may experience pressures from diverse sources. The lives of female users are often characterised by multiple forms of constraint, control and coercion in their relationships with others and the state. They are subject to many forms of coerced treatment and interventions that male users are not. For instance, a choice between engagement in treatment or the loss of child custody cannot realistically be seen as a free choice. Coercive policies fail to take account of the gendered forms of power and control shaping female drug users' lives. Instead, female users are constituted as badly behaved, intractable service users in need of discipline and deserving of coercion. Arguably, while the provision of voluntary treatment is lacking, it is unethical to coerce female users into them. Female users are thus positioned as both badly behaved, intractable service users, deserving of coercion, and also as marginalised, neglected service users.

FIVE

Welfarisation

Welfarisation is another technology of government through which female illicit drug users are governed. It is the process that constructs individuals or groups as needing social support, or that constitutes them as unworthy of it. Governments themselves create welfarisation through the maintenance of structural inequalities, social and economic marginalisation and its 'management'. Certain 'needy' or 'at-risk' groups of individuals are targeted for welfarisation or 'soft policing' through formal and informal social control mechanisms (Worrall, 2001). Welfarisation is in principle, benevolent, and may involve the provision of support with social funds, housing, training, jobseeking or childcare. It may prove to be a lifeline for some individuals, but programmes of welfare have long been identified as having (darker) mechanisms of surveillance and social control embedded within them. This relates to Foucault's concept of the 'carceral continuum' and his view that regulatory techniques permeate 'a whole series of institutions ... well beyond the frontiers of criminal law' involving doctors, social workers and educators (1991 [1975], p 297). Drawing on Foucault's work, Cohen (1985, p 3) argues that liberal capitalist countries such as the UK, Canada and the US all have 'social control systems' embedded in their programmes of 'welfare' and ideologies of treatment.

The idea that policies of welfare also operate as mechanisms of control and surveillance particularly over marginalised groups of individuals has been explored and developed by various writers across a range of disciplines and subjects (see Parton, 1991, on child protection; Carlen, 1988, on young women in care; Carrington, 1993, on juvenile girls; Phoenix, 1999, on sex workers). Interventions into the lives of women who use illicit drugs presented as policies and practices of welfare (concerned with their wellbeing) are often experienced as intrusive, coercive and punitive (see Chapter Seven, pp 238–245 and 253–256). Mechanisms of control and surveillance, including practices of welfare, also serve to enforce gendered expectations of behaviour and to reinforce inequalities of gender. The technology of welfarisation is closely related to that of normalisation discussed in the following chapter (see Part Three, pp 142–144).

This chapter investigates the surveillance and regulation of drug-using women through welfare and social work policies and practices. Some contextual background, including neoliberal policies focusing on risk and responsibility, rather than needs and rights, is provided. How welfarisation policies such as the denial of social security benefits and social work interventions have an impact on female users and their children is also discussed.

Undeserving addicts

An important governmental rationality embedded in the technology of welfarisation is the distinction between the deserving and the undeserving poor. In neoliberal welfare policy, the predominant view is that welfare support should only be provided to those who are doing their best to help themselves. Furthermore, helping those who are in some way responsible for their troubles or who are not making every effort to help themselves is a fundamentally flawed enterprise. It is believed that often people are in receipt of welfare not because circumstances have been against them, but because they are wicked, stupid or lazy. Falling into a state of poverty and staying there is consequently seen as a matter of choice (Bauman, 2005). Within this framework, the institutions of welfarism that, from the end of the 19th century to the 1970s, assured citizens a certain level of security and rights, are seen as dysfunctional and encouraging of dependent, undeserving conduct.

The debate about the role of behaviour in causing poverty has surfaced in various guises over the years (Lister, 1996). The notion of undeservingness is often associated with the 1834 Poor Law in the UK. According to the 1834 Poor Law, the deserving poor were the very old, sick, severely disabled and unwilling unemployed, and the undeserving were unmarried mothers or those capable of working but instead engaged in begging or crime. This idea is also commonly identified with conservative policy analyst Charles Murray and his concept of the underclass that refers not to 'a degree of poverty, but a type of poverty' (Murray, 1996, p 24). Green (1996, p 19) states that this type of poverty is characterised by 'those distinguished by their undesirable behaviour, including drug-taking....'

By virtue of having chosen to use drugs, women and men dependent on drugs are automatically regarded as culpable members of the undeserving poor. This mode of thinking finds expression in contemporary drug policy discourse. Dependency is constituted as *the cause of* poverty, unemployment and delinquency. For instance, the UK Drug Strategy 2010 states: 'Drug and alcohol dependence is a key cause of inter-generational poverty and worklessness' (Home Office, 2010, p 23). Drug-dependent users are thus constituted as responsible for creating their own undesirable condition of poverty and unemployment. As discussed in Chapter Two (see pp 52–55), in neoliberal states, those who do not conform to their role as functioning, disciplined workers in the licit economy are held to account. Social problems such as unemployment, poverty, delinquency and drug use are configured as a matter of individual responsibility, success or failure. Dependent users are rendered 'blameworthy' for their predicament as addiction is constituted as self-induced and users thus as unworthy and undeserving of support.

The view of dependent users as 'undeserving' is evident in the US, where women and men convicted of a drug offence are denied the right to welfare assistance, public housing or student loans on their release from prison. It is also evident in the array of policies and procedures that support the notion that female illicit drug users (particularly if they are poor) do not deserve to have children, that is, child apprehension. The categories of deserving and undeserving also permeate the treatment system, and are evident in drug policies where success in treatment conditions freedom from incarceration. Those who want support may have to earn their right to it by proving their deservingness through success in treatment, finding work, accessing adequate housing and exemplary parental care. The same processes that construct individuals or groups as needing social support may, through responsibilisation, also construct them as un-entitled to or unworthy of it. The process of responsibilisation allows for a justification of a punitive response to an inability to meet conditions imposed in child custody cases or non-compliance with or lack of success in treatment.

As discussed in Chapter Two (see p 56), neoliberal states, welfare and social service provision play as much a role in the social control of poor drug-using women as prohibition and the criminal law. Seddon (2010) conducted a genealogical analysis of the relationship between welfare regimes and drug prohibition. He argues that the emergence of drug prohibition is rooted in the transition from classical to welfare liberalism that took place at the end of the 20th century. Prohibition thus emerged over the same period in which the welfare state was established. While welfarism and prohibition may appear as oppositional regimes, they are closely related, a fact that Seddon (2010, p 133) argues, 'destabilizes our sense of contemporary politics.' This is because 'pro-prohibition "drug warriors" are seen as reactionary right-wingers whilst supporters of the welfare state are considered staunch left-wingers' (Seddon, 2010, p 133). Penal and welfare regimes can be seen as closely intertwined in the governance of illicit drug users. The intertwining of their relationship is related to the ascendance of risk management techniques of governance. Risk management techniques are a key feature of neoliberal strategies of control spanning a range of locales and authorities. As Garland (2001, p 175) argues, since the end of the 1970s, welfare:

> ... as well as becoming more muted, has become more conditional, more offence centred, more risk-conscious.

The philosophy of risk management operates as a governmental continuum, spanning welfare, criminal justice and treatment institutions through which social workers, the police and drugs workers are able to liaise. It has thus increasingly provided the moral element in the medical-legal-moral hybrid equation, whereby social workers and benefit agents have progressively developed into criminal justice and treatment system informers of perceived inadequacy, worthlessness or 'risk'. Risk discourse is thus constitutive of identity. The penal and welfare systems invoke the same stereotypes and assumptions (Garland, 2001). They 'share the same recipes for the identification of risk and the allocation of blame' (Garland, 2001, p 201).

Punitive regulation is activated once individuals make claims on or are forced into the state apparatus, whether through the penal, child protection, medical or welfare benefits systems (Pollack, 2010). Drug users and/or offenders in the US, UK and Canada are assessed and monitored for their eligibility for social security benefits, for their deservingness or un-deservingness by welfare agents. Individuals who attempt to claim financial assistance are assessed for their risk of recidivism and fraud (Pollack, 2010). Drug users as current users and sometimes recovering ex-users who are doing all they can to reform and lead a 'normal', non-drug-using life, are deemed unworthy of social assistance. The techniques of welfarisation discussed here are understood as affecting male and female dependent drug users, although as low-income women and children are the main recipients of social assistance, welfare policy tends to have a disparate impact on them (Allard, 2002; Boyd, 2004).

Denial of social services in the US

A welfare strand of drug policy discourse is largely absent in the US National Drug Control Strategy 2013, as the joint apparatus of the criminal justice system and medical sphere are regarded as the main techniques used in the governance of female and male drug use. The strategy acknowledges that a conducive environment for 'recovery' involves 'access to employment, education, housing, and other economic opportunities' (Executive Office of the President of the United States, 2013, p 58). However, this issue is raised in relation to people leaving jails to facilitate 're-entry' into communities. The possibility of providing preventative support to dependent users in the identified areas is not discussed anywhere in the strategy. How access to employment, education, housing and other economic opportunities might be provided to those leaving jail is not discussed either. The strategy states:

> Neither the criminal justice system nor the public health sector can address the challenges and special needs of heavy users by operating in isolation. (Executive Office of the President of the United States, 2013, p 57)

However, the proposal is not to look to other kinds of provision that might be provided, such as 'economic opportunities', but to 'align the criminal justice and public health systems to intervene with heavy users' (Executive Office of the President of the United States, 2013, p 57). 'Tailored interventions' are proposed which are predominantly criminal justice and medical in orientation, including 'drug courts, in- and outpatient treatment, detoxification, rehabilitation and enhanced probation' (Executive Office of the President of the United States, 2013, p 57). Terms such as 'recovery' and 'rehabilitation' are used in the strategy, but no elaboration on how the strategy envisages such goals might be implemented is provided other than to create some 'interagency partners' to do so (Executive Office of the President of the United States, 2013, p 57). The absence of a discourse of welfare in the US drug strategy is a reflection of welfare policy in relation to drug users. The welfare system is not mobilised to aid in recovery and rehabilitation; rather, quite the opposite takes place.

In the US, drug users convicted of a drug offence and their families face a range of civil penalties that limit their access to social services. These include the loss of rights to welfare benefits and cash assistance, access to public housing and education aid. According to Smith (2007), a growing number of drug organisations, welfare rights groups, public health organisations and elected officials regard these laws as 'cruel, inhumane and counterproductive', and position drug offenders who want to change their lives in 'double jeopardy'. These laws have a disproportionate impact on poor women and children and minority ethnic groups (Allard, 2002; Smith, 2007).

The Welfare Reform Act 1996, more specifically Section 115 of the Personal Responsibility and Work Opportunity Reconciliation Act, imposes a lifetime ban on food stamps and cash assistance (Smith, 2007). This has been estimated to affect 92,000 women and 135,000 children (Allard, 2002).[1] Murder and rape does not result in the loss of these benefits, but possessing or selling a small quantity of drugs does. Victoria Sutherland, 34, in Portland, Oregon, had a drug conviction on her record when she lost her job over a decade later. Victoria had told the police they were drugs belonging to her when they actually belonged to her friend. Although she has served her sentence, she faces a lifetime ban from accessing food stamps. Formerly a manager, when Victoria lost her job she ended up living in a homeless shelter with her five-year-old son (Bapat, 2013). While women are still entitled to welfare benefits for their children, the lifetime welfare ban has a detrimental effect on female drug offenders' ability to look after their children as it means a lower level of subsistence for the family overall. Women who do not qualify for food stamps do not qualify for welfare to work, which offers childcare. This means that women like Victoria are unable to work as they have no one to care for their children (Bapat, 2013). Drug treatment programmes for women are scarce (Boyd, 2004), and the lifetime welfare ban means it is unlikely women will be able to access drug treatment (Allard, 2002). Such a situation can lead to the termination of parental rights as such children are deemed 'at risk' and their mothers as unable to support them, inadequate and blameworthy.

The Housing Opportunity Program Extension Act of 1996 allows public housing agencies the authority to (a) access the criminal records of the applicant or current tenant and (b) access records from drug treatment facilities where that information is solely related to whether the applicant is currently engaging in the illegal use of a controlled substance (Levi and Appel, 2003). The Department of Housing and Urban Development (HUD) enables and actively encourages public housing providers to reject applications and to terminate housing for those with drug-related convictions (Curtis et al, 2013). Public housing authorities or owners can terminate tenancies through the civil courts for suspected drug use or selling or any drug-related criminal conviction

(Curtis et al, 2013). A criminal conviction is not necessary to establish proof for an eviction (Curtis et al, 2013).

A tenant can also lose housing due to the suspected drug use or selling or conviction of a housemate or a guest (Levi and Appel, 2003). Any tenant evicted from housing due to a suspected or actual drug-related criminal activity is not eligible for housing assistance for three years, unless they successfully complete a rehabilitation programme approved by the public housing agency (Public Law, 1996). This policy disproportionately affects single mothers and their children who comprise the majority who occupy public housing in the US (Boyd, 2004). HUD established a Public Housing Drug Elimination Program (PHDEP) in 1989 that provides funds to increase police coverage, hire private security agents and private investigators (Boyd, 2004). HUD has effectively become an enforcement operation that coordinates with SWAT teams throughout the US to police the neighbourhoods of the poor, especially black women (Boyd, 2004). A mother who is evicted from public housing will be at risk of homelessness or living in an unsafe environment, such as with an abusive partner or an overcrowded environment, with limited resources (Allard, 2002). The chances of a woman not recidivating, finding work and staying clean are therefore reduced (Allard, 2002).

Another way that female and male drug users' and offenders' access to social services may be limited is through funding for higher education. The Higher Education Act 1965, reauthorised in 1998, delays or denies federal financial assistance for higher education to anyone who has been convicted of either sale or possession of illicit drugs (Levi and Appel, 2003), including relatively minor drug offences such as possession of small amounts of marijuana. Since the law was passed in 2000, it has been estimated that around 200,000 students have been denied financial aid (Students for Sensible Drug Policy, 2014), many of whom are women. In early 2006, the law was scaled back so that only people who are convicted while in college and receiving financial aid will have their eligibility taken away (Students for Sensible Drug Policy, 2014). This means that people convicted before they decide to go to college are able to do so. Due to further amendments to the Higher Education Act in the 2008 reauthorisation process the penalty was further reduced, and students no longer have to complete a government-approved treatment programme, which is often more expensive than university or college tuition fees, and instead are expected to pass two unannounced drug tests (Students for Sensible Drug Policy, 2014). This is so that students with drug convictions will apparently find it easier to regain eligibility for financial aid than if they had to go through a programme of treatment. However, students convicted on drugs charges are still forced to drop out, which makes them more likely to continue using drugs and to engage in criminal activity (Coalition for Higher Education Act Reform, 2006; Students for Sensible Drug Policy, 2014).

Students on low incomes continue to be most affected, as more well-off students will be able to pay for tuition on their own, as well as hire costly investigators to avoid criminal charges in the first place (Coalition for Higher Education Act Reform, 2006; Students for Sensible Drug Policy, 2014). Disproportionate numbers of women and men convicted for drug offences experience low educational attainment (Allard, 2002; Ramsay, 2003). Limiting female dependent drug users' access to education and training opportunities further marginalises an already disadvantaged group, and makes a continued career of dependent drug use and criminality a more likely outcome. However, it is not just dependent women, but any recreational user who may be deterred from pursuing an education. Many of these recreational drug-using women or men may subsequently end up with poor job prospects, a low income, substandard housing and exposure to dependent drug-using peers as a result of being excluded from educational opportunities. Due to the discriminatory way drug laws operate, black and minority ethnic groups are likely to be most affected by the lack of access to education (Coalition for Higher Education Act Reform, 2006).

The loss of rights to welfare benefits and cash assistance, access to public housing and education aid limits the possibility of women turning their lives around for themselves and for their children. The operation of these welfare policies leads to higher incidences of women and children going hungry, homelessness, criminal justice system involvement, family dissolution and countless hardships. The basic needs of low-income women and their children, particularly black and minority ethnic women (Levi and Appel, 2003), including food, housing, drug treatment, education and job opportunities, are placed in jeopardy (Mauer and McCalmont, 2006).

'Benefit scroungers' in the UK

A welfarisation discourse is more apparent in the UK drug strategy than in the US. However, as discussed in Chapter Four (see p 106), following the US, the Drug Strategy 2010 of the UK coalition government (Home Office, 2010) has adopted a focus on recovery. It outlines plans for the delivery of a recovery-oriented, 'whole systems' approach involving addressing the needs of the 'whole person'. This involves 'working with education, training, employment, housing, family support services, wider health services and, where relevant, prison, probation and youth justice services' (Home Office, 2010, p 20). The dependent user is situated as in need of normalisation through these institutions, enabling 'reintegration into communities' (p 22). However, it should be noted that this assumes previous experience of initial integration in communities that the recovering user may not have.

At the same time, as in US drug policy, the focus on recovery is accompanied by the punitive regulation of welfare recipients. While the UK strategy does not propose to use punitive measures in the same way as the US, the UK has also planned to adopt a sanctioning regime that involves withdrawing social security benefits from drug-dependent claimants who do not engage in treatment. This punitive measure is legitimised by a construction of dependent users as undeserving and blameworthy. While the strategy can be seen to be tackling the issues that are thought to contribute to dependent drug use, at the same time it responsibilises users. The UK strategy highlights the cost to society of a group of unemployed, drug-using benefit claimants. It draws from a study by Hay and Bauld (2008) that estimates that 400,000 benefit claimants (around 8 per cent of all working-age benefit claimants) in England are dependent on drugs or alcohol. The same study estimates that these benefit claimants cost the country £31.6 billion a year. Poverty and unemployment are viewed as caused by drug dependence, and drug-dependent users are thus situated as wholly responsible for their poverty and employment status. Many are engaged in formal employment throughout their drug careers (Bauld et al, 2010). However, according to the Drug Strategy 2010:

> Drug and alcohol dependence is a key cause of intergenerational poverty and worklessness. For example, in England, an estimated 80% of heroin or crack cocaine users are on benefits, often for many years and their drug use presents a significant barrier to employment. (Home Office, 2010, p 23)

The possibility of poverty and worklessness predating or simply cooccurring with drug dependence is not acknowledged. In a study by Luck et al (2004), of 61 female drug users on benefits, the women said they did not feel there was any direct link between their drug use and receipt of welfare, but their welfare dependency was driven by other factors. Furthermore, the strategy does not discuss the possibility of poverty occurring during periods of employment as a result of low-paid, unskilled employment, or that there may be many barriers to employment other than simply drug dependence.

The proposed solution to the problem of 'inter-generational poverty and worklessness' caused by drug dependence is to steer dependent users on benefits to engage with treatment and to find employment. However, this is by no means straightforward, as even assuming appropriate treatment and employment were available, treatment and employment demands may be at odds. The pressure to start work prematurely may hinder the recovery process and lead to relapse (Bauld et al, 2010). Many users on methadone prescriptions are expected to pick it up on a daily basis, making finding work around this difficult (Bauld et al, 2010). Dependent users on benefits may have long histories of disadvantage and social and economic marginalisation. They may have low educational attainment, a lack of skills, limited work experience, histories of abuse, health problems, poor housing, or childcare responsibilities (Bauld et al, 2010). They may be involved in acquisitive crime and/or sex work, negating any incentive to face the kind of low-paid, unskilled work available to them.

Aside from the myriad of social problems creating barriers for dependent drug users to find employment is the issue of the perspective of employers themselves, who are likely to view ex-users of drugs such as crack and heroin as 'the least attractive of potential employees' (UKDPC, 2008a, p 51). Employers are also likely to be unwilling to take on employees with criminal records (Kemp et al, 2004; Payne-James et al, 2005; UKDPC, 2008a).

The strategy aims to offer claimants a choice between sanctions or additional support:

> We will offer claimants who are dependent on drugs or alcohol a choice between rigorous enforcement of the normal conditions and sanctions where they are not engaged in structured recovery activity. (Home Office, 2010, p 23)

Research by Harris (2008) found that dependent users are largely 'invisible' within the benefits system. The prospect of benefit sanctions is unlikely to encourage drug users to disclose their drug use, and in some cases may stop them from seeking drug treatment altogether. There is little evidence that the threat of benefit sanctions improves engagement with treatment or helps drug-dependent users find work (SSAC, 2010, 2013). Drug users are already disproportionately sanctioned within the benefits system, usually because of failing to meet conditions placed on them such as not signing on, attending a medical, completing forms or determination of fitness following a medical (SSAC, 2010). Jobcentre staff work to unofficial targets to sanction as many claimants as possible (Void, 2014). A report by the Citizens' Advice Bureau (CAB) (2013) found that benefit sanctions have led to people attempting suicide, begging and going through bins to find food. They also found a quarter of people sanctioned in their survey had children, and 10 per cent were lone parents. While the strategy of introducing a further sanctioning regime for drug users is apparently intended to avoid the expense of drug-dependent users on benefits, there is an increased risk of poverty, social exclusion and criminal behaviour for those failing to meet the conditions (Release, 2010), and this is likely to cost much more (PwC, 2008).

Benefit conditions in Canada

As discussed in Chapter Three, in Canada in the 1990s onwards, welfare policy became more under the control of provincial governments. Drug users are not directly targeted through the benefits system in Canada. However, in 2001 in Ontario, Premier Harris claimed that women on welfare were drug users (MacDonald et al, 2001 cited in Boyd, 2004). Harris planned to refer welfare recipients for compulsory drug treatment and testing as a condition for receiving benefits. Ontario Minister of Community and Social Services conservative, John Baird, aimed to 'stop people from shooting their welfare cheque up their arm, and to help them shoot up the ladder of success' (Blackwell, 2000). The Centre for Addiction and Mental Health, the Canadian Medical Association and the Medical Reform Group of Ontario publically opposed this move. It was contested that drug testing would go against the Ontario Human Rights Code, would perpetuate negative stereotypes regarding poverty and addiction, and was of unproven efficacy. However, the plans were not realised as the Liberals won the 2003 provincial election. Although in Canada drug users are not explicitly singled out and targeted through the welfare system, the case of Ontario and the existence of a punitive, neoliberal climate demonstrate this could still occur in the future. Cuts to benefits in Canada targeting single mothers will, however, affect many female users (Boyd, 2004).

The loss of benefits for drug-dependent users may lead to poverty, poor nutrition, homelessness, mental health problems, crime and imprisonment. Where punishment and welfare systems meet and mesh, women and children are likely to be the most affected as they constitute the largest proportion of welfare recipients. Destitution may lead some women to resort to desperate measures such as sex work, while other women may become dependent on violent and abusive men. The lack of financial assistance may also have a serious impact on women's ability to provide for their children, leading to family separation or child apprehension.

Welfarisation of drug-using mothers

In the welfare strand of drug policy discourse in the UK, US and Canada, another key problem for government is the risk to children caused by the behaviour of drug-using parents. The governance of pregnant female users through the technology of prohibition and punishment was examined earlier, in Chapter Three (see pp 82–86). This chapter explores the governance of parenting through the technology of welfarisation. The assumption in the welfare strand of drug policy discourse is that the female user is an unfit mother.

In the US National Drug Control Strategy, the problem of the parenting ability of drug users is discussed in terms of the issue of supporting 'addicted mothers and their children' through 'family treatment' (Executive Office of the President of the United States, 2013, p 40). The strategy states that 'alcohol and drug related cases are more likely to result in foster care than are other child welfare cases' (p 41). It is acknowledged that there has been a lack of treatment available to mothers and their children, and this has contributed to a large number of women entering both child welfare and the criminal justice services. Treatment apparently offers 'highly troubled families ... the disruption of intergenerational addiction, violence and poverty' (Executive Office of the President of the United States, 2013, p 41). The implication is that drug 'addiction' is the cause of violence and poverty, and therefore, that addressing a mother's drug-using behaviour through treatment will eliminate these things from her life. Fathers' fitness to parent and their drug treatment are not mentioned. The issue of the absence of fathers from discourse on the governance of parenting is discussed in more detail in relation to child protection policy (see pp 132–133).

In the UK drug strategy, one of the key outcomes for the stated aim of the successful delivery of a recovery-oriented system is outlined as 'the capacity to be an effective & caring parent' (p 20). The problem for government is described as follows:

> A third of the treatment population has childcare responsibilities. For some parents, this will encourage them to enter treatment, stabilise their lives and seek support. For some children it may lead to harm, abuse and neglect and for others it will mean taking on inappropriate caring roles putting their health and/or education at risk. (Home Office, 2010, p 21)

According to the Advisory Council on the Misuse of Drugs (ACMD) in *Hidden harm*, the children of drug-using parents are likely to be exposed to a range of hazards '*as a result of* parental problem drug use' (ACMD, 2011, p 10, emphasis added). These include physical and emotional abuse or neglect, dangerously inadequate supervision, toxic substances in the home and exposure to criminal or other inappropriate adult behaviour. However, also included in the list of problems apparently caused by drug use are poverty, inadequate accommodation and unsatisfactory education (ACMD, 2011). Drug-using parents are therefore responsibilised for a range of social problems they may experience, which are constituted as in their control and as an outcome of their behaviour. The solution to the problem, according to the strategy, is, where it is perceived likely the child will suffer harm, to either remove the child and place them in care through court action, or reduce 'the level of assessed risk' (ACMD, 2011, p 22) by supporting parents to address their drug use while the child remains living with them. While the strategy uses the apparently gender-neutral language of 'parent' rather than mother or father, assessment and practice is usually targeted at mothers and their control and regulation (Kullar, 2009).

In the Canadian National Anti-Drug Strategy, the parenting ability of drug users is not discussed. Parenting is referred to only in relation to the role of parents in the prevention of illicit drug use among young people (Government of Canada, 2014). Since the 1990s, in Canada child protection policy has been more provincially determined, and in places such as Ontario and British Columbia, in relation to drug-using mothers, it has become particularly repressive (Boyd, 2004). In British Columbia, the Ministry of Children and Family Development has established a protocol for working guidelines between child protection and drug services (Boyd, 2004). The protocol features an assessment tool comprising of 23 risk factors for determining whether a child needs protection. As in the UK drug strategy, the gender-neutral language fails to reflect the fact that most 'parents' targeted for surveillance, assessment and control, are mothers (Boyd, 2004).

The approaches underpinning the drug strategies and child protection in the UK, US and Canada are punitive, responsibilising, neoliberal and risk-based. They reflect a wider reconstruction of the welfare state, as outlined in Chapter Three. In the process of the reconfiguration of the welfare state and its policies and practices in the 1980s, professions such as social work were transformed. Social workers witnessed their profession reconfigure from one in which they were expected to respond to need, to one in which risk discourse, risk assessment and management shapes practice. In the context of child protection, Parton (1991, p 203) refers to this reconstruction as a shift from childcare to child protection, and Buchanan and Young (2002, p 196), as a profession moving from an ideology of 'care' to 'control'. Clients managed by social workers and probation workers who, at one time, would have been seen by these workers as 'socially deprived citizens in need of support' (Garland, 2001, p 175), are now more likely to be seen as 'risks who must be managed' (Garland, 2001, p 175). In this process social workers have increasingly become normalising and policing administrators of neoliberal agendas (Thorpe, 1994; Buchanan and Young, 2002). Their role as non-judgemental, compassionate advocates of social justice working to build trust and empower has been undermined (Kullar, 2009).

Thorpe (1994) argues that social work has become a profession more involved in the regulation of parenthood, childrearing practices and the imposition of norms embedded in assumptions about the perceived morality of parents and childrearing practices than about child 'protection' and any actual risk or harm to the child. Welfare policy, similar to criminal justice policy, constructs the interests of the mother and child as in conflict and separate from one another. Although serious, 'at-risk' children constitute only a minority of cases social workers tend to equate drug use with bad mothering (Buchanan and Young, 2002, p 195). The imposition of risk discourses creates 'fixed narratives about the women's "selves"' (Pollack, 2010, p 1271). Female drug users, regardless of their level of drug use, do not adhere to dominant, idealised notions of motherhood. By definition of their drug-using behaviour, drug-using mothers have failed to fulfil their feminine roles, and are consequently judged as 'risky', unfit mothers, and a threat to their children (Buchanan and Young, 2002; Boyd, 2004; Pollack, 2010). In line with official drug policy discourse, social problems such as poverty, inadequate housing, barriers to employment and violence are viewed as caused by drug use, and drug-using mothers are responsibilised and their social conditions viewed as due to 'parental pathology' (Kullar, 2009 p 20). As Thorpe argues, the shift in social work policy and practice can be seen as:

> ... a switch from a view of a child in a context where caregivers are encouraged and supported by the state to look after and protect children, to one where the state "intervenes" to "protect". It sees parents not as nurturing and supporting agents whose difficulties and structural disadvantage require compensation, but as potential threats from which children require protection. (1994, p 199)

The intervention of social services in the lives of drug-using mothers can come in various forms, including surveillance, forced participation in parenting classes, drug treatment or life skills classes, the provision or denial of assistance and child apprehension. Poor women often unknowingly make themselves vulnerable to the surveillance and intervention of social services when they seek welfare assistance (Boyd, 1999). Studies show that social workers who 'have tremendous power over their welfare clients' (Boyd, 2004, p 134) may actively punish as well as regulate their welfare clients (see, for example, Kingfisher, cited in Boyd, 2004). Female drug-dependent mothers are assumed to be bad mothers by virtue of their drug use, and expected to convince social workers that they are abstinent, responsible parents.

Drug-dependent mothers often face coerced treatment or parenting classes, with the threat of the loss of child custody or the promise of reunification as the incentive for abstinence. Information sharing between social workers and treatment services is often a key component of the surveillance and control of female drug users. For instance, in British Columbia, Canada, due to the guidelines of the Ministry of Children and Family Development, social workers have access to the ongoing drug treatment information of their clients and can request drug testing to monitor abstinence (Kullar, 2009). When it comes to child apprehension, studies have noted how family courts are not regulated like criminal courts, according to due process and the assistance of lawyers. Claims made do not have to be proven, and social workers are able to make unsubstantiated claims and arbitrary decisions with little accountability (Boyd, 1999). Social workers mobilise risk discourses and punitive powers, in the area of child protection, to the extent that some women find contact with social services more problematic for them than drug laws (Boyd, 1999).

Risk discourse and risk assessment tools govern and dominate contemporary child welfare social work policy and practice. Risk assessments are deployed to determine whether a child is at risk of future harm, and gain their legitimacy through claims of their objectivity, neutrality and reduction of bias (Krane and Davies, 2000). However, risk assessments are 'highly subjective and moralistic enterprises' (Hannah-Moffat and Shaw, 2003, p 62). They are dependent on the social worker who is conducting them, and his or her values and biases that most often focus on scrutinising mothers (Krane and Davies, 2000). The reliability of risk assessments as accurate measures of potential child abuse is questionable (Corby, 1997). Child abuse is not easily identifiable, detectable or predicable, and there is little evidence that risk assessment tools are better able to discover or avert abuse or neglect (Krane and Davies 2000). Risk thinking disconnects social workers from the context of drug-using women's lives. As Garland (1997, p 182) argues:

> The individual is viewed not as a distinct, unique person, to be studied in depth and known by his or her peculiarities, but rather as a point plotted on an actuarial table.

Poverty, poor nutrition, inadequate housing or homelessness may be categorised as evidence of neglect without further consideration or investigation into the structural reasons for such identified risk factors (Garland, 1997, p 182). However, as Boyd (1999) contends, the majority of women who have experienced class, race and gender inequality could be classified as 'at risk'.

Risk discourse appropriates living conditions as evidence of child neglect or parental pathology and blame (Kullar, 2009). Women's insights into and understanding of their own situation and what they need are ignored and invalidated. Mothers are expected to accept professional 'expert' discourses about their lives and to discard their own perspectives of their experiences (Croghan and Meill, 1998). This is problematic when most social workers tend to be white, middle-class and privileged, and many drug-dependent welfare-dependent mothers are socially disadvantaged, in relationships with violent men, and disproportionate numbers, especially in the US and Canada, are from black and minority ethnic groups (Croghan and Meill, 1998). Risk discourse thus serves the interests of the privileged classes while masquerading as social welfare and obscuring the needs of vulnerable, drug-dependent mothers (Taylor-Gooby, 2001).

Women who use illegal drugs are situated as solely responsible for the health and wellbeing of their children. In the UK, US and Canada, child protection files are frequently under the name of mothers only, and mother blame ensues (Kullar, 2009). Rarely is the role of fathers taken into account, and they are largely absent from discussions about children 'at risk'. The contribution the addiction of the father makes to the family, and the health and wellbeing of children in relation to the fathers' behaviour, are not mentioned. Men are more likely to abuse children than women, and children are more likely to die through the agency of fathers or stepfathers (Milner, 1993). However, social workers continue to assume it is mothers who need to be scrutinised, failing to acknowledge the part played by male care givers (Milner, 1993). Mothers may also be made accountable for neglect in sexual or physical abuse case inquiries for apparently allowing men to abuse when often they are also victims of the abuse (Milner, 1993). Conversely, fathers are not implicated in abuse cases involving mothers (Milner, 1993).

Studies have shown that social workers lack understanding and do not receive adequate training on drug use issues. Research into social work education based on 17 directorates across England found more than a third of social workers did not receive any training on drug use during qualifying training, and of those who did, the majority received less than two days (Galvani and Forrester, 2008). Research participants reported feeling inadequately prepared for practice, and were frustrated by the lack of training they received. In a study by Weaver (2007, p 77) in Canada, it was found that although 69 per cent of the child protection workers' caseloads were comprised of drug-using mothers, the workers rated their knowledge of drug use and treatment as 'relatively poor'. Kullar (2009), working as a child protection worker, describes feeling shocked by the inconsistent approach of social workers towards drug-using women in a specialised maternity unit in Vancouver, Canada. She found that although some social workers were supportive of drug users, others were very punitive, and acted inappropriately towards the mothers.

Drug-dependent mothers invariably describe child protection social workers as ill informed about drug use, addiction, recovery and relapse. They are also frequently experienced as judgemental, insensitive, moralistic and punitive (Boyd, 1999; Buchanan and Young, 2002; Kullar, 2009). Social workers often project negative stereotypes onto drug-using women (Weaver, 2007). Mothers have related how they have lost custody of their children purely because they have histories as dependent drug users. Strengths such as the presence of a mother–child bond, family or other support and parenting skills are ignored in the assessment of risks. Social workers are often reported to have an agenda to remove children from the custody of mothers from the outset, even when the women are no longer using (Boyd, 1999). Mothers describe having to jump through various hurdles in an attempt to regain custody of their children, such as proving themselves in treatment, attending parenting classes and securing housing only to discover that their social worker appeared to have had no intention of returning their children to them (Boyd, 1999). Steps taken by mothers to improve their circumstances often do nothing to change social workers' perspectives of them as incapable of caring for their children (Boyd, 1999; Kullar, 2009) (see Chapter Seven, pp 242–248).

Mothers report how the pressures imposed by social workers are often unrealistic, and are incongruent with the process of recovery. If a mother relapses, it is not understood as part of the process of recovery, but as evidence that the woman was back into her dependency, a 'bad mother', and as justification for child apprehension (Boyd, 1999; Kullar, 2009). Time pressures placed on mothers to get into treatment are often inappropriate due to the chronic lack of accessible and appropriate services available (Hasenback, 2005 cited in Kullar, 2009). The removal of children from their mothers is painful and traumatising, and frequently leads mothers to an escalation of drug use. This often means that they are unable to regain custody of their children, and without support, the view that they are 'bad mothers' may be internalised (Boyd, 1999) (see Chapter Seven pp 194–199).

As a result of changes to social work policy and practice, and the equation of drug use with bad mothering, social workers with minimum knowledge and understanding of drug dependence adopt risk assessment tools to surveil and control drug-using mothers. Social workers are often experienced by their clients as ignorant about drug dependence, judgemental, and as punitive. The reputation of social workers has become such that many drug-using mothers mistrust and wish to avoid contact with them out of fear that their children will inevitably be removed (Buchanan and Young, 2002). Thus, the impact of welfarisation in the case of drug-using mothers is that they may avoid accessing drug treatment, health or other services for fear of social services intervention and losing their children. Consequently, drug-using mothers may not receive the drug treatment, health or social care they need. They and their children may experience unnecessary separation and suffering, and mothers increased drug dependency. This has a disproportionate impact on poor, black women and children in the US, Canada and the UK.

Conclusion

While seemingly benevolent, welfarisation operates to construct female drug users as undeserving of social assistance and as a risk to child welfare. Female users are situated as irresponsible and selfish for choosing to take drugs. Their own behaviour is constituted as the cause of any hardship they experience, which may, in turn, have an impact on their ability to care for their children. Due to their status as undeserving, financial assistance and motherhood may be denied. Drug-using women are responsibilised, and by virtue of this, rendered punishable not simply and exclusively through the criminal justice system. Similar to prohibition and punishment, through the denial of social security and child apprehension, welfarisation plunges female drug users further into precisely the kind of social conditions apparently caused by illicit drug use, including poverty, homelessness, family separation, crime and sex work.

In the US and UK, drug users are situated as undeserving of welfare benefits. In the US, male and female users may lose their right to welfare benefits and cash assistance, access to public housing and education. In the UK, dependent drug users are constructed as undeserving 'benefit scroungers'. Engagement in treatment and ultimately abstinence is set to be a condition of receiving jobseekers' benefits. This is despite the fact that recovery and treatment requirements may be at odds with employment. Furthermore, benefit sanctions have been found to leave people in destitute situations. In Canada, drug users are not currently directly targeted through the benefits system, but provincial governments have proposed such moves. In all three countries, drug-using mothers are constituted as unfit to mother, as 'risks to be managed', and targeted for social services intervention by improperly trained social workers.

While child protection discourse may adopt the neutral language of 'parents' when referring to drug users with children, it is mothers, not fathers, who are targeted for control and regulation. Welfarisation thus reinforces inequalities of gender regarding what is deemed acceptable behaviour for men and women. Due to their drug taking, female users, especially if they are mothers, fail to adhere to prescribed roles of feminine behaviour. They are judged as unfit mothers, and their children are likely to be apprehended regardless of the mother's level of use, the changes they make in their lives, or their positive skills and attributes as parents. Finally, the construction of drug-using women as undeserving of social support and unfit mothers detracts attention from the feminisation of poverty, and the widening gap between the poor and the wealthy in neoliberal states, the lack of accessible treatment for drug-using women, especially if they are mothers, the lack of attention to the role of fathers, violence against women, and the social marginalisation of poor, black and minority ethnic women.

Note

[1] The food stamp programme includes the Supplemental Nutrition Assistance Program (SNAP) offering nutritional assistance to low-income families. The cash assistance programme includes Temporary Assistance for Needy Families (TANF) providing cash assistance to indigent American families with dependent children (Smith, 2007).

Part Three

This part of the book takes a case study approach, and analyses the impact of drug policy on the lives of 40 female drug users. Drug policy is articulated through technologies of power, the affects of which are explored through an examination of detailed life historical interviews focusing on how 40 female illicit drug users see themselves. The stories the women tell about their drug use, with a particular focus on the subject positions they adopt for themselves, are examined. The techniques of power, discussed in Part Two, are taken into account, but there is also a focus on how authoritative discourses shape women drug users' identities by examining the key techniques of the self female users deploy managing their drug-using identities. These include the ascription of characteristics, normalisation and responsibilisation: female users are made visible, defined and categorised through the characteristics ascribed to them through 'authoritative' discourses; and they are also subject to normalisation and responsibilisation at the hands of the 'authorities'. At the same time, the women negotiate alternative identities to those prescribed to them through policy discourse and in this sense their subjectivities serve as sites of resistance.

Technologies of the self

The official discourses of women's drug use not only govern their actual substance use through the governmental technologies of prohibition, medicalisation and welfarisation, but also shape and sustain their using identities. This is made possible through various technologies of the self that operate in the lives of the female users.

Foucault argues that technologies of the self exist in every civilization, and are 'the means by which individuals determine their identity, maintain it or transform it' (Foucault, 2000 [1969], p 87). He describes technologies of the self as:

> ... the techniques and procedures which permit individuals to effect by their own means, or with the help of others, a certain number of operations on their own bodies and souls, thoughts, conduct, and way of being, so as to transform themselves in order to attain a certain state of happiness, purity, wisdom, perfection, or immortality. (2000 [1982], p 225)

Part Two examined the technologies of power – prohibition, medicalisation and welfarisation – through which women users are governed. As discussed, these are technologies of domination or practices of power that 'determine the conduct of individuals and submit them to certain ends' (Foucault, 2000 [1982], p 225). However, Foucault describes governmentality or the 'art of government' as 'the encounter between technologies of the domination of others and those of the self' (p 225). Even when technologies of domination are in operation, they only constitute one side of the system through which individuals are governed (Burchell, 1996). Thus, 'where there is power, there is resistance' (Foucault, 1990 [1976], p 95). Agency and the possibility of resistance to power are therefore always present in power relations, although technologies of the self may be compliant with or resistant to governmental power.

A key feature of technologies of the self is reliance on expertise. 'Experts' make claims based on scientistic truths, and through these, individuals are encouraged to exercise choice with regard to their self-development. They adopt certain ways of being due to the advice, guidance, education, reassurance and encouragement of 'experts' and their claims to objective scientific 'truths'. For instance, drug users often discuss their dependency in quasi-medical terms as an addictive 'illness' or individual pathology that they cannot control (Davies, 1992) rather than as a social problem. They adopt the language of science to describe, and in some cases lend authority to, their condition (Davies, 1992; Reith, 2004). This kind of 'expertise' can be mobilised by governments in an apparently apolitical way. However, technologies of the self involve the internalisation of governmental objectives. They are thus great projects of objectification, knowledge and normalisation turned inwards into a project of self-mastery, self-control and self-discipline.

Technologies of the self interact with governmental technologies in the shaping and maintaining of women drug users' identities. The operations of these three technologies of the self are not exclusive to women who use illicit drugs, although the technologies identified are considered to be particularly pertinent in a description of their lives. They operate in particular ways, producing particular effects on the lives of the women users.

Ascription of characteristics

The ascription of characteristics is a central technology of power operating in the lives of female illicit drug users. For the purpose of this book this is defined as the process through which subjects come to embody particular identities or subjectivities. It is the means by which women are defined, categorised and differentiated from others within various discursive fields and relations of power. In order to understand the operation of the ascription of characteristics as a specific instance of a technique of government, it is important to consider Foucault's understanding of how subjects are constituted, and how this relates to governmental power.

Foucault does not conceive of the subject as a given entity or substance, but as a changing form that is organised, shaped and dislocated in relation to certain technologies of the self, as well as in relation to political technologies aimed at the individual body and the population (Dean, 1994, p 195). The construction of female drug users' identities, according to this technology of power, is thus part of a process Foucault (1990 [1976]) describes as the 'constitution of subjects'. This is the process whereby various intersecting forms of power, knowledge and authority formulate new ways of thinking, understanding and describing types of subjects. It is described by Hacking (1986) as 'making up people', where certain types of people, such as female drug users, are made visible due to the observation, classification and categorisation of their specific features and types of behaviour.

Foucault argues that the dominance and subjugation of individuals cannot be understood through an analysis of the motivations or interests of those who dominate them, but through an analysis of the constitution of subjects as a material instance of their subjection (Foucault, 1980 [1976], p 97). He thus asserts that an analysis of the mechanisms of power should be directed at the multiple and diverse processes through which subjects are constituted:

> We should try to discover how it is that subjects are gradually, progressively, really and materially constituted through a multiplicity of organisms, forces, energies,

> materials, desires, thoughts, etc. (Foucault, 1980 [1976], p 97)

According to Foucault, power originates from and is circulated through a multiplicity of sites and social relationships. In this process, power produces 'effects on the bodies, desires and knowledge of social subjects' (Cooper, 1995, p 13). Individuals thus constitute the effects of power, and are at the same time 'the element of its articulation' (Foucault, 1990 [1976], p 98). In order to gain an understanding of one of the 'prime effects' of power, Foucault recommends that we should attempt to discover how particular subjectivities are generated, that is, how 'certain bodies, certain gestures, certain discourses, certain desires, come to be identified and constituted as individuals' (Foucault 1980 [1976], p 98).

In his genealogy of power, Foucault (1972 [1969]) described the many categories of people constituted during the modern period, including the insane, criminals, and homosexuals. Reith (2004) argues that 'the addict' is another figure in this process. The medical-moral discourse on illicit drug use not only introduced 'new ways of conceiving the consumption of particular substances', but has also 'transformed the consumer into a new type of person – an addict' (Reith, 2004, p 288). Through the authority of 'expert' knowledge on what constitutes this type of person, the technology of medicalisation shapes and maintains the identities of drug users. The identity of the 'addict' is one of deviance, loss of control, lack of will power, loss of autonomy, loss of reason and 'frenzied craving'. The 'addict' thus represents a pathological subjectivity, or an 'other', in a neoliberal society whose core values are those of freedom, choice and autonomy.

The ascription of characteristics as it applies to drug users can be seen as bound up in the process of 'othering' (Young, 2007). This is a way of defining, securing and affirming one's own positive identity through the denigration and stigmatisation of an 'other'. The characteristics ascribed to the 'drug addict' within authoritative and popular discourse are overwhelmingly negative. Ettorre (2004) argues that drug use constitutes a form of 'embodied deviance'. This is when the bodies of individuals who deviate from the ideal are deemed to be socially and morally inferior. 'Normal' bodies 'control their desires, passions and needs', while the bodies of drug users embody 'risk identities' and represent 'a loss of control' (Ettorre, 2004, p 330). 'Drug use "marks" the bodies of individuals and determines their low social status and lack of moral agency' (Ettorre, 2004, p 330).

The 'othering' of the drug taker is gendered. While male users can be seen to comply with hegemonic masculinity (Ettorre,

2004), the identity of the female addict is often constituted as the antithesis of 'normal' womanhood. Women users are typically seen as psychopathological, emotionally disturbed, sexually immoral, polluted, diseased, abnormal, selfish, irresponsible and bad mothers, although in the act of taking drugs, women users may conform to feminine norms to be 'sexually appealing, to relax or to deaden the pain of abusive relationships' (Ettorre, 2007, p 31). However, the denigration and stigmatisation of women users' identities has real objective effects on the lives of the women. For instance, fears about how they may be perceived and treated by professionals may have an impact on their willingness to seek help and/or to access treatment (Klee, 2002).

Particular behaviours, attributes and personalities are ascribed to women drug users by a range of 'authorities', including the criminal justice system, treatment and social services. The characteristics ascribed to them conditions their construction as objects of governance. The making up of their subjectivities and their construction as objects of governance is dependent on the ascription of *contradictory* attributes, so that they can be constituted as amenable to governmental intervention, regulation and transformation. Women users internalise contradictory official constructions of themselves as out of control, irrational and abnormal (for example, as controlled by their drug of choice or as imperfect mothers) *and also* as (potentially) normal, rational and responsible (for example, as essentially the same as non-drug-using women).

However, women users do not, by any means, passively internalise official constructions of their identities. The deviant identities embodied by female users should also be understood as sites of resistance. Lupton (1999) argues that individuals in neoliberal societies rebel against the obligation to be self-controlled and self-regulated by the active and voluntary courting of risks involved in, for example, extreme sports, excess drinking or drug taking:

> There is a sense of heightened living, of being closer to nature than culture, as breaking the rules that society is seen as imposing on people ... participants in such activities may attempt to experience the sublimity of losing their selves in the moment, of transcending the constraints of "civilized" behaviour. (Lupton, 1999, p 152)

Embracing a risk identity can be a positive choice for some women (and men), and may be experienced as a necessary part of 'self-actualisation' and 'self-determination'. The women interviewed for this study described how, in the initial stages, drug use provided them with an escape from the mundane routine of their everyday lives, promising them more wealth, glamour and/or culture. As Lupton (1999) argues about risk taking generally, the pleasure of courting risk through drug taking may also inhere in the ways in which users may find a shared identity and feel a sense of belonging with other like-minded spirits. The women in this study also described how they initially experienced their drug use as something that made them feel included and connected with others.

Women drug users' evasion of official constructions of them not only occurs in the initial stages of use, but is also a continued negotiation in the formation and reformation of their deviant identities. They actively resist stigma, derogatory images and negative constructions by persistently creating alternative identities (Anderson, 2008). Anderson (2008) calls this 'symbolic resistance', which she identifies as one type of agency that women users may deploy to restore to themselves some form of relational and/or structural power:

> Instead of conforming to subordinated or traditional identities, women substance abusers often construct new images or selves, or carefully manage existing ones, in an attempt to convey power and secure desired outcomes. They do this with people in their families and neighbourhoods as well as with criminal justice and social service professionals. (Anderson, 2008, p 6)

The women drug users interviewed for this research deploy 'symbolic resistance' in the management of their identities, and actively reject the negative subjectivities ascribed to them through authoritative discourses. As Anderson (2008) outlines above, they adopt this strategy in all aspects of their everyday lives, with partners, family and friends, as well as in their interactions with professionals. The women interviewed insert themselves into the process of their governance at the level of discourse. They take the subjectivities ascribed to them, and reconstruct them so that they understand themselves as in some ways different from how they are constituted within authoritative discourse.

Normalisation

Another technology of the self operating in the lives of female illicit drug users is normalisation. This, as conceptualised by Foucault, is the process through which deviant subjects are brought into conformity with a constructed norm (1991 [1975], pp 183-4). Technologies of normalisation operate by identifying norms of conduct, and setting up techniques for distinguishing and correcting individuals deviating from these norms (1991 [1975], pp 183-4). In relation to normalisation, Foucault argues that from the beginning of the 19th century a new subject of power emerged, 'the delinquent', whose identity was constructed independently of his/her crimes. Consequently, the focus shifted from acts to be punished to delinquent individuals to be 'normalised'. Hence, Foucault argues that in the 19th century prisons gained a dual function, not only to deprive individuals of their liberty, but also to 'supervise, transform, correct and improve' (1991 [1975], p 303). According to Foucault, techniques of normalisation are not limited to penal incarceration, but operate at 'every level of the social body' (1991 [1975], p 303), and permeate 'a whole series of institutions … well beyond the frontiers of criminal law' (1991 [1975], p 297).

The focal point and target of practices of normalisation in the form of supervision, transformation, correction and improvement is the body. According to Foucault, since the enlightenment, the body has been subject to a new type of power, *biopower*. This is about making bodies normal and conforming in society. As a result of biopower, the body is at the centre of controlling discourses, practices of surveillance, medicalisation and rational control. The normalising power of this new type of power presides over the bodies of men and women in different ways. As biopower produces and normalises female bodies to serve prevailing gender relations, the female drug-using body is shaped and regulated by gendered norms (Ettorre, 2007). A major normalising assumption governing all female bodies is their function as reproducing, care-giving, guardians of morality. As these functions appear to be problematic for drug-using women, they have come to represent the antithesis of 'normal' womanhood. Women users are constituted as failed femininity, polluted women, incapable mothers, lethal foetal containers, selfish, irresponsible and sexually immoral.

Foucault describes the institutions employing disciplinary techniques of normalisation as a 'carceral network' or 'carceral continuum'. The carceral network gained power through the proliferation of new disciplines such as 'medicine, psychology, education, public assistance [and] social work' (1991 [1975], p 308). Foucault argues:

> The judges of normality are present everywhere. We are in the society of teacher-judge, the doctor-judge, the educator-judge, the social worker-judge; it is on them that the universal reign of the normative is based; and

each individual, wherever he may find himself, subjects to it his body, his gestures, his behaviour, his aptitudes, his achievements. (1991 [1975], p 304)

Foucault argues that while it seems that carceral mechanisms are distinct from prison in that they are intended to 'alleviate pain, to cure, [and] to comfort', like prison, they tend 'to exercise a power of normalisation' (p 308) and subject bodies and forces to 'multiple mechanisms of "incarceration"' (p 308). The technology of normalisation operates on multiple levels in the lives of female users. Chapters Six and Seven explore how the lives of women drug users are subject to gendered forms of control, violence and abuse in their relationships with parents, partners, 'punters' and drug-using associates. They examine how the normalising powers of social services, treatment facilities and the criminal justice system often do little to alleviate the pain and discomfort the women experience, but rather expose them further to, and incarcerate them within, these types of experiences, and in some cases, perpetuate and reinforce their victimisation.

Drawing on the work of Foucault, in *Visions of social control* Cohen (1985, p 1) examines social control, that is, the organised ways in which government responds to those it regards as 'deviant, problematic, worrying, threatening, troublesome or undesirable in some way or another.' This response, he argues, appears under many terms, including punishment, deterrence, treatment, welfare and rehabilitation (p 1). He argues that liberal capitalist countries, such as Britain, Canada and the US, all have 'social control systems' embedded in their programmes of 'welfare' and ideologies of treatment (p 3). Techniques for distinguishing and correcting individuals deviating from norms may come in the form of social support, and include helping, teaching, treating, guiding and counselling. Such methods thus appear to operate in the best interests of the individual. However, these modes of governance may be experienced as punishing to individuals who, for whatever reason, find it difficult to, or refuse to, conform. The technology of normalisation is thus closely related to that of welfarisation discussed in Chapter Five.

Responsibilisation

Another technology of power operating in the lives of women who use illicit drugs is responsibilisation. The technology of responsibilisation operates by establishing techniques that constitute individuals and non-state agencies as responsible for meeting the objectives of central government. It is the process through which central government seeks to achieve its objectives, not directly through state agencies (for example, courts, the police, prison), but indirectly, by acting on the action of individuals *and* non-state agencies and organisations (Garland, 1996). Responsibilisation operates as a technology of the self and as a technology of the other. As a technology of the self, it is a way of governing that aims to manipulate the way in which individuals conduct themselves. Through responsibilisation individuals are constructed as rational, free, prudent agents, capable of managing and, if necessary, changing their way of thinking and/or behaving with the help of appropriate 'experts'. Techniques of responsibilisation include persuading, inducing, motivating, teaching and counselling.

The concept of 'responsibilisation' is related to Foucault's (2000 [1984]) notion of 'care for the self' in that it involves being prompted to 'care' for, and be responsible for, the self. For Foucault, 'care for the self' is all the techniques and practices used by the subject in the process of self-formation, and is a practice of freedom (2000 [1984], p 286). Foucault uses the term 'freedom' to mean having power over one's own conduct, 'to master the appetites that threaten to overwhelm one' (2000 [1984], p 285). Responsibilisation is concerned with the practices and techniques the subject uses to manage him or herself. It is also concerned with governing in a way that leaves the subject's freedom intact.

Care for the self is an ethical practice in the sense that it is concerned with 'right conduct' and 'not being a slave to oneself and one's appetites' (Foucault, 2000 [1984], p 286). Responsibilisation involves encouraging people to have control over their own conduct. Foucault asserts that the problem of the relationship with others is present throughout the development of care for the self (2000 [1984], p 287), which 'always aims for the well-being of others' (2000 [1984], p 287). 'Care of others' follows from the care of the self in that 'a person who takes proper care of him or herself would, by the same token, be able to conduct himself properly in relation to others and for others' (2000 [1984], p 287). In so far as responsibilisation is a technique for making people behave responsibly, it implies conduct that is mindful of others.

Drawing on Foucault's notion of care for the self as a practice of freedom, Rose (1996, p 54) argues that advanced liberal democracies act on their subjects by 'shaping and utilising their freedom'. Freedom 'is no "natural" property of political subjects' (Seddon, 2007a), but a constructed concept, dependent on prevailing notions of the subject and its relation to changing modes of governmental power. Within neoliberal societies citizens are conceived of as subjects of freedom, choice and autonomy, and capable of self-government. This conception of the subject is what enables citizens to be responsibilised. As Rose argues:

> Liberal strategies of government become dependent upon devices to create individuals who do not need to be governed by others; but will govern themselves, master themselves, care for themselves. (Rose, 1996, p 45)

Freedom is therefore an obligation as it is not only the way individuals care for and master themselves, but also how they are governed. Rose (1996, p 62) suggests that the 'agnostic relation between liberty and government' is an intrinsic part of what we have come to understand and experience as 'freedom'. The regulation of citizens' conduct becomes a matter of their desire to 'pursue their own civility, wellbeing and advancement' (p 58). While choices are presented to citizens as programmes of self-improvement, health and welfare, their subjectivities are shaped to converge with prevailing ideals of normality, health, consumption and production. Subjects are:

> ... "free to choose", to carve out a lifestyle and an identity from the marketed options available ... but they are also obliged to subjugate aspects of themselves to mould their subjective states and inner desires in accordance with cultural norms and social institutions. (Reith, 2004, p 285)

The free subject is a responsible one who 'is capable of bearing the burdens of liberty' (Rose, 1999, p viii). Responsibilisation thus involves the alignment of individual choice with governmental objectives.

The technology of responsibilisation is related to the ascendance of governmental techniques of risk management and 'actuarialism' (see Feeley and Simon, 1994), in that being responsible involves being aware of and avoiding risks. Risk management techniques attempt to eliminate problems by calculating the effects of problematic actions or potential harms rather than by eliminating causes. Individuals are accorded the responsibility of making rational, prudent, calculated and well-considered choices in order to avoid risk and to safeguard their health and wellbeing as well as that of others. O'Malley (1996) describes this as 'prudentialism'. The basis of the prudent, rational choices individuals are expected to make is the guidance provided by 'experts'.

The advice of 'experts' such as the police or the medical profession enables individuals to act responsibly, 'without recourse to any direct forms of repression or intervention' (Barry et al, 1996, p 14). 'Experts' within the 'psy' sciences, who Rose (1999, p 3) has called 'engineers of the human soul', such as social workers, counsellors and therapists, are able to provide support, advice and encouragement to individuals on almost every aspect of their lives, including relationships, work, emotions and consumption habits. Although in neoliberal societies self-government is regarded as the responsibility of the individual, 'public authorities seek to employ forms of expertise in order to govern society at a distance' (Barry et al, 1996, p 14). Responsibilisation is thus when citizens are provided with advice and information so they are able to manage without interference from the state.

Risk management is an integral aspect of the harm minimisation approach to drug use. This renders illicit drug use a self-governing activity (O'Malley, 1999). All individuals who use drugs are held responsible for controlling their drug consumption. Within this framework:

> The role of state governmental programmes is primarily advisory: to establish and broadcast the so called "recommended safe levels of usage", founded on expert evaluations of actuarial data, so that responsible users may moderate their risk-bearing behaviours in line with an officially endorsed risk calculus. (O'Malley, 1999, p 200)

The assumption is that individuals will make rational decisions that accord with the aims of government, provided they are given 'accurate' information and the skills required to make informed choices. All drug users are therefore responsibilised to manage their drug use sensibly, and to avoid using them problematically or excessively. However, not all users are seen as able to use drugs responsibly. Those who use illicit drugs are constructed as rational, free and autonomous choice makers, and consequently dependent users are viewed as 'author[s] of their own [and others] misfortune' (Rose, 1996, p 59).

Rose (2000) argues that new political rationalities, such as those found within neoliberal societies, are articulated in terms of a distinction between a majority who are responsible and a minority who are not. The majority 'can and do ensure their own well-being and security through their own active self-promotion and responsibility for themselves and their families' (p 331). However, there are also 'those who are outside this nexus of activity: the underclass, the marginalised, the truly disadvantaged, the criminals' (Rose, 2000, p 331). There are therefore individuals who are viewed as responsible, law-abiding and dutiful, who 'either refuse the bonds of civility' or 'are unable to assume them for constitutional reasons, or they aspire to them but have not been given the skills, capacities and means' (Rose, 2000, p 331). Dependent drug users are among those seen as unable to behave responsibly.

As discussed in Chapter Four (see pp 94–95), the concept of addiction is dependent on a distinction between 'normal' and 'pathological' behaviour. According to the disease model, individuals with 'weak' or defective characters are constructed as pathologically prone to addiction. With the emergence of the harm minimisation discourse, this notion of the addict has slightly shifted so that dependent users are constituted as pathological choice makers, unable to responsibly avoid risk. As drug dependency is constituted as the result of a defective choice, it is viewed as brought on by dependent users themselves. Drug users are made responsible for becoming addicted. The issue of the social context in which drug use is initiated and continued is overshadowed by interest in and the scrutinisation of the psychology and cognitive powers of individual users. The association between drug dependency, social and economic marginalisation is consequently obscured. The social and economic deprivation experienced by dependent users is viewed as a result of their individual choices and actions. Through the technology of responsibilisation, the onus on governments to rectify the social ills associated with drug dependency, such as poverty, unemployment and crime, is removed, and instead the spotlight is placed on users themselves.

Individuals are not only considered responsible for becoming dependent on drugs due to defective choice making; they are also constituted as responsible for getting off them by changing and transforming their disordered, irrational way of thinking. That is, those dependent drug users who fail to properly exercise their freedom to choose are prompted to accept their responsibilities as rational, self-regulating consumers. This involves the reshaping of drug users' subjectivities, and the building up of their self-control and agency (Rose, 1999). As Reith (2004, p 296) argues:

> ... the forms of government that contribute to the creation of ... addict identities also attempt to regulate them and return them to their "normal" state.

An individual's 'recovery' from addiction, especially in the treatment of drugs for which there is no substitute, now tends to involve some element of counselling or therapy (Reith, 2004). This can involve motivating, teaching, encouraging, raising self-esteem and boosting the ego. The onus is on the user to transform his or her 'faulty' way of thinking. The provision of support for the social problems a user may face, such as homelessness, violence and poverty, is generally given less consideration.

Rose (1996, p 59) asserts that within advanced liberal democracies, disadvantaged individuals '"excluded" from the benefits of a life of choice and fulfilment' (p 59) (for example, homeless people, drug addicts and unemployed people) come to be seen as 'potentially and ideally' active agents 'in the fabrication of their own existence'. They are not passive victims of a set of social determinations, but 'authors of their own misfortune' (p 59). These disadvantaged individuals are constructed as saveable, educable and trainable through 'a whole array of programmes for their ethical reconstruction as active citizens' (p 60). Programmes of training to improve skills, counselling to restore self-esteem and empowerment to enable individuals to actualise their potential as 'demanding subjects of an advanced liberal democracy' (p 60) are presented as desirable opportunities for self-improvement.

Cognitive behavioural therapy in particular is as a type of counselling that has been adopted in the treatment of dependent users in the UK (Kendall, 2002, p 195). Its aim is to change 'maladaptive' thinking and behaviour. The idea is to transform users' defective ways of thinking and make them rational and responsible. The promotion and adoption of cognitive behavioural therapy allows for 'government at a distance'. While this type of treatment is meant to provide an opportunity for the user to work towards living in a way he or she experiences as more satisfying and resourceful, it also conveniently enables the wills and behaviours of drug users to be aligned with governmental objectives.

In the war on drugs, some drug users are responsibilised more than others. Responsibilisation operates as a class, race and gender-based technology. As discussed in Chapter Three (pp 72–76) earlier, poor and less privileged men and women are more likely to be criminalised for drug offences than high-class users (Cockburn, 1998; Turnipseed, 2000). Black men and women are also more likely to come under the surveillance and control of the criminal justice system, and are grossly over-represented in prison populations in the US, the UK and Canada (Boyd, 2004). Male and female drug users are responsibilised in the war on drugs, but women are made responsible in ways that male users are not.

The assumption underlying the responsibilisation strategy is that government subjects are willing participants in their own regulation. However, more punitive modes of power are reinstated when subjects seem unwilling or fail to take responsibility for their own risk-taking behaviour or self-advancement. As Hannah-Moffat (2001, p 187) argues:

> Where forms of responsibilising government-at-a-distance fail, the powers that be often resort to more sovereign or disciplinary exercises of power. This illustrates the interdependence of multiple forms of power: sovereign, disciplinary and governmental.

Individuals who violate their responsibilities as subjects of moral community and resist 'well intentioned correctional interventions' (Hannah-Moffat, 2001, p 187) (for example, through welfare agencies) may face formal punishments through the criminal justice system.

Hannah-Moffat (2001, p 187) argues that 'irresponsible' individuals tend to be demonised, pathologised and medicalised. The evocation of 'barely human' images of offenders serves to justify the imposition of punitive systems of control (Garland, 2001, p 135). Garland (2001, pp 135-6) argues:

> Crime control policies can invoke images of "the criminal" that depict him (less often her) as profoundly anti-social.... In this inflammatory rhetoric, and in the real policies that flow from it, offenders are treated as a different species ... for whom we have no sympathy and for whom we have no effective help.

Many writers have remarked on the increased punitiveness of the welfare and penal systems, and in particular, on the sharp increase in the prison population in the UK (Garland, 2001). O'Malley (1996) asserts that in neoliberal discourse, a policy of punitiveness or 'just deserts' sentencing is the 'logical corollary' of a policy of responsibilisation. He argues that an increased punitive approach is consistent with a rationality of government based on the idea of responsible, rational, calculative subjects who 'are in command of their own lives and bear the consequences of freely made decisions' (p 198).

The following two chapters focus on the accounts provided by 40 female dependent drug users about their lives, and how they negotiated their identities.

SIX

Psychosocial accounts

Parts One and Two of this book examined how women who use illicit drugs are governed by analysing how they are constituted within official and academic discourse. The operation of three technologies of power as they are expressed through academic and drug policy discourse was explored. Official discourse ascribes multiple and contradictory characteristics to women who use illicit drugs, and in so doing makes them amenable to governmental regulation. Particular norms of behaviour are established through official discourse, and various techniques and tactics are set up to control and regulate female illicit drug users who deviate from these norms. They are constituted as responsible for becoming dependent on drugs, and for the perceived harm they cause to themselves and to others.

How these technologies operate in the lives of the 40 women in this study who use illicit drugs is now explored in an analysis of the subjectivities the women adopt for themselves, in relation to how these are constructed in policy. Their accounts of the characteristics they ascribe to themselves, their view of normality, and what they felt responsible for was in some ways the same, but in other ways different from those constructed within academic and drug policy discourses. The female users in this study imputed new and different meanings to the technologies of power they are subject to by placing themselves into the process of their governance. They take the subjectivities constructed for them and the regulations imposed on them within drug policy discourse, and modify and reshape them at the level of discourse.

This chapter and the next explore the narratives the 40 women provided about their drug use. The women interviewed for this study were taken from three English cities: Bristol, Reading and London.[1] The most dominant stories the women told were psychosocial stories of drug use, in which it featured as a solution to the emotional problems they were experiencing, but which eventually brought them more problems. The women related their experiences of drug use and the social conditions in which this drug use occurred to their psychological wellbeing, reflecting the broader sociopolitical context in which their narratives emerged, wherein illicit drug use is both psychologised and individualised. In other words, the manner in which the women positioned themselves was ultimately and intimately bound up with the way in which official discourse constituted drug users more generally, and female drug users in particular. As discussed in Chapter Five earlier (see p 119), illicit drug use is constructed as a problem arising from the individual due to their bad choice making and lack of employment. The solution to this problem, within current drug policy, is viewed as the promotion of individual psychological and behavioural change with the help of a range of interdisciplinary services. Consequently, the individual drug user and local services are responsibilised.

The psychosocial accounts the women provided of their drug use rendered less dominant other more social stories, which nevertheless were present in their narratives. These more social accounts were tales of gender, poverty and regulation. This chapter explores the psychosocial accounts provided by the women, and how these reflect the wider sociopolitical context in which they occurred. Chapter Seven then examines the social stories embedded within these accounts.

A short-term solution

On the whole, the women described their drug use as a cure or outlet for painful feelings arising from trauma, abuse, isolation, lack of freedom, or self-hatred. However, they all described how their drug use eventually brought them more pain and suffering, due to the impact of their addiction on their lives. They described how their drug taking brought them poverty, illness, involvement in crime and/ or prostitution, separation from friends and family and the loss of children. As one of the women said:

> 'You think, like, that it will solve the problem at the time because it blanks it out, but no, it's just one big problem.' (Jamie, 29)

There were four main stories told by the women in which they explained and justified their involvement in illicit drug use: blocking out pain; fitting in; independence; and self-punishment.

Blocking out pain

All of the women described experiencing some form of abuse, stress or trauma in their childhood or adulthood. They said that they used drugs in order to escape, block out or numb the pain. The women identified many kinds of trauma that had contributed to them beginning or continuing to use heroin, including sexual abuse, rape, bereavement and domestic violence. Many explicitly said that they felt such experiences had caused their addiction. They described how the effects of heroin specifically enabled them to block out and forget past or present experiences of trauma. Many identified this blocking of feelings as why they had first got into heroin, but some did not realise that it would serve this function until they started taking it. Some claimed that it was experiencing one trauma after another that had caused them to experiment with drugs or become addicted to them.

Fitting in

Many of the women said that they started using a particular drug to fit in with a group of friends or a partner. Some said that they had not felt accepted at school, and several had been bullied. Some did not feel wanted or loved by their parents, and described being abused, controlled or made to feel worthless. These women claimed that they experimented with drugs in order to feel accepted and connected with others. Some of them said they had been offered drugs, told "It's nice" and "You should try it" by partners and/or friends. Several of the women who started using drugs with a partner claimed they were completely in love. Some of them whose partners were against them using said they felt they were missing out on something, and wanted to see what it was.

Independence

Many of the women claimed that they got into drugs as part of a struggle to assert their independence and to rebel against strict and controlling parents. They described how their parents had tried to control them in a variety of ways, including by pressuring them to achieve, not allowing them to develop their own interests, forcing them to do endless chores, not allowing them to go out with their friends, watch television or generally do things that other people their age were doing. They described how during their mid to late adolescence in particular, they deliberately started doing things that they knew their parents would not approve of, such as not doing their school work, changing their image, staying out all night, getting involved with people their parents considered 'rough', and taking drugs. Many described how they had never felt loved or accepted by their parents for who they were. They described their early experiences of drug taking as a 'scene' in which they could 'be themselves', feel wanted and accepted by a group of peers, and feel they were part of something that gave them a sense of their own identity.

Self-punishment

Some of the women said they got into particular drugs because they wanted to harm or punish themselves. They described how drug taking gave them an outlet and helped them cope with feelings of self-hatred. All of the women who described using drugs to punish themselves had histories of suicide attempts, self-injury, eating disorders and/or alcohol abuse. They knew what they were getting themselves into but didn't care. They were already at rock bottom. This was connected to heroin being there and the women needing something to cope with a trauma or abuse they had suffered in the past.

Contradictory characteristics

The women's accounts of their experiences of drug use appeared to be linear in character. They described drug use as a cure for pain and isolation that eventually led to the drug use becoming a problem in itself. At the same time, various contradictions emerged from the women's narratives, giving their accounts a less than linear character. As explored in Part Two of this book, the characteristics ascribed to women who use illicit drugs, through the technologies of prohibition and punishment, medicalisation and welfarisation, are contradictory in character. This chapter and the next show that, as in drug policy discourses, the women in this study constructed their subjectivities in contradictory ways. The rest of this chapter explores the contradictions present within the women's accounts, with a focus on the predominant psychosocial aspects of their narratives. The women had somewhat internalised the ways they are situated in contemporary drug policy as hedonistic, bad choice makers, chemically enslaved addicts, dangerous, immoral criminals, irresponsible, unfit mothers, responsible for their dependence and recovery *and also* as recoverable, educable, responsible, changeable and transformable. At the same time, they resisted these constructions, and negotiated more positive, dissenting, albeit inconsistent, identities for themselves.

The focus of this study was on the drug use of women who considered themselves to be or had been dependent on illicit drugs. Most of the women interviewed had become dependent on heroin and/or crack (*n*=38) at some stage in their drug careers. These drugs are commonly viewed as ones that people are known to become dependent on, although some women described themselves at various points in their drug careers as dependent on alcohol, cocaine, amphetamines, methadone, ecstasy, anti-depressants or marijuana. Here it should be acknowledged that, although this study focused on women who at some time or another considered themselves to be 'addicts' and who felt their drug use was a problem, every year millions of women all over the world use illegal drugs 'recreationally', and some experiment with drugs such as heroin and crack and never feel compelled to use repeatedly, consider their drug use to be a problem, or become dependent.

Irresponsible, disordered choice makers

The operation of the technology of medicalisation has real objective effects on the lives of female illicit drug users. In drug policy discourse in the UK, US and Canada, drug use is underpinned by the disease model of addiction, and is understood as a 'disease of the will' (Valverde, 1998; see also Chapter Four, p 95–96, this volume). The construction of drug use as a medical condition forecloses the space for discussion about the role of emotion in drug taking. The possibility of non-problematic, pleasurable, 'recreational' drug use is not expressed. All drug use is situated as risky, dangerous and as causing harm to oneself, to families and to communities. Dependent users have apparently chosen to become addicted through irrational, disordered choice making, and the addiction is constituted as causing illness, unemployment, poverty, homelessness, crime and prostitution.

The women described drug taking as a source of both pleasure and pain. Most, although not all, of the women were motivated by the pursuit of pleasure in the initial stages of their drug use. This was a period when they tended to experiment with a variety of different drugs. In the initial stages of their drug use, and during what they considered to be a recreational stage in the pursuit of pleasure, the women saw themselves as 'normal', rational, responsible, choice makers, consistent with neoliberal constructions of the responsible, rational consumer in a society of risks (see Chapter Two, p 56–57). However, the women eventually became dependent. Although most said they had initially sought pleasure, they stated that they continued to use drugs to manage emotional pain, and considered this to be a rational and reasonable response to their life experiences. They did not see themselves as irresponsible, disordered choice makers; rather, they saw themselves as responsible and rational governors of their pain. Resistant identities to those found within drug policy discourse were embedded in their narratives.

The women described the pleasures of taking drugs, including the euphoric feelings they experienced on different drugs, feeling connected with others, and being able to forget about their problems. The exercise of their free choice as rational, drug-taking consumers was described by the women as pleasurable, although some described how their drug use had always been about governing their emotional pain.

Getting high

Most of the women ($n=36$) described their first experience of drug taking as pleasurable. In the initial stages of their use, the women tended to experiment with a range of different drugs. Drug taking was viewed by them as a 'normal' activity like any other that 'everyone else was doing'. They did not see it as a problem:

> 'I started to smoke cannabis and that a bit when I was at school, just trying it, then mostly when I started going to parties and that, I started doing ecstasy and a bit of base [amphetamine].... I was having a great time. It wasn't really.... I didn't see it as a problem because it was just at the weekends. Everyone was doing it.' (Wendy, 19)

Different drugs were described as pleasurable in different ways, and were used in different environments according to the kind of euphoric feelings they induced. For instance, the women said that ecstasy and cocaine were drugs they mainly used at parties or nightclubs as they made them feel warm, energetic and confident:

> 'I started going out clubbing, I mean E's [Ecstasy] they always give you that extra boost of confidence which was probably what I'd always wanted ... so I could be myself and I felt that when I was on E's and that I was more energetic and confident.' (Sonya, 24)

The women claimed that amphetamine was a drug they took at parties to feel high and to give them energy as well as a drug they might take at home to give them energy to do things:

'It made me feel good, it gave me energy, just made me feel good and happy and like I had the energy to do things in life, I suppose. I wanted it to get on and do normal everyday things, not to just go out and party, but just to get up and take it to feel good for the day.' (Sally, 39)

Heroin and crack were also described as drugs the women experimented with and used recreationally in the initial stages. A few were offered heroin at parties or clubs, and used it alongside other drugs. However, heroin was generally introduced to the women at their own or another person's house by someone who was already an addict, and they mainly used it at home. As found in other studies, some ($n=6$) had tried heroin or crack before trying any other drugs (Taylor, 1993a). However, most had already experimented with a range of other drugs before trying heroin. The women described heroin as a drug that made them feel relaxed, warm and dreamy, rather than energetic and outgoing:

'You're not asleep and you're not awake but you're still dreaming and that's the feeling you're getting, like. It is a lovely warm feeling. It's too nice.' (Jamie, 29)

Many said that they had vomited the first few times they tried heroin, but this did not take away from the good feeling it gave them (see also Taylor, 1993a).

Most of the women who used crack ($n=36$) were introduced to it after they had become addicted to heroin. Crack cocaine was described as a pleasurable drug in that it gave an extremely intense but short-lived high. It was also described as having the opposite effect to that of heroin, in that rather than making the women feel relaxed and peaceful, it made them feel lively, energetic and sociable:

'I get a few minutes buzz and then it makes me chat, not that I don't chat anyway, really, 'cause I do. But I chat even more.' (Lara, 23)

Many of the women ($n=38$) used heroin *and* crack, and many had periods of using one or the other. Most ($n=24$) used heroin to relax them or 'come down' after taking crack, and some ($n=6$) used 'snowballs' – heroin and crack cocaine together – in the same 'hit'. Those who had used 'snowballs' described them as being extremely pleasurable, more so than heroin or crack on their own. According to the women's accounts, 'snowballs' gave them the euphoric feelings of both drugs, and lasted longer:

> 'When I snowball, that's when I get the proper high. The heroin will kick in and the crack will kick in again, so I'll become high again, and then it levels out.' (Lara, 23)

The women described the pleasures derived from taking heroin and crack as temporary and fleeting in character. Although they described deriving pleasure from the euphoric effects of taking heroin, all of them explained that this did not last long:

> 'It's mad to say, but it was a lovely feeling, and I've been chasing that ever since. I can never, ever, ever get it.' (Lara, 23)

The high of crack lasted only a few seconds, and the women explained how the pleasure experienced from taking it was never quite the same as the first time:

> 'You just get a two-minute buzz and then you want more and more.' (Suzi, 31)

> 'It was so good. I tell you, it is a fucking good rush, but you'll never get it again, never. I mean you might give up for six months and then have one and then get it again, but it's still not the same as that first initial rush. (Suzi, 31)

All of the women who used or had used crack ($n=36$) also complained about the high or 'buzz' they felt from using it, which always left them feeling as if they wanted more. Most of the women interviewed for this study had become dependent on heroin and/or crack at some stage in their drug careers. They also described other pleasures they received from taking drugs.

Connecting

Many of the women ($n=23$) explained that they began taking drugs such as marijuana, ecstasy, speed and coke recreationally with a group of friends at parties and nightclubs. They initially associated drug taking with having a good time at the weekend with their friends, and did not then see their drug use as a problem. Many described how their drug use expanded their social options, and provided them with a more exciting lifestyle (see Rosenbuam, 1981; Taylor, 1993a):

> 'So my first experience of drugs was social. I just started meeting a group of friends outside school who I had common interests with, started having a social life, it was sort of when I first left school and home, and life was great and it was just exciting and, you know, I was, it was all hippy stuff, you know.' (Sally, 39)

Many of the women explained that their drug taking made them feel more connected with other users. They described becoming more connected with others as something from which they derived comfort, and it was a prominent aspect of their narratives.

Some of the women ($n=8$) described a certain attraction they felt towards a crowd of people and their lifestyle. They did not see themselves as irresponsible in their decision to use drugs to fit in with a crowd; rather, they saw themselves as governing their relationships in a rational manner in order to be accepted or so as not to be left alone. Lara described her admiration for a group of heroin and crack users she had begun to mix with, and her desire to be like them and be accepted among them:

> 'I think the crowd that I was hanging around with ... because I could see what money they were making and how ... to me, it was sort of like glamorous in a way. It's sad to say, but that's how I saw it, you know. And I wanted to be like that, and I wanted to be accepted.' (Lara, 23)

Nicky was in a bail hostel when she first tried heroin. She decided that she wanted to fit in with the other people there and not be left on her own:

> 'They were just, like, a rough crowd and stuff, and I was on my own, I didn't know anybody when I first moved there, and they asked me if I'd done any heroin before – and I hadn't. I'd never even seen it before in my life but I said yeah 'cause I wanted to get in with the crowd 'coz I didn't want to be on my own, all alone or anything, you know.' (Nicky, 23)

Many of the women described being connected to a particular 'scene' involving others with whom they had shared interests. Their description of a scene might otherwise be thought of as a 'social world'. Rosenbaum used this term in her study of heroin users to denote membership of a group with 'shared symbolisation, experiences and interests' (Rosenbaum, 1981, p 19). In academic and drug policy discourses drug users are constructed as deviant, socially excluded individuals, disconnected from 'the community'. 'Community' in this context denotes integration into a range of social institutions, and an acceptance of the norms and values consistent with neoliberal forms of governance, rather than connection with a group of like-minded others. Ironically, the women described how becoming part of the drug scene enabled them to fit in with a community of others. For some it was an end to loneliness and the first time in their lives they had felt a sense of belonging to a group. They did not view themselves, at least initially, as disconnected from the community, but as members of a community of drug users, albeit a deviant one.

Nine women described the 'rave scene' as a significant period in their lives and a time when they had first experimented with 'recreational' drugs, such as ecstasy and amphetamines. They described the 'rave scene' as an arena in which they felt a sense of community and connection with other young people, and that this feeling of being connected was extremely important to them.

Sonya described her childhood as an unhappy one in which she felt her parents never accepted her for who she was. She also related how she was bullied at school, and claimed that throughout her childhood she had pretended to be someone she wasn't, happy and outgoing, while being deeply depressed underneath:

> 'Everyone used to see this happy person, always trying to be the centre of attention, but it wasn't me. I'd make everyone think that I was alright until in the end, I suppose, it all built up inside me, and I exploded, and I just rebelled against everything.' (Sonya, 24)

At 14 years old, Sonya started taking ecstasy and going out 'raving' with a group of friends who were in their early 20s:

> 'I suppose I was happy, then, in a way, although, like, I was using drugs, I was in, like, quite a big community, and they all used to protect me because I was 14. Once I started getting into the rave scene, I felt like I was in a

group where I could finally, you know, I was happy. I was part of the group and I could be myself and they didn't mind.' (Sonya, 24)

For some of the women (*n*=5) it was the 'hippy scene' that made them feel connected with others and through which they first experimented with drugs such as acid and amphetamines. Sally described her upbringing as strict, and how she was not allowed to go out with friends or develop any of her own interests. She talked about how, after leaving home, she got into a 'scene' where she felt she fitted in and started taking drugs:

'I felt like, you know, I was part of something because I'd never fitted in, you know, with all your make-up and trendy clothes-type people at school. And I found somewhere where I fitted in naturally, the sort of music I was into and all the hippy clothes and that. It was good doing the drugs as well. I suddenly felt I'd found a place in the world.' (Sally, 39)

Some of the women (*n*=5) described how they became part of the 'street scene'. May began to drink heavily from the age of 14. She began hanging around with 'street people' or homeless people at this point in her life, as she knew that she could rely on their company:

'I'd already started going around with the street people and stuff.... I thought it was cool. It was something I could be a part of really, and it was easy 'cos you don't have to have social skills or anything like that, and some of them are nice people, and they are the only people who you can sit around and have a drink all day with.' (May, 21)

May met her boyfriend who was a heroin addict on the streets, and eventually got into using heroin herself.

The women identified various other 'scenes' that they became connected to. These usually involved particular music, clothes, drugs and/or a lifestyle. Many described how the feeling of being connected with other people was initially more important to them than the drugs. As Hope explained:

'Where I lived it was a, like, a surfy sort of place on the coast so, yeah, it was … to socialise, to fit in. I don't …

don't really think I did it for any effect, it was more just to be part of the group really.' (Hope, 35)

Some of the women ($n=14$) described how being involved in a 'drug scene' or accepted within a group of drug takers made them feel more in control of their lives. Lara was 10 years old when she started going 'raving' and taking pills with a group of 18- to 20-year-olds. She described how she felt comfortable with her new group of friends, and was able to confide in them about the abuse she was experiencing at home. It was through her friendship with this group of young drug users that she felt able to stand up to her abuser:

> 'I felt comfortable with them and in control of my life. I could be myself, forget everything that was going on at home.... I spoke to a couple of people I used to knock about with, and it was them that actually told me what was going on.... I knew it wasn't right ... it came to the point where I said to him, "If you touch me one more time I'm gonna phone the police." And he tried it and I moved away from him, and I ended up walking out of the house and running up the road and he never done it since.' (Lara, 23)

Contrary to constructions in official discourse, in which the pleasure of illicit drug use is absent and seen only in disease terms, most of the women described the ways in which illicit drugs had given them immense pleasure. Taking drugs was not a problem for them in the initial stages, and they made rational choices to enjoy the risk of getting high and/or connecting with their others in a drug culture. They therefore did not see themselves as irrational, disordered choice makers, as their decision to experiment with illegal drugs was initially, at least, a positive experience.

Forgetting, blocking and coping

Some of the women ($n=12$) claimed that they did not begin taking drugs to have a good time, party or feel connected with others, but just to take their mind of their problems and to relax. All of the women who had used heroin ($n=36$) described how its effects helped them to block out pain, stress and trauma, and to forget about anything that was troubling them. Many ($n=25$) claimed that taking drugs initially gave them a sense of control over their lives. A few said that stimulant drugs, such as amphetamines or crack, had even helped them lose weight ($n=3$).

The problem of women's illicit drug use within contemporary drug policy is constructed as residing in the individual psychology of female illicit drug users. Dependent users are medicalised and situated as pathological, irrational, disordered choice makers. The problem is to cure them of their faulty or maladaptive way of thinking, and to make them rational and responsible (see Chapter Four, pp 97–98 and Part Three pp 148–149). However, most of the women described their drug taking as a form of escape from psychological distress, from painful memories or ongoing experiences of trauma, abuse and isolation. These experiences pre-dated their illicit drug use, which they viewed as a coping mechanism in that it enabled them to block out emotional pain. The problem for the women was not to be cured of an irrational and disordered way of thinking, but to cope with their psychological trauma. In contrast to constructions found in official discourse, the women viewed themselves as rational and responsible, self-medicating victims of abuse and/or trauma. While 'experts' with the medical authority prescribe legal drugs, serving a normalising function, female illicit drug users lack this medical authority, and their drug use is thus considered immoral and deviant (see Part Two, p 62).

Every one of the women interviewed described experiencing abuse, trauma or isolation in their childhood and/or adulthood, which they said had caused or contributed to their addiction to illicit drugs in that it had provided them with a means of escape. Their experiences included sexual abuse, rape, physical abuse, verbal abuse, witnessing domestic violence, exposure to parental suicide, alcoholism or drug use, having controlling parents, or bereavement. Half of the women ($n=20$) described having felt suicidal as a result of their experiences, and some ($n=12$) had taken an overdose. In addition, half ($n=20$) asserted that they had experienced depression, some ($n=14$) described having low self-esteem, four had suffered from eating disorders, and four had self-injured as teenagers.

Sexual abuse

A quarter of the women ($n=13$) had experienced childhood sexual abuse. They claimed that taking drugs provided them with a means of escape as it enabled them to block out memories of the abuse. Most had suffered abuse for many years until they understood it should not be happening to them. When they told someone about the abuse as children, they were often not believed or were even blamed. The experience of childhood sexual abuse and whether they were believed had a huge psychological impact on their lives, both as they were growing up and throughout their adult lives.

Alanis was abused by her uncle from the age of four until eleven. Alanis's father refused to believe her, and insisted on keeping in contact with his brother. Alanis suffered from nightmares and flashbacks, which became more acute over the years. She recalls a recurring nightmare she had in her 20s:

> 'Basically I'd be in bed – just as I was about to go off to sleep – I used to feel this presence – I'd just see this grey outline of a man – and he'd rape me, start attacking me and raping me and it went on for weeks and weeks – it got to the stage where I was too scared to go to sleep 'coz he would come and get me.' (Alanis, 30)

As a result of experiencing sexual abuse, the women reported having flashbacks, experiencing depression, feeling suicidal, self-blame, guilt, low self-esteem, or self-hatred. As her flashbacks became more acute and Alanis's father continued to stay in touch with her abuser, Alanis began cutting herself to block out the pain. She often felt depressed as a young girl, and had taken several overdoses. Alanis asserted that she used illicit drugs in order to block out or escape the memories of abuse and to punish herself:

> 'I started going clubbing to Dreamers, which I've got no regrets with that scene, 'coz it was one of the best times of my life, but I'd do everything to excess. I wouldn't take one pill or two pills. I'd take seven or eight on top of the speed, on top of the coke until I wouldn't be happy until I was, like, flat out on the floor, totally passed out.... I didn't think about my uncle then until I suppose I was coming down.' (Alanis, 30)

May was sexually abused by her uncle from the age of seven to eight. When she told her parents, her father refused to believe her. Her uncle committed suicide and May's father blamed her and told her she should be going to jail for killing his brother. May became extremely depressed and started smoking marijuana from the age of nine. A year later she took an overdose and continued to do so throughout her young life. She started drinking heavily at 12 as it made her feel good – she traded alcohol for heroin at a point in her life when she felt she "might as well be dead". She had recently been raped by her boyfriend's friend when her boyfriend was in prison, but her boyfriend had interpreted the incident as her being unfaithful to him:

> 'So basically, for about a year, he was treating me like complete dirt, like, which I felt, like, I deserved, which was then that I started getting into the heroin 'cos I just felt like I wanted to kill myself. It's, like, I had to damage myself in some way to punish myself.... I was punishing myself with the drink.... I was still punishing myself because of my uncle really.' (May, 21)

Rape

Half of the women ($n=19$) had been raped. Seven said that this experience had caused their addiction as it provided them with a way of escaping the memories and painful feelings. They had been raped or sexually assaulted by husbands, partners, friends, acquaintances, punters or strangers. As in the case of sexual abuse, after the event many felt unable to tell anyone out of shame and fear of not being believed. When they did tell someone, how that person responded made a great difference. As a result of their experience, they described experiencing shame, guilt, fear, shock, self-blame, anger, dirtiness, panic attacks, insomnia, nightmares and flashbacks. Many described feeling depressed and suicidal after they had been raped.

Sonya was raped by one of the three men her heroin-using boyfriend brought to her flat. Realising he would be unable to get rid of them, her boyfriend had left her alone with the men, telling her to get them out of the flat or the relationship was over. After she was raped, Sonya felt dirty, devastated and betrayed. She could not look at her partner or sleep with him, but at the same time felt that she needed him more than ever:

> 'But 'cause I wouldn't sleep with him, he's sleep in the living room and I wouldn't be able to be left in the room on my own. I'd get anxiety attacks and I'd wake up sweating and screaming and then, you know, I'd be like "Please don't leave me" and I got so clingy on to him that he'd be like "fuck off".' (Sonya, 24)

Sonya's boyfriend left her and took her dog with him. Her panic attacks continued, and she became increasingly isolated, unable to talk to anyone about what had happened to her. Sonya explains the impact this had on her drug use:

> 'Before I was quite a strong-willed person and you know, before, although I was taking heroin, I knew I could stop it, but when that happened, it was just, like, all the life went out of me.... I'd wake up in the morning and I'd be needing it. I'd just need it to get me through the day and it had really got a grasp on me then. That's when I knew I just couldn't come off it, sort of thing. (Sonya, 24)

Lara was gang-raped when she was 17 by a group of men she had never met before:

> 'I got gang-raped four years ago in [city] and they buggered me.... I had 18 stitches on my backside, it was that bad.' (Lara, 23)

Lara describes her life after this happened as her 'lowest point'. She tried to talk to her partner about the rape, but as was so often the case when women told family or partners about what had happened, the response she received was abusive in itself:

> 'Everything had got on top of me – the gang-rape, my ex-partner wouldn't understand or talk about it. He said "Oh you probably asked for it, you dirty slut". I went mad on the crack and I went right downhill.... I nearly gave up on life altogether I just didn't care – I hated myself.' (Lara, 23)

Physical abuse

Some of the women ($n=8$) had experienced physical abuse in childhood. They said that this experience had caused their addiction to illicit drugs as it gave them a means of escape. Jane connected her drug taking with a need to escape childhood memories of physical abuse by her father:

> 'I think most of my drug use was because I wanted to forget. I, like, used it to cut out half my childhood and that, like ... my dad used to hit us a lot. He used to use the belt on us as well.' (Jane, 26)

In Nicky's case, being forced to take drugs was actually part of the abuse she suffered as a child. She was sexually and physically abused by her stepfather from the age of six. From the age of 12 he forced her to inject herself with speed to test its quality before he sold it. Nicky explains:

> 'So, basically, I was his guinea pig and I was so scared of him, so scared I couldn't even tell my mother ... it became a normal thing for me to do every morning for him. If I didn't do it I'd get a beating so I thought, I'll do this – it stops me getting a beating ... and I had so many beatings off him I didn't want any more.' (Nicky, 23)

This continued for four years, and Nicky had to inject herself every day. She has scars from where she had been stabbed with a fork and thrown into a mirror on the rare occasions when she had felt really sick and had tried to refuse to inject herself. When her stepfather was unable to get hold of any speed, Nicky described how in desperation to get some, she went out shoplifting. Her involvement in shoplifting eventually led to her being sent to a bail hostel where she met a young man who introduced her to heroin. She has been using heroin ever since.

Half of the women ($n=20$) described being physically abused by a partner or partners. Most claimed that their experiences had caused their addiction and/or made it difficult for them to stop using drugs. This was because they wanted to escape or block out what was happening to them. Tina suffered constant and severe beatings throughout her relationship with a heroin user. He made her feel "like a bit of dirt in the gutter" and broke her jaw and burnt her legs with an iron:

> 'It got to the stage where he was just making my life hell ... he used to hit me really bad. That was continually going on for about three months.... I just couldn't take any more, I was at my lowest point, like, very depressed, suicidal, I'd say, and he was taking heroin. I thought, right, you know, I need something, and if I took something like that, it would help me, it would block out all them feelings 'coz I could see that he was doing it and falling asleep for hours. I thought, well, if I do some of that, then it would block out ... my head wouldn't be so messed up.' (Tina, 24)

Several of the women said that the physical abuse made it more difficult for them to stop using drugs as they had come to rely on them as a way of blocking out their pain.

Verbal abuse

Some of the women ($n=12$) described being verbally abused or put down by their parents in their childhood. All said that this resulted in them having low self-esteem, lack of confidence and/or motivation. They claimed that illicit drug taking helped them escape these feelings. In most cases the verbal abuse was experienced in a subtle way, that is, through persistent criticism.

Rosy felt that nothing she did was ever good enough in her mother's eyes, who constantly criticised her as she was growing up, and continued to do so throughout her adult life. She described how heroin helped her escape it:

> 'Nothing I've ever done has been good enough for my mother. She's so resentful of me. She puts me down at every opportunity. She's put me down to my daughter.... When I started using I was trying to block it all out. Heroin blanks out memories and makes it so I don't think about reality. I think it's a total escape from reality.' (Rosy, 47)

Fifteen women described being verbally put down, humiliated and made to feel worthless by their partners. They all said that they used drugs to escape painful feelings caused by the abuse, and that in this way the verbal abuse had contributed to the seriousness of their addiction. Sharon recounted how the verbal abuse she endured from her ex-husband was worse for her than the physical abuse:

> 'I went through a very bad time with my ex-husband – mentally, I mean, the head games were actually worse than the physical beatings.... As they say, bruises go away – words don't, and when it came down to mental head games, that man knew exactly where to hurt me. I needed the heroin then more than ever.' (Sharon, 38)

Exposure to parental violence, suicidal behaviour, alcoholism and drug use

Half of the women (*n*=19) described experiencing painful memories of parental violence, suicidal behaviour, alcoholism or drug use. They explained that they experimented with or continued to use illicit drugs in order to escape such memories. Nicky was frequently subjected to the sound of her mother screaming, and her mother being raped and beaten by her stepfather:

> 'When they went to bed, me and my brother was cooched up on the bed cuddling each other, crying, 'coz we couldn't do anything – all we could hear was her screaming "Leave me alone! Leave me alone!" and the next day mum would come down all black between her thighs where he had forced himself on her.' (Nicky, 23)

Nicky told her social worker what was happening, and she ended up going into foster care at the age of seven. It was in foster care a few years later that she first tried illicit drugs. She continued to experiment with drugs, and claimed she needed to take them as they helped her forget about the abuse she had experienced and witnessed as a child.

Cat's father died of a heroin overdose and she swore that she would never take it. She used to see her father beating her mother every week for her wages, to buy heroin with. Cat met a man she really liked, and started seeing him. When he suggested they try some heroin, Cat agreed as she really liked him and felt curious. She decided that she really loved her boyfriend and moved in with him. Cat ended up with a heroin habit. She claimed that taking heroin helped her forget about painful memories from her childhood:

> 'There's not many people you find on heroin haven't had something go wrong.... It numbs the pain of whatever's happened to you. It makes you forget about it and blocks reality.' (Cat, 19)

Controlling parents

Eleven of the women described their parents as strict and controlling. Many of these women claimed that they had experimented with drugs in order to escape feelings caused by their strict childhoods. They described experiencing depression, loneliness, lack of motivation, lack of self-esteem, self-hatred, suicidal thoughts and the need to rebel or 'go off the rails' due to the psychological impact of their childhoods.

Some of the women ($n=5$) who described their parents as controlling were from middle-class backgrounds, and their parents were professionals. In most of these cases they were pressured by their parents to be high achievers, and were prevented from developing their own interests and pursuing leisure activities of their own choosing. Some of the women ($n=6$) from working-class backgrounds were also subject to strict and controlling parents. In these cases the control was not about their academic performance, but, for instance, their contribution to domestic duties, or more generally about their freedom. Most left home as soon as they could.

Sally described her strict upbringing by her GP father and midwife mother. She was not allowed out or to watch television and was expected to "go home and do homework and that was it", and when she'd finished her homework, she was expected to start revising for her exams. She felt she "didn't have the freedom other people had" and that she "didn't have a life". She explained the relentless pressure put on her to achieve:

> 'One summer, when we'd finished our exams, me and my brother, like, maybe we hadn't done so well in some things, my dad really expected us to start revising again for the next year's exams. I mean, not go out celebrating, your exams were over. It was always, like, you should have done better.' (Sally, 39)

Sally connected her 'miserable adolescence' with her later involvement in drugs:

> 'Well, I used to blame everything on my parents, not the fact that I was a drug addict, but the fact that I got into drugs. Maybe the fact that I haven't done other things or got other interests, that I had such a sheltered life, that maybe that was the first thing that came along that I got into; if I'd got into other things, maybe had more interests, maybe I wouldn't have got into drugs.' (Sally, 39)

Bereavement

Ten women described how their drug use began, that it had helped them block out grief and/or had escalated after the death of a loved one. Rosy started using heroin when she was 40. She had always been very close to her father, and loved him a lot. She described how her drug use became more severe after her father's death:

> 'The actual start of my demise into drugs was when my dad died. It was a very significant time for me when my dad died, absolutely.... I was so devastated I think I started losing my grip on life then.' (Rosy, 47)

Rosy had already started to use heroin occasionally when she had lost two children to cot death. She explains how the heroin helped her to cope with her losses:

> 'I'd lost two children, my father.... I just couldn't take anymore. It was just too much and the heroin just blocked everything out without my thinking about it.' (Rosy, 47)

Nicky felt very close to her mother, and when her mother died, her drug use escalated.

> 'When I lost my mother I just took more and more. I know it's not an excuse, but I did do a lot more when my mum died.' (Nicky, 23)

Nicky described how she had begun to feel like she "didn't care anymore", and decided to start doing sex work to support her habit.

According to the narratives of the women in this study, their drug taking provided them with a means of escape from psychological distress. Although initially many had sought pleasure in their experimentation with drugs, they said that they became dependent on heroin not only because of physical addiction, but in order to manage and control emotional pain. They attributed their drug dependency to their experiences of trauma, abuse and isolation. Their accounts therefore reflect the wider sociopolitical context in which drug use is constructed as a problem caused by individual psychology rather than as a social problem within a community. In line with the medicalising discourse of contemporary drug policy, the women saw their individual psychological states as a problem to be governed. However, they did not see themselves as pathological, irresponsible women who needed to be cured of their faulty way of thinking, but rather as rational, responsible, self-medicating victims of abuse and/or trauma.

"All it's brought me is pain, misery and illness"

The women described their drug use as bringing them pleasure or serving a positive function in their lives, such as blocking out pain. Different drugs gave them different pleasures or provided certain benefits according to their different effects. However, all of the women reached a point in their drug-using 'careers' where they began to feel as if their illegal drug use had become a problem, and for some, this was from the outset. Every one of the women explained that the pleasure they had initially experienced through certain drugs, such as heroin, crack cocaine, alcohol or amphetamines, soon turned into pain, misery and illness:

> 'It wasn't long before I realised that there was nothing good about [heroin] at all – absolutely fuck all. And that's the truth 'coz all it's brought me is pain, misery and illness … and I've had enough.' (Lara, 23)

Many described how their first taste of pain, misery and illness due to drug taking was experienced when they realised they were physically or psychologically addicted. They explained that they found both crack and heroin to be highly addictive – heroin was described as being physically and psychologically addictive, and crack cocaine as psychologically addictive.

Most of the women described how they thought that they would just be able to stop using when they wanted (Taylor, 1993a). Many did not know that they were experiencing withdrawal symptoms until a more experienced user told them (Dai, 1937; Rubington, 1967; Lindesmith, 1968; Taylor, 1993a). Rosy said:

> 'You wake up in the morning sweating. You can't breathe. You can't walk. It's terrible. I don't wanna be crawling round the floor like a baby shitting myself 'coz that's what happens. You're damned when you don't have heroin. You get diarrhoea, sickness, you throw up green bile, you get short of breath, your legs are like lead, you can't walk, you can't think, you can't sleep, you can't get comfortable. It's horrible. It's revolting.' (Rosy, 47)

All of the women explained that they continued to use heroin not because it was pleasurable, but because they needed to:

> 'I only buy it and take it if I'm going to be ill. That's the only reason I buy it so I can function on a daily basis.' (Rosy, 47)

Most of the women ($n=36$) said that they regretted ever having tried heroin or crack. Many ($n=10$) described being unaware and uneducated about drugs and the possibility that they would become addicted. Half ($n=20$) described being encouraged by others to use drugs. Nevertheless, as in drug policy discourse, all the women described feeling as if they were solely responsible for getting addicted. They blamed themselves, arguing that they had chosen to continue using drugs, sometimes despite warnings from others. Mandy left home at 15 to work as a childminder for a couple she had met through friends. She lived with them and her mother was paying them rent. The couple were crack and heroin addicts, and Mandy started smoking crack and heroin with them. Mandy described how they then 'turned her out':

> 'I started smoking crack in the end, smoking heroin ... but then, when I decided to leave, they said I owe them £200 and I didn't.... I decided to move on and they said they wanted £200 off me and I said I didn't 'ave that sort of money, being the age I was, so they forced me on the street then ... and ... doing like work and everything ... so I just worked and paid all that money off ... but, like, they used to beat me.... (Mandy, 24)

Mandy continued to use drugs and work on the streets after she had paid the couple off, and insisted that this was a lifestyle she had chosen:

> 'I chose to go on drugs and.... Do you know what I mean, I chose to carry on working. I didn't have to but I did.' (Mandy, 24)

As drug taking was something they had chosen to do, the women were adamant that they were responsible for their pain. Most of the women ($n=31$) described feeling emotional pain due to trauma and abuse suffered prior to their dependency on illicit drugs. However, once drug-dependent, the women commented that they became subjects of more. Many talked about how they suffered poverty, became involved in crime and prostitution, were separated from friends and family, and lost their children. May said her addiction brought her misery for a whole number of reasons that were fairly typical:

'It was a horrible way of living. The people were horrible. It's just waking up every day and having to make that money, really, it's just not knowing where it's gonna come from and the feeling ill all the time…. And the illness…. I had my first day that I didn't have any. The illness was just more horrific than anything I could imagine, like. It was just much worse than I imagined. It was horrible.' (May, 21)

The women talked about experiencing a variety of physical illnesses as a result of smoking or injecting drugs. They described overdosing, having abscesses, nerve and vein damage, hepatitis C, lung damage, deep vein thrombosis and septicaemia. They also said they had suffered physical injuries as a result of violence within the 'drug scene'. Mandy said she had been in intensive care seven times after being beaten up by pimps; other injuries women discussed included a fractured skull, a broken jaw and a broken rib.

Most of the women ($n=37$) described the misery, constant stress and anxiety they experienced trying to get money to support their habits, and the painful withdrawal symptoms they went through if they failed to raise the funds. Most ($n=37$) turned to crime and/or prostitution to support their habits, which brought them further pain and misery. Bridget described how she spent two years living in a 'bin shed' with her partner while she worked as a sex worker, and would disappear for days at a time. The women talked about 'grafting' as hard work and something they dreaded doing when they woke up every morning. Without exception their involvement in street-level sex work meant they were subject to severe forms of physical and sexual violence. Many also discussed how involvement in crimes such as dealing exposed them to violence. It also resulted in imprisonment for many of the women, and for some, this meant they were separated from their children. All of these aspects of the women's lives brought them pain and misery.

"No one to turn to"

The women described becoming increasingly lonely and isolated as a result of their drug taking. Separation from family, friends and children was yet another source of pain. The women saw the underlying cause of their pain and misery as due to their drug taking, and blamed themselves. Most ($n=33$) said their drug taking caused them to become isolated from friends and family. Eleven of them related how they had no one at all to turn to for help or support when they needed it. Sonya described how she fell out with her best friend when she started seeing her heroin-using boyfriend. She started using heroin with him, and explained that she became increasingly isolated:

> 'I started using a bit and I was injecting it and 'erm, yeah, I suppose because I started taking that I started to lose my friends on the clubbing side. I'd split up with my best mate and I was, sort of, alienated with this guy.' (Sonya, 24)

Sonya described her boyfriend as her first love, and that she would have done anything for him. She conned large amounts of money from her father to pay for her boyfriend's habit. After she was raped by a man her boyfriend brought to her flat, it became increasingly apparent to Sonya that her boyfriend did not really care about her, and that he was using her for money. She became increasingly depressed, isolated and dependent on heroin:

> 'I got really depressed and that's when I started getting a habit on gear 'coz I knew he wasn't there for me, and I went really downhill. I'd lost my mates, I knew he didn't care about me, I couldn't face my family because I'd got in a state. And I felt so alone, then, you know, it was sad.' (Sonya, 24)

When Sonya was unable to get money, her boyfriend left her. She felt as if she had no one to turn to and became suicidal.

Most of the women said their drug taking led to loneliness, secrets and lies. Half of the women ($n=20$) related how they tried to keep their drug use a secret from their relatives, friends and/or partners. This was usually out of fear of rejection or to preserve the feelings of those close to them. The women asserted that this secrecy caused them to feel guilty and alone. Nicky described how she kept her drug use a secret from her ex-partner for most of their relationship:

> 'It was wrong of me, but most of the time, I hid it. He only found out the last five to six months we were together. I was just scared about what he would think of me. I didn't want to be rejected, but in a way, I felt so alone that I did want to tell him.' (Nicky, 23)

Alanis described feeling guilty about keeping her heroin use a secret from her husband to the extent that she justified his abusive behaviour towards her. She led him to believe she was only using methadone, but was convinced that he knew anyway:

> 'He must know.... My arms are a right mess. I can't hide it from him all the time. I try to have my arms covered up, but at night he must see them. Your sleeves roll up when you're sleeping. I do feel guilty 'cause I am doing the drugs. He is vile to me, but I sort of justify it ... of course he's gonna get angry, 'course he's gonna get violent with me ... so I let it go on like that.' (Alanis, 30)

Alanis felt as if she needed counselling to help her come off methadone and heroin, but her husband was against it and was not there for her:

> 'He doesn't offer me help or support me. He doesn't like me having counselling. I can't talk to him about anything. There is no one I can talk to.' (Alanis, 30)

Half of the women ($n=20$) described feeling distressed or devastated when relatives found out about their drug use. Many felt that when the truth came out, it damaged their relationships. Jane related how things were never the same between her sister and her after her sister found out she was a heroin user:

> 'Social services told my sister about the drug use, me working as a prostitute, everything.... Me and my sister have always been, like, really close and now like we'll ring each other up – I'll ring her up and she'll send me letters, but, like, it's not the same closeness as it was before that.' (Jane, 26)

Several women ($n=4$) were told they had to leave home before they were 16 when their parents found out they were using heroin.

"I'm embarrassed about myself"

Some of the women ($n=12$) said they deliberately tried to keep a distance from relatives and friends when they were using out of embarrassment, guilt, shame, fear of rejection or upsetting or harming relatives or friends. May felt she needed to leave the town she grew up in once she started using drugs:

> 'I just thought, I've gotta leave Badstone. I was just so embarrassed about my family knowing. I was just embarrassed really so I just decided.... I liked running away it was easier.' (May, 21)

Sky described feeling extremely embarrassed and guilty about being a drug user around her eldest daughter, to the extent that she avoided contacting her:

> 'I tend to keep myself away from my daughter through embarrassment 'cause I'm embarrassed about myself. I mean, she says not to worry about it and she phones me up, or did when I had the phone, and she writes and stuff, but I feel really guilty, loads of guilt around that.' (Sky, 52)

Sky distanced herself from other people in her life in order to protect them. She explained in detail her relationship with one man in particular, and how she felt she should protect him from being exposed to her drug use:

> 'I've just had to put distance between us because he wanted to help me. He wanted to get me out of Badstone and take me away from all the drug using which made sense, but that's not what I wanted ... and he started using stone [crack cocaine] and I could just see how it was going. I care about him too much to do that to him, you know. So I just let the gap widen and haven't contacted him for a couple of years now.' (Sky, 52)

Several women ($n=4$) claimed they led relatives or friends to believe they were clean when they were not, so as to preserve their feelings. They said that this led them to feel more isolated and alone. Sonya explained how she spent two years feeling isolated in a town away from her parents, to avoid letting her mother see she was still taking heroin:

> 'So I was up there for two years and it was more loneliness until I eventually came back to Southstone. I'd phone up my mother and I'd be, like, yes, I'm clean, I'm doing really well and I've got a job, and she was so happy for me, I couldn't face her and let her see I was still using drugs.' (Sonya, 24)

"You don't have friends"

Many of the women (*n*=30) asserted that they had not had many 'real' or 'proper' friends since they had been using heroin and/or crack. As other studies have found, the women considered other addicts untrustworthy, as drugs always came before friendship (Rosenbaum, 1981). As Suzi put it:

> 'You don't have friends. Well, you can, but it's not very often because it's all drug-orientated. I mean, they might be your friend one minute and then they stab you in the back the next by robbing you or something. So, no, you don't really have friends when you're on gear. They are more like acquaintances.' (Suzi, 31)

Lara recalled how devastated she felt at one point when she thought about the number of friends she had:

> 'Erm, to be quite honest, I can't say I've had a single friend in this game, you know, because you're all out for what you can get. I've had people make out they're my friends, but as soon as I'm having a rough patch, they're not there. When I moved into the hostel I thought "How many friends have I got?" and I couldn't even count three. That's sad for a 23-year-old.' (Lara, 23)

Some of the women (*n*=12) described bad experiences they had had with other users they had believed were their friends. They asserted that such experiences caused them to avoid getting friendly with people:

> 'Every time we have something to do with people on gear in Badstone they ... one bloke ended up stealing out of Darren's house ... so we don't have nothing to do with him anymore. So we just, like, sort of keep ourselves to ourselves.' (Cat, 19)

The women seemed to regard a 'real' friend as not only somebody they could trust, but also somebody who would care for them if they needed support or were ill. As Sky put it:

> 'I need someone in my life just to show me that I'm worth something, someone to care for me, someone who cares about me and obviously someone who I respect, preferably

a platonic friendship rather than a relationship. That's what I need, and you just don't meet people like that on this scene 'cause no one's honest.' (Sky, 52)

"You are just partners for drugs"

Some of the women ($n=14$) also said that romantic relationships were not possible between addicts as drugs always came first. As Suzi put it:

> 'When you are on gear there isn't such a thing as boyfriend, girlfriend. You are just partners for drugs, so it's easier just to stay that way with blokes. It's not worth the hassle.' (Suzi, 31)

Eight of these women had resigned themselves to staying single as they had become disillusioned about relationships due to negative experiences with male addicts. Mandy described why she had decided to stay single despite sometimes feeling lonely:

> 'I get lonely now and again, and sometimes I wish someone was there for me but, like.... I ain't into messing about. Fucking end up feeding two people because they're pretending they fucking love you and they don't. I ain't stupid.' (Mandy, 24)

Many of the women ($n=17$) said they had been or were in relationships in which they felt that their partners did not really care about them, as getting and having drugs were put first. Most described feeling isolated and alone within their relationships:

> 'He was just interested in heroin. He didn't care about anything else really, including me. He was extremely greedy with drugs anyway.... "Oh I'm sorry, there's not enough for you I need all that!"... I guess a lot of the time I just felt lonely.' (Sharon, 38)

Half of the women ($n=21$) felt their partners just used them to get drugs, which many described as adding to their loneliness and isolation:

> 'Yeah, so he was my first love, but he din't care about me, he was just there for money. I knew that, but I'd keep getting money.... And I felt so alone, then, that you know,

it's really, I was doing anything to keep him there and he was just taking the piss out of me.' (Sonya, 24)

Most of the women interviewed ($n=34$) said they were extremely isolated. Most felt as if they had no one in their lives whom they could trust or turn to for support. Many of them felt they had to keep their drug use a secret from family and friends, a fact that often made them feel more isolated. Some deliberately kept their distance from loved ones, including their children, in order to protect them and/ or out of embarrassment. Even the other drug users who the women did associate with did not relieve their sense of isolation, as the 'drug scene' was considered no place for 'real' friendships involving trust and mutual support. Within their romantic relationships the women also often felt lonely, unsupported and unloved. Finally, the women faced further isolation in their attempts to get clean when they felt their only choice was to separate themselves from all their friends and sometimes a partner they still loved.

The isolation experienced by the women is a reflection of the criminalisation, medicalisation and welfarisation of drug users, whereby drug use is constituted as an individual, psychological problem, and drug users as diseased, immoral, undeserving 'others'. The women's accounts demonstrate that they had internalised the disease model and had come to feel ashamed of themselves, feared rejection, felt the need to distance themselves from others and felt undeserving of social support. Most ($n=30$) said that their dependency had destroyed their lives. Sky reflected on her life since she had started using heroin:

'It's a pretty nightmare existence.... I've never really been happy with it. I mean, there must have been some point in the beginning, but it's like, when I look at my past up until I was 27, and all my memories are in colour, and then from 27 up until now, it's all sort of grey. My memories are all grey and it has fucked up my life, it really has, and I don't understand why I'm still doing it.' (Sky, 52)

The women explained the highs and lows of their drug use. In contrast to constructions in contemporary drug policy discourse, in which the pleasure of illicit drug use is written out and constituted as a disease, most of the women provided accounts of drug taking as extremely pleasurable and/or as serving important functions in their lives. They described how they made rational choices to experiment with drugs to get high, to connect with others and/or to block out pain. They also described how their drug use eventually led to pain, misery and illness, and rather than helping them to connect with others, they faced increased isolation and loneliness. However, rather than see themselves as pathological, irrational, disordered choice makers, they saw themselves as rational, responsible, self-medicating victims of abuse and/or trauma. As discussed earlier (see p 167), 'experts' with medical authority prescribe legal drugs, serving a normalising function, while female illicit drug users lack this medical authority, and their drug use is thus considered immoral and deviant in drug policy discourse. The more resistant aspect of the women's narratives and the subjectivities they adopted for themselves as responsible governors of pain is examined in more detail next, in Chapter Seven.

Chemically enslaved addicts

Medicalisation gives authority to pathologising discourses of dependent female users who are situated as psychopathological, weak-willed, chemically enslaved, irresponsible, irrational choice makers. In its most extreme configuration, they are positioned as totally out of control, their behaviour controlled by a diseased mind, overtaken by the pharmacological properties of illegal drugs, and driven to illness, crime, prostitution, isolation and child abuse. The accounts of most of the women in this study demonstrated that they had internalised medical discourse of drug use as a disease, and saw themselves through its lens as chemically enslaved 'addicts' who had made the wrong choices. Some of their accounts involved the separation of a 'true self' from an 'addict self' (Kilty, 2011). They described former states of drug-induced behaviour, claiming that it was not their 'true selves' acting, but an immoral, out-of-control 'addict self' that was not really them, or that it was the drug itself. The women felt they were to blame for both becoming addicted to drugs and for the situations they found themselves in. They therefore seemed to somewhat comply with their official constructions in the constitution of their identities.

"I just wouldn't have thought I would ever do that"

As has been found in other studies, most of the women (n=37) asserted that they had initially believed they could control their dependency on heroin and/or crack (Rosenbaum, 1981; Taylor, 1993a). Many (n=31) knew that heroin was supposed to be addictive, but claimed that they did not fully understand or accept how it was going to affect them, and initially believed they were immune to dependency (Rosenbaum, 1981; Taylor, 1993a).

> 'You think you can control it, that it won't happen to you 'cause you don't realise it affects everybody like that.' (Wendy, 19)

Most of them ($n=35$) described how they realised they were physically dependent on heroin when it was too late. Rosy's statement was typical:

> 'I didn't sort of realise at first that I had this habit and that it was gonna take a lot to stop. I thought it was, like, having a spliff.' (Rosy, 47)

The women described how they began to feel controlled by their need for drugs and to behave in ways they had at one time never believed they would. All described how they reached a point when they felt their drug use was out of control, and many described how this seemed to happen very quickly:

> 'I mean, I always said I wouldn't use heroin, but it's so easy just to fall into that, like, circle. Once you've done it once you think, oh, it will be alright, and you do it again and then, before you know it, you've got a full-blown fucking habit and you're out stealing....' (Cat, 19)

The women described their drug use as being out of hand due to issues around using and acquiring drugs. Most ($n=33$) described feeling that their drug taking was out of control when they realised they needed to use every day, and they were physically or psychologically addicted:

> 'It started off just at the weekends, and then I'd take it during the week, and then it was every day. Then one day I realised it was out of control, where I woke up and felt really ill, and I really needed it, physically.' (May, 21)

Some of the women ($n=8$) described how their appetite for a drug had become insatiable, some ($n=4$) when they started injecting, and others ($n=7$) when they had tried to get clean and failed:

> 'I've been on as many as I can get – I'd go out there, I could do 10 or 15 punters. You know £2 or £300 and I'd

be straight out there and every time I'd do a punter I'd do a snowball.' (Lara, 23)

'It all went downhill. I wasn't eating and I wasn't sleeping and, 'erm, I thought "I've gotta get off this".... So I came home and I tried doing it, 'erm.... I didn't know what to expect but it was full on. My mum would be sat up with me all night holding me. I'd be trying to knock myself out, banging my head against the walls and I cun't handle it at all. And, 'erm, in the end I said, "Enough, I can't do it". Before I'd been quite hopeful that I could control it if I really wanted to and things were gonna be ok.' (Sonya, 24)

Many of the women ($n=20$) felt out of control of their drug use when they began to find it difficult to get money for drugs. Some ($n=17$) felt out of control when they started committing crimes to raise money, and others ($n=11$) when they got involved in sex work:

'Basically I couldn't afford it, and I felt, like, I couldn't deal with it no more when I was finding it hard to get money.' (Suzi, 31)

'I knew that was it then.... I couldn't control it anymore when I started having to sell myself to get my drugs.' (Rachel, 21)

The women used disease discourse to talk about their drug use. They appeared to have appropriated and internalised medicalising constructions of drug dependency, and believed that they were enslaved by craving and compulsion over which they had no control. They interpreted their behaviour through the lens of a medicalised condition, and their diseased mind apparently shaped all their experiences. Many of the women ($n=20$) related how their dependency caused them to feel out of control of their behaviour. Some described how they reached a point when they felt as if they did not care anymore, and did things they never thought they would to get money for drugs. Most described how this point was reached when they were at a particularly low point in their lives:

'It wasn't until I came to Badstone and lived on the front line that I really went over-board. I was out of control, like, I'd go shoplifting when I was already on bail and stuff like that, just not really caring, just doing anything to get the money more or less.' (Sky, 52)

Many of the women ($n=17$) told stories of times when they had resorted to doing things that in hindsight they felt were morally wrong, stupid or dangerous. Behaviour viewed in these ways included stealing from family members, crimes such as burglary or mugging, and sex work. These women preserved their identities in the stories they told by separating their 'addict self' and their 'true self'. The 'true self' was the 'real' them, with moral standards, which was distinct from the irrational, irresponsible, chemically driven, 'addict self'. Diane talked about when she had burgled a woman's house and had felt guilty about it after a restorative justice meeting with the victim. She claimed that it was not her who had done the burglary, but the crack she had been smoking:

> 'Yeah, and smoking crack done that. Do you know what I mean? Crack done that. That's not me. I wouldn't go and rob someone's house normal. It controls your life unless you take the control back, which I have done now. It controls you, any which way. It controls what you eat. It controls when you sleep. It controls what you do with your money. 'Cause all you're thinking about is crack, crack, crack, crack. It controls everything, every aspect of your life. It controls whether you have a bath in the morning.… My sister wouldn't lend me a tenner. I just smashed the flat up, just switched. I wasn't like that before, you know what I mean? I was never like that.' (Diane, 23)

As already discussed in this chapter, the women described how they felt their drug use became a source of pain, misery and illness. They recounted experiences of withdrawal symptoms, physical illness and injuries, violence, homelessness, unemployment, crime, sex work, loss of child custody, isolation and poverty. Most saw the cause of these experiences as residing in their fixation on drugs. Similar to the construction of female illicit drug users as chemically enslaved, weak-willed, irresponsible, bad choice makers found within contemporary drug policy, the women viewed themselves as 'author[s] of their own misfortune' (Rose, 1996, p 59) due to them having chosen to use drugs and the power of the drugs over them. The women adopted disease discourse to interpret their own (and other users') behaviour. However, at the same time they regarded themselves as rational and responsible governors of their pain, and thus negotiated resistant identities to those ascribed to them. Chapter Seven explores the ways female drug users also subverted constructions of them as disordered choice makers and authors of their own misfortune.

Dangerous, immoral, criminals, worthy of punishment

Another technology of power operating in the lives of the women in this study was prohibition and punishment. This strand of drug policy discourse in the UK, US and Canada situates dependent female drug users and offenders as bad, immoral and dangerous criminals, worthy of punishment (see Chapter Three). The focus tends to be on a minority of dependent users who are perceived to commit the majority of acquisitive crime through chemically driven behaviour. Female drug offenders and users, along with male drug offenders and dependent users, are constructed as endangering youth, destroying and separating families, and undermining communities through drug use and crime. This identification of the problem to be governed has had a disproportionate impact on poor, marginalised, victimised and black women, with steep rises in the prison populations in all three countries.

The women in this study provided accounts of both their own criminal behaviour and the criminal justice response to it. Adopting policy constructions, they described themselves as chemically driven into acquisitive crime, and as immoral criminals deserving punishment. However, a counter-narrative was embedded in the stories the women told. For some, drug use did not necessarily pre-date their drug dependency, and they became involved in criminal activities *and* drug taking simultaneously with a group of friends or a partner. Many also related how they tried to avoid causing harm to their families and communities, and expressed guilt, shame and regret for harm they had caused. They thus somewhat subverted official discourse situating them as bad, immoral, chemically driven criminals, worthy of punishment.

Grafting

Most of the women ($n=31$) supported their habits through criminal activities, what the women themselves referred to as 'grafting'. Shoplifting, soliciting and dealing were the most common types of crime for women to be involved in. Some ($n=7$) also described their participation in a range of other crimes other than illegal drug possession, such as criminal damage ($n=4$), assault ($n=4$), being drunk and disorderly ($n=3$), or graffiti ($n=1$). Table 6.1 shows the numbers of women involved in each type of crime used to support their drug habits.

Table 6.1: Crimes of women

Type of crime[a]	N
Shoplifting	26
Soliciting	16
Dealing	13
Burglary	8
Chequebook fraud	6
Begging	5
Mugging	5
Credit card fraud	4
Robbery	3
Drug running	1
Mortgage forgery	1
Total	89

Note: [a] Some women were involved in more than one type of crime.

Drug policy discourse has tended to insist on a straightforward link between drug use and crime, and has situated drug users as chemically driven into acquisitive crime. Many studies have also inferred this link (see, for example, Plant, 1990; Inciardi et al, 1993; Koester and Swartz, 1993). Many of the women's narratives ($n=20$) appeared to substantiate such constructions of female drug users. Some of the women provided accounts of how they had been driven to commit crimes to support their habits, and how their criminal activity had escalated as their drug habits increased. The women dependent on crack, in particular, described cravings that they felt led to them engaging in binges of criminal activities to get more and more money:

> 'Soon as you smoke one pipe, that's it, you want more until your money's gone and then when your money's gone, you think, aw ... how can I get some more money? At the height I could spend a thousand pounds a night ... all you wanna do is earn money. I used to rob fruit machines and go shoplifting.' (Diane, 23)

At the same time, embedded in the women's accounts were alternative understandings of their involvement in criminal activities. The dependent drug use of some of the women ($n=6$) did not pre-date their involvement in criminal activities, and for some ($n=10$), it happened around the same time that they invested emotionally in relationships with a group of friends or a partner. In many cases ($n=8$), the women said they became involved in criminal activities almost accidentally, through friends, partners or acquaintances. Ivy described how at 13 she got involved in graffiti, 'fighting', shoplifting, drinking and smoking 'weed' with a gang of older boys in her neighbourhood. Drug taking, truancy and criminal activities were group behaviours that she joined in with when she befriended them:

> 'At 12, 13, I started to rebel quite strongly.... I started hanging around with a group of guys that lived around my area. We smoked a lot of weed, drank on a Friday night, and it felt really cool. They were always bunking off school. They were into graffiti and a bit of shoplifting, and it just seemed so much more appealing.' (Ivy, 28)

In the prohibition strand of drug policy discourse, female (and male) users and offenders are situated as dangerous and immoral criminals who deserve to be punished. Some of the women ($n=7$) in this study described committing crimes that they felt harmed others. Lara discussed the burglaries she had committed:

> 'In a way I raped people by going in their house and going through their personal things.... I abused them in a way – old people I conned, the bag snatches, the fear I put into that person through snatching their bag, 'erm, you know – I hurt so many people.' (Lara, 23)

Diane described how a restorative justice meeting with the victims of one of her burglaries had stuck in her head.

> 'The woman said she didn't go home for over a month because I'd been in her house. That's horrible.... There are people who don't turn to crime but there are people that do ... like me, for crack. I have ruined lives, and I know I have, but I've changed all that now.' (Diane, 23)

However, most of the women held firm moral ideas about what crimes they were willing to commit to pay for their drugs. For example, some thought that stealing from banks and shops was acceptable, but that stealing from old people or family and friends was not:

> 'If I need crack and there's someone walking up the road and I see an opportunity to get money, I'm doing it. Don't

matter what it is ... some people rob old grannies for crack, go and tie up their Nan for money for crack, that's disgusting. I've never done things like that, but there are people out there that do it for drugs.' (Diane, 23)

Many (*n*=12) asserted that they were comfortable with stealing from banks and shops because "it's not hurting anybody":

'I only ever shoplifted so I'd think, well, I'm not hurting anyone because it's only the shops.... I'm not stealing off people, I'm not hurting them. And then it was the credit cards, and I'd think, well, I'm just stealing off the bank because credit cards, they get it back. So it's only the bank that's losing money.' (Sonya, 24)

Those women who had committed certain crimes, despite their sense that these crimes were immoral, expressed guilt, shame and regret, and saw their behaviour as morally reprehensible. Half of the women (*n*=19) recalled times when they had stolen from family and friends. Every one of them described feeling terrible about their behaviour:

'Then I stole all my daughter's gold one day when I was in Badstone. I stole all my daughter's gold and made out my mum's house had been burgled, that was dreadful.' (Sky, 52)

'I took £95 of my Nan's Christmas money on Christmas night. She's passed away now. T'was horror for me 'coz she was like a mum to me ... and what I done to her was shit, was shit. Yeah – Xmas night – took the Xmas money from her ... [quiet]. After all my family's done for me.... (Mandy, 24)

Some of the women (*n*=12) described getting involved in certain criminal behaviours they felt were morally wrong. These kinds of behaviours left them feeling ashamed and guilty. Lara described her feelings about the crimes she had committed:

'I think back then I lost all sense of right and wrong. All the burglaries I did, when I sit and think the things that I stole from people's houses– not material things, but sentimental things they can't get back, I hurt a lot of people like that.' (Lara, 23)

However, as found in other studies (see, for example, Carlen 1988), the majority of the crimes the women had got involved in were typically petty, non-violent. Not all of the women became involved in crime and sex work, and supported their habits through 'grafting'. Some (*n*=4) managed to support their habits through legitimate work or through benefits for many years, and a few of them throughout their drug career.

Most of the women who had committed crimes (*n*=32) eventually came into contact with the criminal justice system. Two women were only ever cautioned, but most (*n*=30) received some kind of punishment. The numbers of women receiving different types of sentence is summarised in Table 6.2.

Table 6.2: Sentences received by women

Type of sentence[a]	N
Prison	19
Fine	7
Probation	3
Conditional discharge	3
Bail	4
Total	19

Note: [a] Some women received more than one type of sentence.

As shown in Table 6.2, the most common form of punishment experienced by the women was imprisonment. A total of 19 women had been in jail. The main crime the women had been jailed for was shoplifting. Three women had received a prison sentence for chequebook fraud, two for robbery, another for assault, and another for mugging a punter. The women were thus mainly jailed for petty non-violent crimes.

As discussed in the first part of this chapter, for the most part the women saw themselves as 'author[s] of their own misfortune' (Rose, 1996, p 59), as to blame for their 'out-of-control' behaviour, their subsequent demise, and they were thus worthy of punishment:

> 'Maybe going back to jail is the best thing for me. My life is a horrible mess and I don't have anybody. But then, I only have myself to blame. I mean, no one forced me down this path, did they? I wish I could take back the pain I caused people, especially my mum. All the thieving and lying; I've done some horrible things to people.' (Kelly, 27)

However, some of the women were already punishing themselves. They said they started using drugs as they wanted to harm themselves out of guilt, self-loathing and desperation. Some said they took drugs because they hated themselves. Most had histories of suicide attempts, eating disorders and alcohol abuse. Their desire to punish themselves was linked to experiences of childhood abuse. Their need to punish themselves was reinforced within official technologies that construct female illicit drug users as immoral, irresponsible and punishable. This aspect of the women's accounts is discussed in more depth in Chapter Seven, in 'Unacknowledged victims' and 'Victims of policy' (see pp 233–237).

Irresponsible, unfit mothers

Welfarisation was another technology of power that operated to control and regulate the women in this study. In drug policy discourse, women who use drugs while pregnant or who have children are situated as unfit mothers who place their foetuses or children at risk of harm (see Chapters Three and Five). Pregnant female drug users are criminalised in the US and may be subjected to mandatory drug treatment programmes. In the UK and Canada, women may have their children removed from their care (possibly at birth) if the child is deemed to be in need of protection. Twenty-two of the 40 women interviewed for this study had children. Between them they had 36 children. Five women were pregnant at the time of interview. The ages of the children ranged from 11 months to 13 years. Fifteen of the children lived with their mother, three were looked after by their grandmother, and ten had their children taken into care. One woman was in the process of losing custody of her child at the time of interview. The women were conscious of perceptions of them as 'bad mothers', and some seemed to have taken on the identity of the 'bad mother' when they described their relationships with their children:

> 'I did really screw up bringing up my son because he … I've got three kids and the last one has grown up with me as an addict.… I got busted and then I had to go to this court hearing to see whether he needed to be placed in care. And it was court that it was all sort of brought home to me, my lifestyle and what my son was involved in and how it affected him. And 'erm [voice breaking up] … he went into care and he was only five [crying]. (Sky, 52)

Sky described how she felt she had "fucked up" her son by being a user when he was growing up:

> 'They do worry a lot, children of parents who are addicts. The parents don't realise how much their children know or what their feelings are around the drug situation. I mean, I didn't realise at the time, but I do now. It's too late and it's really screwed him up.... He's 22 now but my drug use has really fucked him up.... He's got all the traits of an addict, but he doesn't use, he gambles...his behaviour and irresponsibility around money and stuff like that. It's all what he's seen me doing.' (Sky, 52)

Sky described how her son put himself into care when he was 13 because of her drug use, and how he continued to keep himself out of her life:

> 'When he was 13 he left and put himself into care. He saw my life getting in a mess and took himself off, and I've only seen him a few times. He has cut himself off from me in order to protect himself, in order to get on with his own life. He's had to.... I think he went to NA or Al-Anon or Al-Ateen or something. It's for children of addicts.' (Sky, 52)

All of the women who had lost custody of or contact with their children blamed themselves and their drug dependency, and expressed immense guilt and self-loathing. They saw themselves as responsible for the health and wellbeing of their children, and blamed themselves for any harm that their children suffered. When Shelly found out she was pregnant, she stopped taking heroin and started taking a low dose of methadone instead. Her plan was to reduce, but was advised that this would be too dangerous for the baby. When her daughter was born, Shelly realised she was withdrawing. She described this as her lowest point:

> 'Having my daughter born addicted was probably my lowest point. I felt like a piece of shit, like I didn't deserve to have her.' (Shelly, 35)

Wendy was in a Mother and Baby Unit at the time of interview, where she had been referred by social services for not seeking pre-natal care. She had used heroin for two-and-a-half years before getting a place at the unit, and had three other small children, twins aged four, and another child aged two, who were all in the care of her mother while she was at the unit. Wendy felt her drug use had negatively affected her ability to parent:

> 'My children haven't had the upbringing they should have done because of my drug use. One time I had to take them to my mum's and I missed their first day at school. I will always have to live with that.... It doesn't automatically make you a bad mother but it does affect your parenting. If you haven't got your gear how can you look after your baby ... because you've got no money for a start, and when you're ill, how are you going to look after the baby? You think they don't see things, you think they don't know things, and of course they do. They're not stupid.' (Wendy, 19)

Wendy said she felt guilty about that time, and wanted to have all of her family together. The women's accounts involved an acceptance of the prescribed role of motherhood, whereby women are seen as solely responsible for the wellbeing of their children, and the behaviour of fathers and the state are not. However, embedded within the women's narratives were alternative understandings of their subjectivities that challenged official constructions of female illicit drug users as 'bad mothers'. Many ($n=10$) described how they had done everything they could to care for and protect their children. Some ($n=6$) had stopped taking illegal drugs when they found out they were pregnant. Many said that their priority was still their children, even when they were using, that they only used a minimum amount just to feel well, and were not getting high or 'gauging out'. Some said that during periods of use they did their best to hide their drug use from their children, and that they tried to educate their children about drugs in order to discourage them from trying it themselves:

> 'I always made sure I spent quality time with them and we had shopping and everything, but it's not really easy. They just think that I was ill sometimes, and that now I'm getting better.' (Cherry, 25)

> 'We always did our drugs away from our daughter. I used to go in the bathroom for a hit. We didn't have a lot to live on but she was never without food or love.' (Shelly, 35)

Some of the women suggested that their problems with mothering were not so much to do with their drug use, which they felt they had under control, but more to do with poverty, housing, violent and abusive partners, lack of support and prejudiced family members and professionals. Their drug dependency was, for these women, just one problem among many. Sharon had been in a violent marriage for 15 years when her husband left her for a much younger woman. However, her ex-husband continued to visit her council flat and beat her regularly. She said at one point he "beat me five times in five evenings". Sharon went to the council to be rehoused, and was housed in a one-bedroom flat with a security gate, but this meant her 11-year-old daughter had to live with her violent, ex-husband and his new partner in his two-bedroomed house. At the time of interview Sharon was still waiting to be rehoused in a two-bedroom house, and had been waiting 12 weeks. Not only was the flat she had too small; it was also damp, and she was unwell, with hepatitis C:

> 'It's been 12 months weeks and I've had no offer whatsoever and they haven't come round and done the repairs, and every time my daughter comes round it's like, "Mum, I think it's really bad that they're making you live somewhere like this, it smells damp, it smells old and you're not well".... My daughter's getting more and more frustrated because she wants to spend more time with me.' (Sharon, 38)

Sharon also said there was a neighbour upstairs with mental health problems who had attacked both her and her new partner and who had propositioned her daughter. Her ex-husband had also beaten up and continued to intimidate her new partner. Sharon had been on methadone for 11 years, since her daughter was born, and described how much she hated it and wanted to get off it. However, for years her major concern had been to avoid beatings, and now to be housed, and so her drug use was just one problem among many.

Shelly, a qualified nurse, had a nine-year-old daughter who had been living with her mother for the last 18 months. She said that as far as social services were concerned, she had unlimited access, but her mum had cut her off. She said her mother had never liked her husband, and once she found out they were addicts, that was it in terms of their relationship:

> 'My mum did everything she could to get my daughter off me.... Social services said I could see her every day.

They don't have a problem with it, as long as she lives at my mum's, I can go whenever I like, I can take her out, anything. My mother won't allow it. She's cut off even my daughter's friends at school.' (Shelly, 35)

Shelly explained that her social worker had packed up his job and left after he had to deal with her and her husband, as he had promised them they would keep their daughter, and their daughter that she would not be taken away. "As far as he was concerned our daughter was well cared for and was a happy little girl." However, Shelly said a senior protection worker took an instant dislike to her and "made up lies" that her and her husband were incapable of looking after her daughter:

'They said "We had a phone call from a neighbour that we can't identify and they said we were drunk and on methadone every day and she was wandering the streets at 11 am at night, not fed." None of this is true, but those things have been said, so the judge hears that and no proof has to be provided.' (Shelly, 35)

Shelly said she wanted to go to court to try and get access to her daughter, but her and her husband had many problems. They had lost everything, were "in debt up to [their] eyeballs", had warrants out for their arrests, and Shelly had resorted to working as a sex worker. Every day Shelly was at risk of assault, rape, murder, sexually transmitted disease, arrest, going to jail, homelessness, overdose or withdrawal. She said she wanted to come off drugs ideally by doing a detox. However, her drug issues were not her immediate or primary concern.

Child welfare discourse equates drug use with bad parenting, and treats female users as legitimate targets for intervention, regardless of their positive skills and attributes as parents, the level of use, or the changes they make in their lives. However, the women in this study showed self-awareness about their limitations as parents, and in some cases gave their children to partners or relatives to look after to protect them from exposure to their drug use. Rosy explained why she had felt she had to send her 11-year-old daughter to live with her ex-husband:

'I had Lucy with me at first, then I had to face the fact that the quality of her life was not very good. I wish to god I could take away that decision to let her go with her dad, but I realised that I actually had a habit and I couldn't wake up in the morning and not have any. When I realised that, I felt I had no choice.' (Rosy, 47)

Seven women said they separated themselves from their children as they felt they could no longer offer them the quality of life they deserved because of their drug use. Some ($n=5$) described feeling unable to contact or face their children until they were clean. Sky related that this was the situation with her son:

'I need to write to him but I just feel, what's the point of writing to him while I'm still using, you know. I tried to tell him that the person I was then is not the person I am now, but he just kept saying "Yeah, but you're still using, you're still using".' (Sky, 52)

Many of the women had somewhat internalised constructions of themselves found in the child welfare strand of drug policy. However, embedded in their narratives were resistant identities to those prescribed to them. Chapter Seven explores the more social aspects of the women's accounts, and in particular, their experiences of social services intervention.

Recoverable, programmable, changeable and transformable

Current drug policy discourse situates dependent drug users as bad choice makers, suffering from a disease of the mind and 'author[s] of their own misfortune' (Rose, 1996, p 59). At the same time, they are constructed as educable, saveable, programmable and transformable. Most women in this study internalised these constructions of their identities, and saw themselves as responsible for their predicament, describing how they wanted to believe they could stop taking drugs and start a new life. At the same time, many saw themselves as trapped in dependency and a drug-using lifestyle. They wanted to see themselves as changeable, transformable and recoverable. However, they described how they feared coming off heroin, not only because of anticipation of painful withdrawal symptoms, but also the fear of not having heroin to block out painful feelings caused by trauma and abuse. They also explained how they experienced their drug use as inescapable, as they could not imagine a life without drugs, and their only friends and/or partners were drug users.

"I'll come off it one day"

All of the women in this study still using drugs ($n=27$) described how they wanted to stop. Most insisted that they were going to come off drugs at some point in the future:

> 'I know I'll come off it one day. Do you know what I'm saying? I know I will, like. I'm determined to. But it's when that day will come, like. But I know I will. I don't wanna be doing this for the rest of my life. Do you know what I'm saying? Definitely not.' (Jamie, 29)

The women wanted to believe that their lives could be transformed and they could be reprogrammed. Most insisted that they had chosen to use drugs, and were therefore responsible for getting themselves off them. Tina started using heroin when she was 17, after moving in with her violent heroin-using partner. She started shoplifting to support their habits, and consequently has been in and out of jail. She eventually split up with her partner and had recently moved to Badstone, where she started work as a sex worker:

> 'It is very sad and I never want anyone to feel sorry for me because I got myself in this predicament and I've got to get myself out of it.' (Tina, 24)

Most of the women said that getting help, support and/or treatment from appropriate services was a precondition of them being able to come off drugs. Ultimately they had faith in helping agencies or 'experts', who they believed would one day in the future help them transform their faulty ways of thinking and acting:

> 'But there's got to be the help there, there's got to be the help. And my hope is that I succeed in doing that, but I need the help to do it. I cannot do it on my own at the moment. There's not enough help out there for me to do it. When there is enough help out there and I'm ready to come off, I will do it. Until then I cannot do it.' (Tina, 24)

Although the women had faith that they could be helped, there was little consensus about what kind of support or treatment would help them get off drugs. Many ($n=34$) had experience of being on a methadone prescription, but most ($n=33$) said that it had not been helpful. Counselling was viewed by many of the women as a service that was helpful (see Chapter Seven, p 260).

"People tell me I don't love myself enough"

Despite wanting to believe they could stop taking drugs, many felt unable to do so, as if they were trapped in dependency. Many of the women ($n=25$) described how they had spent years trying to get off drugs but to no avail, and were extremely frustrated with their situation and with themselves. They blamed themselves, saying that it was their flawed way of thinking or behaving that prevented them from coming off drugs. Sky insisted that the NA (Narcotics Anonymous) programme worked, but that she had 'sabotaged' her own recovery three times:

> 'I've been to treatment three times to try and come off gear and, 'erm, it might sound weird, but NA. Do you know about NA treatment? The 12-step programme. It is really good. It is really good. It din't work for me 'cause I sabotaged my own recovery, really. But, 'erm, it does work.' (Sky, 52)

Sky, like many of the women, felt that it was not loving herself enough that prevented her from getting off drugs. She explained how counsellors had told her this:

> 'It's a horrible existence, and I suppose I can change it. I could change it if I really wanted to. I don't know what it is. People tell me that I don't love myself enough. Well, all the counsellors always say that I don't love myself enough, but I don't know. I don't know what it is that stops me from going for help … it would be not thinking I'm worth it or something. I don't feel that but I've been told that, and I think that they're right, otherwise why aren't I doing something about it? I'm not happy where I am, I don't enjoy using anymore.' (Sky, 52)

To her frustration and despair, Sky was unable to stay off drugs:

> 'I'm not happy where I am, I don't enjoy using anymore. I hate myself every time I spend my last tenner on a stone. I fucking hate myself…. I just hate myself when I do it. I don't get off on it anymore.' (Sky, 52)

All of the women still using claimed that the only reason they continued was because they were psychologically or physically addicted. Nineteen of the 27 still using drugs ($n=19$) said that they no longer took drugs for pleasure, to feel high or for a buzz, but to feel 'normal'. As Rosy explained:

> 'As long as I'm well, I'm happy. I don't take the drug for a buzz. I don't take it to get a good gauge. I take it to feel normal. I take it so that I don't have diarrhoea and sickness and legs, like I can't walk, basically.' (Rosy, 47)

Many related how they were afraid to come off heroin because they anticipated not only excruciating withdrawal symptoms, but also the return of painful memories. Many of the women ($n=29$) described feeling trapped in their addiction to heroin because they were afraid of not having it to block out painful feelings caused by trauma and abuse. Suzi said that there was nothing good about heroin, and no reason for her to be taking it anymore, except to stop herself from "clucking and hurting":

> 'It's just blocking the memories out at the moment. Well, the memories are still there, but they just don't hurt. They're just not painful. That's the only thing that's scaring me from getting clean is all these emotions and things come rushing back.' (Suzi, 31)

For some women, a drug-using lifestyle was mostly the way they lived their lives, and they couldn't actually imagine what they would do or feel without their drug of choice. Lara had started injecting heroin at the age of 13. She explained that she felt strange and experienced a lack of confidence when she was 'straight':

> 'I can't handle being normal, straight. I'm not used to it. I've been using so long; to have nothing in my system and be completely abstinent is not … it feels so strange…. I feel absolutely bare…I can't talk to people, I have no confidence to start conversations.' (Lara, 23)

For years, many of the women's lives ($n=22$) had revolved around earning money to get drugs, scoring them and using them, and some of these women ($n=9$) could not imagine living 'normal' lives. They feared boredom, and couldn't imagine how they were going to fill their time:

> 'When I'm actually getting clean I need something to occupy me so I don't fall back into what I did before because of pure boredom. The main reason most people do relapse is because of the boredom of not having nothing [sic] to do.' (Suzi, 31)

Most of the women ($n=30$) described feeling trapped in their addiction to heroin and/or crack because all their friends and/or acquaintances were also drug users (Taylor, 1993a). Wendy explained why she had found it so difficult to get clean:

> 'I never met anybody straight or anything 'cause when you're using, everybody you meet's a drug addict – it just seems like nobody gets off of it and nobody – it's not that they don't, it's just that you don't see them afterwards, I suppose. It just seems like nobody does at the time. So everyone I met was to do with it.' (Wendy, 19)

Some of the women ($n=11$) also described being locked into their addiction, as their partners were also users. As has been found in other studies, this seriously jeopardised their resolve to come off and stay off drugs (Kaufman, 1985; Stewart, 1987; Parker et al, 1988; Taylor, 1993a). Half of the women ($n=20$) described how they had been in a relationship like this in the past. Most of these relationships were described as partnerships completely based on a drug-using lifestyle, where they spent all their time scoring, grafting and using together. Some of the relationships were described as co-dependent, where the addiction of the partnership was as strong as the drug addiction. If one partner went away and got clean, they would soon relapse when reunited with the other. All of the women who were in or had been in relationships with users described how it was difficult for them and their partners to come off and then stay off drugs at the same time. None of the women had ever successfully come off drugs at the same time as a partner. May explained the typical scenario described by the women:

> 'I just realised that I did still really love him but neither of us were gonna get off the drugs if we were together, like. Because, like, one of us would be strong and the other one

would want to get drugs, and then it would be the other way round, and it was just, yeah, virtually impossible.' (May, 21)

Most of the women blamed themselves for the situation they found themselves in, wanted to believe they could stop taking drugs and were saveable and changeable. However, the most dominant subjectivity they adopted for themselves was that of being trapped in dependency and a drug-using lifestyle. Their accounts demonstrated that getting off heroin and/or crack was, for them, not simply about making a choice. They explained how they felt enmeshed in illicit drug use due to physical and/or psychological dependence, the fear of having nothing to block their feelings, not being able to imagine a life without drugs, and having only drug-using friends and partners. The women's narratives also contained other stories about why they felt trapped in a life of drug taking. As discussed in Chapter Seven next, poverty, social regulation and a lack of access to treatment characterised their experiences.

Conclusion

The women in this study were governed through three mutually reinforcing technologies of power: prohibition and punishment, medicalisation and welfarisation. These operate at the level of discourse by constructing the subjectivities of female illicit drug users in particular ways, making them amenable to control and regulation. The narratives of the women demonstrated that they had, to some extent, internalised governmental constructions and made themselves complicit in their own regulation. Through technologies of the self, the women somewhat accepted negative constructions of their identities, rendering them 'abnormal' and at the same time responsible for their predicament. Their accounts of their lives were largely psychosocial and contradictory, reflecting the wider sociopolitical context and an inherently contradictory drug policy.

The women had taken on the disease model of dependent drug use, and saw themselves as chemically enslaved, controlled by the pharmacological properties of drugs. Consequently they interpreted much of their behaviour as something they were unable to control and, at the same time, blamed themselves because this was a life they had chosen. They saw the pain, misery and illness they experienced and caused others as solely due to a disease of the mind which was not their 'true self'. The crimes they had committed, the families they had hurt, the children they had lost, their bodies they had sold, and the poverty and isolation they found themselves in, was seen as due to a faulty way of thinking caused by drugs. The women viewed themselves as 'authors of their own' misfortune. They wanted to be reprogrammed, changed and saved, to be 'normal' non-using women, and trusted in 'experts' to help them.

Embedded in the women's accounts were alternative perspectives of their subjectivities resistant to the pathologising constructions emanating from policy discourse. The women discussed the role of emotion in their drug taking, which is precluded within the medical model and policy discourse. As well as seeing themselves as chemically driven, they also discussed their pleasure and pain. They were not motivated by a hedonistic, chemically driven pursuit of selfish pleasure, which might be implied by pathologising constructions of the 'diseased mind', but by the desire to escape and block out painful emotions caused by trauma, abuse, violence or illness. These experiences were often the result of them being the victims of serious crimes of violence. The women saw themselves as responsible, self-medicating, governors of their pain.

Although many of the women had done things they were ashamed of, and committed crimes to fund their habits, they did not exactly see themselves as dangerous, immoral criminals and a threat to communities, families and young people. They described the ways in which they had tried to keep their morals and principles and avoid harming others, committing predominantly low-level, minor crimes, such as shoplifting, and eventually turning to sex work, which they perceived as only harming themselves. They did not regard themselves as unfit mothers by virtue of their drug use, and described how they stopped or reduced their drug use when they discovered they were pregnant, cared for their children and protected them from their drug use as best they could. They wanted to see themselves as changeable, saveable and recoverable, but described the ways they felt trapped in dependency and a drug-using lifestyle. Coming off drugs for the women was not simply about making the 'right' choices.

The psychosocial accounts the women provided about their lives showed the ways in which they were malleable to governmental constructions. Through the authority of 'expert' knowledge on what constitutes the female 'addict', she embodies loss of control, autonomy, willpower, reason, morality and femininity. She represents the 'other' in neoliberal societies whose governments preach freedom, choice, autonomy and family values. The women's narratives demonstrated they were subject to governmental regulation. However, as Foucault argues, agency and the possibility of resistance to power are always present in power relations (see p 138). The female users in this study did not passively internalise authoritative constructions of their identities or accept attempts to normalise and responsibilise them. Chapter Seven now explores how the women evaded official constructions, and negotiated and reconstructed more positive, resistant identities for themselves, taking account of the social contexts of their lives.

Note

[1] See Appendix 1 for a discussion of the research methods used in this study. Names have been anonymised to protect the identity of the respondents.

SEVEN

Social stories

Introduction

Preliminary analysis of the women's narratives demonstrated that their accounts were largely psychosocial. Chapter Six focused on how the women related their experiences of drug use, and the social conditions in which this drug use occurred, to their psychological wellbeing. These most dominant stories the women told reflect the broader sociopolitical context in which their narratives emerged, wherein illicit drug use is both psychologised and individualised. The psychosocial accounts the women provided of their drug use rendered less dominant other more social stories, which, nevertheless, were present in their narratives. The social stories the women told about their drug use are tales of gender, poverty and regulation. The contradictory aspects of their narratives identified in Chapter Six, but with an emphasis on their more social meanings, are revisited here.

The subjectivities the women in this study adopted for themselves, and hence the way they saw themselves, were shaped and framed by governmental technologies. The women had somewhat assimilated governmental constructions, and unknowingly colluded in their own control and regulation. At the same time, they twisted the subjectivities and regulations imposed on them by 'the authorities' at the level of discourse. They inserted themselves into the process of governance that they are the subjects of, and ascribed new and different meanings to their subjectivities. Although they had absorbed and complied with dominant, psychosocial constructions of their subjectivities, through which they are responsibilised for their predicament, embedded within their narratives were more social stories that undermine and subvert dominant and official understandings of them.

Unrecognised pain

There was a paradox inherent in the women's accounts of their illicit and licit drug use. This was evident from some of their accounts of their experiences of prescription drugs as compared to their experiences of heroin and crack in the context of contemporary drug policy. Their accounts draw attention to the incongruent character of contemporary drug policy. All of the women in this study explained how their drug use functioned as a form of escape from experiences of trauma, abuse and isolation (see Chapter Six, p 163–171). While female users are not authorised to govern their emotional pain with illegal drugs, some described how they were encouraged to use legal drugs prescribed by doctors for depression.

The women came to view illicit drug use as a coping mechanism rather than as a source of pleasure, as discussed earlier in Chapter Seven. The problem for them was not to be cured of an irrational and disordered way of thinking, but to cope with and block out painful memories or experiences. As Sonya asserted:

> 'It takes away the guilt, and the depression, and the pain, and things like that. It's a painkiller.' (Sonya, 24)

Aside from methadone prescriptions to come off heroin, many of the women were identified by their GPs as individuals who needed prescribed drugs to help them function 'normally' within their lives. Five of the women in this sample were prescribed anti-depressants; four were prescribed them before they had tried heroin or crack, and one when she was no longer using heroin for post-natal depression. Some of the women who had experience of being prescribed drugs for depression saw a parallel between their use of prescribed drugs and their use of illegal drugs. Unlike the construction of dependent drug users in contemporary drug policy, the women in this study did not view their illicit drug use as irrational and irresponsible. Suzi argued that the drugs she had been prescribed by her doctor were similar to heroin and crack. Apart from the issue of their legality, she asserted that taking crack and heroin was actually more rational than taking prescription drugs due to the 'side effects' she experienced from the latter. Suzi started using heroin when she became depressed after she lost her children, she split up with her partner and became homeless. She wanted to come off heroin and went to see her doctor:

> 'So what they done was put me on anti-depressants – desipramine, and it's got like a mild sleeper in it. So with the anti-depressants they're doing exactly the same as what crack and heroin's doing because they are giving me an upper with the anti-depressant and then they are giving me a sleeper which is a downer. The only difference is it's prescribed. It's legal. But I'll tell you what, though the prescribed drugs have got a damn sight more side effects. I was getting really bad mood swings on desipramine.' (Suzi, 31)

As a heroin user Suzi viewed herself as a responsible pain governor who wanted to get off heroin if it was not for her need to block her emotions:

> 'It's just blocking the memories out at the moment. Well, the memories are still there, but they just don't hurt. They're just not painful. That's the only thing that's scaring me from getting clean is all these emotions and things come rushing back.' (Suzi, 31)

Like Suzi, Jane began using drugs that were not mediated by the medical profession, and considered herself to be self-medicating:

> 'It makes me, like, forget my problems. It's, like, it shuts your emotions off, but you don't actually think of anything.' (Jane, 26)

She saw herself as a rational choice maker, deciding to take heroin to put herself to sleep and to feel well:

> 'I don't know, it's just the faintest noise and I'll be awake. Anybody moves in a room, I'm awake. It's a sleep problem … that's always the problem with me…. Like some days I'll wake up at 7 o'clock in the morning, have a hit and then just go back to sleep and that lot 'coz I'm still tired.' (Jane, 26)

Jane had just come out of hospital and had come off heroin and crack while she was pregnant. She was living with her partner who had continued to use heroin. As they were known to be drug users, Jane and her partner were visited twice a week by a social worker and two community service team workers. Jane described how she ended up using heroin again, and her perception of her social worker's attitude towards her:

> 'When I come back out of hospital because my bloke was still doing the drugs and that lot, it was in front of me all the time so I just thought, "Oh I'll have a bit just to help me sleep" and that lot. So I did that and then we managed with the babies fine, everything they needed was done for them and that lot. But the social worker sees that if you are on drugs, you have gotta be out of your face which doesn't necessarily mean it, half the time you take it just to feel well and that lot. You just don't feel like the gauging anymore, you just feel like you need it just to be well for that day. But she saw it, like, if you took the drug you would be out of your face and can't cope with the babies and that lot. But every appointment they needed to go to everything that needed to be done for 'em was done for 'em.' (Jane, 26)

Jane's daughters were taken into foster care despite the fact that she insisted throughout the interview that she had looked after her babies well, and had not 'gauged out' since they were born.

Rachel suffered from post-natal depression after the birth of her daughter, so her doctor prescribed the anti-depressants diazepam and amitriptyline. Despite their legality, Rachel said she was unable to look after her children on the drugs that were prescribed to her:

> 'When I first started taking them, they would knock me out for days, so for, like, three solid days I'd be on the sofa fast asleep and my partner was there coping with the new-born and our eldest one who was coming up to two years. So it was quite difficult for him then. When I'd come round from the tablets, I'd take more and then he started smoking [heroin] where he had all the stress.' (Rachel, 21)

Ironically, while Rachel was prescribed drugs that put her to sleep so she was literally unable to look after her children, Jane had her children taken away from her due to the 'risk' that she posed to her children because of her heroin dependency. Jane continued to see her heroin use as a way of coping with emotional pain, this time caused by having her children taken away:

'I just stayed on the drugs just to shut off the emotions, like.' (Jane, 26)

These accounts of the women's experiences of their licit and illicit drug use draw attention to the contradictory character of contemporary drug policy. Rationales and justifications for the illegal status of heroin and crack centre around them being constructed as dangerous drugs. They are viewed as such because they are seen as highly addictive, harmful to the health of users, and render users irresponsible and/or incapable of functioning normally. As shown by the accounts of the women in this study, these are also the characteristics of legally prescribed drugs. Fundamental to the public approbation of illegal drug taking is the constitution of this drug use as irresponsible. As long as women comply with drug use being administered by 'experts', regardless of the relative addictiveness or harmfulness of the drugs prescribed, their normality, rationality and responsibility is considered to be restorable. Although the technology of normalisation operates to maintain female users within the subject position of irresponsible, bad choice makers, they ascribe new and different meanings to their subjectivities by seeing themselves as responsible, rational governors of their emotional pain. The women were thus able to resist the subjectivities ascribed to them in official discourse.

Rational, adaptive, caring, resourceful women

In drug policy discourse, female drug users are situated as diseased, out-of-control addicts who, in the selfish, hedonistic, pursuit of pleasure, have apparently chosen to become and continue to be addicted through irrational, disordered choice making. Any problems experienced by dependent users are constituted as caused by the disease of addiction, weak will and irrational choice making. The problems users experience have apparently been brought on by themselves, including pain, misery, illness, unemployment, poverty, homelessness, crime and prostitution (see Part Three, p 148). Although the women in this study saw themselves to some extent as chemically enslaved 'addicts' who had made the wrong choices and were to blame for their predicament, they considered their drug taking as a rational and reasonable response to their life experiences. The women saw themselves as rational governors of their pain rather than irrational, disordered choice makers, and thus somewhat resisted official understandings of them.

This resistant aspect of the women's narrative is now explored in more depth as the social stories told by the women are explored. In their pursuit of drugs and a drug-taking lifestyle the women not only wanted to escape psychological pain and trauma, but also social disadvantage. They discussed the social and economic contexts of their lives prior to their involvement in sustained illicit drug use. Their accounts of themselves as socially disadvantaged prior to their involvement in the 'drug scene' poses a challenge to the construction of them as the 'author[s] of their own misfortune' (Rose, 1996, p 59). The women initially saw the 'drug scene' as providing them with more social and economic options and a means of escape from poverty and abuse. By seeing themselves as socially disadvantaged women who have made rational choices, they resist the subjectivities ascribed to them within the current drug policy discourse.

The women provided accounts of their attempts to stay in control of their drug use, their behaviour and their lives. In response to the feeling that they were losing control, they found themselves redefining their moral and behavioural standards to adapt to their changing circumstances. They preserved their identities by distinguishing themselves from 'other' dependent drug users who were unlike themselves. In so doing, they subverted official constructions of themselves as irrational, and out of control, instead seeing themselves as rational and responsible, adapting to their changing situations. Finally, rather than behaving selfishly and hedonistically and putting their desire for drugs before others, despite their addictions most of the women exhibited unselfish, caring and nurturing behaviour in their relationships with others. This was most evident in some of women's narratives, where they risked their freedom, wellbeing and safety to financially support the drug habit of a partner through crime, sex work or sharing benefits.

The women described the social conditions they inhabited prior to their sustained use of illicit drugs. They discussed their family background, education and formal labour force participation. For many of the women, experiences of gendered abuse provided the context for their need to escape through drug taking. However, their need to escape usually occurred within a range of constraining economic and social conditions. The women provided accounts of their involvement in the 'drug scene' as a widening of social and economic options. The 'drug scene' initially seemed to provide them with an escape from poverty and abuse, as it appeared to be lucrative, glamorous and cultured.

Family background

Most of the women in this sample (*n*=32) grew up in relatively poor homes, and described themselves as coming from working-class backgrounds. Their parents, if they worked, had blue-collar and menial jobs. Two of the women grew up in care. Four of the women spent some of their childhoods in foster care. One spent her childhood in a children's home. Eight of the women described themselves as well provided for and middle-class. Their parent/s were qualified professionals, such as doctors, teachers and solicitors. Less than half of the women (n=18) were raised by both birth parents. A third of the women (*n*=13) were raised by their mother and a stepfather. Two were raised in a single-parent family by their mothers.

Most of the women, whether from middle- or working-class backgrounds, described experiencing an abusive home life as children (see Chapter Six). Half of the women (*n*=19) witnessed parental violence, suicidal behaviour, alcoholism or drug use, a quarter (*n*=13) were sexually abused, 12 were verbally abused or put down, 11 described their parents as strict and controlling and 8 were physically abused by their parents. As discussed in Chapter Three (see pp 67–68), in drug policy discourse families are constructed as in need of protection from harm from dangerous drugs and drug users. However, this discourse fails to acknowledge the ways in which families are often sites of harm and abuse for female drug users.

According to the women's narratives, their childhood experiences meant that they were likely to spend a lot of time away from their family home, outside, on the streets, 'outside shops', or in parks with friends or in their homes or in pubs and nightclubs with older friends. These women were likely to be exposed to drugs at an early age. More than half of the women (*n*=21) had experimented with drugs by the age of 16. Some of these women (*n*=12) had started smoking or injecting heroin or crack by the age of 16:

> 'I'd go to school and as soon as school had finished, that's it, off with school uniform and down to the flats where I had friends and then…. Yeah, things at home were bad. I was practically not really there, you know, I'd go there to get a shower and change and I'd be off for the night.' (Sonya, 24)

> 'I dunno, I just sort of, like, withdrew into myself and er, started mixing with people that were older than me. I got into the rave scene. And 'erm, I started up on drugs when I was 10.' (Lara, 23)

Many of the women ($n=16$) asserted that they had left their parent's home at the earliest opportunity, some before they were 16, because of an oppressive family life and/or to be with a partner. Seven said they left home to live with a partner they had fallen in love with, six left because of a stepfather they did not get on with or who had abused them, and three left due to conflict over their freedom. Some of these women ($n=11$) moved out of their parents' homes into housing in which they were immediately exposed to and became involved in drug taking. All of the women who left home to live with boyfriends discovered that their boyfriends were heroin addicts and/or violent.

All of the women described their drug taking in psychosocial terms as functioning to provide them with an escape from trauma, abuse and isolation (see Chapter Six, p 163). As discussed in Chapter Three, research indicates a disproportionate number of dependent drug users have experiences of sexual abuse, rape and trauma (Gilbert et al, 2001; Becker and Duffy, 2002; Agrawal et al, 2005; Brady and Ashley, 2005). The women's need to escape often occurred within the context of violent and abusive relationships. A quarter of the women ($n=13$) had experienced childhood sexual abuse, half ($n=19$) had been raped, and half ($n=20$) described being physically abused by a partner or partners (see Chapter Six, pp 163–168). It was within such social contexts that all the women began using drugs such as heroin and/or crack as a form of escape. Such experiences are *gendered* experiences, that is, they disproportionately affect women. They occur in specific social contexts that the women share with 'normal' or non-drug-using women. However, this aspect of the women's narratives, so prominent and central to their accounts of their lives and explanations for their dependence, is not recognised in drug policy discourse.

Education

Women who have been incarcerated for drug or drug-related offences are more likely than non-incarcerated women to have lower educational attainment (see Chapter Three, p 73). Many of the women described how they truanted from school and/or did not complete or continue with their education. A third of the women ($n=13$) said that they had truanted from school. This was usually because it interfered with their social lives. All of the women who truanted from school were from working-class backgrounds. Some of these women ($n=5$) explained that their truanting was instrumental in them being exposed to and experimenting with drugs:

> 'I started bunking off school and then I started using but I only started using drugs 'cause everybody else was doing it.' (Mandy, 24)

Some of the women (*n*=8) described how their drug taking had led them to start truanting from school as they became more connected with a new group of friends and/or embedded in a drug-using lifestyle:

> 'I started going out clubbing and taking E's and that and I was out raving round the country and lost interest in school. I was in, like, a community, and they all used to protect me when I started getting into the drug scene because I was 14.' (Sonya, 24)

Only six women continued their education after the age of 16. Several women who started using drugs while still at school recalled how they struggled to keep up their attendance and academic performance due to their drug-using lifestyle:

> 'I'd lost weight, I was skin and bone, about seven stone, never ate and slept once a week sort of thing, but I'd go to school and I'd be half asleep in my lessons and I wouldn't be able to concentrate.' (Sonya, 24)

Leaving home early for most of these women meant a disrupted education. A third of the women (*n*=13) did not finish school or sit their GCSEs or 'O' levels. Many of the women left school at the age of 16 (*n*=26). A quarter (*n*=14) of the women attempted educational courses after leaving school, but most found they were unable to motivate themselves, to attend and/or keep up with the work because of their drug use:

> 'About three years ago I signed up to do one of those access things at college ... but because, like, at the time I was still into drugs and that lot, there was no way that, like, I was gonna get there for, like. 9 o'clock in the morning.' (Jane, 26)

Four of the women were successful in completing their courses, and one was in the process of doing so. One became a qualified psychiatric nurse, one a qualified horse-riding instructor, one a drugs counsellor and one woman was in her final year of a university degree. The latter two women were in recovery. As Rosenbaum (1981, p 25) found in her study, the lack of education of most of the women in this sample meant that they experienced 'reduced options for non-menial work to which they might become committed.' It was within such constraining circumstances the women felt they needed to escape.

Formal labour force participation

The stifled education of most of the women in this sample meant that their occupational options were limited. A third of the women ($n=14$) had never held a legitimate job. The majority of those who had been employed in the formal labour force had worked in low-paid menial jobs. A summary of their formal sector work experience is provided in Table 7.1.

Table 7.1: Formal work experience

Type of job[a]	N
Shop manager	2
Care worker	3
Barmaid	4
Receptionist	1
Shop assistant	8
TEFL teacher	1
Child minder	2
Supermarket cashier	3
Factory worker	1
Catering assistant	1
Waitress	1
Bank worker	1
Psychiatric nurse	1
Cosmetics consultant	1
Gardener	1
Office worker	2
Clothes designer	1
Drug counsellor	1
Welder	1
Total	36

Note: [a] Some women had experience of more than one type of work.

Only one woman in the sample was in formal employment during the fieldwork period. The rest were unemployed, and one was a student. Hope was a drugs counsellor and had been clean for eight years. Most of the women thus became embedded in drug-taking lifestyles as their lack of education and lack of work experience meant that alternative lifestyles were not readily available to them.

The 'drug scene': lucrative, glamorous, cultured

As Rosenbaum (1981) and Taylor (1993a) found in their studies of heroin users, the women's involvement in a 'drug scene', or in friendships or relationships with drug users, initially seemed to provide them with more social and economic options. Part of the women's perception of this widening of options came from their involvement in crime and sex work. The women found that these activities were considerably more lucrative than any legitimate work that was accessible to them. Many initially experienced their involvement in crime or sex work as a way out of poverty. As Rosenbaum (1981, p 26) argued in her study of heroin-using women:

> Due to their initially reduced options resulting from poverty, lack of viable goals, work, and education, these women became enmeshed in social worlds that they felt could increase their options.

In this study, many of the women said that their involvement in a 'drug scene' or their ties with drug users were either more lucrative, glamorous, cultured or interesting than other options they had. The women saw themselves as 'normal' rational choice makers in a world where, as poor and/or abused individuals, they faced limited options. By seeing themselves as socially disadvantaged women making rational choices, they were able to actively contest and redefine constructions of them as pathological, maladaptive women who have made the wrong choices.

Rosy described how, during her childhood, her family was very close, but they "din't have much materially". She was expected to spend most of her time doing domestic chores, cooking, cleaning and babysitting, and when she reached her teens she began to feel as if she "was being put upon". She also described her childhood as culturally impoverished:

> 'We didn't have a painting on the wall, we din't have a bookshelf.... I had no musical instruments.' (Rosy, 47)

Rosy also explained how she was expected to leave school at 16 and get a job. There was no question of her continuing her education. In addition, the kind of job she was expected to do was limited:

> 'I'd never heard the word "career". I was expected maybe to get a job in an office or a bank or be a nurse or a shop assistant, and that was really the limit, that was the limits you were given.' (Rosy, 47)

Rosy described how during her late teens she got into the 'hippy scene' where she started mixing with 'cultured', upper middle-class hippies, and began to experiment with drugs. She said that she had found her 'niche', and described how she began to feel resentful of her background:

> 'The people that I started taking drugs with were, like, ex-university students, upper middle class, and I mean I had a boyfriend who had a Rolls-Royce when I was 21. I thought, "This is the life" you know. "My parents are so uncultured" and I became very resentful and ashamed of them in some ways.' (Rosy, 47)

The hippy scene thus provided Rosy with a lifestyle that seemed attractive, both in terms of the wealth and the culture she experienced within it.

Most of the women took measures to control their addiction. All of them had tried to get clean at some point. Coming off and going back onto drugs was an integral part of their lives as drug users, however (Waldorf, 1970; Brown et al, 1971; Pearson, 1987; Robertson, 1987; Stewart, 1987; Parker et al, 1988; Taylor, 1993a). Half of the women ($n=20$) had tried to get clean three times or more:

> 'And it's always been, like, a never-ending circle. I mean, I've spent a lot of time trying to get clean. I've always wanted to get clean and I've tried and I've tried, and I've tried so many times through my life to get clean.' (Sonya, 24)

Many of the women ($n=16$) described how they tried to keep their drug use to a minimum, and only used enough to feel 'normal':

'Now I've learnt to calm myself down, like. Like, before every time I scored I'd always buy crack and heroin at the same time. But now I just buy crack and, like, limit myself to the heroin as long as I've got something for the morning. A bit in the afternoon praps, and someing [sic] for the evening and I'm happy with that. Whereas before I'd have to have it all the time and all the way through, like.' (Jamie, 29)

Most of the women ($n=19$) supported their habits through criminal activities or sex work, what the women themselves referred to as 'grafting'. They were not *driven* into crime by some uncontrollable, addictive urge, as many studies have inferred (see, for example, Plant, 1990; Inciardi et al, 1993; Koester and Swartz, 1993). The women in this study, as in Taylor's (1993a), made pragmatic choices about how to raise money. Activities such as shoplifting, credit card fraud, dealing and sex work provided them with the high earnings necessary to support their habits. In most cases, the women described how they became involved in criminal activities accidentally, through friends, partners or acquaintances. The women initially felt that their involvement in crime and sex work was an easier and more lucrative way of raising funds than the kind of low-paid work that was accessible to them or any other methods that were an option. These kinds of activities thus initially provided them with an escape from poverty. This is discussed in detail later in this chapter (see pp 222–224). Far from acting irrationally, the women saw themselves as rational and responsible in their desire to escape social disadvantage as well as psychological pain and trauma. Hence, they were able to contest and redefine the meanings ascribed to them through drug policy.

"I've kept my morals"

All of the women at points in their 'drug careers' said they felt chemically enslaved and blameworthy, as they are situated in drug policy discourse (see Chapter Six, pp 181–184). They recounted behaving in ways that they were ashamed of, and in ways they never thought they would. At the same time, they placed certain limits on their own drug use and standards on their behaviour in order to stay in control. Although they did not always succeed in keeping their behaviour within the limits and standards they had set for themselves, they continued to redefine these according to their changing situation. In so doing, far from seeing themselves as the completely chemically dependent, out-of-control, maladaptive individuals they are constructed as being within official discourse, they considered themselves to be adaptive, rational and responsible.

Many of the women (*n*=26) said that even when they considered their drug use to be out of control, they were still in control of their behaviour. They compared themselves with 'other' drug users who would do 'anything' to get their drug. According to the women, these 'other' drug users engaged in criminal, dangerous or immoral behaviours that they stated they would never engage in. They viewed these behaviours as an indication of having an addiction that was out of control. By not doing certain things, the women were able to view themselves as in control, rational, responsible and 'normal':

> 'Well, most people are 'erm … sly, thieving; er … they do anything to get the drug, you know. I mean, I'm proud to say I've kept my morals, I wun't steal off anyone. I wouldn't go shopping to get someone's drugs for them if they couldn't make it down the road 'coz they were too ill and take half of it away from them. I think it's disgusting doing things like that.' (Rosy, 47)

The women's views about what behaviours were immoral were very different, however. Some thought that stealing from individuals, especially family and friends, was unacceptable. Sharon said that she felt fine about stealing from large companies, but not from friends:

> 'I've always been a heroin addict and I've always kept my scruples and my principles through being addicted. I've never stolen off my friends…. But yes, there are things that I've done. I've stolen from big corporations and companies 'cause the way I see it, they're insured, it's not hurting anybody and I don't see it as much of a problem … all I was doing was trying to keep my head above water and keep myself well.' (Sharon, 38)

The women redefined their moral standards in response to their changing situation. Shelly described how her and her partner burgled a house out of desperation, something she never thought she would do. However, she maintained she would never do it again, and drew the line at taking anything out of the children's bedrooms:

> 'I never thought I'd do anything like that, but we were desperate.... I got the hammer and smashed the window and said, "fuck it if we're gonna do it" and I know it sounds really weird but they obviously had kids ... they had PlayStations the lot in their bedrooms ... and I said "That's it, none of that goes, it's gonna be bad enough when they come back from holiday, front room video and telly's gone, but whatever's in the boys' bedrooms stays. We don't go in there, we don't touch it".' (Shelly, 35)

Begging and sex work were other behaviours that some women (n=15) asserted they considered to be too dangerous, immoral and/or undignified. Again, by not engaging in these behaviours, the women viewed themselves as in control:

> 'I've never worked on the street, 'cause, like, to me that's selling my soul.... There's no way that I could tolerate ... no, I just couldn't, it's just not me, it's not me. I'd rather someone drop me through a skylight and say "Go and take that computer", yeah. Leg it and hope for the best. I'd feel safer doing that than getting in a car with some total stranger and them expecting me to have sex with them.' (Sharon, 38)

Another way in which some of the women (n=9) considered themselves to be in control compared to 'other' users was through taking care of their appearance:

> 'We're both very, like.... I think if you were to place us next to some other heroin addicts I think we look fairly fucking tidy. I think, because I've always liked to look nice and I've always liked the nice things in life, like Steve has, and I think that it's not hard just to have a bath and keep yourself up together. Do you know what I mean?' (Cat, 19)

"Keep[ing] my head above water"

Rather than seeing themselves as irrational and out of control, the women rationalised their behaviour, viewing themselves as adaptive and responsible individuals. They redefined their moral and behavioural standards, making their behaviour acceptable to themselves in some way. This enabled them to retain a sense of control. They rationalised their behaviour in various ways including by asserting it was a one-off, only temporary, that it was not as bad as some other behaviour, not as bad as it could be, that it was an unavoidable part of the situation they had found themselves in, or had benefits that made it bearable. Jamie described the benefits of sex work, and that as far as she was concerned, her current situation was a temporary one:

> 'It's not very nice, like, but a lot of it ain't sex. A lot of it is … a lot of people want company and the money's good. But, like I said, I don't wanna be in it forever, you know what I mean?' (Jamie, 29)

As explored in Chapter One (pp 27–31) earlier, in academic discourse female dependent drug users are constructed as likely to do anything for a hit, and likely to spread disease due to their immoral, irresponsible, risky sexual behaviour. In response to the threat of HIV/AIDS, the control and regulation of 'risky' female sexual behaviour was central to harm minimisation policy and practice in the UK (see Chapter Four, pp 99–101). The stories told by the women about themselves in this study did not correlate with these constructions of female users. Some of the women who were sex workers regarded themselves as 'responsible' and seemed to take pride in the professional manner in which they carried out their work, something that they felt distinguished them from 'others':

> 'Then you get ones that, like … that have had bad experiences with the girls out there … like they've ripped 'em off and that lot. 'Coz that's one thing I've always made sure, I've never ripped anybody off and that lot. I've got some punters that come back because they realise that, like, I don't rip 'em off and they can spend time with me and that lot, instead of, like, being rushed.' (Jane, 26)

Some described how they would only do certain things, and others made a point of saying that they always practiced safe sex:

> 'But I wear safe protection anyway, I don't do nothing without a condom. Everything I do a condom is used. I know they are not 100% but at the same time I'm not doing nothing without one, it's as simple as that.' (Tina, 24)

Caring women

Rather than behaving selfishly and hedonistically, and putting their desire for drugs before others, despite their addictions, most of the women exhibited unselfish, caring and nurturing behaviour in their relationships with others. This was most apparent in the accounts provided by some of the women ($n=12$) who willingly supported their male partner's drug habit out of 'love' or a sense of responsibility to look after him. Although four of the women claimed they were forced to go out 'grafting' due to violence and/or intimidation from their partner, the majority of those who said they had supported a partner's habit were at least initially quite willing to do so.

Many recent studies have found that women frequently finance a partner's drug use through sex work (Taylor, 1993; Cusick et al, 2003; Hunter et al, 2004). As one of the women in this study stated, "it's almost like they're pimped by their partners". Contrary to the findings of other studies, sex work was not the primary means through which women financed their partner's drug habits. Five of the women in this sample funded their own and a partner's drug use by working on the street. In all but one of these cases the women had initially supported their partner's habit through shoplifting, and had moved on to sex work when they became too well known by security guards. Table 7.2 below shows the forms of income through which the women financed a partner's drug use.

Table 7.2: Form of financial support

Type of income[a]	N
Shoplifting	9
Sex work	5
Legitimate work	4
Credit card fraud	3
Begging	3
Income Support	3
Other	1
Total	28

Note: [a] Some women had supported a partner's habit through more than one type of income.

The most common way in which the women in this study supported their men's drug habit was through shoplifting. Some supported their partner's drug use through legitimate work. This was usually in the early stages of a relationship, when the women were not using drugs themselves. Several women supported their partner's habit through credit card fraud and several through begging. A few paid for their partner's drugs while they were on benefits. Supporting their partners meant that many of the women lived in more serious poverty:

> 'I got another job, again just in retail, and then it went right downhill ... we just could not afford it – £50 a day, 250 quid a week, which isn't that much for the two of us but still too much to live – we'd have no food in the house, we wouldn't have any electricity 'cause we had an electric key. It just got so dire ... in the end he went back to his ex-girlfriend, which, I should have seen it coming.... I was in a right state then.... I lost everything.... I ended up in a hostel.' (Alanis, 30)

Despite the women's need to escape from poverty and abuse, they took what they perceived to be their responsibilities for others seriously. They seemed prepared to sacrifice a better quality of life for love. In this sense they can be seen as responsible, caring, giving individuals. This way of seeing themselves is in direct contrast to their construction as irresponsible, selfish and hedonistic, as they are situated in academic and drug policy discourses. All of the women claimed to be in love and/or said they felt they should look after their partner. Nine women said they financed the drug taking of a partner as they were in love:

> 'I loved him a lot and I'd have done anything to be with him.' (Cat, 19)

> 'I'd do anything to keep him there because he was, like.... I was just sort of holding on, I suppose.' (Sonya, 24)

Six women claimed they felt they had to look after a partner. In all these cases the arrangement seemed more immediately practical, often because it appeared to be 'easier' for the women to earn the money. In most of these instances the women viewed themselves as the most 'responsible' or capable ones within their relationships. Jane had financed her and her partner's habit through sex work for three years. She explained that her partner could not get a job, and every time he went out shoplifting, he got caught. Jane thus seemed to be in the position of 'breadwinner' as she saw herself as the most capable earner. She explained how initially sex work had seemed like an easy way of earning money:

'This girl who lived in the hostel was telling me how easy it was out there and that lot. It was the first time I went out there it was so easy 'coz I only stood out there for 10 or 20 minutes and got one straight away.' (Jane, 26)

Suzi said that financing her partner's habit while living on the street gave her a purpose. She also found that as a female beggar she was able to make more money in a shorter period of time:

'It was alright because it was sort of, like, replacing my children with him to be honest [laughs]. 'Coz he was only young I was looking after him. It was giving me a reason to get up every morning….' (Suzi, 31)

Contrary to the construction of women drug users within the academic literature as dependent 'parasites', unable to support their drug use without a man (see Chapter One, pp 32–33), according to the women in this study it seemed that it was the men who were more likely to behave like 'parasites'. Only five of the women said they had had their drug use supported by a partner, compared with 16 who had supported their partner's drug use. Of the partners of the five women who had their habits supported, only two did so without question. Alanis's partner made her pay him back out of her benefits after he had gone off with his ex-girlfriend. Lara's partner was physically and verbally abusive, and taunted her that she would never survive on her own. Diane's partner was also physically and verbally abusive, and 'controlled' her with crack.

Poverty and gendered abuse sometimes pre-dated the women's drug use. They faced initially reduced options due to their family backgrounds, disrupted educations, limited job prospects and gendered abuse. For many of the women, their early involvement in a 'drug scene', in friendships or relationships with drug users, seemed to provide them with more social and economic options. The majority of the women in this study not only wanted to escape psychological pain, but also social disadvantage that they experienced prior to their involvement in regular drug use. The subjectivities the women adopted for themselves challenge their construction as maladaptive women responsible for their social disadvantage, as found in current drug policy. They saw themselves as rational, adaptive, resourceful women, resisting social and economic marginalisation. In response to feeling out of control, they redefined their moral and behavioural standards. Despite the fact that the dependent women in this study described feeling out of control of their drug use and behaviour at various points in their drug careers, they redefined their moral and behavioural standards, and retained certain behavioural standards in order to stay in control and preserve their identities. Finally, they demonstrated that they were often caring, giving and supportive of others despite their dependence, rather than selfish and hedonistic.

Victims of policy: criminals versus victims

Chapter Six explored how in line with policy discourse the women saw themselves, as chemically driven criminals, causing harm to their families and communities, as 'authors of their own misfortune', responsible for their 'out-of-control' behaviour, and thus deserving of punishment. This was reinforced by the fact that some of the women said they were already punishing themselves due to feelings of guilt, self-hatred and self-loathing connected to childhood experiences of abuse. The need to punish was reinforced by official technologies that situate female users as criminal, dangerous, immoral, irresponsible and punishable. At the same time, embedded in the women's accounts were resistant understandings. The vast majority of the women were involved in petty non-violent offending, and could hardly be described as dangerous. They also described how they sought to keep their morals in attempts to avoid causing harm to their families and communities, and expressed guilt and regret for harm they had caused.

In what follows, the women's experience of crime and punishment in its wider social and political context is examined. Three major themes emerged from the women's narratives. First, the women were not simply driven into crime through chemical enslavement, but made rational choices to escape poverty and to raise money. Second, most of the women in this sample were punished through the criminal justice system for being 'criminals', for crimes they had committed to avoid poverty, and for money to fund their drug habits. At the same time, most of them were 'victims' of crimes of violence and abuse, the perpetrators of which have never been punished. Third, the interventions of the criminal justice system served to reinforce and compound the poverty, unemployment, homelessness, family separation and susceptibility to abuse and violence experienced by the women.

Perpetrators

Most of the women ($n=31$) in this study admitted to committing some kind of crime to pay for their drug habit. Criminal activities initially provided them with an escape from poverty. Crime was experienced as more lucrative than the kind of low-paid work that was accessible to them. The women saw themselves as rational and responsible in their desire to escape social and economic disadvantage. Their drug use and criminal behaviour can be seen as a rational response to poverty as well as abuse, trauma or controlling parents (see Chapter Six).

Natalie had a full-time job working as a sales assistant. Her heroin-using friends would ask her to drive them around while they went 'grafting'. Natalie's friends offered her half the profits in exchange for driving. Natalie gave up her job when she found that being a 'driver' for her friends was more lucrative and easier than going to work. Her decision to give up work and be a driver made sense to her:

> 'I was the driver 'coz I had the car. They used to say, "Take me out and whatever I earn I'll give you half". That was a lot easier than going to work all day for 20 or 30 quid when I could earn 100 quid in an hour. I was the driver. It would be "Natalie, could you pop round so and so's? I've got this to sell. I'll sort you out". So off I'd go. It's easier init, than getting up and going to work? I gave up my job. I was pissed off with going to work every day.' (Natalie, 28)

Natalie's involvement with other drug users provided her with an escape from the tedium of her low-paid job. At this point she was dabbling with heroin. After she gave up her job and her heroin use became daily, she started shoplifting to support her habit. As her habit grew, she found herself shoplifting more and more. Shoplifting was the most popular crime for the women in this sample to become involved in. Most of the women ($n=26$) started shoplifting to fund their habits. Natalie, like most of the women who had shoplifted ($n=26$), eventually became known to store detectives and the police. Consequently, the women had to find alternative means of supporting their habits.

Another way in which some of the women ($n=13$) had supported their habits was through drug dealing. Sally described how ever since she had dropped out of university, she had never known what she wanted to do for a career, and said, "I've always been frightened or scared of the commitment of a full-time job anyway". Sally had only ever had temporary or part-time jobs, but explained that she made more money and was more comfortable as a dealer. She got into dealing without really intending to through her flat mate. Her involvement seemed to her to be a rational one at the time:

> 'Where I was living there was a guy downstairs who was dealing and he was often out and he would leave me stuff to sell and then he left, so I got loads of customers straight away, people would.... I didn't want to go into dealing, I didn't think about it but people kept asking me for it so, you know, I was making plenty of money.' (Sally, 39)

Some of the women also became involved in other crimes that they found lucrative. These crimes included burglary ($n=8$), mugging ($n=5$), begging ($n=5$), chequebook fraud ($n=6$), robbery ($n=4$), credit card fraud ($n=3$), drug running ($n=1$) and mortgage forgery ($n=1$).

Many of the women ($n=16$) started doing sex work as a way out of poverty. All of them described this decision as a last resort, but a logical one. Shelly explained how, in a state of poverty, she made the decision to start doing sex work:

> 'There was no gas on the meter, we had a little bit of electric, but soon we would be on candles. So we had no hot water, no heating, no cooking, no food in the cupboards, three bailiff letters arrived from the same company demanding twelve hundred quid, and I thought, well, there's fuck all left for them to take, I've got nothing to sell, I've got no way of making any money and I've got this, I was working at this job in a call centre where you cold call people trying to sell double glazing for £4.10 an hour. By the time I'd signed on I'd lost my rent and benefit, it wasn't worth me doing it, I was on less money than I was on the dole. So I did that for a couple of months, and then, as I say, I got these letters one morning and I thought, well, I've only got me left to sell, that really is my only option, you know, otherwise we're going to have no food after today, no gas, we're going to be sick, strung out, stuck in bed. We're literally going to starve in our bed in the cold.' (Shelly, 35)

The women were not simply *driven* into crime by some uncontrollable, addictive urge. The women in this study, as in Taylor's (1993a), made pragmatic choices about how to raise money. However, once dependent, activities such as shoplifting, credit card fraud, dealing and sex work provided them with the high earnings necessary to support their habits.

Hidden victims

Most of the women in this sample were victims of crime, and in most cases the crimes were not reported to the police. These crimes included childhood sexual abuse, rape, domestic abuse and assault. These were crimes that many of the women said had caused their initial use of illicit drugs, and were at the root of their subsequent involvement in criminal behaviour. The women provided a range of explanations for why the police were not informed of the crimes committed against them, including feeling ashamed, wanting to forget, being in love, their own involvement in crime, the response from their family, fear of further attacks and their perception of the police and/or the criminal justice system.

However, unlike in the case of non-drug users, some asserted that they did not want to involve the police because they did not want to draw attention to themselves or be seen as a 'grass'. As Taylor (1993a, p 82) argued, a sense of belonging to a 'drug world' involves following certain 'rules designed to protect the subcultural group from outsiders', the most important one of which is to not be a 'grass'. In her study of injecting female drug users:

> To expose or denounce another drug user to straight society, particularly but not exclusively to law enforcement agents, even to save oneself, was a serious misdemeanour. (Taylor, 1993a, p 82)

The women's membership of a 'drug world' involved secrecy about criminal activities. Sky described how when she was raided she kept quiet despite being offered money and being threatened with social services:

> 'I was getting raided every year and the drug squad wanted me to give information and stuff like that and offering money and threat ... and they threatened me with my son, Fred. Like, when he was little when I was first raided the first three or four years, every time they offered money for information. When you don't agree to do that, then they can get nasty, and he did, and he threatened me with the social services and eventually he did it.' (Sky, 52)

When Sky was a victim of domestic violence, like other women, she was reluctant to contact the police. In addition, for many of the women their only experience of the police was as perpetrators of crime, which prevented them from viewing or having faith in the police as a possible source of support. Lara described how she was well known by the police for her attitude:

> 'Because of my stepdad being a criminal, whenever I used to get arrested I'd be straight away, "No comment" and I'd be really cocky because of being young and that. So I've got a reputation with the police, I'm quite well known by the police and I do give them a lot of grief. I fight them if they arrest me.' (Lara, 23)

Lara had been in a series of relationships in which she was beaten up, but never turned to the police for help.

Again, many of the women were involved in crime or had partners who were, and did not want to draw attention to themselves. Sonya's boyfriend had brought three men he had met in rehab back to Sonya's flat. He left her with them, too afraid to go back and to phone the police:

> 'I mean, like, I was raped and he din't tell the police. He din't do anything. He left me in that flat with them for three days. He knew they were there and he just said that he was too scared to come back. He din't wanna phone the police 'coz there were stolen things in the flat. So he just left them to it.' (Sonya, 24)

Eight-and-a-half months pregnant, and describing herself at the time of the interview as suicidal, Betty described how her partner, who smokes crack and 'batters' her, had nearly blinded her in one eye:

> 'I was being beaten and stuff throughout this pregnancy, and my womb, I got kicked in my stomach, and my womb was dislodged basically, and subsequently I suffer from low blood pressure … and he [partner] used to make me go on the road and whore, but I said "I don't want to, I'm tired". He would say "Go and whore, go and whore and make some money" and he would chaperone me and stuff.' (Betty, 29)

Betty was the only woman in the sample who identified herself as a 'victim':

> 'I've been a victim for far too long now, I've been a victim of rape, sexual abuse, molestation, bullying, domestic violence, mental battery … and I can't get a break.' (Betty, 29)

The lifestyles of the women as heroin and/or crack users meant they were more likely to become subject to precisely the kinds of experiences they initially started using drugs to escape from, such as physical abuse and rape. All of the women who suffered violence and abuse within the 'drug world' claimed they continued to use drugs as an escape to block out these experiences. They thus seemed to be trapped in lives of drug addiction, trauma and abuse, caught in a vicious cycle.

Within the 'drug world' the women inhabited, they became subject to all kinds of trauma, violence and abuse. Some said that they used heroin to escape experiences of physical abuse from a parent or partner (see Chapter Six, pp 166–167). Due to their membership of the 'drug world', in which violence and intimidation are common currency (Maher, 1997), the women seemed to be even more vulnerable to physical abuse. Many of the women in this sample ($n=20$) said that they had been assaulted within the heroin and crack world in non-domestic situations by dealers, other drug users and members of the public. Ten women had been assaulted by dealers. Three were unable to pay the dealer what they owed. Rosy was involved in dealing herself when she was robbed of all the drugs. She had no money to pay her supplier the money she owed him, and he was not sympathetic:

> 'I was terrified of him 'cause he said he was gonna box me down, do this and do that to me if he didn't get his money.... Now I was walking through St Stevens one night and he jumped out on me and said, "Where's my loot?" and slashed my face and that's the scar that I have here. It went straight through my cheek. He opened my cheek up completely.' (Rosy, 47)

A few of the women were assaulted as they were under suspicion of stealing from a dealer. Jamie was blamed for missing drugs:

> 'I got a broken rib from a dealer. He had a drug stash in the house and put me responsible, but little did he know there was like about four other people who knew where

the stash was. Er, one of the boys had gone in there and took a bit out of each one. Because I knew where it was I had the blame. He kicked me in the ribs.' (Jamie, 29)

Many of the women described how in the 'drug world' users frequently robbed from one another. Most of the women (*n*=30) had been robbed by other drug users. The women were also subject to violence from other drug users. In most cases they said that these drug users were people who they thought were their friends. Rosy was robbed while carrying drugs:

> 'I was selling for this chap and I was.... I had the bags on me, I had eight 10 pound bags on me, street value 80 pound ... and I was mugged at the top of Slim Street and I suffered a slight fracture to my skull, resulting in the fact that I don't have a sense of smell anymore.' (Rosy, 47)

Suzi described how she was treated by 'normal' male members of the public as a homeless woman on her own:

> 'When you are on the streets you get a lot of shit from blokes that are just members of the public. Yeah, because the amount of blokes that have asked how much I charge for service and stuff like that, is unbelievable, and the amount of blokes that have tried kicking shit out of me or urinate on me when I've been asleep in shop doorways is ridiculous.' (Suzi, 31)

All of the 16 women who were sex workers had been raped and assaulted while they were working. None of the women reported these crimes to the police and, as found in other studies (see Hunter et al, 2004), many considered such incidents to be an occupational hazard. Most of the women claimed that they did not think the police would take them seriously. Suzi's perception of the police, although not a sex worker herself, was relatively typical:

> 'A lot of it the police don't wanna know because they just say, "Oh it's alright. It's just another working girl, he didn't pay her so she's screaming rape".' (Suzi, 31)

Many of the women claimed they used drugs to block out past experiences of sexual and physical abuse. As many of them ended up turning to sex work to finance their drug use, they became subject to more such experiences. They seemed to be trapped in a life in which they were to be repeatedly abused and victimised. Fourteen of the women said that they had been raped by a punter, 16 said they had been assaulted and 8 were held or taken somewhere against their will. Mandy had been raped in the course of her work so many times that she had begun to see it as a 'normal' aspect of the work:

> Mandy: 'I've been raped loads of times … but that don't seem to bother me, do you know what I mean? It's happened so many times, 'coz I've been working for 10 years, it's jus' like another customer that ain't payin.'
>
> *Interviewer: 'Right – so you're kind of desensitised to it now?'*
>
> Mandy: 'Yeah, yeah … yeah, but it's not easy.' (Mandy, 24)

Mandy later referred to the times that she had been raped as some of the 'lowest points' in her life. All of the other women emphasised the violent aspects of their experiences, and the various ways in which punters forced them into doing things they had not agreed to do.

Some of the women described how they were locked or tied up for hours by a punter. Shelly described how she was tied up and tortured:

> 'I got held in The Rainbow Hotel, tied up for five hours while a bloke tortured me, basically. A middle-class businessman who was seriously into S&M. He burnt me, he put my head – he tied carrier bags over my head with tights round my neck until I was passing out from suffocation and all sorts of nasty things. He put broken bottles up my ass, he tried to make me eat his shit, all sorts of things.' (Shelly, 35)

Many of the women ($n=16$) complained of having their money or drugs taken from them regularly by a partner, pimp or associate. This study supported the claim made by Maher (1997) in her study of sex workers in Brooklyn, that one of the recent changes in street-level sex work has been the declining significance of the 'pimp'. Only one of the women had worked for 'pimps' in the formal sense. As discussed in Chapter Six, Mandy was 'turned out' at 16 by a young couple who claimed she had to pay them back for crack and heroin she had smoked with them.

Mandy continued to work on the streets to get money to buy crack and heroin. However, she then had problems getting picked up by punters when she had pimps 'hanging around' her, wanting her to work for them. She ended up working for these pimps who started off pretending to be friends:

> 'They was making me think they was my friends and they were just pimps, basically, so I was working for them.... I was buying people to befriend, d'you know what I mean … and I realised … that they ain't my friends – I knew all along they wasn't my friends.' (Mandy, 24)

After some time, Mandy began to resent having her money taken off her, but when she did not hand over the money she earned, she was beaten up:

> 'If I would go out and do a punter for 40 quid, I would end up with about fucking … £10 of it, not even that … and if I didn't go back with the money, I would get found and beat up and put in hospital.... I've been in intensive care seven times.' (Mandy, 24)

Some of the women also described being witness to violence towards others. Sky described how she watched a friend of hers being stripped naked and tortured:

> 'I saw him on the kitchen floor, face down naked, with boiling water being poured down his back out of the kettle, and they were wanting to know where his money and stash was. 'Erm, and he ended up in hospital that night for quite some time. They did terrible things to him.' (Sky, 52)

Finally, many of the women said that they used drugs to block out the pain from having lost a loved one. Ironically, due to the high rate of illness and risk of overdose among drug users, a few of the women had lost or lived in fear of losing a loved one within the 'drug world'.

Suzi described how most of the people she had known living on the streets had died:

> Suzi: 'But, like, I've seen so many people die. Like most of the people that have been on the streets as long as I have

or longer they're all dead or they've moved on but most of them are dead.'

Interviewer: 'What do they die of?'

Suzi: 'Erm, hepatitis c, septicaemia, deep vein thrombosis, abscesses.' (Suzi, 31)

The women viewed all of these experiences as something to be expected within the 'drug world', and not as a matter for the police. They described how their lives seemed to be characterised by trauma and abuse and a need to escape such experiences. However, this need to escape only seemed to cause them to become further entrapped in precisely the kind of trauma and victimisation they had originally claimed they used drugs to escape from.

Punishment

Most of the women ($n=32$) eventually came into contact with the criminal justice system. As discussed in Chapter Six (see p 189), the most common form of punishment experienced by the women was imprisonment – a total of 19 women had been in jail. Most of these women ($n=14$) had received more than one prison sentence in their lives. Several ($n=7$) had been in prison more than three times. For these women, imprisonment had started to become an expected aspect of their lives. Rachel said that she would be "in and out of jail" numerous times before she got the support she needed to come off heroin:

> 'I don't want to go back to jail and do it back in jail. I want to do it on my own to prove to myself I can do it … but that's how it's going to end up, me going to prison again.' (Rachel, 21)

The main crime the women had been jailed for was shoplifting, and petty non-violent crime. All of the women who had been fined were fined for shoplifting. Several complained that as they were shoplifting because they had no money to begin with, this punishment made no sense:

> 'I thought it was daft, really, because I wun't be out pinching stuff if I had money to pay a fine. I mean, I asked them for a bit of probation or something and they said "No,

because if we give you probation now, Rosy, then if you get caught again, then it will be an immediate custodial sentence"'. (Rosy, 47)

Most of the women who had come into contact with the criminal justice system turned to sex work to fund their habit. All of these women asserted that this was partly because they felt they were less likely to get arrested and sent to jail for doing it – sex work in the UK itself is not against the law, although soliciting is. Sentences for crimes such as shoplifting tend to be much harsher than that for soliciting, which is usually punished with a fine. As Sky put it:

'If you weigh up the difference in terms of the legal system, you're better off selling your body.' (Sky, 52)

Tina had turned to sex work after being in and out of prison for shoplifting numerous times. She argued that it was easier in that it meant avoiding prison. She said that the police were less concerned as the risk of harm was to the women themselves:

'Well, you can't get sent to prison for it, for a start. There's nothing they can do, really. I mean, what can the police do? You are stood there, you are not doing no harm. The way they see it, is that you are taking that risk by getting into that car.' (Tina, 24)

As discussed earlier in this chapter, all the women who were sex workers had been the victims of rape and physical abuse in the course of their work. The current legal system thus operates so that women who use drugs, who, as already shown, are a victimised group of women, find it easier to support their habits by being victimised further. As Sharon stated:

'What makes me sick about it law wise is, yeah, basically, I could go and break the law, yeah, in a way that I would feel safe for myself, yeah, where I wasn't gonna be hurt and where I wasn't hurting anybody else, yet if it came to prison sentences, I'd probably end up having to do three times longer than someone that's working the street. So it's easier for women to do something that's harming them.' (Sharon, 38)

Most of the 19 women who had been to prison had received more than one prison sentence in their lives (*n*=17). For these women imprisonment had started to become an expected aspect of their lives. The women in this study did not support the idea that harsh punishment in the form of imprisonment may serve as some sort of deterrent for these female 'criminals'. Mandy said that she enjoyed going to prison as it provided her with a welcome break from drug taking:

> 'I been in and out of prison for shoplifting. So ... prison ain't nothing to me. It's nothing really. It just takes away your freedom for a while. Do you know what I mean? I love it. It's a break from drugs and everything 'coz I don't always get drugs brought up to me. It's just nice to have a break 'coz you've got no choice but to come off the drugs. Do you know what I mean? Out here 'coz you know you can get them, you just don't want to come off 'em.' (Mandy, 24)

For some of them, being in jail was a haven in that it was the only place where they had experienced being clean and felt they could get clean.

Unacknowledged victims

Most of the women were perpetrators of crime, albeit largely petty non-violent crime, and were punished within the criminal justice system. At the same time, most were victims of crime, many of them before they were ever perpetrators. These were crimes that the women were too ashamed or afraid to report. The women in this sample can thus be seen as unrecognised and unacknowledged victims of crime. Most of the perpetrators of the sexual abuse, domestic abuse, rape and assault of the women, unlike the women themselves, were never punished for their crimes. According to the women's accounts, their punishment within the criminal justice system only seemed to steer them into sex work, causing them to be victimised even further. If the women were victims, the question is, why are we punishing them? A justice system that disproportionately incarcerates female drug-dependent, economically marginalised, victimised, low-level drug and property offenders, while perpetrators of domestic violence, rape and sexual abuse continue to be under-represented, can only be described as a gendered injustice system (see Chapter Three, pp 88–89).

As demonstrated in Chapters Three and Four earlier, current drug policy both punishes and treats drug users who are constituted as both victims and criminals (see Chapter Three, pp 86–88). This paradoxical way of seeing and responding to illicit drug use reflects a general cultural ambivalence and uncertainty about drug use. Arguably, this is not a new ambivalence, and reflects a historical response to 'the poor' as either 'deserving' or 'undeserving'. The construction of women drug users as both victims and criminals is also reflected in criminological debates on women's crime and deviance, and within research and theory on female drug users. As Maher has argued, these discourses tend to dichotomise agency, and women are either seen as passive victims devoid of choice or agency, or as active criminals seeking to maximise deviant and criminal opportunities. As Maher (1997) found in her study of women drug users, the women in this sample were by no means merely passive victims devoid of agency or active criminals out to maximise criminal opportunities, and most did not see themselves as such. As Sally commented:

'I didn't think of myself as a criminal, I didn't wanna be a criminal. I just slipped into it through circumstances.' (Sally, 39)

Arguably, through their construction as criminals, the women are responsibilised not only for the crimes they have committed, but also for being victims of crime. That is, their status as victims of crime is not recognised and understood as involving any diminished responsibility that might effect a change in the way they are dealt with within the criminal justice system.

The victim/criminal dichotomy, in which women drug users are constituted as treatable criminals and punishable victims, apparent within the discourse of drug policy and evident within the institutional practices used to deal with women drug users, does not 'fit' the women in this study. Rather than seeing themselves as victims or criminals, the women understand themselves as normal, rational, adaptive women, responsibly governing their pain, managing their relationships and providing for their partners and children. Notwithstanding the women's own displacement of victim or criminal status, their stories also give vindication to the argument that they are indeed socially disadvantaged victims of abuse, victimised further by the rationalities and technologies constituting contemporary drug policy rather than simply bad mothers, pathological, selfish and hedonistic, out-of-control, irresponsible women, worthy of punishment. In what follows, some of the women's accounts of the impact of the criminal justice system on their lives are explored. The very control mechanisms brought into place to bring discipline into the women's lives actually plunged their lives further into being out of control and in chaos.

Victims of policy

Some of the women ($n=18$) complained about the chaos in their lives caused by their contact with the criminal justice system. They described how going to prison had impaired their future employment opportunities, and how it had interrupted and damaged their relationships, especially with their children. In addition, although many of them were able to get clean in prison, after getting out, their lives were often thrown into chaos and destitution through homelessness, unemployment and social isolation.

Rachel was living with her heroin and crack-using partner who she got together with when she was 15. They had two young children. Rachel started smoking heroin and crack after getting post-natal depression. She started shoplifting to support her and her partner's habits, got caught, and received a jail sentence. As a result of her contact with the criminal justice system, her life has taken a downturn. She has been separated from her children, has had difficulty staying clean after getting out of prison, and in finding and keeping legitimate employment. When she went to prison, her children went to live with her mother. She has been in and out of prison ever since. Rachel described how she missed her children and that they were always on her mind:

> 'Every day I think about it, I missed their first days at school. I think of them playing around my mother's house when they should be playing round my house. I should be cooking their tea on my cooker and things like that.' (Rachel, 21)

After coming out of prison the first time, Rachel managed to find a job in a cafe working for cash in hand. She struggled to pay off debts she had left behind, and eventually started using, and stealing from her work. Her plans to provide a stable home for her children were then destroyed:

> 'When I last got out of jail, this time, I got myself a job so I was working, it was cash in hand, but still I was working. I was starting to pay off rent arrears that I got 'coz I owe £4 grand worth in rent arrears, damages and everything else to the flat being smashed up. So I was starting to pay

off that. If the council had of seen regular payments, they would have offered me a new flat, which then I could have started decorating out for me to have my girls back, but I started on the gear and I started stealing from my works. I was only working in the cafe. The money wasn't brilliant, it was only £4 per hour, but someone just being out of prison, it was good. Especially cash in hand as well. So I was making a really good start and effort for myself.' (Rachel, 21)

Rachel was caught and has just served another jail sentence. After getting out of jail clean for the second time, she started smoking heroin again. Her mother kicked her out of her house where she was staying with her children. At the time of interview the police had a warrant for her arrest as she had broken her bail conditions. She was working as a sex worker and is staying with an elderly male crack addict who lets her stay in his house in exchange for crack. Rachel complained about the chaos of her situation:

'I'm sick of going out selling myself to get money for my drugs, I'm sick of waking up every morning and feeling like shit. And I am damn right sick of living up on Brown Road away from my kids.' (Rachel, 21)

Rachel claimed that her heroin and crack habit is now worse than ever.

Shelly got into doing chequebook fraud when she was pregnant. She and her husband were in debt, and Shelly's husband had been made redundant. After her daughter was born, Shelly gave up her criminal activities and started working again, as a psychiatric nurse. When she was tempted to do another chequebook fraud, she got caught. As a result of her contact with the criminal justice system, she lost her daughter and her career. When she was about to go to jail, her mother took the opportunity to arrange a meeting with social services to get custody of Shelly's daughter:

'The day before I was due to go inside, my mum phoned social services and convened a meeting with child protection and they said "If you don't put your daughter into voluntary care we're going to take her into care when you go into prison tomorrow. You'd better go home and tell your daughter she's not going to be with daddy".' (Shelly, 35)

Shelly's mother now has custody of Shelly's daughter and does not allow her access:

> 'I'm not allowed to phone, I'm not allowed to write and I see her about three times a year.' (Shelly, 35)

When Shelly was caught shoplifting, she decided to hand in her notice rather than be fired from her job. This marked the end of her career as a psychiatric nurse. She now works selling sex. Shelly fears that when she goes to jail she and her husband will lose their flat.

These accounts show that the criminal justice system not only punishes the women by taking away their freedom, but also damages their relationships with their children, destroys their careers and/or job prospects and causes them to become homeless. The very government agency drawn on to control the women ends up plunging their lives into further chaos. As discussed in Chapter Five (p 119), drug users are constituted as responsible for their predicament and 'author[s] of their own misfortune' (Rose, 1996, p 59). However, the women's view of themselves as 'victims of policy', with lives thrown into chaos by the criminal justice system, challenges this construction.

Through their construction as criminals the women are responsibilised not only for the crimes they have committed, but also for being victims of crime. That is, their status as victims of crime is not recognised and understood as involving any diminished responsibility that might effect a change in the way they are dealt with within the criminal justice system. A contradictory policy that treats women as victims and criminals is manifested in the way female drug users are treated so that they are able to get 'treatment', that is, detox and counselling within the institutions designed to punish them, and they end up feeling punished by those designed to help them.

Although the women had committed a range of criminal offences, the 'bad', dangerous, criminal featured in policy discourse threatening young people, families and communities did not quite fit the women in this study. Most of the women faced social and economic marginalisation before they had ever committed a criminal offence. The pull of quick money was thus attractive for these women, who saw their choice to commit crimes to raise money as rational in the face of alternative legitimate ways that they saw as an option for them. Most of the women were victims of serious crimes of violence and abuse, which is a silenced aspect of drug policy discourse, and demonstrates the gendered impact of disciplinary powers. The criminal justice system exacerbated the women's social and economic marginalisation and vulnerability to abuse, damaged their relationships with their children, caused them to become homeless and plunged their lives into chaos. The women were victims of abuse and also victims of a punitive drug policy. Nevertheless, they navigated an identity for themselves as adaptive, rational and resourceful women, who were responsibly governing their pain and providing for their partners and children.

Disciplined, normalised and punished mothers

The psychosocial aspects of the women's narratives, discussed in Chapter Six, demonstrated that some of the women somewhat accepted negative constructions of themselves as incapable of looking after their children due to their drug dependence. At the same time, they described how they cared for their children, and discussed the strategies they used to protect their children from exposure to their drug use. This chapter explores the more social aspects of the women's accounts, and in particular, their experiences of social services intervention in their lives that they experienced as punitive. In the welfare strand of drug policy discourse, female drug users are constituted as bad mothers and expected to convince social workers that they are abstinent, responsible parents. They are not only situated as unfit mothers, but at the same time, as changeable, saveable, educable mothers who need treatment, education and training. Such a construction inheres in the assumption that motherhood is a 'natural' state for all women, which women drug users simply need help in realising. Controlling discourses, practices of surveillance and control operate to normalise female bodies to serve prevailing gender relations. The accounts of the women in this study show that social workers actively punish as well as regulate their welfare clients, creating a 'carceral continuum' with criminal justice and medical regimes.

Many of the women in this sample ($n=18$) had come into contact with social services because of their children. Most ($n=13$) felt they were seen as 'bad' and punished for being drug users. They described how social workers treated them with a lack of understanding, and were judgemental and rude. Social workers operated as the judges of normality, employing disciplinary techniques to ensure adherence to gendered norms of appropriate feminine behaviour. Many said that they had initially trusted their social workers, who they felt had misled and been dishonest with them. They described how their children were taken away from them, which left all of them feeling as if their lives were no longer worth living. Some of the women's accounts of social services as a mechanism used to punish them are now explored.

As discussed in Chapter Six, Wendy was in a Mother and Baby Unit. She explained that as she did not seek pre-natal care she had been sent there by the family courts on an interim care order for neglect. Wendy did not agree with this assessment of the situation:

> 'Well, I'd had three children, and I've been through three pregnancies, so if I'd been ill, I would have gone to the hospital but, like, she was moving. If there was anything physically wrong with her, I don't see what they were going to do then, because I didn't realise until I was six months pregnant. If she was going to be born with two heads ... anyway, I don't think you can say that is neglect.' (Wendy, 19)

First, Wendy was very positive about being at the unit, and said that all the staff there were very helpful. However, when confidentiality was reiterated, her account began to change. She said that she did not have a choice about going to the Mother and Baby Unit, and had to go along with it because she did not want to lose her children. Risk discourse in child protection appropriates living conditions as evidence of child neglect or parental pathology and blame (see Chapter Five, p 132). Wendy felt that she was approached with prejudice from the outset for being a drug user and for living in a squat:

> 'I was living in a squat then, when the social met me it was, like, "Oh actually, you're not like that." Because they met my little girl Fleur, and they thought she was going to be, like, undernourished and in, like, dirty clothes and she wasn't. She was in clean clothes and she was really happy. The squat had a plumbed-in toilet, running water, gas and electric and everything.' (Wendy, 19)

Wendy said that while she was at the unit she did not like the feeling of being constantly judged and watched, missed her other children, and would rather she was not unnecessarily separated from them. She claimed some of the staff were rude and patronising towards her, and the parenting classes were a "waste of time".

Jane and her partner had twins and were using just enough heroin to make them feel 'normal'. She had come off heroin when she was pregnant, but said she had got back on it as her partner was still using and she had trouble sleeping. Jane explained that her support workers had said to her that if ever her and her partner needed anything, to ask them. Jane had asked them for help when her and her partner had no money left for nappies before their giro day. Jane said that the support workers came round with nappies and food for the weekend, but the next time they came round, they reprimanded her:

> 'On the Monday when they come again, they started hassling us about it, "We shouldn't have had to do that" and I goes, "You lot say if we ever need anything just to ask you and that lot and then when we ask, you moan". Then it got to September, it was…. I wasn't gonna ask 'em again because I couldn't be doing with them making me feel bad about it … so I decided to go out working that weekend.' (Jane, 26)

Jane had stopped working the streets but decided to go out just for the weekend. Information sharing between social workers and treatment, health or criminal justice services is often a key component of the surveillance and control of female drug users. Jane found out that one of the drugs workers at the drugs service she used had seen her and phoned social services. The following Monday her social worker and support workers arrived for an impromptu visit and told her:

> '"We know you've started working again. We are going to take these kids in foster care. You can either give them over to us now or we will get the police and take them off you".' (Jane, 26)

Jane said she was shocked and upset as she loved her children, and thought that she always gave them everything they needed. She maintained that:

> 'Every appointment they needed to go to, everything that needed to be done for 'em was done for 'em.' (Jane, 26)

Jane thought that if the police were involved, it would get her children upset, so she agreed to them being taken. She felt that the social service workers were dishonest with her, had wanted to take her children from her all along, and were looking for faults:

> 'It felt like, all the way along they wanted to take the kids off me and that lot. And 'erm … it's the way, like … even after they took 'em off us one of the community support team turned round and goes, "If it had been up to me, you

wouldn't even have taken 'em out of the hospital, we'd have put them into foster care straight away".' (Jane, 26)

As discussed in Chapter Five (see pp 132–134), despite the fact that drug users are likely to comprise a sizeable proportion of social workers' clients, they typically receive inadequate training on drug issues and therefore lack understanding. Jane described her perception of her social worker's attitude towards her: as a drug user and therefore an incapable mother.

> 'The social worker ... she saw it, like, if you took the drug you would be out of your face and can't cope with the babies and that lot.... They think all drug users can't look after kids, which is not right, if you're just taking it to be normal every day.' (Jane, 26)

Women's insights into their own situation and what they need are ignored and invalidated, and they are expected to accept professional 'expert' discourses about their lives. Jane said that she felt that social services should have been more honest about their intentions from the beginning, and that the report about her and her partner that was used in court was "full of lies". Women have described feeling deceived by prejudiced social workers who had an agenda to remove children from drug-using women's care all along in other studies (Buchanan and Young, 2002; Kullar 2009; Pollack 2010). Like Jane, many of the women complained about the court process concerning the custody of their children. As Shelly asserted:

> 'They don't have to prove any allegation they make. It's not like a court of law where when they make an allegation, it has to be proven with fact. They can just make statements left, right and centre, to weigh their case and the judge will hear all this.' (Shelly, 35)

Jane said she trusted social services and was open with them and felt betrayed. At the time of interview, she still had all her babies' pictures and clothes and things around their flat:

> 'So I'd had about four or five months with them, then all of a sudden they are not there anymore. So I think that's another reason I just stayed on the drugs, just to shut off the emotions, like. 'Cause every time like I feel clucking

in the morning or something, it all just hits me 'cause I've got the pictures hanging up on my walls in my front room and that lot. And I just burst into tears and that lot and it's like, as if, like, "Why am I crying" and then you realise why.' (Jane, 26)

Whenever Jane sees twin babies in the street, she wonders if they are hers. Since losing hers she has been suicidal, and her and her partner's drug use has escalated:

'When we lost them, I felt really down. I wanted to use more, we wanted it more just to, like, try and shut out the emotions and that, because we'd had enough. Half the time I just wanted to kill myself, it was that bad. And now it's just like.... I just need to get past every day without thinking about it.' (Jane, 26)

Jane felt her babies gave her life meaning and she has nothing to live for anymore.

At 21 years old, Fleur found out she was five months pregnant. She was advised by a professional not to give up using heroin or it would hurt her baby. Once her baby was born, she felt she could not stop using as she was frightened she would not cope, and didn't have anyone to look after the baby. When her son was 14 months old, Fleur and her boyfriend had an argument and "came to blows". Social services intervened, stated that Fleur's son was at risk and placed him under an interim care order. At the time of the interview, Fleur shared parental responsibility with her local authority. She was told that her drug use and mental health problems meant that she was incapable of looking after her son. Fleur had been diagnosed with depression when she was 17, and social services told her that if she wanted custody of her son, she had to address her drug problem. She went to a drug agency for help, and came off heroin. Social services then told her she had to address her mental health problems. Fleur went to see a psychologist who said that she should be given a chance after a series of assessments, but Fleur was still not allowed custody of her son:

'They said "If you address your drug issue you can have him back". I did that, but then they started saying I had to address my mental health problems. I had to go and see people, I went and did that. I've seen five different psychologists all saying we should be given a chance, but it's got us nowhere. Then they tried started saying my asthma would be a problem. They're trying to find anything.' (Fleur, 25)

Fleur complained that her and her partner had been "looked at under a microscope" by social services, but to no avail:

'Me and Dean say we wouldn't have done what we've done for the past year, assessments and everything, if it's all for nothing. They look at you under a microscope, every detail, your past, what you're doing now, every problem. It's none of their business but we've done it willingly. Yet they're still not prepared to give us a break. What's the point? I'm fed up with kissing everyone's fucking arse.' (Fleur, 25)

Fleur is still waiting for a decision from social services concerning the custody of her son. The women thus felt punished by services that were supposed to help them. So, while it may seem that welfare agents can be distinguished from criminal justice agents in that they are intended to 'alleviate pain, to cure [and] to comfort', like police and prison officers they tend to 'exercise a power of normalisation' (Foucault 1991 [1975], p 308). While appearing to help, teach and counsel the 'deviant' mothers in this study, social services employed disciplinary techniques of normalisation forming a 'carceral continuum' in their lives.

Normalise, discipline and punish

The normalising powers of social services did little to alleviate the pain, discomfort, social and economic marginalisation and gendered victimisation the women in this study experienced, but rather seemed to perpetuate, reinforce and expose them further to it. A third of the women in this sample ($n=13$) complained about how their lives were left in chaos after social services intervention. They explained how their lives were damaged by the threat of or actually having their children taken away. Sky was living on the road in a convoy with her two-year-old son when she moved to Badstone. She had got into heroin several years previously, in Thailand. She described how her life changed when the local social services forced her to get housed:

'The local social services were saying to get housed or they'd take my kid off me because I din't have a toilet and stuff like that in the caravan. So I got housed and that's really when the nightmare started, here in Badstone. It was really bad. I got housed but I got housed right on the front line.' (Sky, 52)

Sky was housed in the main scoring area of the city, and her drug use escalated. She explained how she ended up doing all kinds of things for money, to buy heroin, and her life ended up in chaos:

'It wasn't until I came to Badstone and lived on the front line that I really went over board. I was out of control, like, I'd go shoplifting when I was already on bail and stuff like that, and not really caring, just doing anything to get money, more or less.' (Sky, 52)

Sky started selling drugs in order to raise money, which attracted the attention of the local drug squad. She was raided every year for the next three years, and threatened with social services. When the drug squad eventually reported her to social services, she was advised by her social worker to put her son into voluntary care. Sky described how her life was plunged into further chaos when she lost her son:

'Well, he went into care, after that, he went into care, and he was only five [crying], six, and it was voluntary care which meant that I could get him back providing I was alright. But what happened was, because he'd gone into care, my life just fell to bits, it really did, that's when I went on to the streets and 'erm, I din't realise how much he'd been holding me together. And when he'd gone, I just had nothing and 'erm, that's when I went onto the streets and just did stupid, stupid things. My life went crazy, it just sort of plummeted really.' (Sky, 52)

Suzi was living with her partner and her three children when she started smoking heroin in the evenings to relax. She explained that her four-year-old son had really bad temper tantrums since he'd had an operation, and he took it out on her disabled daughter. When Suzi's daughter had 12 non-accidental bruises on her, social services refused to believe that they were caused by Suzi's son, and threatened to take her children into care. Suzi's boyfriend took the blame so that Suzi would not lose her children. Suzi had a nervous breakdown because of "all the upset and depression", and ended up having to put her three children into voluntary care. Suzi was then illegally evicted from her home. She described the chaos she found herself in:

> 'I felt like life wasn't worth living because I'd lost my kids. There was nothing left for me. I'd had to put my children into voluntary care. What else was there? I'd lost my bloke because of it, because they weren't believing it ... then I ended up on the streets.' (Suzi, 31)

The first night that Suzi's son went into care, he broke one of the foster carer's arms and one of her ribs. Consequently, all of the charges against Suzi's boyfriend were dropped. However, Suzi's life was already in chaos at this point due to the intervention of social services in her life. Suzi blamed them for the state her life was in:

> 'I lost my children, I lost my house, I lost my boyfriend. I'd lost everything and everything just caved in at once. So, like, the gear was the best escape for me because I had nothing else.... They ruined a big part of my life, to be honest.' (Suzi, 31)

The accounts of these women demonstrate that rather than improving their situation, social services operated to plunge their lives into further chaos. Rather than seeing themselves as 'chaotic', irrational and irresponsible, the women saw themselves as victims of prejudiced social services.

Saveable, changeable, programmable and recoverable

In the psychosocial accounts the women provided, they blamed themselves for their dependence and the situation they found themselves in. At the same time, they wanted to believe they could stop taking drugs and were saveable, changeable, transformable and programmable. However, the most dominant subjectivity they adopted for themselves was that of being enmeshed in dependency and a drug-using lifestyle. Their accounts demonstrated that getting off heroin and/or crack was, for them, not simply about making a choice. They explained how they felt enmeshed in illicit drug taking because of physical and/or psychological addiction, the fear of having nothing to block their feelings, not being able to imagine a life without drugs, and having only drug-using friends and partners. The women's narratives also contained other stories about why they felt trapped in a life of drug dependence and a drug-using lifestyle. They also described feeling unable to stop using and to escape the drug world due to social and economic marginalisation, social regulation and a lack of services to fit their needs.

Socially and economically marginalised women

Policy discourse responsibilises female users through the language of 'reintegration' and 'recovery' (see Chapter Four, pp 105–110 and Chapter Five 126–127). The assumption is of a previous state to which the dependent user must return in which one does not use drugs, has a supportive family, a home and a job. All the user apparently has to do is to get treatment and find work to 'reintegrate' and 'recover'. Failure by a dependent user to 'recover' is regarded as faulty thinking, individual weakness and pathology, rather than a consequence of social and economic disadvantage, lack of service provision or practical support. However, the women's accounts provided resistant understandings of their struggle to change their lives that cannot be reduced to making the right, 'rational' choices, accessing treatment and finding work.

All of the women who were still using ($n=28$) described wanting to feel included within the 'straight world', which they expressed in terms of a wish to be 'normal'. This meant different things for different women. For all of them, inclusion involved getting 'clean', and for most, it meant having a happy family, a home, furthering their education, getting a job and financial security:

> 'I wanna go back to college. I wanna do hair and beautician.' (Nicky, 23)

> 'At the end of the day I wanna get off the drugs, get a little job, a little normal ... not normal, you know what I'm saying. I just wanna get a nice little life going, like, but.... I dunno what sort of job. I dunno what really I want, but just something that I can live comfortably and be contented.' (Jamie, 29)

For some of the women, being 'normal' involved being with someone they loved. Some wanted 'normal' friendships with non-users who they felt cared about them:

> 'I just want to be happy. I want both of us to get clean. Just get little jobs and lead a normal life.' (Sonya, 24)

Some of the women stated that they wanted to have a family or be reunited with the family they had:

> 'That is my dream for the future is to be able to come off drugs and to live a normal sense of life, to be able to get a little job and to be able to settle down with a man and have a family, you know. I don't want to be like this for the rest of my life.' (Tina, 24)

Several women specified that having a 'normal' life involved them having financial security:

> 'I'd like to become clean and to have a family of my own and a nice little house of my own and a job and just to be normal, really, and not to have money worries.' (Cat, 19)

At the same time, as discussed in Chapter Six (see pp 198–199), for most of the women in the sample, a drug-using lifestyle was the way most of them had lived their adult lives. They could not imagine a 'normal' life without drugs and a drug-using lifestyle, as they had limited or no experience of it. For example, Lara said she "had no confidence" and "felt absolutely bare" without drugs (see Chapter Six, p 198). She said that she had started trying drugs when she was 10 years old, and became dependent on heroin at 13. She played truant from school, had been suspended four times and left school at 15 with no qualifications. She had left a six-year relationship with a verbally abusive heroin dealer and user, and was working as a sex worker. She seemed to consider this to be positive, as she saw it as 'standing on her own two feet'. Lara had never had a 'normal' job and has a criminal record. In relation to her previous existence when she had been using more, weighed five-and-a-half stone and was dependent on her ex, she felt she was doing well:

> 'I'm standing on my own two feet 'cause he always said to me, "You won't survive on your own without me". So I thought, "Right I'll show you". You know, and I have got myself together and I've got my habit right down to what it was. It used to be £250 a day and now it's 20 or 30 quid's worth. So I'm doing quite … really well.' (Lara, 23)

Lara had a new partner and was pregnant. She said she wanted a home and to get clean. However, a change to her life cannot be reduced to one of making the right choices to seek treatment and employment. She said she had been through rehabilitation eight times, but did not feel at the time she was ready to come off heroin and crack, and now she would be refused funding. Lara has no qualifications, work experience and limited job prospects due to her criminal record. Rather than reintegration and recovery, invention, discovery and integration may be a more accurate description of what Lara needs. This seemed to be the case for many of the women in this study who had never known a different life to be reintegrated into.

For most of the women still using, getting off drugs, giving up criminal activities and finding work did not necessarily involve an end to their social and economic marginalisation or relegation to living on the fringes of society, as they saw it. Having a 'normal' life for them involved poverty, unemployment and/or low-paid work, and thus a return to the kind of lifestyle they had originally used drugs to escape from. Many of the women had grown up in care, were from relatively poor, working-class backgrounds, or single-parent families. Such women face specific barriers when trying to come off drugs to do with their initial social and economic marginalisation that cannot be reduced to problems with their current drug use or access to employment. These women's lives never involved having many choices. Arguably, the construction of the solution to 'problem' drug users as that of reprogramming them to make the *right* choices is setting them up to fail.

Many described feeling disillusioned by what inclusion within the 'straight world' and their perception of what a 'normal' lifestyle had to offer them. Many had led criminal lifestyles to fund their habits and had left school with no qualifications, so the kind of low-paid jobs they felt able to get were not at all appealing. Mandy had left school with no qualifications, and had limited work experience. She described her attitude to the lifestyle she saw as the alternative to her current one as a drug user:

> 'Yeah – I ain't ready to give it up now. Do you know what I mean? I mean, what's normal life? It's boring. I don't particularly wanna sit behind a till for 40 hours a week for 200 quid when I can make it out 'ere in a night! Then again – do I still wanna be a prostitute for the rest of my life? No I don't. But now I'm pretty confused, very confused.'
> (Mandy, 24)

Some described how they had trouble adjusting to a non-drug-using lifestyle when they had tried. Mandy revealed that she could not resist taking money from her work when she was a barmaid:

> 'Trouble is, though, if I sit behind a till, do you know what I mean? [laughs].... I'm likely to take the money out ... [laughs].... To tell you the truth. I did when I worked in a pub, I used to take a hundred pound out every night.'
> (Mandy, 24)

Significantly, the women interviewed who saw themselves as 'in recovery' were more likely to be from middle-class backgrounds, and their movement between the 'drug world' and the 'straight world' had continued throughout their drug careers. These women were more likely to have pursued an education and worked in legitimate jobs prior to their drug careers, and were less likely to have been involved in the criminal justice system. For example, Hope was from a middle-class background, was privately educated, and had worked in a bank for 10 years. She supported her heroin and crack habit through financial scams she learned while working in a bank, and never got caught. After leaving her job, she moved on to dealing with her partner. Hope was able to get a part-time job as a cashier once she decided she wanted to get off heroin, to 'create some structure' in her life. After several attempts at getting clean with her heroin-using partner, Hope left him, moved to a rural area where she didn't know anyone, got a methadone prescription, and made some new non-using friends. She had been clean for eight years at the time of interview, and was working as a drugs counsellor.

The middle-class women's involvement in crime and/or sex work tended to come much later in their drug careers. Most ($n=8$) supported their habits through legitimate work for many years before they lost or left their jobs, and turned to crime and/or sex work. Only two working-class women in this study had supported their habits through legitimate work for some time before losing or leaving their jobs.

The middle-class women's education and employment status meant they were able to move more freely between the 'drug world' and the 'straight world'. For instance, Shelly supported her habit through her normal wage as a psychiatric nurse for many years before she turned to credit card fraud when she became pregnant. After she had her daughter, she gave up all criminal activity and started working again as a nurse. When she and her partner were short of money, they decided to raise money again through crime.

In contrast, the social and economic marginalisation experienced by the working-class women due to their involvement in crime and sex work tended to be more sustained and acute than that experienced by the middle-class women. Once the working-class women became part of the 'drug world', they were more likely to become stuck within it and locked out of the 'straight world'. Jane started selling sex for money when introduced to the idea through a friend. As Rosenbaum (1981, p 11) found in her study of heroin-using women from working-class backgrounds:

> Ultimately the woman addict is locked into the heroin life and locked out of the conventional world.... Typically, she begins life with a status of relatively reduced options and then drifts into the heroin world; the conditions associated with this life steadily, almost inevitably, narrow her options further.

Most of the women who became involved in crime, whether from middle-class or working-class backgrounds, ended up with criminal records. This meant exclusion from the jobs market for many of them. Shelly described how being caught doing chequebook fraud caused her to lose her career as a psychiatric nurse, which for her, was also the loss of 'normality':

> 'I realised it fucked up my career and that was it, fuck it. I've lost normality now. I won't be going to work. Hiding this secret, admittedly, but outwardly portraying that I was a normal person, and that's gone now.' (Shelly, 35)

Involvement in crime also led to time in prison for most of the women, which reinforced social and economic marginalisation through further exclusion from the jobs market, homelessness, discrimination, social isolation and separation from children. The women gradually began to see themselves as less and less recoverable, changeable and saveable.

Lack of social support and social networks

The women were subject to social and economic marginalisation prior to and increasingly during their drug careers due to a lack of social support and a lack of social networks. This has been termed 'network poverty', whereby individuals are deprived of the social support and informal help needed to participate in community life (Pierson,

2002). Pierson (2002) distinguishes between networks for 'getting by' and those for 'getting ahead'. Networks for getting by are those found within relationships between family members, close friends and neighbours. These can provide emotional support, help and support during illness, childcare, somewhere to stay, small loans and cash in emergencies, or to make ends meet. The middle-class and working-class women in the sample both experienced a lack of social networks for getting by and getting ahead, but the situation was worse for the working-class women, especially in terms of networks for getting ahead.

The women experienced their drug taking as a source of separation from others, loneliness and isolation (see Chapter Six, pp 174–181). The majority of them thus had few networks for getting by. However, some did receive support from their families, whether they were from middle-class or working-class backgrounds. Several ($n=4$) said that they could always rely on their mothers for support, and they had done so throughout their drug career. These women received emotional support, financial assistance, somewhere to live and help with childcare when they needed it:

> 'My mum's such a nice person, she'd do anything for anyone. She done so much for me and I'd treated her so shitty over the years, but she'd still stuck by me no matter what, and I'd put her through so much.' (Cat, 19)

A few women spoke of other family members such as fathers, grandmothers, or aunties who had helped them in difficult times with particular needs, such as financial assistance and childcare.

Although the women inhabited social worlds comprised mostly of other addicts, only two women said they had a friend within the 'drug world' they inhabited whom they could trust and received support from. A few ($n=4$) said they had partners who supported them in some way. Only a few of the women said they had friends who were non-drug users. Cat described how being friends with non-drug users was important to her as they helped her feel 'normal' and hence not so excluded from the straight world:

> 'I've got some friends where I live now who aren't users but a lot of 'em don't know I use so it's just.... I go out with them every now and again.... And like they come round and it's quite nice because it's a bit of like just normalness. Do you know what I mean? 'Cause we'll just go out and have a drink and just be normal sort of thing, so.... (Cat, 19)

Most of the women (*n*=27) gave accounts in which their drug taking caused them to become isolated from friends and family (see Chapter Six, pp 174–179). Apart from the family support and friendships discussed above, most ended up having little contact with non-users, and mixed only with other addicts. The women thus had few social networks for getting by. As Rosenbaum found in her study:

> A separate social world is formed, composed almost exclusively of addicts, and the longer the addict is part of this social world, the more isolated from the non-addict world she becomes. (Rosenbaum, 1981, p 53)

Half of the women still using (*n*=14) claimed that they had no one at all to turn to for help or support when they needed it. As Sky said:

> 'I wish I'd known better or I wish I'd had some help or someone helping to direct me, you know.' (Sky, 52)

Most of the women lacked social support for getting by. This meant that their options for getting ahead were also limited. These involve the provision of information and opportunities for individuals concerning employment opportunities, education, training and advancing their interests (Pierson, 2002). Networks for getting by and for getting ahead were not mutually exclusive but were interdependent. Most of the women lacked social networks for getting ahead. The main social networks for getting ahead used by the working-class women seemed to be ones they had formed within the 'drug world'. These provided the women with an education in and introduction to criminal activities and sex work. For most of them such networks were formed early in their drug careers, and in some cases, during their early teens. Nicky, like other women, was introduced to crime and/or sex work by others who told her what to expect:

> 'When I was here last time, which was a year ago, I had a friend called Debbie and she just took me down to the beat in Green Parade. So if I started working I could get a bit of money from there. And she said, "Come with me, put something nice on and put these condoms in your pocket".' (Nicky, 23)

Most of the middle-class women formed social networks for getting ahead within the 'drug world' later in their drug careers, after they had lost legitimate work. Shelly described how she had become involved in chequebook fraud:

> 'When I had a salary to cover my addiction I didn't commit any crime. I'd never been in trouble with the police. It was only after I'd had my daughter and I was on maternity leave that I started doing cheque fraud. I was working for a woman who I met in the maternity hospital who was coming in selling half-price nappies and tins of baby milk and stuff to the mums in the maternity hospital. I wondered why, and we got chatting. She introduced me to cheque fraud and taught me how to do it really.' (Shelly, 35)

Due to either the financial support they received from parents and/or their employment status, the middle-class women tended to move more freely between the 'drug world' and the 'straight world'. They were thus more likely to keep or form new networks in the 'straight world' throughout their drug career. These networks gave them access to training and work for getting off drugs and getting ahead. Compared to poor, working-class women, these women were less socially and economically marginalised to begin with, and thus more amenable to programmes of change and 'recovery'. Conversely, poor working-class women were more likely to struggle to make it in the 'straight world', and with that, more likely to be responsibilised for their failure to abstain. Social and economic marginalisation was an important factor in the women's entry into and exit out of a drug-using lifestyle. However, medicalisation gives authority to pathologising constructions of female users in policy discourse so that structural issues are individualised and female users continue to be seen as 'authors of their own misfortune'.

Disciplined women

The ways in which the women in this study were punished, disciplined and regulated through the criminal justice system and social services has already been discussed. The women were also subject to punitive and disciplinary treatment in their use of the public health service and in drug treatment. This was an obstacle to women seeing themselves as changeable, recoverable and saveable. Apparently benevolent services designed to help them were experienced as punitive and demoralising, and made them feel as if they were undeserving. They experienced health and drug treatment services as punitive and demoralising in various ways, including by being excluded from them, being dismissed and treated with contempt, and having their access to services or medication obstructed, stopped or withheld. This reflects drug policy discourse that situates female users as badly behaved, irresponsible service users, deserving of disciplinary treatment and/or coercion.

Many of the women complained they were denied primary healthcare services as well as being judged and discriminated against by health and social care professionals for being drug users. They described being treated as if they were time wasters, not normal or out to get something, by GPs, and nurses in particular. This discrimination conditioned the healthcare the women received. Some complained they were denied primary healthcare services. They found they had difficulty in accessing support from GPs in particular. The women were told certain GPs did not accept drug users, which the women described as making them feel unworthy and undeserving – punishment for being an "addict":

> 'You get doctors who say, "We don't take drug users in our surgery. I think you'd better go somewhere else". It makes you feel like shit.' (Sonya, 24)

Shelly said that GPs assume that addicts are out to get something:

> 'I mean GPs and stuff, if you're an addict, you really don't count in that they automatically think you are out to get something from them.' (Shelly, 35)

Shelly described the consequences of the discriminatory attitude she had received from GPs:

> 'I've been rushed into hospital three times this year by ambulance, each of the three times I've been in, I've been to the doctors three or four days beforehand, telling them I am unwell, there's something really not right, and every time they fob me off really not wanting to know, and it's got to the point where I've actually collapsed and had to be rushed into hospital with a kidney problem, a heart problem and, 'erm, a lung problem.' (Shelly, 35)

Fleur described how she was sent away from a psychiatric unit when they discovered she was a drug user. She had originally been admitted to hospital because she had taken an overdose after being gang-raped:

'I went down the police station but started crying and told them about the overdose I took. I was admitted to the hospital. I walked out but went back 12 hours later and asked to be sectioned ... it was the only way I could see a future.... I got told at Barrow they didn't want my sort there because I was a drug user and I got discharged.... I had nowhere to go.' (Fleur, 25)

Shelly was told that she was "not fit to be a mother" by a nurse at a maternity ward where she had just had a baby. The nurse threatened to break confidentiality, report Shelly to her employers, and get her deregistered:

'One nurse decided it was an utter disgrace that I was a nurse.... It was really hard as she told me I wasn't fit to be a mother, and she gave me a really hard time.' (Shelly, 35)

A consequence of the dismissive and contemptuous treatment the women received and another way in which they experienced a punitive approach was by having their access to services or medication obstructed. Several complained about having services or treatment withheld from them because they were drug users. Nicky explained how she was punished for being "a dirty smack head" by being made to wait for her medication which was withheld from her at a maternity ward:

'I was treated like I was a freak, a dirty smack head. When I asked for my methadone when I was in hospital, "Oh you got yourself into this situation, you'll have to wait". You know, and when you need your methadone, you need your methadone there and then, not later, now, you need it, you know.' (Nicky, 23)

Several women objected to how they were asked to leave treatment programmes, and had their methadone stopped suddenly by drug agencies. This made the women ill and they had to use more heroin to get through the withdrawal. Sharon described how she had witnessed other people withdrawing from methadone after it had been stopped suddenly:

'I've seen people who've been on 50mg a day and then been cut to nothing and then been left to get on with it.

Now I've seen them rolling round in a ball for three, four, five weeks, and everyday runs into another day that runs into a week, a month and it is four times worse to come off than any opiate substance that is naturally coming from the earth.' (Sharon, 39)

Rosy was thrown off a programme for using heroin on top of methadone. She insisted that she had not used heroin, and explained why having her methadone supply cut off suddenly was experienced as punitive:

'You still withdraw even though you use heroin, you still withdraw from methadone badly. That's why I have to use more heroin at the moment. They just cut me straight off dead! "Ta da, Rosy, you've lost your prescription".' (Rosy, 47)

Since Rosy's methadone prescription was stopped, her heroin habit is worse than ever. These disciplinary measures were not experienced by the women as for their own good, but rather made their attempts to deal with their health needs, difficult times and managing their dependency and recovery extremely onerous.

Neglected women

As outlined in Chapter Six (p 196), all of the women in this study still using drugs ($n=27$) said they wanted to stop. They wanted to believe they could be reprogrammed and transformed, and had faith in helping agencies or 'experts' that would one day help them do so. At the same time, most of the women who had tried, found it difficult to access satisfactory treatment services, and saw themselves as trapped in dependency. While there is some acknowledgement in policy discourse that women's treatment needs may not fit current services, failure by women to 'recover' is constructed as due to individual weakness and bad choice making rather than a lack of service provision. Most of the women who wanted to come off drugs complained about the difficulty they had in getting clean due to a lack of services. Rather than being bad choice makers, they felt there was a distinct lack of choices:

'It's a shame 'cause there's a lot of people out there that are ruining themselves that want help but they can't get it 'cause it's not there for them.' (Tina, 24)

'I just feel that there's not so much help there. You have to really go out and fucking search for it, in the fucking woods. Do you know what I mean? I seem to be searching forever.' (Cat, 19)

Many said that support within the community was largely limited to methadone prescribing, and users had to 'prove themselves' on a methadone prescription before they could access support to do a detox. Current UK policy is oriented to the promotion and facilitation of more 'recovery' and abstinence-based treatments (see Chapter Four, p 105). Such an orientation was supported by many of the women in this study who complained about the lack of detox services in the community that they wanted access to:

'I would like to just be able to go in. I don't want to be on methadone to be honest. I would rather just go in through my heroin use, go in and just do my 10-day detox. Come straight off the heroin. The withdrawal from methadone, I find worse than the withdrawal from heroin.' (Shelly, 35)

'I've tried speaking to people about detox, but no one seems to want to help, saying that I've got to go through loads and loads of meetings.' (Rachel, 21)

Most of the women who had been prescribed methadone ($n=17$) said they found methadone substitution unhelpful in helping them get off heroin. This was largely to do with the way it was administered. Some said the amount prescribed was not enough to prevent them from feeling ill:

'You end up losing your script because you are using on top. Any addict will tell you they don't give you enough and it will take months of putting it up 5mls a month to get to a dosage that will keep you well for 24 hours. Most of them under-medicate you.' (Shelly, 35)

Some women, especially those who had been on methadone long term, said it was a harmful drug:

'Methadone is worse; it kills your insides.' (Tina, 24)

Many (*n*=16) said that it was counterproductive as they ended up with a double habit:

> 'You're trying to get off one thing and you end up getting on another thing, and you're in more of a mess than you was at the start.' (Cat, 19)

The idea that methadone has been used as a form of social control and regulation was supported by many of the women's accounts. Many criticised the stringent rules and regulations attached to receiving a methadone prescription, which they thought were unnecessary and counterproductive:

> 'I think methadone is really bad, I really do. I think it's a really poor substitute. It makes people suffer profusely. I think the people who actually prescribe the methadone are too forceful and their conditions are absolutely unreal. If they knew what it was like to actually be on it and they had to cope with the rules and laws, they'd realise how hard it was for someone who has that type of addiction.' (Sharon, 38)

Sharon had been prescribed methadone for 12 years. She complained about how receiving a prescription meant that she had to stay in one place because of having to pick up a weekly prescription. This was a particular problem for her while she was married to her violent husband and when trying to escape from him:

> 'In the end I escaped from the house and like an idiot I left my medication at home. I went without my methadone for four days and I ended up collapsing on the road and I ended up being taken into hospital. And the hospital they wouldn't give me any medication either because I'd already had my medication allocated to me for that period of time and it was in my house and I was scared to go back 'cause I thought I'm gonna go straight back into what I've just left.' (Sharon, 38)

Some complained about having to take their methadone at the chemist all in one go:

> 'Let me take it in two lots rather than one, because you are well for 12 hours, then you're sick and you're waiting to get to the chemist.' (Shelly, 35)

Hope was the only woman interviewed who had successfully been reduced on methadone and stayed clean. She explained that she was ready to stop using and went to her GP who she said knew very little about dependency but gave her a fixed schedule that she followed:

> 'She was like, "Well I'll give you this one chance but if you don't do it, that's it. So this is how we're going to do it: reduce it by 5ml a fortnight …" and so on, and there was no crossing her. She was only a tiny little woman, but you knew she meant what she was saying, and it just worked.' (Hope, 35)

The other 10 women who saw themselves as 'in recovery' had mostly managed this without the help of formal treatment services by detoxing by themselves, except for one who had attended a rehabilitation centre. Several said they had done this with the help of a non-using partner, family or a friend. All of these women said the key to their continued 'recovery' was their attendance at NA meetings, and the fact that they had acquired a whole network of ex-users for support.[1] Critics of the move towards the provision of more abstinence-based treatments have claimed there is a risk this will be at the expense of methadone prescribing and other harm reduction services, and will involve pressure for users to achieve abstinence before they are ready to do so (see Chapter Five, pp 105, 126). A few of the respondents said they had heard about cuts to harm minimisation and outreach services. Bridget, who had been 'clean' for a year and regularly attended NA, said this was what she had heard about an outreach needle and condom exchange service she had used when she had been a sex worker, and described how crucial this service had been to her survival:

> 'One of the most important things for me was the Outreach Team who brought me the needles. There was someone who cared enough that I was alive to come and look for me because I had some really bad abscesses and infections. You know there's no point paying someone to go to rehab six or seven times, but when they are ready, then, yeah. Until people want to change it's just about supporting

people till they're ready and having the services available to them.' (Bridget, 39)

Bridget discussed the risks she had taken using used needles and having sex without condoms when they were not available. She said that the harm reduction services were not only important for preventing harm, but also because they provided a stepping-stone for the people using them towards recovery:

> 'It's important that the services are there, but not just that, those services are a stepping-stone to the next stage. Once we get used to going to these places and find out that they are alright, then we might make that next step then.' (Bridget, 39)

Many of the women said they believed counselling would help them because they had so many issues relating to past trauma and abuse that they needed to address. However, they said it was difficult to get counselling because most services do not accept drug users, and counselling provided by drug agencies is usually short term. Some complained that services exposed them to too many involuntary users who were still using, and this made them vulnerable to relapse. Many of the women said that the help they had received was not sustained, and so it was easy for them to complete a drug programme or come out of a rehabilitation centre and then relapse. They wanted long-term support, tailored to their individual needs.

Many of them complained about the lack of services tailored for women. Several said that there was a lack of services with childcare provisions that made it impossible for them to access them. Some discussed how they experienced services as male-dominated, and how this made them feel uncomfortable. A few said they had difficulty accessing supported housing and thought there should be more available for women.

Many of the women said that they had to wait too long to get access to treatment when they wanted it. Rachel described what happened when she wanted to get clean:

> Rachel: 'Every time I goes to someone about going off the drugs and getting into detox and then rehab or getting a script they just don't wanna know. With my doctors it takes up to six months. With Badstone Drugs Project, I don't

know, I've kept going backwards and forwards, backwards and forwards to see them.'

Interviewer: 'And what do you want, a script? You want detox?'

Rachel: 'I wants either a script or detox, I want anything. Anything to get me off this.' (Rachel, 21)

She described what she saw as the importance of not having to wait for support within the community:

'When a heroin addict does want to come off, that's when they should get things organised for them. This thing where you have got to wait six months, heroin addicts, like myself, can turn round and say, well bollocks to it, what's the fucking point? What's the point in smoking another six months and by that time I'm going to be in and out of jail I don't know how many fucking times, so I may as well do it there.' (Rachel, 21)

Some also complained about the time it took for them to get into a rehabilitation centre. Sonya was told she would have to wait for a year before she could get funding to go. The women found it hard to get help at the time that was right for them to come off drugs. Betty thought services for female users in general were poor, and this amounted to governmental neglect:

'I think the services are ill-equipped and not organised ... neglecting me mentally and physically and not offering me the support I need. People think neglect just happens in the family, but society plays its game of neglect. The government neglects; it happens in health services, schools, the workplace. So when people have to take something, even cigarettes, to comfort them, it shows what type of society we are living in. They said, I was neglecting my son, but they need to look up what neglect means.' (Betty, 29)

While female users are situated as badly behaved, irresponsible service users, and at the same time responsible for changing their faulty way of thinking and becoming drug-free, services to facilitate this in the community are lacking.

Treatable criminals

The women described how in prison they were able to get the type of help they wanted for getting off drugs, that is, detox and counselling. As outlined previously (see p 237), for some of them prison was the only place where they had ever been clean since becoming dependent:

> 'The only time I've come off is in prison. I have had no outside help at all which I am trying to do at the moment and it still ain't going nowhere.' (Rachel, 21)

All of the women who had been in prison identified the help they had received to come off drugs there as the best kind of help they had received. Several explained that this was because they were able to do a detox straight away with medication to help them withdraw such as DFs and Valium, receive regular counselling and attend group counselling. Many complained about the fact that this kind of support was not available in the community:

> 'You shouldn't have to be sent to prison to get good counselling and help like that. Why should you go out and commit crimes and be put in prison just to get help?' (Tina, 24)

Some described how they deliberately committed crimes to be sent to prison in order to get clean, as Sonya explained:

> 'Everything got on top of me. I handed myself in and I said, "Send me to prison" and the judge who was there he actually said, "Look, your crimes aren't serious enough. We're not going to send you to prison". He said, "I'm going to adjourn it for a pre-sentence report but don't expect to get prison". So I didn't turn up to the pre-sentence report, I didn't turn up to court the next time. I did everything I could to get sent down. Then I got arrested again, and I said, "Look, send me to prison". I was just so desperate to get clean.... I thought, if rehab doesn't work, I can't do it out on the streets, I can't do it living with this guy. It just seemed like the only option.' (Sonya, 24)

However, prison was not always described as being a positive experience, and according to the women's accounts, facilities for doing a detox and counselling were variable from prison to prison. Sonya was not given detox the first time she went to prison. She described how she reached a point when she wanted to commit suicide:

> 'I was claustrophobic and I wasn't used to being locked up. It was like 23-hour lock-up at a time. It was horrific…. Simon didn't send me any clothes so I only had one change of clothes the whole time I was prison. I used to have to wash them out with soap every night, and I'd be shitting myself and throwing up. So I'd say "I've had a problem" but they wouldn't open the doors and give you any fresh clothes. So if you shit yourself, you just had to wash it out and hope you get through the next 24 hours. It was terrible and it got to the stage where I was ready to kill myself.' (Sonya, 24)

Sonya described how a girl in a neighbouring cell actually did kill herself:

> 'There was a girl, 21 I think she was. It was her first time in prison. And it could have been me, because they give you a shit detox, they don't take care of you. She hung herself; they didn't find her until 7 o'clock the next morning. This was like Christmas Eve or something like that. I was in the cell opposite her and I'd actually been talking to her the night before, and she was going, "I can't handle it." I said, "Hang in there, I was like that. You can handle it. You'll get through it". Anyway, she was found dead the next morning. There should have been more support there, if she was suicidal and she was in that much trouble.' (Sonya, 24)

The women said that the support they did receive in prison was rarely followed up in the community:

> 'You get a drug counsellor, so you do have a fair few meetings in prison with counsellors, but then they just don't organise it when you get out. As soon as your release date is up, they bump you off out the gates and that's it, you're off.' (Rachel, 21)

Having access to drugs again was experienced by many of the women as a reward they received when they got out of prison. Most started using again as soon as they were released in celebration of their freedom. For some of the women these experiences seemed to characterise a never-ending and self-perpetuating cycle of movement to and from custody. The governmental strategies, that is, treatment and social services used to help the women, were often experienced as punitive and those designed to punish, that is, imprisonment, was often experienced as a reward. This is an effect of a contradictory drug policy in which women drug users are constituted as 'bad' punishable victims *and* as treatable criminals.

Conclusion

The women in this study were able to contest, redefine, challenge and reconstruct the subjectivities that are ascribed to them in contemporary drug policy and academic discourse. The accounts the women provided of their lives posed a direct challenge to many of the negative, stigmatising constructions of dependent female users found in policy, and their medicalisation, welfarisation and punishment. While to some extent the women saw themselves as reprehensible, 'authors of their own misfortune' and responsible for harming themselves and others, their narratives involved alternative insights. They were able to negotiate and salvage positive identities for themselves as adaptive, rational and responsible despite their social and economic marginalisation, gendered violence and regulation, and governmental control and punishment.

Contemporary drug policy discourse constructs dependent female users as immoral, weak-willed bad choice makers in a society of risks, and responsible for their predicament as they chose to use drugs. All the dependent women in this study explained how they use drugs to block out emotional pain from experiences of trauma, abuse and isolation. They saw themselves as rational, responsible governors of their pain. While female illicit drug users are not authorised to govern their emotional pain with illegal drugs, some described how they were encouraged to use legal drugs prescribed by doctors for depression. Their accounts draw attention to the contradictory character of contemporary drug policy.

Female drug users are further positioned in policy discourse as immoral, chemically enslaved, out-of-control 'addicts' who have chosen to become dependent through irrational, disordered choice making. Problems experienced by them they have apparently brought on themselves, including illness, unemployment, poverty, homelessness, crime and sex work. Although the women in this study saw themselves in this way, at the same time they considered their drug taking as a rational and reasonable response to their life experiences. According to the psychosocial stories the women told, they saw themselves not as irresponsible, bad choice makers, but as rational, responsible, self-medicating governors of emotional pain caused by trauma, abuse and isolation.

The social accounts embedded within the women's narratives highlighted that for many of them, social and economic marginalisation pre-dated their drug use. Their early involvement in a 'drug scene', in friendships or relationships with drug users, seemed to provide them with more social and economic options. They wanted to escape their social disadvantage and made rational choices to do so. Furthermore, in response to feeling out of control of their drug use and behaviour at various points, the women retained certain moral and behavioural standards in order to stay in control and preserve their moral identities. To do so, they distinguished themselves from 'other' dependent drug users who were unlike themselves, and their 'true selves' from their 'addict selves'. Finally, they demonstrated that they were often caring, unselfish, giving and supportive of others, rather than selfish, immoral, drug-enslaved addicts. They risked their freedom, wellbeing and safety to financially support the drug habit of a partner through crime, sex work or sharing their benefits.

Drug policy discourse situates female drug users as 'bad', dangerous, irresponsible, immoral, criminal women who cause harm to young people, families and communities. The psychosocial accounts the women provided about their lives showed that, to some extent, they identified with this construction of their identities. Many had supported their habits through criminal activities and had committed crimes that they were ashamed of. Many described this as chemically driven behaviour that at times they were unable to control. However, despite this, they described the ways in which they had tried to keep their morals and principles and avoided harming others, committed predominantly low-level, minor crimes such as shoplifting, and eventually turning to sex work that they saw as only harming themselves.

The social stories the women told demonstrated that they were often socially and economically marginalised prior to their involvement in crime. The women were not simply chemically driven into crime, but instead made rational choices to escape poverty and raise money. They saw criminal activity as a rational, easier, more lucrative and attractive way of raising funds than the kind of low-paid work that was accessible to them. Most of the women were punished within the criminal justice system for crimes they had committed to fund their drug habits. However, they were not only criminals but also 'victims' of crimes of violence and abuse, the perpetrators of which have never been punished. They were thus subject to a gendered injustice system. The criminal justice system not only punished the women by taking away their freedom, but also damaged or severed their relationships with their children, destroyed their job prospects or careers, caused them to become homeless and reinforced their vulnerability to abuse and violence. The women were socially disadvantaged victims of abuse, victimised further by the rationalities and technologies constituting contemporary drug policy. However, resisting official constructions, they did not see themselves as victims or criminals, but as adaptive, rational and resourceful women, responsibly governing their pain and providing for their partners and children.

Female drug users are constituted as 'bad', unfit, irresponsible, incapable, undeserving mothers within drug policy discourse. The predominant psychosocial aspects of the women's accounts demonstrated that some women seemed to have taken on the identity of a 'bad mother' when they described their relationships with their children, and some had lost custody of or contact with their children. Their accounts involved an acceptance of the prescribed role of motherhood, whereby women are seen as solely responsible for the wellbeing of their children and the behaviour of fathers and the state are not. All of them saw themselves as responsible for the health and wellbeing of their children, and blamed themselves for any harm that their children suffered. At the same time, many said they did not regard themselves as unfit mothers by virtue of their drug use, and described how they stopped or reduced it when they realised they were pregnant, cared for their children and did their upmost to protect them from their drug use. Their narratives showed that their drug use was only one obstacle to their mothering among many, including domestic violence, sub-standard housing, poverty, lack of support and prejudiced family members and professionals.

Policy discourse also constructs drug-using mothers as educable, saveable, and changeable mothers who, with the help of welfare agents, can stop using and become 'normal', responsible and capable. The women discussed the interventions of social services in their lives. They said they felt judged, misled, punished and betrayed by uninformed social workers who they felt had an agenda to take their children from them all along. The normalising powers of social services did little to alleviate the pain, discomfort, social and economic marginalisation and gendered victimisation the women in this study experienced, but rather seemed to perpetuate, reinforce and expose them further to it. Rather than seeing themselves as irrational and irresponsible unfit mothers, the women began to see themselves as victims of prejudiced social services.

While drug policy discourse situates female drug users as chemically enslaved, 'bad', immoral criminals, unfit mothers and irresponsible, irrational, bad choice makers, they are simultaneously constituted as recoverable, changeable, educable and saveable. All the women in this study still using drugs said they wanted to stop. They wanted financial security, a stable home, employment, friendships, acceptance and to be 'normal'. They wanted to believe they could be reprogrammed and transformed, and had faith in helping agencies or 'experts' that would one day help them do so. The women explained how they felt enmeshed in illicit drug use due to physical and/or psychological dependence, the fear of having nothing to block their feelings, not being able to imagine a life without drugs and having only drug-using friends and partners.

The social accounts they provided showed that their desire to be 'normal' conflicted with their alienation from the 'straight world' through social and economic marginalisation, social regulation and a lack of services to fit their needs. For most of the women still using, getting off drugs, giving up criminal activities and finding work did not necessarily involve an end to their social and economic marginalisation. Having a 'normal' life for them involved poverty, unemployment and/or low-paid work, and thus a return to the kind of lifestyle they had originally used drugs to escape from. Many had grown up in care, were from relatively poor, working-class backgrounds, or single-parent families. Their initial social and economic marginalisation meant they faced specific barriers when trying to come off drugs that are not reducible to problems with their current drug use or access to employment. These women's lives never involved having many choices. The working-class women were less able to move between the 'drug world' and the 'straight world', and were more likely to lack the social networks for getting ahead. They were thus more likely to be responsibilised and held to account for their predicament.

Apparently benevolent services designed to help the women were experienced as punitive and demoralising. The women were excluded from services, dismissed and treated with contempt, and had their access to medication obstructed, stopped or withheld. They also experienced a lack of accessible treatment services. While there is some acknowledgement in policy discourse that women's treatment needs may not fit current services, failure by women to 'recover' is constructed as due to individual weakness and bad choice making rather than a lack of service provision. Rather than being bad choice makers, the women felt there was a distinct lack of choices. For this reason, some felt that jail was the easiest place for them to detox and get drug counselling. They were punished in treatment services and supported in the criminal justice system.

Note

[1] A total of 10 women were accessed through NA.

Conclusion

The aim of this book was to explore the ways in which the governance of illicit drug use shapes female dependent drug users' lives. Their subjectivities, and hence their experiences, are shaped and regulated by drug policies. The relationship between the social regulation of female drug users and the construction of their subjectivities has been explored, which involved, first, an investigation into the ways in which women who are identified as having 'problematic' drug use are positioned in academic discourse and in official governmental policy. Second, it involved an analysis of the dominant governmental technologies of power from which the key constructions of women as 'problematic' drug users emanate in the UK, US and Canada – punishment and prohibition, medicalisation and welfarisation. The construction of female users' subjectivities in policy discourse and the impact the characteristics ascribed to them have on their experiences have also been examined. Third, it investigated the meanings that women who identify as having dependent drug use attach to their drug use and to themselves. Insights were gathered from the in-depth accounts of 40 female drug users in the UK. Finally, the ways in which dependent female drug users position themselves vis-à-vis the ways in which they are positioned in governmental technologies was explored. This involved an examination of the operation of three technologies of the self operating in the lives of the 40 female drug users – the ascription of characteristics, normalisation and responsibilisation.

An analysis of the punishment and prohibition, public health and welfare strands of drug policy discourse, and how female users are constructed as a problem to be governed within them, was conducted. This was based on the assumption that objects of government are discursively constructed, and it is these constructions that make female users amenable to governmental intervention and regulation. It was found that the discourses of drug policy are not mutually exclusive, but interweave, overlap and combine in different ways to make particular subject positions available to female users. These emanate from the operation of governmental technologies operating in the UK, US and Canada, which intersect, intertwine and reinforce each other in the regulation of female illicit drug users. An analysis of detailed life historical interviews with 40 female users focused on how they saw themselves, and also explored how they both internalised and resisted governmental constructions of themselves.

An analysis of drug policy and academic discourse on women's illicit drug use showed that women drug users are constituted in contradictory ways, and their interviews showed that the way in which they see themselves was also marked by contradiction. So, the analysis of authoritative discourse asserted the following:

- Public health discourse situates female users as immoral, weak-willed, bad choice makers, or as the psychopathological clients of 'expert' doctors or nurse prescribers who have the medical knowledge/power to 'cure' them. Women who use illegal drugs are considered deviant and immoral when drugs are self-administered, while 'experts' with the medical authority may prescribe legal drugs to women, serving a normalising function. Once the women comply with their drug use being administered through the medical profession, regardless of the relative addictiveness or harmfulness of the drugs prescribed, their normality, rationality and responsibility is considered to be restorable.
- Public health discourse grounded in the disease model constructs female users as *both* psychopathological, chemically enslaved addicts, faulty thinkers and choice makers *as well as* rational, responsible, educable, free choice makers. Such a contradiction is resolved in the call to intervene (usually through education and counselling) in ways that help the women make the *right* choices, that is, drug abstinence.
- Public health discourse also constitutes female users as 'polluted', promiscuous, immoral, disease-spreading prostitutes *as well as* moral protectors of communities and safe sex practices. Female drug users are frequently equated with prostitutes, and consequently seen as carriers of medical and moral disease, targeted for intervention. At the same time, they are given the major responsibility for preventing HIV/AIDS, the sexual health and moral standards in the heterosexual community, and allocated the role of safer sex educators.
- Prohibition and punishment and public health discourse constructs female users as *both* 'bad', dangerous, criminal women who pose a threat to young people, families and communities *and also* psychopathological victims of abuse and trauma, devoid of choice,

agency and accountability. Poor women, often victims of abuse, are constituted as punishable, while their status as victims of male violence is a low priority for investigation and punishment.
- Prohibition and punishment, public health and welfare discourses constitute female drug users as *both* 'bad', 'unfit', 'irresponsible' mothers *and also* as responsible mothers. Within the academic and drug policy discourse, female drug users are constructed as 'abnormal', ignorant, irresponsible, undeserving, incapable mothers. In its most extreme configuration, they are situated as criminal child abusers and murderers. At the same time, they are constructed as normal 'responsible' mothers who need education and training. Such a construction inheres in the assumption that motherhood is a 'natural' state for all women, and that women drug users simply need help in realising this.
- Public health discourse also situates female users as badly behaved, bad choice makers, responsible for their dependence and recovery, deserving of disciplinary treatment and/or coercion *and also* as neglected service users whose needs do not fit the existing structure of services. Failure by women to 'recover' is constructed as due to individual weakness rather than lack of service provision. Female users are responsibilised for their predicament, for their dependence and experiences of poverty, violence and psychological trauma. While the provision of voluntary treatments, especially for women, is lacking, female users continue to be constructed as worthy of coercion.
- Welfare discourse situates female drug users as benefit scroungers, undeserving of social support *and also* as changeable, saveable and educable. The solution to the problem of underserving, dependent users is to steer them into treatment and employment.

This book also explored how the women saw themselves. The relationship between how the women are constructed and regulated by 'the authorities', and how they see themselves, is a dialectical and mutually constitutive one. Drug policy is partially determined by how female users think, act and define themselves, and the values, beliefs and experiences of female users are, to some extent, shaped by drug policy. This book has demonstrated that, at least for those who were interviewed, female users internalised many of the negative constructions of themselves found in the official discourses of drug policy. Notwithstanding this, they also found ways to resist, redefine and contest these negative constructions. To this end, official discourse (as emanating from drug policy and academic research) creates the space for female users to position themselves in the following ways:

- As responsible for causing themselves and others pain, misery and illness *and also* as responsible, rational governors of their emotional pain. Specifically, the women saw themselves as bringing pain, misery and illness on themselves due to poverty, involvement in crime and prostitution, physical illness, separation from family and friends and the loss of children. Despite this, they saw themselves as behaving rationally in managing their pain.
- As rational, free choice makers, escaping emotional pain and social disadvantage *and also* as trapped in dependency and a drug-using lifestyle. The women viewed themselves as rational and responsible self-medicating victims of trauma, abuse and isolation. Despite wanting to believe they could get off drugs and that they were saveable, educable, programmable and transformable, the dominant idea many of the women had of themselves was as trapped in dependency on drugs.
- As in control of their lives, as adaptive, rational, responsible providers *and also* as out of control of their lives due to poverty, social and economic marginalisation and social regulation. In response to feeling out of control of their lives in the context of changing circumstances, the women continuously redefined their moral and behavioural standards in order to retain a sense of control. In this way they saw themselves as adaptive, rational and responsible. At the same time, they experienced their lives as out of control and in chaos because of poverty, social and economic marginalisation, and the intervention of government agencies in their lives.
- As worthless women deserving punishment *and also* as victims of abuse victimised further by official technologies. Some of the women claimed that they used drugs to punish themselves out of feelings of worthlessness, guilt, self-loathing and desperation. Some saw themselves as deserving of punishment, and this was reinforced within official discourse constituting them as punishable criminals. Most of the women had been victims of childhood abuse, domestic violence and rape. Their victimisation was reinforced directly by the agents of drug policy through criminalisation, imprisonment and the removal of their children. Their victimisation and social and economic marginalisation was further entrenched by poor and insecure housing, violence from dealers and clients, poverty brought about by the high cost of their drug dependency, exclusion from

the jobs market and the loss of employment, discrimination, and separation from friends and family.

The manner in which the women who were interviewed positioned themselves was ultimately and intimately bound up with the way in which official discourse constituted drug users more generally, and female drug users in particular. Within the discourse of 'the authorities', drug users are situated as 'author[s] of their own misfortune', and the problem of their illicit drug use is constituted as an individual, psychological problem, a disease of the will. This is reflected in the way the women viewed themselves.

Within the predominant psychosocial strand of their narratives, the women viewed themselves in various paradoxical ways that rendered them responsible for their own predicament. They saw themselves as chemically driven addicts with faulty ways of thinking, causing pain, misery and illness to themselves and to others. They themselves appeared to believe that their 'misfortunes', their poverty, unemployment, homelessness and the loss of their children, were all a result of their *own* actions, and that it was their *own* responsibility to change their lives. They also saw themselves as changeable, saveable and recoverable. The women looked to various 'experts' from whom they desperately wanted help in transforming their faulty ways of thinking and acting. In a similar fashion, they understood and explained their poverty and marginality as resulting out of their own choice and strategy.

At the same time, they were able to negotiate different subjectivities for themselves at the discursive and practical level. The women inserted themselves into the process of their governance, and ascribed new and different meanings to the characteristics attributed to them. In so doing, the characteristics the women ascribed to themselves, their view of 'normality' and what they felt 'responsible' for was at odds with how they are constructed, what is constituted as normal, and what they are held responsible for within academic and drug policy discourse.

So, for instance, within their psychosocial accounts, the women saw themselves as 'normal', responsible governors of their emotional pain, rather than irresponsible bad choice makers. While they viewed themselves as chemically enslaved addicts, to some extent, they also saw themselves as responsible governors of their own lives, behaviour and relationships with others. They described how they protected family, friends and their children from being harmed by the knowledge of, or the effects of, their drug use. Many supported their partner's habits, which exacerbated their poverty.

The women provided alternative accounts of their situation to that of the problematic drug user through more social stories that relocated their lives in particular social and economic contexts. These undermined and resisted the dominant and official understandings of the women. Hence, they saw themselves as rational choice makers in the context of economic and social disadvantage. They faced initially reduced options due to poverty, a disrupted education and limited job prospects. In the discourse of 'the authorities', female users' maladaptive thinking, rather than their social circumstance, is seen as the cause of their drug dependence. However, they did not see themselves as maladaptive or pathological. Instead, they interpreted their behaviour as adaptive, normal and understandable, given the poverty and marginalisation that characterised their lives.

Although involvement in crime and sex work initially seemed to provide the women with an escape out of poverty, they became trapped in a cycle of grafting, scoring and using, and continued to live 'hand to mouth' every day. Within policy discourse female drug users have been situated as out-of-control, irresponsible, chemically driven addicts. In addition, as chemically driven, they have been positioned as bad, unfit mothers and disease-spreading prostitutes. The women in this study regarded themselves not out of control, but as predominantly in control, rational, moral individuals. They identified poverty, social and economic marginalisation and social regulation as the causes of their loss of control, and not their chemical enslavement.

In relation to the intervention of social services and the criminal justice system, the women experienced the very control mechanisms brought into place to deal with the perceived chaos in their lives as plunging them into being out of control and in chaos. The criminal justice system not only punished the women by taking away their freedom, but also damaged their relationships with their children, destroyed their careers and/or job prospects, and caused them to become homeless. Most of the women in the study had been punished through the criminal justice system for committing crimes to get money for drugs. At the same time, they had been victims of crimes of violence and abuse, of childhood abuse, domestic violence and rape. Their victimisation was reinforced directly by the agents of drug policy through criminalisation, imprisonment and the removal of their children. Those mechanisms used to 'help' the women, that is, treatment and social services, were often experienced as punitive, and those that were designed to punish, that is, imprisonment, were often experienced as a reward. The women did not see themselves as immoral criminals, deserving of punishment, but as normal, rational adaptive women in the face of poverty, marginalisation, violence and victimisation.

The women expressed a desire to be 'normal', that is, to have a stable home, a job and/or a family. In the discourse of current drug policy, women drug users are constructed as socially excluded, but as saveable, programmable and changeable through the provision of education and/or employment. The women described a range of difficulties in overcoming social and economic marginalisation, including a lack of services to fit their needs, disillusionment about what a life without drugs could offer them, and being unable to imagine a life without drugs. Their accounts suggest that various issues hinder drug users when trying to get off heroin and/or crack that cannot be reduced simply to problems with access to treatment and employment.

In summary, in the governance of dependent drug-using women, particular subjectivities are constructed which, in themselves, become part of the narrative, sustaining women in their 'problematic' drug use. The dominant stories the women told were psychosocial accounts reflecting the broader sociopolitical context, wherein drug dependency is individualised and psychologised, and users' responsibilised for their predicament. Female users experience drug policy as something that exacerbates their social disadvantage, and contributes to their lives being plunged into further poverty, marginalisation and victimisation. Although they internalise many of the negative constructions of themselves found in policy discourse, they also find ways to resist them.

The women negotiate their subjectivities through a broad range of contradictory choices, adaptations and resistances. Their resistances were explored through an examination of the pleasurable and painful aspects of the women's drug use – as a means of escape from trauma, abuse and oppressive social circumstances; the agency, rationality and resourcefulness wielded in the face of social and economic marginalisation and gendered control and regulation; and the women's response to the negative impacts of the treatment, welfare and criminal justice systems. In this process, the aim is to subvert popular misconceptions of female users that condition oppressive interventions, and to contribute to the formulation of drug policies based on empowerment, gender equity and social justice.

The research has shown that the contradictory basis of drug policy has real objective effects in the lives of female illicit drug users. The dichotomous programmable victim versus punishable, criminal approach to drug policy is to a large extent fruitless. What is needed is a more integrated approach to drug policy that does not criminalise drug using women or see them as maladaptive individuals who can or need to be reprogrammed. The contradictory axis on which drug policy is constituted means that a more holistic approach to dealing with drug users is not an option. For as long as drug policy is based on a contradiction, too many dependent, female, drug users are likely to continue to feel their lives are hopeless and drug policy itself will remain a hopeless cause.

Appendix: Research methods

The way in which a sample is accessed ultimately affects the kind of respondents the researcher will interview. There were three cohorts from three different English cities: Bristol, Reading and London. The 21 women from Bristol were interviewed for part of the researcher's PhD. Most of these women were contacted through a drugs project, some responded to a poster, four were contacted through the snowballing method, and a few through other means (such as on the street, or through a friend of a friend). The second cohort of nine women came from a Drug and Alcohol Team (DAAT)-funded study on stimulant services in Reading, and were accessed mainly through two of the DAAT-funded drug services in Reading. Forty-two men and women in total were interviewed during the fieldwork for the stimulant study, and nine of them were women. Only the women's interview data was used for this study. The third cohort of 10 women were all accessed in courtyards or doorways at the beginning of Narcotics Anonymous (NA) meetings in South or East London locations. This final sample were accessed with the intention of finding more women who were 'in recovery'.

The 40 women who came forward to be interviewed were very much an 'opportunity sample'. While the researcher attempted to gain a sample of women with a range of experiences, the women who did agree to be interviewed represented only a fraction of those involved in dependent drug using in Bristol, Reading and London. In addition, all of them were willing and able to discuss their experiences (although some did not find it easy). This raised the question of whether the accounts of the women who volunteered to be interviewed might be substantially different to those who did not. However, the aim of finding a 'representative' sample is a positivist concern displaced by the theoretical framework adopted in this study.

This study does not make any claims that the sample used was 'representative'. No generalisations have been made about women who use crack and heroin based on the accounts of the women in this sample. For instance, at some stage most of the women funded their heroin or crack habit through crime or sex work. This doesn't mean that all women who become dependent on drugs fund their drug use in either of these ways – it simply means that most of the women who came forward to be interviewed happened to be those who had become involved in crime and/or sex work. This, however, doesn't mean that their accounts cannot provide us with insights into the social world beyond them. As Maher (1997) has argued:

> The search for representativeness ... obscures what the anomalous or the marginal can reveal about the centre and the critical insights atypical voices can yield into power relations of domination and, perhaps most crucial of all, strategies of resistance. (p 29)

The 40 drug-dependent respondents were a heterogeneous group of women of different ages and backgrounds, coming from different places (some from Bristol, Reading or London, but some were from other places), struggling with a diverse range of circumstances and experiences. The only ways in which these dependent women's lives seemed to be similar were through their engagement in illicit drug taking, how they made sense of their involvement in illicit drug taking, and the material, social and ideological conditions they inhabited.

Bibliography

ACMD (Advisory Council on the Misuse of Drugs) (1988) *AIDS and drug misuse, Part 1*, London: HMSO.
ACMD (1989) *AIDS and drug misuse, Part 2*, London: HMSO.
ACMD (1993) *AIDS and drug misuse, Update*, London: HMSO.
ACMD (2003) *Hidden harm: Responding to the needs of children of problem drug users*, London: Home Office.
ACMD (2011) *Hidden harm: Responding to the needs of children of problem drug users*, ACMD inquiry reports, London: Home Office.
ACOG (American College of Obstetricians and Gynaecologists) (2005) 'Maternal decision making, ethics and the law', ACOG Committee Opinion, No 321, November, Washington, DC: ACOG.
Addiction Services Team: Bentinck Centre (1995) *Women and drugs: Information for women who use drugs illegally*, Kilmarnock: Ayrshire and Arran Community Health Care NHS Trust.
Adlaf, E. and Smart, R. (1983) 'Risk-taking and drug use behaviour: an examination', *Drug and Alcohol Dependence*, vol 11, pp 287-96.
Adler, F. (1975) *Sisters in crime: The rise of the new female criminal*, New York: McGraw Hill.
Agar, M. (1973) *Ripping and running: A formal ethnography of urban heroin addicts*, New York: Seminar Press.
Agrawal, A., Gardner, C., Prescott, C. and Kendler, K. (2005) 'The differential impact of risk factors on illicit drug involvement in females', *Social Psychiatry and Psychiatric Epidemiology*, vol 40, no 6, pp 454-66.
Alexander, B.K. (1998) 'Reframing Canada's "drug problem."', *Policy Options*, vol 19, no 8, pp 28-30.
Alexander, B.K. (2001) *The roots of addiction in free market society*, Vancouver, BC: Canadian Centre for Policy Alternatives (www.policyalternatives.ca).
Allard, P. (2002) *Life sentences: Denying welfare benefits to women convicted of drug offences*, Washington, DC: The Sentencing Project.

Allen, R., Levenson, J. and Garside, R. (2003) *A bitter pill to swallow: The sentencing of foreign national drug couriers*, London: Rethinking Crime and Punishment (http://rethinking.org.uk/informed/pdf/briefing5.pdf.pdf).

Alroomi, L., Davidson, J., Evans, T., Galea, P. and Howat R. (1988) 'Maternal narcotic abuse and the newborn', *Archive of Disease in Childhood*, vol 63, no 1, pp 81-3.

Amato, H. (1995) 'Love, sex and power: considering women's realities in HIV prevention', *American Psychology*, vol 50, pp 437-47.

Amato, L., Davoli, M., Minozzi, S., Ali, R. and Ferri, M. (2005) 'Methadone at tapered doses for the management of opioid withdrawal', *Cochrane Database of Systematic Reviews*, 20 July, no 3, CD003409.

Amnesty International (1999) *'Not part of my sentence': Violations of the human rights of women in custody*, Amnesty International: Rights for All: Amnesty International's Campaign in the United States of America (www.amnesty.org/en/library/asset/AMR51/019/1999/en/7588269a-e33d-11dd-808b-bfd8d459a3de/amr510191999en.pdf).

Anderson, E. (1990) *Streetwise: Race, class and change in an urban community*, Chicago, IL: University of Chicago Press.

Anderson, K. (2000) *A recognition of being: Reconstructing native womanhood*, Toronto, ON: Second Story Press.

Anderson, S. with Cairns, C. (2011) *The social care needs of short sentence prisoners*, A literature review commissioned by the North-East Public Health Observatory, London: Revolving Doors Agency (www.revolving-doors.org.uk/documents/the-social-care-needs-of-short-sentence-prisoners).

Anderson, T. (2008) *Neither villain nor victim: Empowerment and agency among substance abusers*, New Brunswick, NJ: Rutgers University Press.

Andreas, P. (1999) 'When policies collide: market reform, market prohibition, and the narcotization of the Mexican economy', in H.R. Friman and P. Andreas (eds) *The global economy and state power*, New York: Roman & Littlefield, pp 125-40.

Anglin, M., Hser, Y. and McGlothlin, W. (1987) 'Sex differences in addict careers, 2: Becoming addicted', *American Journal of Drug and Alcohol Abuse*, vol 13, pp 253-80.

Appleton, L.M. (1995) 'Rethinking medicalization: alcoholism and anomalies', in J. Best (ed) *Images of issues: Typifying contemporary social problems* (2nd edn), New York: Aldine de Gruyter, pp 58-90.

Arendt, R., Short, E., Singer, L., Minnes, S., Hewitt, J., Flynn, S., Carlson, L., Min, M., Klein, N. and Flannery, D. (2004) 'Children prenatally exposed to cocaine: developmental outcomes and environmental risks at seven years of age', *Journal of Developmental and Behavioral Pediatrics*, vol 25, no 2, pp 83-90.

Armstrong, D. (2004) 'A risky business? Research, policy, governmentality and youth offending', *Youth Justice*, vol 4, no 2, pp 100-16.

Arnold, R. (1990) 'Processes of victimization and criminalization of black women', *Social Justice*, vol 17, no 3, pp 153-66.

Aron, W. and Daly, C. (1976) 'Graduates and splitees from therapeutic community drug treatment programs: a comparison', *International Journal of the Addictions*, vol 11, no 1, pp 1-18.

Auld, J., Dorn, N. and South, N. (1986) 'Irregular work, irregular pleasures: heroin in the 1980s', in R. Matthews and J. Young (eds) *Confronting crime*, London: Sage Publications, pp 166-87.

Austin, R. (1992) 'The black community, its lawbreakers, and a politics of identification', *Southern California Law Review*, vol 65, pp 1769-817.

Avert (2006) 'UK HIV & AIDS history: 1981-1995', Horsham: Avert (www.avert.org/uk-aids-history.htm).

Awiah, J., Butt, S., Dorn N., Pearson, G. and Patel, K. (1992) *Race, gender and drug services*, London: Institute for the Study of Drug Dependence.

Bagnall, G., Plant, M. and Warwick, W. (1990) 'Alcohol, drugs and AIDS-related risks: results from a prospective study', *AIDS Care*, vol 2, pp 309-17.

Baker, P. and Carson, A. (1999) '"I take care of my kids": mothering practices of substance-abusing women', *Gender and Society*, vol 13, no 3, pp 347-63.

Balisy, S. (1995) 'Maternal substance abuse: the need to provide legal protection for the fetus', *South Californian Law Review*, vol 60, pp 1209-38.

Ball, A., Rana, S. and Dehn, K. (1998) 'HIV prevention among injecting drug users: responses in developing and transitional countries', *Public Health Reports*, June, vol 113, p 1.

Bapat, S. (2013) 'Welfare reform insanity: banning convicted drug offenders from food stamps for life', Alternet, 29 August (www.alternet.org/food/welfare-reform-insanity-banning-convicted-drug-offenders-food-stamps-life).

Barr, H., Oltenberg, D. and Rosen, A. (1973) 'A two year follow up study of 724 drug addicts and alcoholics treated together in an abstinence community', Fifth National Conference of Methadone Treatment, 17-19 March, New York.

Barry, A., Osborne, T. and Rose, N. (eds) (1996) *Foucault and political reason: Liberalism, neo-liberalism, and rationalities of government*, Chicago, IL: The University of Chicago Press.

Barton, A. (1999) 'Sentenced to Treatment? Criminal Justice Orders and the Health Service', *Critical Social Policy*, vol 19, no 4, pp 463-83.

Bashevkin, S. (2002) *Welfare hot buttons: Women, work, and social policy reform*, Toronto, ON: University of Toronto Press.

Baskin, D., Sommers, I. and Fagan, J. (1993) 'The political economy of female violent street crime', *Fordham Urban Law Journal*, vol 20, pp 401-7.

Batty, D. (2002) 'Drug charities back police proposals', *The Guardian, Society*, 2 May.

Bauld, L., Hay, G., McKell, J. and Carroll, C. (2010) *Problem drug users' experiences of employment and the benefit system*, DWP Research Report No 640, London: Department for Work and Pensions.

Bauman, Z. (1988) *Freedom*, Milton Keynes: Open University Press.

Bauman, Z. (2005) *Liquid life*, Cambridge: Polity Press.

Bays, J. (1990) 'Substance abuse and child abuse: impact of addiction on the child', *Paediatric Clinics of North America*, vol 37, pp 881-904.

Bean, P. (2002) 'Drug courts, the judge, and the rehabilitative ideal', in J. Nolan (ed) *Drug courts in theory and in practice*, New York: Aldine de Gruyter, pp 235-53.

Bean, P. (2004) *Drugs and crime* (2nd edn), Cullompton: Willan Publishing.

Bean, P. (2010) *Legalising drugs: Debates and dilemmas*, Bristol: Policy Press.

Bearak, B. (1992) 'A room for heroin and HIV', *Los Angeles Times*, 27 September.

Beatty, P., Petteruti, A. and Ziedenberg, J. (2007) *The vortex: The concentrated racial impact of drug imprisonment and the characteristics of punitive counties*, Washington, DC: Justice Policy Institute, 4 December (www.justicepolicy.org/research/1953).

Becker, J. and Duffy, C. (2002) *Women drug users and drug service provision: Service-level responses to engagement and treatment*, DPAS Paper 17, London: Drugs Strategy Directorate, Home Office.

Beckett, K. (1995) 'Fetal rights and "crack moms": pregnant women in the war on drugs', *Contemporary Drug Problems*, vol 22, no 4, pp 587-612.

Belenko, S. (1998) *Research on drug courts: A critical review*, New York: National Center on Addiction and Substance Abuse, Columbia University.

Belenko, S. (2001) *Research on drug courts: A critical review: 2001 update*, New York: National Center on Addiction and Substance Abuse, Columbia University.

Belknap, J. (2001) *The invisible woman: Gender, crime and justice*, Belmont, CA: Wadsworth Publishing Co.

Berger, C., Sorenson, L., Gendler, B. and Fitsimmonds, J. (1990) 'Cocaine and pregnancy: a challenge for health care providers', *Health and Social Work*, vol 15, no 4, pp 310-14.

Berman, G. (2012) *Prison population statistics, SN/SG/4334*, London: House of Commons, Social and General Statistics.

Berridge, V. (1984) 'Drugs and social policy: the establishment of drug control in Britain 1900-30', *British Journal of Addiction*, December, vol 79, no 4, pp 17-29.

Berridge, V. and Edwards, G. (1981) *Opium and the people: Opium use in nineteenth-century England*, London: Allen Lane and St Martin's Press.

Bertram, E. (1996) *Drug war politics: The price of denial*, Oakland, CA: University of California Press.

Bewley-Taylor, D., Hallam, C. and Allen, R. (2009) *The incarceration of drug offenders: An overview*, Oxford and London: The Beckley Foundation, International Centre for Prison Studies and King's College London.

Bhargava, S. (2000) 'Challenging punishment and privatization: a response to the conviction of Regina McKnight', *Harvard Civil Rights-Civil Liberties Law Review*, vol 39, pp 513-42. (www.law.harvard.edu/students/orgs/crcl/vol39_2/bhargava.pdf).

Binion, V. (1977) *A descriptive comparison of the family of origin of women heroin users and non-users*, Bethesda, MD: Women's Drug Research Project, National Institute on Drug Abuse.

Binion, V. (1979) *Addicted women: Family dynamics, self-perceptions and support system*, Bethesda, MD: National Institute on Drug Abuse.

Black, M., Basile, K., Breiding, M., Smith, S.G., Walters, M., Merrick, M., Chen, J. and Stevens, M. (2011) *The National Intimate Partner and Sexual Violence Survey (NISVS): 2010 Summary Report*, Atlanta, GA: National Center for Injury Prevention and Control, Centers for Disease Control and Prevention.

Blackwell, T. (2000) 'Civil rights group may challenge drug testing', *National Post*, 15 November, A27.

Blair, T. (1997) 'Bringing Britain together', Prime Minister's Speech for the Launch of the Social Exclusion Unit, Stockwell Park School, South London, 8 December.

Blair, T. (2002) 'Full text of Tony Blair's speech on welfare reform', *The Guardian, Society*, Monday 10 June (www.theguardian.com/society/2002/jun/10/socialexclusion.politics1).

Blakeslee, S. (1989) 'Crack's toll amongst babies: a joyless view even of toys', *New York Times*, 17 September.

Blenheim Project (1988) *Changing gear: A book for women who use drugs illegally*, London: Blenheim Project.

Blinick, G., Inturrisi, C. and Jerez, E. (1975) 'Methadone assays in pregnant women and progeny', *American Journal of Obstetrics and Gynaecology*, vol 1, pp 617-19.

Blinick, G., Wallach, C. and Jerez, E. (1969) 'Pregnancy in narcotics addicts treated by medical withdrawal', *American Journal of Obstetrics and Gynaecology*, vol 105, pp 997-1003.

Blom, M. and van den Berg, T. (1989) 'A typology of the life and work styles of "heroin prostitutes": from a male career model to a feminized career model', in M. Cain (ed) *Growing up good: Policing the behaviour of girls in Europe*, Newbury Park, CA: Sage Publications, pp 55-69.

Bloom, B. and Chesney-Lind, M. (2000) 'Women in prison: vengeful equity', in R. Muraskin (ed) *It's a crime: Women and criminal justice* (2nd edn), Upper Saddle River, NJ: Prentice Hall, pp 183-204.

Bloom, B. and Steinhart, D. (1993) *Why punish the children?*, Oakland, CA: National Council on Crime & Delinquency.

Bloom, B., Chesney-Lind, M. and Owen, B. (1994) *Women in California prisons: Hidden victims of the war on drugs*, San Francisco, CA: Center on Juvenile and Criminal Justice.

Bloor, M.J., McIntosh, J., McKeganey, N.P. and Robertson, M. (2008) '"Topping up" methadone: an analysis of patterns of heroin use among a treatment sample of Scottish drug-users', *International Journal of Drug Policy*, vol 19, no 3, pp 248-54.

Blume, S. (1990a) 'Alcohol and drug problems in women: old attitudes, new knowledge', in L. Sederer (ed) *Treatment choices for alcoholism and substance abuse*, Lanham, MD: Lexington Books, pp 183-93.

Blume, S. (1990b) 'Chemical dependency in women: important issues', *American Journal of Drug and Alcohol Abuse*, vol 16, nos 3 and 4, pp 297-309.

Boumanhuis (1997) 'Women and drugs', *Boumanhuis Newsletter*, vol 3, no 2, pp 1-26.

Bourgois, P. (1989) 'In search of Horatio Alger: culture and ideology in the crack economy', *Contemporary Drug Problems*, vol 16, no 4, pp 619-49.

Bourgois, P. (1995) *In search of respect: Selling crack in El Barrio*, Cambridge, MA: Harvard University Press.

Bourgois, P. and Dunlap, E. (1993) 'Exorcising sex-for-crack: an ethnographic perspective from Harlem', in M. Ratner (ed) *The crack pipe as pimp*, Lanham, MD: Lexington Books, pp 97-132.

Bowie, C. (1982) *Prisoners, 1925-81*, Washington, DC: Office of Justice Programs, Bureau of Justice Statistics.

Box, S. (1987) *Recession, crime and punishment*, London: Tavistock.

Box, S. and Hale, C. (1983) 'Liberation and female criminality in England and Wales revisited', *British Journal of Criminology*, vol 23, pp 35-49.

Box, S. and Hale, C. (1985) 'Unemployment, imprisonment and prison overcrowding', *Contemporary Crises*, vol 9, pp 208-28.

Boyd, S. (1994) 'Women and illicit drug use', *International Journal of Drug Policy*, vol 5, no 3, pp 185-9.

Boyd, S. (1999) *Mothers and illicit drugs: Transcending the myths*, Toronto, ON: University of Toronto Press.

Boyd, S. (2002) 'Women and illicit drug use', Drug Text (www.drugtext.org/Gender-issues/women-and-illicit-drug-use-1.html).

Boyd, S. (2004) *From witches to crack moms: Women, drug law and policy*, Durham, NC: Carolina Academic Press.

Boyd, S. (2006) 'Representations of women in the drug trade', in G. Balfour and E. Comack (eds) *Criminalizing women: Gender an (in)justice in neo-liberal times*, Halifax, NS: Fernwood Publishing, pp 131-51.

Boyd, S. and Faith, K. (1999) 'Women, illegal drugs and prison: views from Canada', *The International Journal of Drug Policy*, vol 10, pp 195-207.

Brady, T. and Ashley, O. (2005) *Women in substance abuse treatment: Results from the Alcohol and Drug Services Study* (ADSS), HHS Publication No SMA 04-3968, Analytic Series A-26, Rockville, MD: Substance Abuse and Mental Health Services Administration, Office of Applied Studies.

Braithwaite, J. (2000) 'The new regulatory state and the transformation of criminology', in D. Garland and R. Sparks (eds) *Criminology and social theory*, Clarendon Studies in Criminology, Oxford: Oxford University Press, pp 47-70.

Braithwaite, J. (2008) *Regulatory capitalism: How it works, Ideas to make it work better*, Cheltenham: Edward Elgar.

Brannen, J. (1988) 'The study of sensitive subjects', *Sociological Review*, vol 36, pp 552-63.

Brannen, J. (1992) *Mixing methods: Qualitative and quantitative research*, Aldershot: Avebury.

Brannen, J. (1993) 'Research note: The effects of research on participants: Findings from a study of mothers and employment', *Sociological Review*, vol 41, no 2, pp 328-46.

Brecher, E. and the Editors of Consumer Reports Magazine (1972) *Licit and illicit drugs*, The Consumers Union Report on narcotics, stimulants, depressants, inhalants, hallucinogens, and marijuana including caffeine, nicotine, and alcohol, Schaffer Library of Drug Policy (www.druglibrary.org/schaffer/library/studies/cu/cumenu.htm).

British Library Public Debate (2013) '"Addictive personality": myth or reality?', Guest post from Stephanie Minchin with Professor Nutt, Professor Reith and Professor Withington, 26 March (http://britishlibrary.typepad.co.uk/socialscience/2013/03/addictive-personality-myth-or-reality.html#sthash.Tl4Fkv12.dpuf).

Brook, H. and Stringer, R. (2005) 'Users, using, used: a beginner's guide to deconstructing drugs discourse', *International Journal of Drug Policy*, vol 16, no 5, pp 316-25.

Brooks, C., Zuckerman, B., Bamforth, A., Cole, J. and Kaplan-Sanoff, M. (1994) 'Clinical issues related to substance-involved mothers and their infants', *Infant Mental Health Journal*, vol 15, no 2, pp 202-17.

Broom, D. and Stevens, A (1990) 'Doubly deviant: women using alcohol and other drugs', *International Journal on Drug Policy*, vol 2, pp 25-7.

Brown, B., Gauvey, S., Meyers, M. and Stark, S. (1971) 'In their own words: addicts' reasons for initiating and withdrawing from heroin', *The International Journal of the Addictions*, vol 6, no 4, pp 635-45.

Brown, V. and Weissman, G. (1994) *Women and men injecting drug users: An updated look at gender differences and risk factors*, Westport, CT: Greenwood Press.

Buchanan, J. and Young, L. (2000) 'The war on drugs – a war on drug users', *Drugs: Education, Prevention Policy*, vol 7, no 4, pp 409-22.

Buchanan, J. and Young, L. (2002) 'Child protection: social workers' views', in M. Jackson, H. Klee and S. Lewis (eds) *Drug misuse and motherhood*, London: Routledge, 195-210.

Burchell, G. (1996) 'Liberal government and techniques of the self', in A. Barry, T. Osborne and N. Rose (eds) *Foucault and political reason: Liberalism, neo-liberalism, and rationalities of government*, Chicago, IL: The University of Chicago Press, Chapter 1.

Bush-Baskette, S. (1998) 'The war on drugs as a war on black women', in S. Miller (ed) *Crime control and women: Feminist implications of criminal justice policy*, Thousand Oaks, CA: Sage Publications, pp 113-21.

Bush-Baskette, S. (1999) 'The "war on drugs": a war against women?' in S. Cook and S. Davies (eds) *Harsh punishment: International experiences of women's imprisonment*, Northeastern Series on Gender, Crime, and Law, Boston, MA: Northeastern University Press, pp 211-29.

Bush-Baskette, S. (2004) 'The war on drugs as a war against black women', in M. Chesney-Lind and L.J. Pasko (eds) *Girls, women and crime: Selected readings*, Newbury Park, CA: Sage Publications, pp 185-94.

Bush-Baskette, S. (2010) *Misguided justice: The war on drugs and the incarceration of black women*, Bloomington, IN: iUniverse.

CAB (Citizens' Advice Bureau) (2013) *Punishing poverty: A review of benefits sanctions and their impacts on clients and claimants*, Manchester: CAB Service.

Cain, M. (ed) (1989) *Growing up good: Policing the behaviour of girls in Europe*, Newbury Park, CA: Sage Publications.

Cameron, D. (2012) 'David Cameron's Conservative Party Conference Speech: In full', *The Telegraph*, 10 October (www.telegraph.co.uk/news/politics/conservative/9598534/David-Camerons-Conservative-Party-Conference-speech-in-full.html).

Campbell, A. (1987) *The girls in the gang*, Oxford: Basil Blackwell.

Campbell, N. (1999) 'Regulating "maternal instinct": governing mentalities of late twentieth-century US illicit drug policy', *Signs*, vol 24, no 4, pp 895-923.

Campbell, N. (2000) *Using women: Gender, drug policy and social justice*, London: Routledge.

Canadian Human Rights Commission (2003) *Protecting their rights: A systematic review of human rights in correctional services for federally sentenced women*, Ottawa: Canadian Human Rights Commission.

Caputo, G. (2008) *Out in the storm: Drug addicted women living as shoplifters and sex workers*, Boston, MA: Northeastern University Press.

Carlen, P. (1983) *Women's imprisonment*, London: Routledge & Kegan Paul.

Carlen, P. (1988) *Women, crime and poverty*, Milton Keynes: Open University Press.

Carlen, P. (1990) *Alternatives to women's imprisonment*, Milton Keynes: Open University Press.

Carlen, P. (1998) *Sledgehammer: Women's imprisonment at the millennium*, London: Macmillan Press.

Carlen, P. (2002) *Women and punishment: The struggle for justice*, Cullompton: Willan.

Carlen, P. and Cook, D. (1989) *Paying for crime*, Milton Keynes: Open University Press.

Carpenter, C., Mayer, K., Stein, M., Leibman, B., Fisher, A. and Fiore, T. (1991) 'Human immunodeficiency virus infection in North American women: experience with 200 cases and a review of the literature', *Medicine*, vol 70, no 5, pp 307-25.

Carr, J.N. (1975) 'Drug patterns among drug-addicted mothers: incidence, variance in use, and effects on children', *Paediatric Annals*, July, vol 4, issue 7, pp 65-77.

Carrington, K. (1993) *Offending girls: Sex, youth and justice*, St Leonards, NSW: Allen & Unwin.

Carvel, J. (2002) 'Support for drug addicts "too badly run to help"', *The Guardian, Society*, 28 February.

CDC (Centre for Disease Control and Prevention) (2005) 'Syringe exchange programs', December (www.cdc.gov/idu/facts/aed_idu_syr.pdf).

CDC (2008) 'HIV/AIDS among women', CDC HIV/AIDS Fact Sheet (www.cdc.gov/hiv/topics/women/resources/factsheets/pdf/women.pdf).

Chads, K. and Simes, J. (2002) *April 2002, Monthly prison population brief*, London: Home Office.

Chadwick, C. (1988) 'Drug use during pregnancy', *Mersey Drugs Journal*, vol 1, no 5, pp 8-9.

Chambers, C. (1974) 'Narcotic addiction and crime: an empirical review', in J.A. Inciardi and C.D. Chambers (eds) *Drugs and the criminal justice system*, Beverly Hills, CA: Sage Publications, pp 125-142.

Chambers, C., Hinsely, R. and Moldestad, M. (1970) 'Narcotic addiction in females, a race comparison', *The International Journal of the Addictions*, vol 5, no 2, pp 257-78.

Chambliss, W. (1995) 'Another lost war: the costs and consequences of drug prohibition', *Social Justice*, vol 22, no 2, pp 101-24.

Chandler, R., Fletcher, B. and Volkow, N. (2009) 'Treating drug abuse and addiction in the criminal justice system: improving public health and safety', *JAMA: Journal of the American Medical Association*, vol 301, pp 183-90.

Chapman, J. (1980) *Economic realities and the female offender*, Lanham, MD: Lexington Books.

Chasnoff, I., Burns, K. and Burns, W. (1987) 'Cocaine use in pregnancy: perinatal morbidity and mortality', *Neurotoxicology and Teratology*, vol 9, pp 291-3.

Chasnoff, I., Landress, H. and Barrett, M. (1990) 'The prevalence of illicit drug or alcohol use during pregnancy and discrepancies in mandatory reporting in Pinellas County, Florida', *New England Journal of Medicine*, vol 322, pp 1202-6.

Chasnoff, I., Burns, W., Schnoll, H. and Burns, K. (1985) 'Cocaine use in pregnancy', *New England Journal of Medicine*, vol 313, pp 666-9.

Chasnoff, I., Hunt, C., Kletter, R. and Kaplan, D. (1989) 'Prenatal cocaine exposure is associated with respiratory pattern abnormalities', *American Journal of Disabled Children*, vol 148, pp 583-7.

Chein, I., Gerard, D., Lee, R. and Rosenfield, E. (1964) *The road to H: Narcotics, juvenile delinquency, and social policy*, New York: Basic Books.

Chesney-Lind, M. (1995) 'Rethinking women's imprisonment: a critical examination of trends in female incarceration', in B. Price and N. Sokoloff (eds) *The criminal justice system and women: Offenders, victims, and workers* (2nd edn), New York: McGraw-Hill, pp 105-17.

Chesney-Lind, M. (1997) *The female offender: Girls, women and crime*, Thousand Oaks, CA: Sage Publications.

Chesney-Lind, M. and Pasko, L. (2004) *The female offender: Girls, women, and crime*, Thousand Oaks, CA: Sage Publications.

Chesney-Lind, M. and Rodriguez, N. (1983) 'Women under lock and key', *Prison Journal*, vol 63, pp 47-65.

Chesney-Lind, M. and Shelden, R.G. (1992) *Girls, delinquency and juvenile justice*, Pacific Grove, CA: Brooks/Cole Publishing Company.

Chigwada-Bailey, R. (2003) *Black women's experiences of criminal justice – Race, gender and class: A discourse on disadvantage*, Hook: Waterside Press.

Chitwood, D. (1993) 'Epidemiology of crack use among injection drug users', in B.S. Brown and G.M. Beschne (eds) *Handbook on risks for AIDS: Injection drug users and sexual partners*, Westport, CT: Greenwood Press, pp 155-69.

Chomsky, N. (1998) '"The drug war industrial complex": Noam Chomsky interviewed by John Veit', *High Times*, April (www.chomsky.info/interviews/199804--.htm).

Chrisholm, C. (1929) 'Alcohol and drug addiction in relation to women and children', *British Journal of Inebriety*, vol 26, no 4, pp 207-17.

Christie, N. (1993) *Crime control as industry* (revised edn), London: Routledge.

Christmas, J. (1978) 'Women, alcohol and drugs: issues and implications', in *Drug abuse: Modern trends, issues and perspectives*, Proceedings of the second National Drug Abuse Conference, Inc., New Orleans, Louisiana, 1975, New York: Dekker.

Church, S., Henderson, M., Barnard, M. and Hart, G. (2001) 'Violence by clients towards female prostitutes in different work settings: questionnaire survey', *British Medical Journal*, vol 332, pp 524-5.

Cicero, T. (1994) 'Effects of paternal exposure to alcohol on offspring development', *Alcohol Health and Research World*, vol 18, no 1, pp 37-41.

Cicourel, A. (1964) *Method and measurement in sociology*, Glencoe, IL and New York: Free Press.

Clancey, G. and Howard, J. (2006) 'Diversion and criminal justice drug treatment: mechanism of emancipation or social control?' *Drug and Alcohol Review*, vol 25, no 4, pp 377-85.

Clark, A. (1987) *Women's silence men's violence: Sexual assault in England 1770-1845*, London: Pandora Press.

Clinic Social Workers Group (1987) *Proposed procedure and policy guidelines for work with pregnant women who misuse drugs*, London: Standing Conference on Drug Abuse.

Cloud, W. and Granfield, R. (2008) 'Conceptualizing recovery capital: expansion of a theoretical construct', *Substance Use and Misuse*, vol 43, nos 12-13, pp 1971-86.

Coalition for Higher Education Act Reform (2006) 'Background on the Higher Education Act Drug Provision', Washington, DC (www.raiseyourvoice.com/Backgrounder.pdf).

Cockburn, A. (1998) 'The drug war: A war on poor lower classes', *The Los Angeles Times*, Thursday 11 June (www.hartford-hwp.com/archives/28/088.html).

Coffin, P. (1996) *Cocaine & pregnancy*, New York: The Lindesmith Center (www.drugpolicy.org/docUploads/cocaine_pregnancy.pdf).

Cohen, J., Haver, L. and Wofsey, C. (1989) 'Women and intravenous drugs: parental and heterosexual transmission of human immunodeficiency virus', *Journal of Drug Issues*, vol 19, pp 39-56.

Cohen, S. (1985) *Visions of social control: Crime, punishment and classification*, Cambridge: Polity Press.

Coles, C., Platzman, K., Smith, I., James, M. and Falek, A. (1992) 'Effects of cocaine and alcohol use in pregnancy and neonatal growth and neurobehavioural status', *Neurotoxicol Teratology*, vol 14, pp 23-33.

Colten, M. (1977) *A descriptive and comparative self analysis of self perceptions and attitudes of heroin addicted women*, Bethesda, MD: Women's Drug Research Project, National Institute on Drug Abuse.

Collins, W. (1916) 'The ethics and law of drug and alcohol addiction', *British Journal of Inebriety*, vol 13, p 141.

Colten, M. (1980) 'A comparison of heroin-addicted and nonaddicted mothers: their attitudes, beliefs and parenting experiences', in National Institute on Drug Abuse Services Research Report, *Heroin-addicted parents and their children: Two reports*, Washington, DC: US Department of Health and Human Services, Public Health Service, Alcohol, Drug Abuse, and Mental Health Administration, pp 1-18.

Colten, M. (1982) 'Attitudes, experiences, and self-perceptions of heroin-addicted mothers', *Journal of Social Issues*, vol 38, no 2, pp 77-92.

Commission on Systemic Racism in the Ontario Criminal Justice System (1995) *Report of the Commission on Systemic Racism in the Ontario Criminal Justice System: A community summary*, Toronto, ON: Queen's Printer for Ontario.

Conference on Women and Drugs, Birmingham (1995) *Women and drugs: Conference report*, 15 March, Oldbury, Glasgow, Newham and Birmingham: West Midlands Regional Drugs Training Unit, Glasgow Women's Reproductive Health Service, Newham Drugs Advice Project and Women's Interagency Group.

Connaughton, J., Reeser, D., Schut, J. and Finnegan, L. (1977) 'Parental addiction: outcome and management', *American Journal of Obstetrics and Gynaecology*, vol 9, pp 679-86.

Connors, J. (1990) 'Women, drug control and the law', *UN Bulletin of Narcotics*, vol 42, no 1, pp 41-7.

Conrad, P. (1992) 'Medicalization and social control', *Annual Review of Sociology*, vol 18, pp 209-32.

Conrad, P. (2007) *The medicalization of society: On the transformation of human conditions into treatable disorders*, Baltimore, MD: Johns Hopkins University Press.

Conrad, P. and Schneider, W. (1992) *Deviance and medicalization: From badness to sickness*, Philadelphia, PA: Temple University Press.

Cook, D. (1988) 'Rich law, poor law: differential response to tax and supplementary benefit fraud', Unpublished PhD thesis, University of Keele.

Cooper, D. (1995) *Power in struggle: Feminism, sexuality and the state*, Buckingham: Open University Press.

Corby, B. (1997) 'Risk assessment in child protection work', in H. Kemshall and J. Pritchard (eds) *Good practice in risk assessment and risk management*, London: Sage Publications, pp 13-30.

Corby, N., Wolitski, R., Thornton-Johnson, S. and Tanner, W. (1991) 'AIDS knowledge, perception of risk, and behaviours among female sex partners of injection drug users', *AIDS Educational Review*, vol 3, no 4, pp 353-66.

Corkery, J. (2001) 'Drug seizure and offender statistics, United Kingdom, 1999', *Statistical Bulletin 5/01*, London: Home Office.

Cornwell, J. (1984) *Hard earned lives*, London: Tavistock Publications.

Correctional Service Canada (2002-03) *Departmental Performance Report (2002-03)* (www.csc-scc.gc.ca/text/pblct/dpr/2003/section_3_overview_of_changes_e.shtml).

Coupe, J. and Glass, I. (eds) (1991) 'Why women need their own services', in I. Belle Glass (ed) *The International Handbook of Addiction Behaviour*, London: Routledge, pp 168-74.

Covington, J. (1985) 'Gender differences in criminality among heroin users', *Journal of Research in Crime and Delinquency*, vol 22, no 4, pp 329-54.

Covington, J. (1988) 'Crime and heroin: the effects of race and gender', *Journal of Black Studies*, vol 18, pp 486-506.

Covington, S. (1998) 'Women in prison: approaches in the treatment of our most invisible population', *Women and Therapy Journal*, Haworth Press, vol 21, no 1, pp 141-55.

Covington, J. (2008) 'Evaluation of a trauma-informed and gender-responsive intervention for women in drug treatment', *Journal of Psychoactive Drugs*, SARC Supplement 5, November.

Cregler, L.L. and Mark, H. (1986) 'Medical complications of cocaine abuse', *New England Journal of Medicine*, vol 315, pp 1495-500.

Crites, L. (ed) (1976) *The female offender*, Lanham, MD: Lexington Books.

Croghan, R. and Miell, D. (1998) 'Strategies of resistance: "bad" mothers dispute the evidence', *Feminism & Psychology*, vol 8, no 4, pp 445-65.

Cullen, F., Golden, K. and Cullen, J. (1979) 'Sex and delinquency: a partial test of the masculinity hypothesis', *Criminology*, vol 17, pp 301-10.

Cunningham, A. and Baker, L. (2004) *Invisible victims: The children of women in prison*, December, San Diego, CA: Voices for Children, Centre for Children & Families in the Justice System.

Curtis, M., Garlington, S. and Schottenfeld, L. (2013) 'Alcohol, drug and criminal history restrictions in Public Housing', *Cityscape: A Journal of Policy Development and Research*, vol 15, no 3, U.S. Department of Housing and Urban Development, Office of Policy Development and Research.

Curtiss, M. (2004) 'Brain dependence: the debate over the addictive personality and gender implications', Biology 202, Serendip (http://serendip.brynmawr.edu/bb/neuro/neuro04/web1/mcurtiss.html).

Cusick, L., Martin, A. and May, T. (2003) *Vulnerability and involvement in drug use and sex work*, Findings 207, London: Home Office Research, Development and Statistics Directorate.

Cuskey, W. (1982) 'Female addiction: a review of the literature', *Journal of Addictions and Health*, vol 3, no 1, pp 1752-69.

Cuskey, W., Berger, L. and Densen-Gerber, J. (1977) 'Issues in the treatment of female addiction: a review and critique of the literature', *Contemporary Drug Problems*, vol 6, pp 307-71.

Cuskey, W., Premkumar, T. and Sigel, L. (1972) 'Survey of opiate addiction among females in the US between 1850 and 1870', *Public Health Reviews*, vol 1, pp 8-39.

Dai, B. (1937) *Opium addiction in Chicago*, Shanghai: Commercial Press.

DAIS (Drug Advice and Information Service) (1990) *Why women and drugs?*; *Women, HIV, AIDS and drug use; Cannabis?*; *Amphetamine Sulphate*, Brighton: DAIS.

Daniel, R. (1962) *Women, dope and murder*, London: Wright and Brown.

Daniels, C. (2006) *Exposing men: The science and politics of male reproduction*, New York: Oxford University Press.

Datesman, S. (1981) 'Women, crime and drugs', in J. Inciardi (ed) *The drugs crime connection*, Beverly Hills, CA: Sage Publications, pp 85-104.

Davies, J.B. (1992) *The myth of addiction: An application of the psychological theory of attribution to illicit drug use*, Abingdon: Taylor Francis.

Davis, A. (1998) 'Masked racism: reflections on the prison industrial complex', Colorlines, Thursday 10 September (http://colorlines.com/archives/1998/09/masked_racism_reflections_on_the_prison_industrial_complex.html).

Davis, A. (1999) *The-prison-industrial-complex*, Oakland, CA: A K Pr Distribution.

DAWN (Drugs Alcohol Women Nationally) (1984a) *Women and tranquillisers*, London: DAWN.

DAWN (1984b) *Women and heroin and other opiates*, London: DAWN.

DAWN (1986) *Women and stimulants: Amphetamines and cocaine*, London: DAWN.

DAWN (1987) *HIV and AIDS: Facts for women who use drugs*, London: DAWN.

DAWN (1989) *Black women and dependency: A report on drug and alcohol abuse*, London: DAWN.

DAWN (1994) *When a creche is not enough: A survey of drug and alcohol services for women*, London: DAWN.

Dawson, D. (1996) 'Correlates of past-year status among treated and untreated persons with former alcohol dependence', *Alcoholism: Clinical and Experimental Research*, vol 20, pp 771-9.

DCPC (Drugs and Crime Prevention Committee) (2010) *Inquiry into the impact of drug-related offending on female prisoner numbers*, October, Parliament of Victoria, Australia (http://catalogue.nla.gov.au/Record/5013790).

Dean, M. (1994) *Critical and effective histories: Foucault's methods and historical sociology*, London: Routledge.

Deehan, A. and Saville, E. (2003) *Recreational drug use among clubbers in South East England*, Findings 208, London: Home Office.

Degenhardt, L., Mathers, B., Vickerman, P., Rhodes, T., Latkin, C. and Hickman, M. (2010) 'Prevention of HIV infection for people who inject drugs: why individual, structural and combination approaches are needed', *The Lancet*, vol 376, no 9737, pp 285-301.

de Leon, G. (1974) 'Phoenix House: psychopathological signs among male and female drug free residents', *Addictive Diseases: An International Journal*, vol 1, no 2, pp 135-51.

Deng, K., Liu, Z., Lin, Y., Mu, D., Chen, X., Li, J., Li, N., Deng, Y., Li, X., Wang, Y., Li, S. and Zhu, J. (2013) 'Periconceptional paternal smoking and the risk of congenital heart defects: a case-control study', *Birth Defects Research Part A, Clinical and Molecular Teratology*, April, vol 97, no 4, pp 210-16.

Densen-Gerber, J. and Rohrs, C. (1973) 'Drug-addicted parents and child abuse', *Contemporary Drug Problems*, vol 2, no 4, pp 683-96.

Densen-Gerber, J., Weiner, J. and Hochstedler, R. (1972) 'Sexual behaviour, abortion and birth control in heroin addicts: legal and psychiatric considerations', *Contemporary Drug Problems*, vol 1, no 4, pp 783-93.

Departmental Committee Report (1926) *British Medical Journal*, 1926 Feb 27, 1(3400), pp 391-93.

Deren, S. (1986) 'Children of substance abusers: a review of the literature', *Journal of Substance Abuse Treatment*, vol 3, pp 77-94.

DH (Department of Health) (1996) *The Task Force to review services for drug misusers – Report of an Independent Review of Drug Treatment Services in England*, London: The Stationery Office.

DH (1998) *Tackling drugs to build a better Britain: The government's 10-year strategy for tackling drug misuse*, London: The Stationery Office.

DH (1999) *Drug misuse and dependence: Guidelines on clinical management*, London: The Stationery Office.

DH (2000) *No secrets: Guidance on developing and implementing multi-agency policies and procedures to protect vulnerable adults from abuse*, London: Department of Health.

Dilner, L. (2004) 'Why millions of women are hooked on the happy pills', *The Observer*, Sunday 18 April.

Dobash, R. and Dobash, R. (1980) *Violence against wives*, London: Open Books.

Dodge, M. and Pogrebin, M. (2001) 'Collateral costs of imprisonment for women: complications of reintegration', *The Prison Journal*, vol 81, no 1, pp 42-54.

Donzelot, J. (1979) *The policing of families*, London: Hutchinson.

D'Orban, P. (1970) 'Heroin dependence and delinquency in women: a study of heroin addicts in Holloway Prison', *British Journal of Addiction*, vol 65, no 1, pp 67-78.

Dorfman, L., Derish, P. and Cohen, J. (1992) 'Hey girlfriend: an evaluation of AIDS prevention among women in the sex industry', *Health Education Quarterly*, vol 19, no 1, pp 25-40.

Dorn, N., James, B. and Lee, M. (eds) (1992) *Women, HIV, drugs: Criminal justice issues*, London: Institute for the Study of Drug Dependence.

Dorris, M. (1990) 'A desperate crack legacy', *Newsweek*, 25 June.

DPA (Drug Policy Alliance) (2010) 'Drug war statistics'; 'Drug war facts' (www.drugpolicy.org/drug-war-statistics).

DPA (2013) 'Race and the drug war' (www.drugpolicy.org/race-and-drug-war).

DrugScope (2005) 'DrugScope Policy Briefing: Using women', DrugScope: London (www.drugscope.org.uk/Resources/Drugscope/Documents/PDF/Policy/polwomenprison.pdf).

DrugScope (2010) 'The 2010 Drug Strategy Consultation: Response from DrugScope', 30 September (www.drugscope.org.uk/Resources/Drugscope/Documents/PDF/Policy/DSResponse2010DrugStrategyConsultation.pdf).

Duelli-Klein, R. (1983) 'How to do what we want to do: thoughts about feminist methodology', in G. Bowles and R. Duelli-Klein (eds) *Theories of women's studies*, London: Routledge & Kegan Paul, pp 88-104.

Dunlap, E., Johnson, B., Manwar, A. and Maher, L. (1997) 'Who they are and what they do: female crack sellers in New York City', *Women and Criminal Justice*, vol 8, no 4, pp 25-55.

Durkheim. E. (1952 [1897]) *Suicide*, London: Routledge & Kegan Paul.

Durkheim, E. (1964 [1895]) *The rules of sociological method*, Glencoe, IL: Free Press.

Du Rose, N. (2006) 'Talking about drugs: gender, discourse and women's drug use', Unpublished doctoral thesis, Bath: University of Bath, pp 23-44.

Du Rose, N. and Keene, J. (2009) *Stimulant drug use in Reading: Report for the Drug and Alcohol Action Team*, Reading: Drug and Alcohol Action Team.

Dwyer, R., Richardson, D., Ross, M.W., Wodak, A., Miller, M.E. and Gold, J. (1994) 'A comparison of HIV risk between women and men who inject drugs', *AIDS Education and Prevention*, vol 6, no 5, pp 379-89.

Economist, The (2009) 'How to stop the drug wars', 5 March.

Edlin, B., Irwin, K., Ludwig, D., Faruque, S., McCoy, C., Serrano, Y., Inciardi, J., Bowser, B., Schilling, R. and Homberg, S. (1994) 'Intersecting epidemics – crack cocaine use and HIV infection among inner-city young adults', *New England Journal of Medicine*, vol 331, pp 1422-7.

Edwards, R. (1993) 'An education in interviewing: placing the researcher and researched', in C.M. Renzetti and R.M. Lee (eds) *Researching sensitive topics*, London: Sage Publications, pp 181-96.

Edwards, S. (1996) *Sex and gender in the legal process*, London: Blackstone.

Egami, Y., Ford, D., Greenfield, S. and Crum, R. (1996) 'Psychiatric profile and sociodemographic characteristics of adults who report physically abusing or neglecting children', *American Journal of Psychiatry*, vol 153, no 7, pp 921-8.

Ehrenreich, B. and English, E. (1974) *Witches, midwives and nurses – A history of women healers*, London: Compendium.

Ehrlich, J. (2008) *Breaking the law by giving birth: The war on drugs, the war on reproductive rights, and the war on women*, New York: New York University Review of Law and Social Change.

Ekstrand, L. and Blume, J. (2000) *US Customs Service: Better targeting of airline passengers for personal searches could produce better results*, Washington, DC: General Accounting Office.

Eldred, C. and Washington, M. (1976) 'Interpersonal relationships in heroin use by men and women and their role in treatment outcome', *The International Journal of the Addictions*, vol 1, no 1, pp 117-30.

Ellinwood, E., Smith, W. and Valliant, G. (1966) 'Narcotic addiction in males and females: a comparison', *The International Journal of the Addictions*, vol 1, pp 33-45.

EMCDDA (European Monitoring Centre for Drugs and Drug Addiction) (2000) 'Problems facing women drug users and their children', in *EMCDDA 2000 annual report on the state of the drugs problem in the European Union*, Lisbon: EMCDDA.

Erickson, P. and Watson, V. (1990) 'Women, illicit drugs and crime', *Research Advances in Alcohol and Drug Problems*, vol 10, pp 251-72.

ESPAD (European School Survey Project on Alcohol and Other Drugs) (1999) *Alcohol and other drug use among students in 26 European countries*, Stockholm: Swedish Council on Alcohol and other Drugs.

Ettorre, E.M. (1985) *Survey of facilities for women using drugs (including alcohol) in London*, London: Drugs Alcohol Women Nationally.

Ettorre, E. (1992) *Women and substance use*, Basingstoke: Macmillan.

Ettorre, E. (2004) 'Revisioning women and drug use: gender sensitivity, embodiment and reducing harm', *The International Journal of Drug Policy*, vol 15, pp 327-35.

Ettorre, E. (2007) *Revisioning women and drug use: Gender, power and the body*, London: Palgrave Macmillan.

Ettorre, E. and Riska, E. (2001) 'Long-term users of psychotropic drugs: embodying masculinized stress and feminized nerves', *Substance Use & Misuse*, vol 36, nos 9-10, pp 1187-211.

Evensen, D. *Fetal Alcohol Consultation and Training Services*. FAS Alaska (www.fasalaska.com/).

Executive Office of the President of the United States (2013) *National Drug Control Strategy 2013* (www.whitehouse.gov/sites/default/files/ondcp/policy-and-research/ndcs_2013.pdf).

Fagan, J. (1994) 'Women and drugs revisited: female participation in the cocaine economy', *Journal of Drug Issues*, vol 24, no 2, pp 179-225.

Fagan, J. (1995) 'Women's careers in drug use and drug selling', *Current Perspectives on Aging and the Life Cycle*, vol 4, pp 155-90.

Faith, K. (1993) *Unruly Women*, Vancouver: Press Gang Publishers.

Famularo, R., Kinscherff, R., Bunshart, D., Soivak, T. and Fenton, L. (1989) 'Parental compliance in court-ordered treatment interventions in cases of child maltreatment', *Child Abuse and Neglect*, vol 13, p 507.

Farabee, D., Prendergast, M. and Anglin, M. (1998) 'The effectiveness of coerced treatment for drug-abusing offenders', *Federal Probation*, vol 62, no 1, pp 3-10.

Farkas, M. (1976) 'The addicted couple', *Drug Forum*, vol 5, no 1, pp 81-7.

Farmer, P., Connors, M. and Simmons, J. (1996) *Women, poverty, and AIDS: Sex, drugs, and structural violence*, Monroe, ME: Common Courage Press.

Farrant, F. (2001) *Troubled inside: responding to the mental health needs of children and young people in prison*, London: Prison Reform Trust.

Faupel, C. (1991) *Shooting dope: Career patterns of hard-core heroin users*, Gainesville, FL: University of Florida Press.

Feeley, M. and Simon, J. (1994) 'Actuarial justice: the emerging new criminal law', in D. Nelken (ed) *The futures of criminology*, London: Sage Publications, pp 173-201.

Feinman, C. (ed) (1992) *The criminalisation of a woman's body*, New York: Haworth Press.

Feinman, C. (1994) *Women in the criminal justice system*, Westport, CT: Praeger Publishers.

Feldman, H. (1968) 'Ideological supports to becoming and remaining a heroin addict', *Journal of Health and Social Behaviour*, vol 9, pp 131-9.

Fellner, J. and Vinck, P. (2008) *Targeting Blacks: Drug law enforcement and race in the United States*, New York, NY: Human Rights Watch.

Fentiman, L. (2008) *Pursuing the perfect mother: Why America's criminalization of maternal substance abuse is not the answer*, Pace Law Faculty Publications Paper 488, New York: Pace Law.

Fernandez, H. and Libby, T.A. (2011) *Heroin: it's history, pharmacology, and treatment* (2nd edn), Center City, MN: Hazelden.

Feucht, T., Stephens, R. and Romans, S. (1990) 'The sexual behaviour of intravenous drug users: assessing the risk of sexual transmission of HIV', *Journal of Drug Issues*, vol 20, no 2, pp 195-213.

Fiddle, S. (1976) 'Sequences in addiction', *Addictive Diseases: an International Journal*, vol 2, no 4, pp 553-68.

File, K. (1976) 'Sex roles and street roles', *The International Journal of the Addictions*, vol 11, no 2, pp 263-8.

File, K., McCahill, T. and Savitz, L. (1974) 'Narcotics involvement and female criminality', *Addictive Diseases: an International Journal*, vol 1, no 2, pp 177-8.

Finch, J. (1993) '"It's great to have someone to talk to": ethics and politics of interviewing women', in M. Hammersly (ed) *Social research: Philosophy, politics and practice*, London: Sage Publications.

Finnegan, L. (1975) 'Narcotics dependence in pregnancy', *Journal of American Psychedelic Drugs*, 7 (July-September), 3.

Finnegan, L., Connaughton, J. and Emich, J. (1972) 'Comprehensive care of the pregnant addict and its effect on maternal and infant outcome', *Contemporary Drug Problems*, vol 1, p 795.

Flavin, D. and Frances, R. (1987) 'Risk taking behaviour: substance abuse disorders and the Acquired Immune Deficiency Syndrome', *Advances in Alcohol and Substance Abuse*, vol 6, pp 23-32.

Fleetwood, J. (2014) *Drug mules: Women in the international cocaine trade*, London: Palgrave Macmillan.

Fonnow, M. and Cook, J. (1991) *Beyond methodology: Feminist scholarship as lived research*, Bloomington, IN: Indiana University Press.

Fontana, V. (1971) *The maltreated child*, Springfield, IL: Charles C. Thomas.

Ford, C., Hepburn, M. and Beaumont, B. (eds) (1997) 'Caring for the pregnant drug user', in B. Beaumont (ed) *Care of drug users in general practice: A harm-minimization approach*, Abingdon: Radcliffe, pp 107-22.

Forrester, D. (2000) 'Parental substance misuse and child protection in a British sample: a survey of children on the child protection register in an inner London District Office', *Child Abuse Review*, vol 9, pp 235-46.

Fortenberry, J., Orr, D., Katz, B., Brizendine, E. and Blythe, M. (1997) 'Sex under the influence: a diary self-report study of substance use and sexual behaviour among adolescent women', *Sexually Transmitted Diseases*, July, vol 24, no 6, pp 313-18.

Foucault, M. (1972 [1969]) *The archaeology of knowledge*, London: Routledge.

Foucault, M. (1980 [1976]) *Power/knowledge: Selected interviews and other writings 1972-1977* (edited by C. Gordon), Brighton: Harvester Press.

Foucault, M. (1990 [1976]) *The will to knowledge: The history of sexuality, Volume 1*, London: Penguin Books.

Foucault, M. (1991 [1975]) *Discipline and punish: The birth of the prison*, London: Penguin Books.

Foucault, M. (2000 [1969]/[1982]/[1984]) *Ethics: Subjectivity and truth: Essential works of Foucault, 1954-1984, Volume 1* (edited by J. Faubion), London: Penguin Books.

Foucault, M. (2002 [1978]/[1982]) *Power: Essential works of Foucault, 1954-1984, Volume 3* (edited by J. Faubion), London: Penguin Books.

Foucault, M. (2006 [1965]) *Madness and civilization – A history of insanity in the age of reason*, New York: Vintage Books.

Franco, C. (2010) *Drug courts: Background, effectiveness, and policy issues for Congress*, Report for Congress, Washington, DC: Congressional Research Service, 12 October (http://fpc.state.gov/documents/organization/150203.pdf).

Fraser, A. (1976) 'Drug addiction in pregnancy', *Lancet*, 23 October, vol 2, pp 896-9.

Friedman, J. and Alicea, M. (1994) 'Women and heroin: the path of resistance and its consequences', *Gender and Society*, vol 9, no 4, pp 432-49.

Gallagher, J., (1989) 'Fetus as patient', in S. Cohen and N. Taub (eds) *Reproductive laws for the 1990s*, Totowa, NJ: Humana Press, pp 185-235.

Galvani, S. (2004) 'Responsible disinhibition: alcohol, men and violence to women', *Addiction Research and Theory*, vol 12, no 4, pp 357-71.

Galvani, S. and Forrester, D. (2008) *What works in training social workers about drug and alcohol use*, Coventry and Luton: University of Warwick and University of Bedfordshire.

Galvani, S. and Humphreys, C. (2007) *The impact of violence and abuse on engagement and retention rates for women in substance use treatment*, London: NHS National Treatment Agency for Substance Misuse.

Garland, D. (1985) *Punishment and welfare: A history of penal strategies*, Aldershot: Gower.

Garland, D. (1996) 'The limits of the sovereign state: strategies of crime control in contemporary society', *The British Journal of Criminology*, vol 36, no 4, pp 445-71.

Garland, D. (1997) '"Governmentality" and the problem of crime: Foucault, criminology, sociology', *Theoretical Criminology*, vol 1, no 2, pp 173-214.

Garland, D. (1999) 'Governmentality and the problem of crime', in R. Smandych (ed) *Governable places: Readings in governmentality and crime control*, Advances in Criminology Series, Aldershot: Ashgate Publishing Ltd, Chapter 2.

Garland, D. (2001) *The culture of control: Crime and social order in contemporary society*, Chicago, IL: University of Chicago Press.

Geiger, B. (2006) 'Crime, prostitution, drugs, and malingered insanity: female offenders' resistant strategies to abuse and domination', *International Journal of Offender Therapy and Comparative Criminology*, October, vol 50, no 5, pp 582-94.

Gerada, C. (1995) 'Pregnancy and drug abuse: complications and management issues', *European Addictions Resource*, vol 1, pp 146-50.

Gerstein, D., Judd, L. and Rovner, S. (1979) 'Career dynamics of female heroin addicts', *American Journal of Drug and Alcohol Abuse*, vol 6, no 1, pp 1-23.

Giddens, A. (1982) *New rules of sociological method*, London: Hutchinson.

Gilbert, L., El-Bassel, N., Rajah, V., Foleno, A. and Frye, V. (2001) 'Linking drug-related activities with experiences of partner violence: a focus group study of women in methadone treatment', *Violence and Victims*, vol 16, pp 517-36.

Gilbert, N. (ed) (1993) *Researching social life*, London: Sage Publications.

Gilfus, M.E. (2002) 'Women's experiences of abuse as a risk factor for incarceration', Harrisburg, PA: National Online Resource Center on Violence Against Women (www.vawnet.org/research/print-document.php?doc_id=412&find_type=web_desc_AR).

Gillman, D. (1989) 'The children of crack', *New York Times*, 31 July.

Gilman, M. (1988) 'Joining the professionals', *Druglink*, March/April, pp 10-11.

Glaze, L. and Maruschak, L. (2010) *Parents in prison and their minor children*, Statistics Special Report, Washington, DC: Bureau of Justice.

Glesne, C. and Peshkin, A. (1992) *Becoming a qualitative researcher: An introduction*, New York: Longman.

Glucksmann, M. (1994) 'The work of knowledge and the Knowledge of women's work', in M. Maynard and J. Purvis (eds) *Researching women's lives from a feminist perspective*, London: Taylor & Francis, pp 149-65.

Goldstein, P. (1979) *Prostitution and drugs*, Lanham, MD: Lexington Books.

Gomberg, E. (1986) 'Women: alcohol and other drugs', *Drugs and Society*, vol 1, no 1, pp 75-109.

Gomby, D. and Shiono, P. (1991) 'Estimating the number of drug exposed infants', *Future Child*, vol 1, no 1, pp 17-25.

Gomez, C. and van Oss, M. (1996) 'Gender, culture, and power: barriers to HIV-prevention strategies for women', *Journal of Sex Research*, vol 33, no 4, pp 355-62.

Gomez, L. (1997) *Misconceiving mothers: Legislators, prosecutors, and the politics of prenatal drug exposure*, Philadelphia, PA: Temple University Press.

Gordon, C. (1991) 'Governmental rationality: an introduction', in G. Burchell, C. Gordon and Miller, P. (eds) *The Foucault effect: Studies in governmentality*, Chicago, IL: Chicago University Press, pp 1-51.

Gordon, D. (1994) *Return of the dangerous classes: Drug prohibition and policy politics*, New York: W.W. Norton & Co Inc.

Gossop, M. (1986) 'Drug dependence and self-esteem', *The International Journal of the Addictions*, vol 11, no 5, pp 741-53.

Gossop, M. and Strang, J. (1991) 'A comparison of the withdrawal responses of heroin and methadone addicts during detoxification', *The British Journal of Psychiatry*, vol 158, pp 697-9.

Gossop, M., Powis, B., Griffiths, P. and Strang, J. (1995) 'Female prostitutes in South London: use of heroin, cocaine and alcohol and their relationship to health risk behaviours', *AIDS Care*, vol 7, no 3, pp 253-60.

Gostin, L. (1991) 'Compulsory treatment for drug-dependent persons: justifications for a public health approach to drug dependency', *Milbank Quarterly*, vol 69, pp 561-93.

Government of Canada (2014) *National anti-drug strategy*, Canada.ca: Government of Canada (http://healthycanadians.gc.ca/anti-drug-antidrogue/index-eng.php Accessed on 12/11/2014).

Graham, H. (1984) 'Surveying through stories', in C. Bell and H. Roberts (eds) *Social researching: Politics, problems, practice*, London: Routledge, pp 104-24.

Grant, B., Furlong, A., Hume, L., White, T. and Doherty, S. (2008) *Women offender substance abuse programming: Interim research report*, Ottawa, ON: Correctional Service Canada.

Gray, J. (2001) *Why our drug laws have failed and what we can do about it: A judicial indictment of the war on drugs*, Philadelphia, PA: Temple University Press.

Green, A., Day, S. and Ward, H. (2000) 'Crack cocaine and prostitution in London in the 1990s', *Sociology of Health & Illness*, vol 22, no 1, pp 27-39.

Green, C., Polen, M., Dickinson, D., Lynch, F. and Bennett, M. (2002) 'Gender differences in predictors of initiation, retention and completion in an HMO-based substance abuse treatment program', *Journal of Substance Abuse Treatment*, December, vol 23, no 4, pp 285-95.

Green, D. (1996) 'Foreword: The emerging British underclass', in R. Lister (ed) *Charles Murray and the underclass: The developing debate*, London: Health and Welfare Unit, Institute of Economic Affairs, pp 19-22.

Green, P. (1996) *Drug couriers: A new perspective*, Howard League handbooks, London: Quartet Books.

Greenfield, S., Brooks, A., Gordon, S., Green, C., Kropp, F., McHugh, R., Lincoln, M., Hien, D. and Miele, G. (2007) 'Substance abuse treatment entry, retention, and outcome in women: a review of the literature', *Drug and Alcohol Dependence*, 5 January, vol 86, no 1, pp 1-21.

Greenleaf, V. (1989) *Women and cocaine: Personal stories of addiction and recovery*, Los Angeles, CA: Lowell House.

Gregg, J., Davidson, D. and Weindling A. (1988) 'Inhaling heroin during pregnancy: effects on the baby', *British Medical Journal*, vol 296, no 6624, p 754.

Grella, C., Joshi, V. and Hser, Y. (2000) 'Program variation in treatment outcomes among women in residential drug treatment', *Evaluation Review*, vol 24, no 4, pp 364-83.

Guy, P. (2009) 'Race and the "drug problem": more than just an enforcement issue' (www.drugtext.org/Minorities/race-and-the-drug-problem-more-than-just-an-enforcement-issue.html).

Gyngell, K. (2011) *Breaking the habit: Why the state should stop dealing drugs and start doing rehab*, Guildford: Centre for Policy Studies, University of Surrey.

Gyngell, K. (2012) 'Will the coalition get to grips with the state sponsored addiction it inherited from Labour?', Mail Online, Blog, 13 January (http://gyngellblog.dailymail.co.uk/2012/01/will-the-coalition-get-to-grips-with-the-state-sponsored-addiction-it-inherited-from-labour.html).

Hacking, I. (1986) 'Making up people', in T. Heller and C. Brooke-Rose (eds) *Reconstructing individualism: Autonomy, individuality, and the self in Western thought*, Stanford, CA: Stanford University Press, pp 222-36.

Haddon, C. (1984) *Women and tranquillisers*, London: Sheldon Press.

Hall, M. (1968) 'Mental and physical efficiency of women drug addicts', *Journal of Abnormal and Social Psychology*, vol 33, pp 322-45.

Hall, W. and Lucke, J. (2010) 'Legally coerced treatment for drug using offenders: ethical and policy issues', *Contemporary Issues in Crime and Justice*, no 144, September, Crime and Justice Bulletin, Parramatta, NSW: NSW Bureau of Crime Statistics and Research (www.bocsar.nsw.gov.au/agdbasev7wr/bocsar/documents/pdf/cjb144.pdf).

Hammersley, M. and Atkinson, P. (1987) *Ethnography principles in practice*, London: Routledge.

Hammersmith and Fulham Social Services (1993) 'Child protection (and) women, pregnancy and drug use', *Links*, November, vol 6, pp 8-10.

Hannah-Moffat, K. (2000) 'Prisons that empower: neo-liberal governance in Canadian women's prisons', *British Journal of Criminology*, vol 40, pp 510-31.

Hannah-Moffat, K. (2001) *Punishment in disguise: Penal governance and federal imprisonment of women in Canada*, Toronto, ON: University of Toronto Press.

Hannah-Moffat, K. and Shaw, M. (2000) 'Prison for women: theory, reform, ideals', in K. Hannah-Moffat and M. Shaw (eds) *An ideal prison? Critical essays on women's imprisonment in Canada*, Halifax, NS: Fernwood Press, pp 11-27.

Hannah-Moffat, K. and Shaw, M. (2003) '"The meaning of risk" in women's prisons: a critique', in B. Bloom (ed) *Gendered justice: Addressing female offenders*, Durham, NC: Academic Press, pp 69-96.

Hansard (2000) Written Answers 'Drugs and alcohol (women)', 14 February.

Hanslope, J. (1994) 'Healthy women', *Druglink*, vol 9, no 2, pp 16-17.

Harding, T. (2008) 'Gender, drugs and policy', in R. Hughes, R. Lart and P. Higate (eds) *Drugs: Policy and politics*, Maidenhead: Open University Press, pp 18-30.

Harper, R., Solish, G., Purow, H., Sand, E. and Panepinto, W. (1974) 'The effect of a methadone treatment program upon pregnant heroin addicts and their newborn infants', *Paediatrics*, vol 54, pp 300-5.

Harris, M. and Fallot, R. (2001) *Using trauma theory to design service systems*, San Francisco, CA: Jossey-Bass.

Harris, N. (2008) *Getting problem drug users (back) into employment. Part one: Social security and problem drug users: Law and policy*, London: UK Drug Policy Commission.

Harrison, P. (1989) 'Women in treatment: changing over time', *International Journal of the Addictions*, vol 24, pp 655-73.

Hartnoll, R., Mitcheson, M., Battersby, A., Brown, G., Ellis, M., Fleming, P. and Hedley, M. (1980) 'Evaluation of heroin maintenance in controlled trial', *Archives of General Psychiatry*, vol 37, pp 877-84.

Hasenbeck, E. (2005) *Substance abuse recovery and reunification in the child welfare system: Mothers' stories of success*, M.S.W. dissertation, California State University, Fresno, United States.

Haslam, B. (2004) Memorandum submitted by Barry Haslam (P176) Select Committee on Health Minutes of Evidence, House of Commons, UK Parliament, Health Committee Publications.

Hawke, J., Jainchill, N. and de Leon, G. (2000) 'The prevalence of sexual abuse and its impact on the onset of drug use among adolescents in therapeutic community drug treatment', *Journal of Child & Adolescent Substance Abuse*, vol 9, no 3, pp 35-49.

Hay, G. and Bauld, L. (2008) *Population estimates of problematic drug users in England who access DWP benefits: A feasibility study*, DWP Working Paper No 46, London: Department for Work and Pensions.

Health Canada (2013) 'Heroin and other dangerous drugs are banned from health Canada's special access programme', News Release, October 3, 2013.

Heidensohn, F. (1985) *Women and crime*, New York: New York University Press.

Henderson, P. (1998) *Tackling drugs together: Report of a conference*, London: Community Development Foundation.

Henderson, S. (1990) *Women, HIV, drugs: Practical issues*, London: Institute for the Study of Drug Dependence.

Henderson, S. (1993) *Young women, sexuality and recreational drug use: A research and development project*, Manchester: Lifeline Project.

Henderson, S. (1995) *Drugs and pregnancy*, London: Institute for the Study of Drug Dependence.

Henderson, S. (1999) 'Drugs and culture: the question of gender', in N. South (ed) *Drugs: Cultures, controls and everyday life*, London: Sage Publications, pp 36-48.

Henderson, S. and Goode, J. (2001) 'Women's outreach 2001: responding to women's drug use: the development of an outreach service in North Nottinghamshire', Unpublished, North Nottinghamshire Health Authority, North Nottinghamshire Drug Action Team.

Henderson, S., Doyal, L., Naidoo, J. and Wilton, T. (eds) (1994) 'Time for a makeover? Women and drugs in the context of AIDS', in L. Doyal, J. Naidoo and T. Wilton (eds) *AIDS: Setting a feminist agenda*, London: Taylor & Francis, pp 183-95.

Hepburn, M. (1993) 'Drug misuse in pregnancy', *Current Obstetrics and Gynaecology*, vol 3, pp 54-8.

Hepburn, M. (1996) 'Drug use in pregnancy: sex, drugs and fact 'n' fiction', *Druglink*, vol 11, no 4, pp 12-14.

Hepburn, M. (1999) 'Women and drug use, Bolton Document', cited in M. Simpson, and J. McNulty (2008) 'Different needs: Women's drug use and treatment in the UK', *International Journal of Drug Policy*, vol 19, no 2, pp 169-75.

Hepburn, M., Stark C., Kidd, B.A. and Sykes, R.A.D. (1999) 'Working with women who use drugs', in C. Stark, B.A. Kidd and R.A.D. Sykes (eds) *Illegal drug use in the United Kingdom: Prevention, treatment and enforcement*, Aldershot: Ashgate, pp 131-40.

Hessler, R. (1992) *Social research methods*, St Paul, MN: West Publishing.

Hicks, C. (1999) 'More addictive than heroin', *Sunday Express Magazine*.

Higgins, J., Tanner, A. and Janssen, E. (2009) 'Arousal loss associated with condoms and risk of pregnancy: implications for women's and men's sexual risk behaviours', *Perspectives on Sexual and Reproductive Health*, vol 41, no 3, pp 150-7.

Hiller, M., Knight, K., Broome, K. and Simpson, D. (1998) 'Legal pressure and treatment retention in a national sample of long-term residential programs', *Criminal Justice and Behavior*, December, vol 25, pp 463-81.

Hinchliff, S. (2000) 'Mad for it: ecstatic women', *Druglink*, vol 15, no 5, pp 14-17.

Hinchliff, S. (2001) 'The meaning of ecstasy use to women in the late 1990s', *International Journal of Drug Policy*, vol 12, nos 5-6, pp 455-68.

Hindess, B. (1973) *Use of official statistics in sociology: Critique of positivism and ethnomethodology*, London: Macmillan.

HIT (1997) *Get set: Information for women who use drugs*, Liverpool: HIT.

HM Government (2012) *Putting full recovery first – A new agenda* (www.gov.uk/government/uploads/system/uploads/attachment_data/file/98010/recovery-roadmap.pdf).

HM Inspectorate of Prisons (2009) *Race relations in prison: Responding to adult women from black and minority ethnic backgrounds*, London: HM Inspectorate of Prisons.

Hoffman, J., Klein, H. and Crosby, H. (2000) 'Frequency and intensity of crack use as predictors of women's involvement in HIV-related sexual risk behaviors', *Drug and Alcohol Dependence*, 1 March, vol 58, no 3, pp 227-36.

Hoigard, C. and Finstad, L. (1992) *Backstreets: Prostitution, money and love*, Oxford: Polity Press.

Home Office (2001) 'Communities against drugs', booklet, London: Home Office (www.crimereduction.gov.uk/drugsalcohol20.htm).

Home Office (2002a) *Updated drug strategy 2002*, London: Home Office.

Home Office (2002b) *Tackling crack: A national plan*, London: Home Office.

Home Office (2003) *Cul-de-sacs and gateways: Understanding the positive futures approach*, London: Home Office.

Home Office (2010) *Reducing demand, restricting supply, building recovery: Supporting people to lead a drug-free life*, Drug Strategy 2010, London: Home Office.

Home Office (2012) *Putting full recovery first: the recovery roadmap*, London: Home Office.

Hopkins, E. (1989) 'Childhood's end', *Rolling Stone*, 18 October.

Howard League (2011) *No winners: The reality of short-term prison sentences*, London: Howard League.

Hser, Y. and Anglin, M.D. (2011) 'Addiction treatment and recovery careers', *Addiction Recovery Management Current Clinical Psychiatry*, pp 9-29.

Hser, Y., Anglin, M.D. and Booth, M. (1987a) 'Sex differences in addict careers 3: Addiction', *American Journal of Drug and Alcohol Abuse*, vol 13, no 3, pp 231-51.

Hser, Y., Anglin, M.D. and McGlothlin, W.H. (1987b) 'Sex differences in addict careers 1: Initiation of use', *American Journal of Drug and Alcohol Abuse*, vol 13, no 1, pp 33-57.

Hser, Y., Huang, D., Teruya, C. and Anglin, D. (2003) 'Gender comparisons of drug abuse treatment outcomes and predictors', *Drug and Alcohol Dependence*, vol 72, no 3, pp 255-64.

Huggins, L. (2005) *Drug law deadlock: The policy battle continues*, Stanford, CA: Hoover Institution, Stanford University.

Huling, T. (1995) 'Drug couriers: sentencing reform for prisoners of war', *Criminal Justice*, vol 15, pp 15-27.

Human Rights Watch (2000) *Punishment and prejudice: Racial disparities in the war on drugs*, May, vol 12, no 2, New York: Human Rights Watch (www.hrw.org/reports/2000/usa/).

Human Rights Watch (2002) *Collateral casualties: Children of incarcerated drug offenders in New York*, New York: Human Rights Watch (www.hrw.org/reports/2002/usany/).

Human Rights Watch (2008) *Targeting blacks: Drug law enforcement and race in the United States*, 5 May, New York: Human Rights Watch (www.hrw.org/reports/2008/05/04/targeting-blacks).

Humphries, D., Dawson, J., Cronin, V., Keating, P., Wisniewski, C. and Eichfield, J. (1992) 'Mothers and children, drugs and crack: reactions to maternal drug dependency', in C. Feinman (ed) *The criminalisation of a woman's body*, New York: Haworth Press, pp 203-21.

Hunt, G., Evans, K. and Karas, K. (2007) 'Drug use and meanings of risk and pleasure', *Journal of Youth Studies*, February, vol 10, no 1, pp 73-96.

Hunt, N. and Stevens, A. (2004) 'Whose harm? Harm reduction and the shift to coercion in UK drug policy', *Social Policy and Society*, vol 3, pp 333-42.

Hunter, G. and Judd, A. (1998) 'Women injecting drug users in London: the extent and nature of their contact with drug and health services', *Drug Alcohol Review*, vol 17, no 3, pp 267-76.

Hunter, G., May, T. and the Drug Strategy Directorate (2004) *Solutions and strategies: Drug problems and street sex markets: Guidance for partnerships and providers*, London: Home Office.

Hurley, D. (1991) 'Women, alcohol and incest: an analytical review', *Journal of Studies on Alcohol*, vol 52, no 3, pp 253-62.

Husak, D. (1992) *Drugs and rights*, Cambridge: Cambridge University Press.

ICSDP (International Centre for Science in Drug Policy) (2010) *Effect of drug law enforcement on drug-related violence: Evidence from a scientific review*, Vancouver, BC: ICSDP.

IDPC (International Drug Policy Consortium) (2010) *Drug policy guide*, Edition 1, March.

Iglehart, A. (1985) 'Brickin' it and going to the pan: vernacular in the black inner-city heroin lifestyle', in B. Hanson, G. Beschner, J. Walters and E. Bovelle (eds) *Life with heroin: Voices from the inner city*, Lexington, MA: D.C. Heath, pp111-33.

Inciardi, J. (ed) (1981) *The drugs-crime connection*, Beverly Hills, CA: Sage Publications.

Inciardi, J. (1995) 'Crack, crack house sex, and HIV risk', *Archives of Sexual Behaviour*, vol 24, no 3, pp 249-69.

Inciardi, J., Lockwood, D. and Pottieger, A. (1993) *Women and crack cocaine*, New York: Macmillan.

Irvine, J., Miles, I. and Evans, J. (eds) (1979) *Demystifying social statistics*, London: Pluto Press.

ISDD (Institute for the Study of Drug Dependence) (1993-94) *Drugs and you*, Information for women from ISDD, Parts 1 and 2, Factsheets 4 and 5, London: ISDD.

ITN (2000) 'Drugs killing more than heroin', ITN News Review.

James, J. (1976) 'Prostitution and addiction: an interdisciplinary approach', *Addiction Disorders*, vol 2, pp 601-18.

James, J., Gosho. C. and Whol, R. (1979) 'The relationship between female criminality and drug use', *The International Journal of the Addictions*, vol 14, no 2, pp 215-19.

Jansson, L., Svikis, D., Lee, J., Paluzzi, P., Rutigliano, P. and Hackerman, F. (1996) 'Pregnancy and addiction: a comprehensive care model', *Journal of Substance Abuse Treatment*, vol 13, pp 321-9.

Jeffery, C. (no date) 'Dads and birth defects: the inside story' (http://fasalaska.com/DadsBirthDefects.html).

Jeffries, S. (1983) 'Heroin addiction: beyond the stereotype', *Spare Rib*, July, pp 6-8.

Johnsen, D. (1992) 'Shared interests: promoting healthy births without sacrificing women's liberty', *Hastings Law Journal*, vol 43, no 3, pp 569-614.

Johnson, H. (2006) 'Factors associated with drug and alcohol dependency among women in prison', *Trends and Issues in Crime and Criminal Justice*, no 318, Canberra, ACT: Australian Institute of Criminology.

Johnson, T. (1993) 'Expertise and the state', in M. Gane and T. Johnson (eds) *Foucault's new domains*, London: Routledge, pp 139-52.

Johnstone, F. (1990) 'Drug abuse in pregnancy', *Contemporary Review of Obstetrics and Gynaecology*, vol 2, no 2, pp 96-103.

Jolly, S. and Cornwall A. (2006) ***Sexuality matters***, Brighton: Institute of Development Studies (www.ids.ac.uk/publication/sexuality-matters).

Jones, D., Irwin, K., Inciardi, J., Bowser, B., Schilling, R., Word, C., Evans, P., Faraque, S., McCoy, H. and Edlin, B. (1998) 'The high-risk sexual practices of crack-smoking sex workers recruited from the streets of three American cities', *Sexually Transmitted Diseases*, vol 3, pp 187-93.

Jones, S. (1985) 'Depth interviewing', in R. Walker (ed) *Applied qualitative research*, London: Gower, pp 45-55.

Kadaba, L. (1990) 'Crack's costly legacy', *Boston Globe*, 1 July.

Kandall, S. (1999) *Substance and shadow: Women and addiction in the United States*, Cambridge, MA: Harvard University Press.

Kandall, S., Albin, S., Lowinson, J., Berle, B., Eidelman, A. and Gartner, L. (1976) 'Differential effects of maternal heroin and methadone use on birthweight', *Paediatrics*, vol 58, pp 681-5.

Kaufman, E. (1984) *Substance abuse and family therapy*, New York: Grune & Stratton.

Kearney, P. and Ibbetson, M. (1991) 'Opiate dependent women and their babies: a study of the multi-disciplinary work of a hospital and a local authority', *British Journal of Social Work*, vol 21, no 2, pp 105-26.

Keat, R. (1979) 'Positivism and statistics in social science', in J. Irvine, I. Miles and J. Evans (eds) *Demystifying social statistics*, London: Pluto Press, pp 75-86.

Kelly. L. (1988) *Surviving sexual violence*, Cambridge: Polity Press.

Kelley, S. (1992) 'Parenting stress and child maltreatment in drug exposed children', *Child Abuse and Neglect*, vol 16, pp 317-28.

Kemp, K., Savitz, B., Thompson, W. and Zanis, D. (2004) 'Developing employment services for criminal justice clients enrolled in drug user treatment programs', *Substance Use and Misuse*, vol 39, pp 2491-511.

Kendall, K. (2002) 'Time to think again about cognitive behavioural therapy', in P. Carlen (ed) *Women and punishment: The struggle for justice*, Cullompton: Willan, pp 182-98.

Kennedy, H. (1992) *Eve was framed*, London: Vintage.

Kerr, J. (1998) 'Two myths of addiction: the addictive personality and the issue of free choice', *Human Psychopharmacology Clinical and Experimental* (Impact Factor: 2.1), 12/1998, 11(S1):S9.

Kilman, P. (1974) 'Personality characteristics of female narcotics addicts', *Psychological Reports*, vol 35, pp 485-6.

Kilty, J. (2011) 'Tensions in identity: notes on how criminalized women negotiate identity through addiction', *Aporia*, vol 3, no 3, pp 5-15.

Kim, M., Marmot, M., Dubin, N. and Wolfe, H. (1993) 'HIV risk-related sexual behaviors among heterosexuals in New York City: associations with race, sex and intravenous drug use', *AIDS*, vol 7, pp 409-14.

Kinder, D. and Walker, W. (1986) 'Stable force in a storm: Harry J. Anslinger and United States narcotic foreign policy, 1930-1962', *The Journal of American History*, vol 72, no 4, March, pp 908-27.

King, E. (1994) 'The use of the self in qualitative research', in J.T.E. Richardson (ed) *Handbook of qualitative research methods for psychology and the social sciences*, Oxford: BPS Blackwell, pp 175-88.

King, R. (2008) *Disparity by geography: The war on drugs in America's cities*, Washington, DC: The Sentencing Project.

Kingfisher, C. (2001) 'Producing disunity: The constraints and incitements of welfare work', in J. Goode and J. Maskovsky (eds), *The new poverty studies: The ethnography of power, politics, an impoverished people in the United States*, New York, NY: New York University Press, pp 273-92.

Kinnel, H. (1989) *Prostitutes, their clients and risks of HIV infection in Birmingham*, Occasional Paper, Birmingham: Department of Public Health Medicine, University of Birmingham.

Kitsuse, J.I. and Cicourel, A.V. (1963) 'On the use of official statistics', *Social Problems*, vol 11, no 2, pp 131-9.

Klee, H. (1993) 'HIV risks for women drug injectors: heroin and amphetamine users compared', *Addiction*, vol 88, no 8, pp 1055-62.

Klee, H. (1997) 'Amphetamine injecting women and their primary partners: An analysis of risk behaviour', in J. Catalan, L. Sherr, and B. Hedge (eds) *The impact of AIDS: Psychological and social aspects of HIV infection*, Harwood Academic Publishers, Amsterdam, pp 115-26.

Klee, H. (2002) 'Women, family and drugs', in H. Klee, M. Jackson and S. Lewis (eds) *Drug misuse and motherhood*, London: Routledge, pp 3-14.

Klee, H. and Council of Europe (eds) (1995) 'Women's first experiences with illicit drugs: retrospective accounts by drug using women', Women and Drugs: Focus on Prevention: Proceedings of a Symposium, Bonn, 6-7 October, Strasbourg: Council of Europe, pp 45-59.

Klee, H., Lewis, S. and Jackson, M. (1996) 'Pregnant drug users: are their fears real or imaginary?', *Archive of Public Health*, vol 54, pp 103-16.

Klenka, H. (1986) 'Babies born in district general hospital to mothers taking heroin', *British Medical Journal*, vol 293, pp 745-6.

Knight, D.K., Hood, P.E., Logan, S.M. and Chatham, L. (1999) 'Residential treatment for women with dependent children: one agency's approach', *Journal of Psychoactive Drugs*, vol 31, pp 339-51.

Koester, S. and Schwartz, J. (1993) 'Crack, gangs, sex and powerlessness: a view from Denver', in M. Ratner (ed) *Crack pipe as pimp: An ethnographic investigation of sex-for-crack exchanges*, Lanham, MD: Lexington Books, pp 187-203.

Kohn, M. (1992) *Dope girls: The birth of the British drug underground*, London: Lawrence & Wishhart.

Kohn, M. and Gootenberg, P. (eds) (1999) 'Cocaine girls: sex, drugs, and modernity in London during and after the First World War', in P. Googenberg (ed) *Cocaine: Global histories*, London: Routledge, pp 105-22.

Krane, J. and Davis, L. (2000) 'Mothering and child protection practice: rethinking risk assessment', *Child & Family Social Work*, vol 5, no 1, pp 35-45.

Krutilla, J. (1993) 'School expectations from drug using family: assisting and understanding the child and the home', Paper presented at the Meeting of the South Carolina Council for Exceptional Children, Myrtle Beach, SC, 27 February (http://eric.ed.gov/?id=ED357307).

Kruttschnitt, C. (2010) 'The paradox of women's imprisonment', *Daedalus*, vol 139, no 3, pp 32-42.

Kruttschnitt, C. and Rosemary G. (2003) 'Women's imprisonment', in M. Tonry (ed) *Crime and justice: A review of research*, vol 30, Chicago, IL: University of Chicago Press, pp 55-135.

Kullar, S. (2009) 'The social construction of substance using women in BC's child welfare system', MA Social Work thesis, University of British Columbia.

Langan, N. and Pelissier, B. (2001) 'Gender differences among prisoners in drug treatment', *Journal of Substance Abuse*, vol 13, pp 291-301.

Lapidus, L., Luthra, N.A., Verma, A., Small, D., Allard, P. and Levingston, K. (2005) *Caught in the net: The impact of drug policies on women and families*, New York and Berkeley, CA: American Civil Liberties Union, Break the Chains: Communities of Color and the War on Drugs, Brennan Center at NYU School of Law (www.ccjrc.org/pdf/Caught_in_the_Net.pdf).

Larimer, M. and Kilmer, J. (2000) 'Natural history', in G. Zernig, A. Saria, M. Kurz and S. O'Malley (eds) *Handbook of alcoholism*, Boca Raton, FL: CRC Press, pp 13-28.

Larner, W. and Walters, W. (2004) *Globalisation as governmentality*, Special edition of *Alternatives* (edited by M. Dean and P. Henman), vol 29, no 5, pp 495-514.

Lee, A. and Schofield, S. (1994) 'Drug use in pregnancy: general principles', *Pharmacology Journal*, vol 253, no 6796, pp 27-30.

Leifer, M., Shapiro, J. and Kassem, L. (1993) 'The impact of maternal history and behaviour upon foster placement and adjustment in sexually abused girls', *Child Abuse and Neglect*, vol 17, pp 755-66.

Leitner, M., Shapland, J. and Wiles, P. (1993) *Drug usage and drugs prevention: The views and habits of the general public*, London: HMSO.

Leshner, A.I. (1999) 'Research shows effects of prenatal cocaine exposure are subtle but significant', *NIDA Archives*, NIDA Notes, Director's Column, September, vol 14, no 3 (http://archives.drugabuse.gov/NIDA_Notes/NNVol14N3/DirRepVol14N3.html).

Levi, R. and Appel, J. (2003) *Collateral consequences: Denial of basic social services based upon drug use*, Berkeley, CA: Office of Legal Affairs, Drug Policy Alliance.

Levine, H.G. (2001) 'The secret of world-wide drug prohibition: the varieties and uses of drug prohibition', *Hereinstead*, October (www.cedro-uva.org/lib/levine.secret.html/).

Levitas, R. (1998) *The inclusive society? Social exclusion and New Labour*, London: Macmillan.

Levy, S. and Doyle, K. (1974) 'Attitudes toward women in a drug treatment program', *Journal of Drug Issues*, vol 4, pp 423-4.

Levy-Pounds, N. (2006) 'Children of incarcerated mothers and the struggle for stability', *The Modern American*, vol 2, issue 2, Summer (Commemorative Sylvania Woods issue).

Lewis, D. and Watters, J. (1991) 'Sexual behaviour among heterosexual intravenous drug users: ethnic and gender variations', *AIDS*, vol 5, pp 67-73.

Lewis, S., Klee, H. and Jackson, M. (1995) 'Illicit drug users' experiences of pregnancy: an exploratory study', *Journal of Reproductive and Infant Psychology*, vol 3, pp 219-27.

Lievore, D. (2002) *Non-reporting and hidden recording of sexual assault: An international literature review*, Canberra, ACT: Australian Institute of Criminology.

Lind, B., Chen, S., Weatherburn, D. and Mattick, R. (2005) 'The effectiveness of methadone maintenance treatment in controlling crime: an Australian aggregate-level analysis', *Journal of Criminology*, vol 45, no 2, pp 201-11.

Lindesmith, A. (1968) *Addiction and opiates*, Chicago, IL: Aldine de Gruyter.

Liriano, S. and Ramsay, M. (2003) 'Prisoners' drug use before prison and the links with crime', in M. Ramsay (ed) *Prisoners' drug use and treatment: Seven research studies*, Home Office Research Study 267, pp 7-22.

Lister, R. (ed) (1996) *Charles Murray and the underclass: The developing debate*, London: Health and Welfare Unit, Institute of Economic Affairs.

Lockyer, K. (2013) *Future prisons – A radical plan to reform the prison estate*, London: Policy Exchange.

Logan, T., Leukefeld, C. and Farabee, D. (1998) 'Sexual and drug behaviours among women crack users: implications for presenting AIDS', *Educational Preview*, vol 10, no 4, pp 327-40.

Longshore, D., Prendergast, M.L. and Farabee, D. (2004) 'Coerced treatment for drug-using criminal offenders', in P. Bean and T. Nemitz (eds) *Drug treatment: What works?*, New York: Routledge, pp 110-22.

Luck, P.A., Elifson, K.W. and Sterk, C.E. (2004) 'Female drug users and the welfare system: a qualitative exploration', *Drugs: Education, Prevention and Policy*, vol 11, pp 113-28.

Lupton, D. (1999) *Risk: Key ideas*, London: Routledge.

Lutiger, B., Graham, K., Einarson, T. and Koren, G. (1991) 'Relationship between gestational cocaine use and pregnancy outcome: a meta-analysis', *Teratology*, vol 44, no 4, pp 405-14.

MacDonald, S., Bois, C., Brands, B., Dempsey, D., Erickson, P. and Marsh, D. (2001) 'Drug testing and mandatory treatment for welfare recipients', *International Journal of Drug Policy*, vol 12, pp 249-57.

MacDonald, V. (1997) 'Prescribed drugs do more harm to babies than heroin', *Sunday Telegraph*, 21 September.

MacGregor, S. (1999) 'Drugs and culture: the question of gender', in N. South (ed) *Drugs: Cultures, controls and everyday life*, London: Sage Publications, pp 36-48.

MacGregor, S. (2000) *Drugs research funded by central government: A review*, London: Social Policy Research Centre, Middlesex University.

MacGregor, S. and Lipow, A. (eds) (1995) *The other city: People and politics in New York and London*, Atlantic Highlands, NJ: Humanities Press.

Macrory, F. (1997) *Drug use, pregnancy and care of the newborn*, St Mary's Hospital for Women and Children and Manchester Drug Service.

McCoy, H. and Inciardi, J. (1993) 'Women and AIDS: social determinants of sex-related activities', *Women Health*, vol 20, no 1, pp 69-86.

McCoy, H., Miles, C. and Inciardi, J.A. (1995) 'Survival sex: inner city women and crack cocaine', in J.A. Inciardi and K. McElrath (eds) *The American Drugs Scene: An Anthology*, Los Angeles, CA: Roxbury, pp 172-77.

McCusker, C. and Davies, M. (1996) 'Prescribing drug of choice to illicit heroin users: the experience of a UK community drug team', *Journal of Substance Abuse Treatment*, vol 13, pp 521-31.

McGrath, R. (1993) 'Health education and authority', in V. Harwood (ed) *Pleasure principles: Politics, sexuality and ethics*, London: Lawrence & Wishart, pp 158-83.

McGregor, K. and Makkai, T. (2003) *Self-reported drug use: How prevalent is under-reporting?*, Canberra: Trends and Issues in Crime and Criminal Justice, Australian Institute of Criminology.

McIntosh, J. and McKeganey, N. (2000) 'Addicts' narratives of recovery from drug use: constructing a non-addict identity', *Social Sciences & Medicine*, vol 50, pp 1501-10.

McKee, L. and O'Brien, M. (1983) 'Interviewing men: "taking gender seriously"', in E. Gamarnikow et al (eds) *The public and the private*, London: Heinemann, pp 147-76.

McKeganey, N., Neale, J. and Robertson, M. (2005) 'Physical and sexual abuse among drug users contacting drug treatment services in Scotland', *Drugs: Education, Prevention and Policy*, vol 12, issue 3, pp 223-32.

McKeganey, N., Barnard, M., Leyland, A., Coote, I. and Follet, E. (1992) 'Female street-working prostitution and HIV infection in Glasgow', *British Medical Journal*, vol 305, pp 801-4.

McKormack, P. (2007) 'Essays: Noam Chomsky on drugs: Part IV' (www.petemccormack.com/essays_NCdrugs4.htm).

Maden, A., Swinton, M. and Gunn, J. (1990) 'Women in prison and use of illicit drugs before arrest', *British Medical Journal*, 17 November, vol 301, p 1133.

Maher, L. (1990) 'Criminalizing pregnancy: the downside of a kinder, gentler nation?', *Social Justice*, vol 17, no 3, pp 111-35.

Maher, L. (1992) 'Punishment and welfare: crack cocaine and the regulation of mothering', in C. Feinman (ed) *The criminalization of a woman's body*, New York: Haworth Press, pp 157-92.

Maher, L. (1995a) 'In the name of love: women and initiation to illicit drugs', in R. Dobash, R. Dobash and L. Noaks (eds) *Gender and crime*, Cardiff: University of Wales Press, pp 132-66.

Maher, L. (1995b) 'Dope girls: gender, race and class in the drug economy', Doctoral dissertation, Rutgers University, Ann Arbour, MI: University Microfilms International.

Maher, L. (1997) *Sexed work: Gender, race and resistance in a Brooklyn drug market*, Oxford: Clarendon Press.

Maher, L. (2002) 'Don't leave us this way: ethnography and injecting drug use in the age of AIDS', *International Journal of Drug Policy*, vol 13, pp 311-25.

Maher, L. and Curtis, R. (1992) 'Women on the edge of crime: crack cocaine and the changing contexts of street-level sex work in New York City', *Crime Law Social Change*, vol 18, no 3, pp 221-8.

Maher, L. and Daly, K. (1996) 'Women in the street level drug economy', *Criminology*, vol 34, pp 465-91.

Makkai, T. and McGregor, K. (2002) 'Drugs and crime: calculating attributable fractions from the DUMA project', in D.J. Collins and H.M. Lapsley, *Counting the cost: Estimate of the social costs of drug abuse in Australia in 1998-99*, Monograph Series No 49, Canberra: Commonwealth Department of Health and Ageing, Appendix D.

Malloch, M. (2000) *Women, drugs and custody: The experiences of women drug users in prison*, Winchester: Waterside Press.

Malloch, M. (2004a) 'Not "fragrant" at all: criminal justice responses to "risky" women', *Critical Social Policy*, vol 24, no 3, pp 385-405.

Malloch, M. (2004b) 'Missing out: gender, drugs and justice', *Probation Journal*, vol 51, no 4, pp 295-308.

Malloch, M. (2004c) 'Women, drug use and the criminal justice system', in G. McIvor (ed) *Female offenders and female offending*, Research Highlights in Social Work 44, London: Jessica Kingsley Publishers, pp 246-66.

Mann, C. (1995) 'Women of color and the criminal justice system', in B. Price and N. Sokoloff (eds) *The criminal justice system and women: Offenders, victims, and workers* (2nd edn), New York: McGraw-Hill, pp 118-35.

Margulies, M. (1972) 'Women and drugs', *Parade Magazine*.

Marsh, J. (1982) 'Public issues and private problems: women and drug use', *Journal of Social Issues*, vol 38, no 2, pp 1-8.

Marsh, J., D'Anino, T. and Smith, B. (2000) 'Increasing access and providing social services to improve drug abuse treatment for women and children', *Addiction*, vol 95, no 8, pp 1237-48.

Mathers, B., Degenhardt, L., Phillips, B., Wiessing, L., Hickman, M., Strathdee, S., Wodak, A., Panda, S., Tyndall, M., Toufik, A. and Mattick, R. (2008) 'Global epidemiology of injecting drug use and HIV among people who inject drugs: a systematic review', *Lancet*, 15 November, vol 372, no 9651, pp 1733-45.

Mathias, R. (1992) 'Developmental effects of prenatal drug exposure may be overcome by postnatal environment', *NIDA Notes*, vol 7, no 1, pp 14-17.

Matthews, L. (1993) 'Outreach on the front line – crack's damaging impact on the lives of Liverpool's street prostitutes', *Druglink*, vol 8, no 2, pp 14-15.

Matthews, L. (1995) 'Outreach work with female sex workers in Liverpool', in C. Siney (ed) *The Pregnant Drug Addict*, Hale: Books for Midwives Press, pp 83-91.

Matthews, L. and Plant, M. (eds) (1990) 'Outreach work with female prostitutes in Liverpool', in M.A. Plant (ed) *AIDS, drugs and prostitution*, London and New York: Routledge, pp 76-87.

Mattick, R., Breen, C., Kimber, J. and Davoli, M. (2009) *Methadone maintenance therapy versus no opioid replacement therapy for opioid dependence (Review) Cochrane Collaboration*, The Cochrane Library 2009, issue 3, Wiley and Sons.

Mauer, M. (2013) *The changing racial dynamics of women's incarceration*, Washington, DC: The Sentencing Project.

Mauer, M. and Huling, T. (1995) *Young black Americans and the criminal justice system: Five years later*, Washington, DC: The Sentencing Project.

Mauer, M. and McCalmont, V. (2013) *A lifetime of punishment: The impact of the felony drug ban on welfare benefits*, Washington, DC: The Sentencing Project.

Mauer, M., Potler, C. and Wolf, R. (1999) *Gender and justice: Women, drugs and sentencing policy*, Washington, DC: The Sentencing Project.

May, T., Harocops, A. and Hough, M. (2000) *For love or money: Pimps and the management of sex work*, PRCU Paper 134, London: Policing and Reducing Crime Unit, Home Office.

Meade, G. (2004) 'GPs turning millions into prescription drug addicts', *The Scotsman*, 4 February (benzo.org.uk/scotsman1.htm).

Measham, F. (2002) '"Doing gender" – "doing drugs": conceptualizing the gendering of drug cultures', *Contemporary Drug Problems*, vol 29, pp 335-73.

Merleau-Ponty, M. (1967) *Phenomenology of perception*, London: Routledge.

Merlo, A. and Pollock, J. (eds) (2006) *Women, law, and social control* (2nd edn), Boston, MA: Allyn & Bacon.

Messerschmidt, J. (1986) *Capitalism, patriarchy and crime*, Lanham, MD: Rowan & Littlefield.

Metsch, L., McCoy, C., Shultz, J., Page, J., Phillipe, E. and McKay, C. (1999) 'Gender comparisons of injection drug use practices in shooting galleries', *Population Research and Policy Review*, vol 18, pp 101-17.

Metzger, D., Woody, G., McLellan, A., O'Brien, C., Druley, P., Navaline, H., DePhilippis, D., Stolley, P. and Abrutyn, E. (1993) 'Human immunodeficiency virus seroconversion among intravenous drug users in- and out-of-treatment: an 18-month prospective follow-up', *Journal of Acquired Immune Deficiency Syndromes*, September, vol 6, no 9, pp 1049-56.

Mieczkowski, T. (ed) (1991) *Drugs and crime: A reader*, Boston, MA: Allyn & Bacon.

Mieczkowski, T. (1994) 'The experiences of women who sell crack: some description data from the Detroit Crack Ethnography Project', *Journal of Drug Issues*, vol 24, nos 1 and 2, pp 227-48.

Mies, M. (1983) 'Towards a methodology for feminist research', in G. Bowles and K. Renate Duelli (eds) *Theories of women's studies*, London: Routledge & Kegan Paul.

Miles, I. and Irvine, J. (1979) 'The critique of official statistics', in J. Irvine, I. Miles and J. Evans (eds) *Demystifying social statistics*, London: Pluto Press, pp 113-29.

Miller, B., Downs, W., Gondoli, D. and Keil, A. (1987) 'The role of sexual abuse in the development of alcoholism in women', *Violence and Victims*, vol 2, no 3, pp 157-72.

Miller, E. (1986) *Street women*, Philadelphia, PA: Temple University Press.

Miller, P. and Rose, N. (1990) 'Governing economic life', *Economy and Society*, vol 19, 1 February.

Miller, P. and Rose, N. (1992) 'Political power beyond the state: problematics of government', *British Journal of Sociology*, vol 43, no 2, pp 173-205.

Miller, P. and Rose, N. (1993) 'Governing economic life', in M. Gane and T. Johnson (eds) *Foucault's new domains*, London: Routledge, pp 75-106.

Miller, W. and Muñoz, R. (2005) *Controlling your drinking*, New York: Guilford Press.

Milloy, C. (1989) 'A time bomb in cocaine babies', *Washington Post*, 17 September.

Mills, S. (2003) *Michel Foucault*, London: Routledge.

Milner, J. (1993) 'A disappearing act: the differing career paths of fathers and mothers in child protection', *Critical Social Policy*, vol 13, pp 48-63.

Ministry of Justice (2013) *Story of the prison population: 1993-2012 England and Wales*, London: Ministry of Justice.

Miron, J. (2004) *Drug war crimes: The consequences of prohibition*, Oakland, CA: The Independent Institute.

Mondanaro, J. (1987) 'Strategies for AIDS prevention: motivating health behaviour in drug-dependent women', *Journal of Psychoactive Drugs*, vol 19, no 2, pp 143-8.

Mondanaro, J. (1989) *Chemically dependent women: Assessment and treatment*, Lanham, MD: Lexington Books.

Mondanaro, J. (1990) 'Community based AIDS prevention interventions: special issues of women intravenous drug users', in C.G. Leukfield, R.G. Battjes and Z. Amsel (eds) *AIDS and intravenous drug use: Future directions for community-based prevention research*, National Institute on Drug Abuse Research Monograph 93, Rockville, MD: US Department of Public Health.

Morgan, P. and Joe, K. (1997) 'Uncharted terrain: contexts of experience among women in the illicit drug economy', *Women and Criminal Justice*, vol 8, no 3, pp 85-103.

Morningstar, P.J. and Chitwood, D.D. (1987) 'How women and men get cocaine: sex-role stereotypes and acquisition patterns', *Journal of Psychoactive Drugs*, vol 19, no 2, pp 135-42.

Morris, L. (1994) *Dangerous class: The underclass and social citizenship*, London: Routledge, Taylor & Francis Group.

Morrison, C.L. and Siney, C. (1996) 'A survey of the management of neonatal opiate withdrawal in England and Wales', *European Journal of Paediatrics*, vol 155, pp 323-6.

Moser, C. and Kalton, G. (1971) *Survey methods in social investigation*, Aldershot: Gower.

Moses, D., Huntington, N. and D'Ambrosio, B. (2004) *Developing integrated services for women with co-occurring disorders and trauma histories: Lessons from the SAMHSA women with alcohol, drug abuse and mental health disorders who have histories of violence study*, Washington, DC: National Center on Family Homelessness.

Muller, R., Fitzgerald, H., Sullivan, L. and Zucker, R. (1994) 'Social support and stress factors in child maltreatment among alcoholic families', *Canadian Journal of Behavioural Science*, vol 26, no 3, pp 438-61.

Murphy, J. (2007) 'The intersection of the criminal justice system and the medical treatment establishment in the labelling and managing of substance abuse problem', Paper presented at the Annual Meeting of the American Sociological Association, New York, 11 August.

Murphy S. (1987) 'Intravenous drug use and AIDS: notes on the social economy of needle sharing', *Contemporary Drug Problems*, vol 14, pp 373-95.

Murphy, S. and Rosenbaum, M. (1987) 'Women and substance abuse. Introduction', Special Edition, *Investigations into Psychoactive Drugs*, vol 20, no 4.

Murray, C. (1996) 'The emerging British underclass', in R. Lister (ed) *Charles Murray and the underclass: The developing debate*, London: Health and Welfare Unit, Institute of Economic Affairs, pp 23-52.

Naeye, R.L., Ladis, B. and Drage, J.S. (1976) 'Sudden infant death syndrome: a prospective study', *American Journal of Disease in Childhood*, vol 130, pp 1207-10.

Naeye, R.L., Blanc, W., Leblanc, W. and Khatamee, M. (1973) 'Fetal complications of maternal heroin addiction: abnormal growth, infection and episodes of stress', *Journal of Paediatrics*, vol 83, pp 1055-61.

Naffine, N. (1987) *Female crime: The construction of women in criminology*, London: Allen & Unwin.

Najavits, L., Weiss, R. and Shaw, S. (1997) 'The link between substance abuse and posttraumatic stress disorder in women', *American Journal on Addictions*, vol 6, no 4, pp 273-83.

NAPW (National Advocates for Pregnant Women) (2010) 'Prenatal exposure to illegal drugs and alcohol: media hype and enduring myths are not supported by science', 24 March, New York: NAPW (http://advocatesforpregnantwomen.org/main/publications/fact_sheets/_prenatal_exposure_to_illegal_drugs_and_alcohol_media_hype_and_enduring_myths_are_not_supported_by_science.php).

NASADAD (National Association of State Alcohol and Drug Abuse Directors) (2008) *Guidance to states: Treatment standards for women with substance use disorders*, Washington, DC: NASADAD.

National Center for Injury Prevention and Control (2010) *The National Intimate Partner and Sexual Violence Survey*, 2010 summary report, Division of Violence Prevention.

Navarro, V. (1976) *Medicine under capitalism*, New York: Croom Helm.

NCSL (National Conference of State Legislatures) (2010) *Fetal homicide laws*, Washington, DC: NCSL (www.ncsl.org/research/health/fetal-homicide-state-laws.aspx).

Neaigus, A., Miller, M. and Friedman, S. (2001) 'Potential risk factors for the transition to injecting among non-injecting heroin users: a comparison of former injectors and never injectors', *Addiction*, vol 96, pp 847-60.

Nelson-Zlupko, L., Kauffman, E. and Dore, M.M. (1995) 'Gender differences in drug addiction and treatment: implications for social work intervention with substance-abusing women', *Social Work*, vol 40, pp 45-54.

Nelson-Zlupko, L., Dore, M.M., Kauffman, E. and Kaltenbach, K. (1996) 'Women in recovery', *Journal of Substance Abuse Treatment*, vol 13, pp 51-9.

Neuberg, R. (1970) 'Drug dependence and pregnancy: a review of the problems and their management', *Journal of Obstetrics and Gynaecology of the British Commonwealth*, vol 77, no 12, pp 117-22.

Newburn, T. and Pearson, G. (2002) *Drug use among young people in care*, Sheffield: Youth Citizenship and Social Change Programme.

Newcombe, R. (1996) 'Live and let die: is methadone more likely to kill you than heroin?', *Druglink*, vol 11, no 1, pp 9-12.

Newham Drugs Advice Project (no date) *Women rock users: Women partners of rock users*, London: Newham Drugs Advice Project, leaflet.

Newman, R.G. (1974) 'Pregnancies of methadone patients', *New York State Journal of Medicine*, vol 1, pp 52-4.

NIDA (National Institute on Drug Abuse) (2005) 'Pregnancy and drug use trends', NIDA InfoFacts (www.nida.nih.gov/Infofacts/pregnancytrends.html).

NIDA (2011) 'Prenatal exposure to drugs of abuse', A research update from the National Institute on Drug Abuse, May, Bethesda, MD: NIDA (www.drugabuse.gov/sites/default/files/prenatal.pdf).

NIDA (2012) 'What are the effects of maternal cocaine use?' (www.drugabuse.gov/publications/research-reports/cocaine/what-are-effects-maternal-cocaine-use).

NIDA (2014) 'Drugs, brains and behaviour: the science of addiction' (www.drugabuse.gov/publications/drugs-brains-behavior-science-addiction/preface).

Norfolk Mental Healthcare NHS Trust (1997) *Pregnancy and drug use protocol: Recommended procedure and policy guidelines for inter-agency working*, Norfolk: NHS Trust Norfolk.

NTA (National Treatment Agency) (2002) *Models of care for the treatment of adult drug misusers*, London: NTA for Substance Misuse (www.nta.nhs.uk/uploads/nta_modelsofcare2_2002_moc2.pdf).

NTA (2010) *Women in drug treatment: What the latest figures reveal*, London: NTA for Substance Misuse (www.nta.nhs.uk/uploads/ntawomenintreatment22march2010.pdf).

NTA (2012) 'Drug treatment in England: The road to recovery', London: NTA for Substance Misuse (www.nta.nhs.uk/uploads/dtie2012v1.pdf).

Oakley, A. (1974) *The sociology of housework*, Oxford: Martin Robertson.

Oakley, A. (1981a) *From here to maternity*, Harmondsworth: Penguin.

Oakley, A. (1981b) 'Interviewing women: a contradiction in terms', in H. Roberts (ed) *Doing feminist research*, London: Routledge & Kegan Paul, pp 30-61.

O'Connell Davidson, J. and Layder, D. (1994) *Methods, sex and madness*, London: Routledge.

O'Halloran, T. (1984) 'Women in jail getting dosed to the eyeballs', *New Statesman*, 5 October, p 5.

O'Leary, A. (2000) 'Women at risk for HIV from a primary partner: balancing risk and intimacy', *Annual Review of Sex Research*, vol 11, pp 191-234.

O'Malley, P. (1992) 'Risk, power and crime prevention', *Economy and Society*, vol 21, no 3, pp 252-75.

O'Malley, P. (1996) 'Risk and responsibility', in A. Barry, T. Osborne and N. Rose (eds) *Foucault and political reason: Liberalism, neo-liberalism, and rationalities of government*, Chicago, IL: The University of Chicago Press, Chapter 9.

O'Malley, P. (1999) 'Consuming risks: harm minimization and the government of drug users', in R. Smandych (ed) *Governable places: Readings on governmentality and crime control*, Aldershot: Ashgate Publishing Ltd, pp 103-31.

O'Malley, P. (2002) 'Drugs, risks and freedoms', in G. Hughes and E. McLaughlen (eds) *Crime prevention and community safety: New directions*, Milton Keynes: Open University Press, pp 279-96.

O'Malley, P. (2008) 'Neoliberalism and risk in criminology', in T. Anthony and C. Cunneen (eds) *The critical criminology companion*, Leichhardt, NSW: Federation Press, pp 55-67, Sydney Law School Research Paper No 09/83 (http://ssrn.com/abstract=1472862).

O'Malley, P. and Valverde, M. (2004) 'Pleasure, freedom and drugs: The uses of 'pleasure' in liberal governance of drug and alcohol consumption', *Sociology*, vol 38, no 1, pp 25-42.

ONDCP (Office of National Drug Control Policy) (2010) *Office of National Drug Control Policy*, Washington, DC: The White House.

Oppenheim, C. (1998) 'An overview of poverty and social exclusion', in C. Oppenheim (ed) *An inclusive society: Strategies for tackling poverty*, London: Institute for Public Policy Research, pp 11-28.

Oppenheimer, E. (1991) 'Alcohol and drug misuse among women – an overview', *British Journal of Psychiatry*, vol 158, no 10, pp 36-44.

Oppenheimer, E., Strang, J. and Gossop, M. (eds) (1994) 'Women drug misusers: a case for special consideration', in J. Strang and M. Gossop (eds) *Heroin addiction and drug policy: The British system*, Oxford: Oxford University Press, pp 79-99.

Ostrea, E., Chavez, C. and Strauss, M. (1976) 'A study of factors that influence the severity of neonatal narcotics withdrawal', *Journal of Paediatrics*, vol 88, pp 642-5.

Owen, B. (1998) *'In the mix': Struggle and survival in a women's prison*, New York: SUNY Press.

Owen, B. (2000) 'Women and imprisonment in the United States: the gendered consequences of the US imprisonment binge', in S. Cook and S. Davies (eds) *Harsh punishments: International experiences of women's imprisonment*, Boston, MA: Northeastern Press, pp 81-98.

Pagliaro, A.M. and Pagliaro, L.A. (1999) *Substance use among women: A reference and resource guide*, Philadelphia, PA and London: Taylor & Francis.

Paltrow, L. (1992) *Criminal prosecutions against pregnant women: National update and overview*, Reproductive Freedom Project, American Civil Liberties Union Foundation, April.

Paltrow, L. (1993) *Criminal prosecutions against pregnant women: National update and overview*, American Civil Libraries Union Foundation, April.

Paone, D. and Alperen, J. (1998) 'Pregnancy policing: policy of harm', *International Journal of Drug Policy*, vol 9, pp 101-8.

Paone, D., Chavkin, W., Willets, I., Fried-Mann, P. and Des Jarlais, D. (1992) 'The impact of sexual abuse: implications for drug treatment', *Journal of Women's Health*, vol 1, pp 149-53.

Parker, H. and Measham, F. (1994) 'Pick n mix: changing patterns of illicit drug use amongst 1990s adolescents', *Drug Education Prevention and Policy*, vol 1, pp 5-13.

Parker, H. and Kirby, P. (1996) *Methadone maintenance and crime reduction on Merseyside*, Police Research Group – Crime Detection and Prevention Series Paper 72, London: Home Office.

Parker, H., Aldridge, J. and Measham, F. (1998) *Illegal leisure: The normalisation of adolescent recreational drug use*, London: Routledge.

Parker, H., Bakx, K. and Newcombe, R. (1988) *Living with heroin*, Milton Keynes: Open University Press.

Parton, N. (1991) *Governing the family: Childcare, child protection and the state*, London: Macmillan.

Passaro, C., Little, R., Savits, D., Noss, J. and the ALSPAC Study Team (1998) 'Effect of paternal alcohol consumption before conception on infant birth weight', *Teratology*, vol 57, pp 294-301.

Patton, C. (1985) *Sex and germs*, Boston, MA: South End Press.

Paul-Emile, K. (1989) 'Charleston policy: substance or abuse', *4 Mich Journal of Race and Law*, vol 325 (http://ir.lawnet.fordham.edu/cgi/viewcontent.cgi?article=1394&context=faculty_scholarship).

Payne-James, J., Wall, I. and Bailey, C. (2005) 'Patterns of illicit drug use of prisoners in police custody in London, UK', *Journal of Clinical Forensic Medicine*, vol 12, pp 196-8.

Pearce, J., Marlow, A. and Pearson, G. (1999) 'Selling sex, doing drugs and keeping safe', in A. Marlow and G. Pearson (eds) *Young people, drugs and community safety*, Lyme Regis: Russell House Publishing, pp 118-26.

Pearson, G. (1987) *The new heroin users*, Oxford: Basil Blackwell.

Pearson, G. (1999) 'Drugs at the end of the century', *British Journal of Criminology*, vol 39, no 4, pp 477-87.

Pearson, G. (2001) 'Normal drug use: ethnographic fieldwork among an adult network of recreational drug users in Inner London', *Substance Use and Misuse*, vol 36, nos 1 and 2, pp 167-200.

Pearson, G., Gilman, M. and McIver, S. (1986) *Young people and heroin: An examination of heroin use in the North of England*, London: Health Education Council.

Perneger, T.V., Giner, F., del Rio, M. and Mino, A. (1998) 'Randomised trial of heroin maintenance programme for addicts who fail in conventional drug treatments', *British Medical Journal*, vol 317, no 7150, pp 13-18.

Perry, L. (1979) *Women and drug use: An unfeminine dependency*, London: Institute for the Study of Drug Dependence.

Perry, L. (1987) 'Fit to be parents?', *Druglink*, vol 2, no 1, p 6.

Perry, L. (1991) *Women and drug use: An unfeminine dependency*, London: Institute for the Study of Drug Dependence.

Pettinati, H., Rukstalis, M., Luck, G., Volpicelli, J. and O'Brien, C. (2000) 'Gender and psychiatric comorbidity: impact on clinical presentation of alcohol dependence', *American Journal on Addictions*, vol 9, no 3, pp 242-52.

Pettiway, L.E. (1987) 'Participation in crime partnerships by female drug users: the effects of domestic arrangements, drug use and criminal involvement', *Criminology*, vol 25, no 3, pp 741-66.

Peyrot, M. (1984) 'Cycles of social problem development', *Sociology Quarterly*, vol 25, pp 83-96.

Philips, K. (1986) 'Neonatal drug addicts', *Nursing Times*, 19 March, pp 36-8.

Phoenix, A. (1994) 'Practicing feminist research: the intersection of gender and "race" in the research process', in M. Maynard and J. Purvis (eds) *Researching women's lives from a feminist perspective*, London: Taylor & Francis, 49-71.

Phoenix. J. (1997) 'Making sense of prostitution today', PhD thesis, Bath: University of Bath.

Phoenix, J. (1999) *Making sense of prostitution*, London: Palgrave.

Pierson, J. (2002) *Tackling social exclusion*, London: Routledge.

Plant, A. (ed) (1990) *AIDS, drugs, and prostitution*, London and New York: Tavistock-Routledge.

Plant, M. (1975) *Drugtakers in an English town*, London: Tavistock.

Plant, M., Plant, M., Peck, D. and Setters, J. (1989) 'The sex industry, alcohol and illicit drugs: implications for the spread of HIV infection', *British Journal of Addiction*, vol 84, pp 53-9.

Polit, D., Nuttal, R. and Hunter, J. (1976) 'Women and drugs: a look at some of the issues', *Urban Social Change Review*, vol 9, no 2, pp 9-16.

Political Research Associates (2005) *How the criminal justice system is anti-women: Factsheet*, Defending Justice, An Activists Resource Kit, Somerville MA (http://www.publiceye.org/defendingjustice/pdfs/factsheets/14-Fact%20Sheet%20-%20System%20as%20Anti-Women.pdf).

Pollack, S. (2010) 'Labelling clients "risky": social work and the neoliberal state', *British Journal of Social Work*, vol 40, pp 1263-78.

Poole, N. (2004) 'Working with women concurrently on substance use, experience of trauma and mental health issues', *Visions: BC's Mental Health and Addictions Journal*, vol 2, no 1, Winter, pp 29-30.

Poole, N. and Dell, C.A. (2005) *Girls, women and substance use* (www.addictionresearchchair.ca/wp-content/uploads/Girls-Women-and-Substance-Use.pdf).

Poole, N. and Isaac, B. (2001) *Apprehensions: Barriers to treatment for substance-using mothers*, Vancouver: BC Centre of Excellence for Women's Health.

Positively Women (1990) *Women and AIDS: 4 Women, drugs and HIV*, London: Positively Women, leaflet.

Powers, K. and Anglin, M.D. (1993) 'Cumulative versus stabilizing effects of methadone maintenance', *Evaluation Review*, vol 17, no 3, pp 243-70.

Powis, B., Gossop, M., Bury, C., Payne, K. and Griffiths, P. (2000) 'Drug-using mothers: social, psychological and substance use problems of women opiate users with children', *Drug and Alcohol Review*, vol 19, no 2, pp 171-80.

Preble, E. and Casey, J.J. (1969) 'Taking care of business – the heroin user's life on the street', *International Journal of the Addictions*, vol 4, pp 1-24.

PRNewswire (2004) 'GPs admit to over-prescribing', *News Release*, Tuesday 30 March (www.prnewswire.co.uk/news-releases/gps-admit-to-over-prescribing-154838665.html).

Prochaska, J. and DiClemente, C. (1992) *Stages of change in the modification of problem behaviors*, Newbury Park, CA: Sage Publications.

PRT (Prison Reform Trust) (2000) *Justice for women: The need for reform*, Report of the Committee on Offending, London: PRT.

PRT (2004) *Forgotten prisoners – The plight of foreign national prisoners in England and Wales*, London: PRT.

PRT (2010) 'Women in prison', London: PRT (www.prisonreformtrust.org.uk/uploads/documents/Women%20in%20Prison%20August%202010.pdf)

PRT (2013) 'Prison: the facts', Bromley Briefings, Summer 2013 (www.prisonreformtrust.org.uk/Portals/0/Documents/Prisonthefacts.pdf).

Public Accounts Committee (2010) *Tackling problem drug use, Thirtieth report of Session 2009-10*, London: House of Commons.

Public Law (1996) *Housing Opportunity Program Extension Act of 1996*, 104th Congress, 104-120, 28 March.

PwC (PricewaterhouseCoopers) (2008) *Review of prison-based drug treatment funding*, London: Ministry of Justice.

Radcliffe, P. and Stevens, A. (2008) 'Are drug treatment services only for "thieving junkie scumbags"? Drug users and the management of stigmatised identities', *Social Science & Medicine*, October, vol 67, no 7, pp 1065-73.

Rajegowder, B.K., Glass, L., Evans, H.A., Maso, G., Swartz, D.P. and LeBlanc, W. (1972) 'Methadone withdrawal in new-born infants', *Journal of Pediatrics*, vol 81, no 3, pp 532-4.

Randolph, M., Pinkerton, S., Bogart L., Cecil, H. and Abramson, P. (2007) 'Sexual pleasure and condom use', *Archives of Sexual Behaviour*, vol 36, no 6, pp 844-8.

Ramsay, M. (ed) (2003) *Prisoner's drug use and treatment: Seven research studies*, Research Study 267, London: Home Office.

Ramsay, M., Baker, P., Goulden, C., Sharp, C. and Sondhi, A. (2001) *Drug misuse declared in 2000: Results from the British Crime Survey*, Home Office Research Study 224, London: Home Office.

Ratner, M. (ed) (1993) *Crack pipe as pimp: An ethnographic investigation of sex for crack exchanges*, Lanham, MD: Lexington Books, pp 187-203.

Reed, B. (1985) 'Drug misuse and dependency in women: the meaning and implications of being considered a special population or minority group', *International Journal of Addictions*, vol 20, no 1, pp 13-62.

Reed, B. (1991) 'Linkages: battering, sexual assault, incest, child sexual abuse, teen pregnancy, dropping out of school and the alcohol and drug connection', in P. Roth (ed) *Alcohol and drugs are women's issues, Volume 1: A review of the issues*, Metuchen, NJ: Women's Action Alliance and The Scarecrow Press Inc, pp 130-49.

Reilly, J. (2010) 'State-sponsored heroin addicts costing us €20m', *Irish News*, 29 August (http://m.independent.ie/irish-news/statesponsored-heroin-addicts-costing-us-20m-26675936.html).

Reiman, R. (1979) *The rich get richer and the poor get prison*, London: Wiley.

Reith, G. (2004) 'Consumption and its discontents: addiction, identity and the problems of freedom', *British Journal of Sociology*, vol 55, no 2, pp 283-300.

Regan, D.O., Ehrlick, S.M. and Finnegan, L.P. (1987) 'Infants of drug addicts: at risk for child abuse, neglect and placement in foster care', *Neurotoxicology and Teratology*, vol 9, no 4, pp 315-19.

Release (1979) Women and Drugs News Release, vol 6, no 2, pp 11-12.

Release (2010) 'Release's response to the government's Drug Strategy Consultation Paper 2010', London: Release: Drugs, The Law and Human Rights (www.release.org.uk/sites/default/files/pdf/publications/Response_Drug_Strategy_20101%20public.pdf).

Rementeria, J.L. and Nunag, N.N. (1973) 'Narcotic withdrawal in pregnancy', *American Journal of Obstetrics and Gynaecology*, vol 116, pp 1052-6.

Reuter, P. and Stevens, A. (2007) *An analysis of UK drug policy: A monograph prepared for the UK Drug Policy Commission*, London: UK Drug Policy Commission.

Reuter, P. and Trautmann, F. (2009) *A report on global illicit drug markets 1998-2007*, European Commission, Trimbos Instituut, Rand Europe (www.trimbos.org/~/media/Programmas/Internationalisering/AF0880%20Report%20on%20Global%20Illicit%20Drug%20Markets%201998%20-%202007%20Final.ashx).

Rhoads, D. (1983) 'A longitudinal study of life stress and social support among drug abusers', *International Journal of Addiction*, vol 18, no 2, pp 195-222.

Rhodes, T., Donoghoe, M., Hunter, G. and Stimson, G. (1994) 'HIV prevalence no higher among female drug injectors also involved in prostitution', *AIDS Care*, vol 6, no 3, pp 269-76.

Ribbens, J. (1989) 'Interviewing – an "unnatural situation"?', *Women's Studies International Forum*, vol 12, no 6, pp 579-92.

Ribbens, J. (1998) *Feminist dilemmas in qualitative research: Public knowledge and private lives*, London: Sage Publications.

Rice, M. (2000) 'Sex and drugs', *Observer Magazine*, 26 March, pp 14-20.

Richardson, D. and May, H. (1999) 'Deserving Victims?', *The Sociological Review*, vol 47, no 2, pp 308–33.

Roberts, C. (1989) *Women and rape*, Hemel Hempstead: Harvester Wheatsheaf.

Roberts, D. (1991) 'Punishing drug addicts who have babies: women of colour, equality, and right of privacy', *Harvard Law Review*, vol 194, pp 1419-82.

Roberts, M., Trace, M. and Klein, A. (2004) *Thailand's 'war on drugs'*, London: The Beckley Foundation.

Robertson, R. (1987) *Heroin, AIDS and society*, London: Hodder & Stoughton.

Romero-Daza, N., Weeks, M. and Singer, M. (2003) '"Nobody gives a damn if I live or die": violence, drugs, and street-level prostitution in Inner City Hartford, Connecticut', *Medical Anthropology: Cross-Cultural Studies in Health and Illness*, vol 22, no 3, pp 233-59.

Room, G. (1995) *Beyond the threshold: The measurement and analysis of social exclusion*, Bristol: Policy Press.

Root, M. (1989) 'Treatment failures: the role of victimization in women's addictive behaviour', *American Institute of Orthopsychiatry*, vol 59, no 4, pp 542-9.

Rose, N. (1990) *Governing the soul: The shaping of the private self*, London: Routledge.

Rose, N. (1996) 'Governing "advanced" liberal democracies', in A. Barry, T. Osborne and N. Rose (eds) *Foucault and political reason: Liberalism, neo-liberalism, and rationalities of government*, Chicago, IL: The University of Chicago Press, Chapter 2.

Rose, N. (1999) *Powers of freedom: Reframing political thought*, Cambridge: Cambridge University Press.

Rose, N. (2000) 'Government and control', *British Journal of Criminology*, vol 40, pp 321-39.

Rose, N. and Miller, P. (1992) 'Political power beyond the state: problematics of government', *British Journal of Sociology*, vol 43, no 2, pp 173-201.

Rose, N., O'Malley, P. and Valverde, M. (2006) 'Governmentality', *Annual Review of Law and Social Science*, vol 2, pp 83-104.

Rosenbaum, M. (1979) 'Difficulties in taking care of business: women addicts as mothers', *American Journal of Drug and Alcohol Abuse*, vol 6, no 4, pp 431-46.

Rosenbaum, M. (1981) *Women on heroin*, New Brunswick, NJ: Rutgers University Press.

Rosenbaum, M. (1995) *Women: Research and policy*, San Francisco, CA: Drug Policy Alliance (http://gos.sbc.edu/r/rosenbaum.html).

Rosenbaum, M. and Murphy, S. (1987) 'Not the picture of health: women on methadone', *Journal of Psychoactive Drugs*, vol 19, no 2, pp 217-26.

Rosenbaum, M. and Murphy, S. (1998) *Pregnant women on drugs: Combating stereotypes and stigma*, New Brunswick, NJ: Rutgers University Press.

Rosenberg, H. (1993) 'Prediction of controlled drinking by alcoholics and problem drinkers', *Psychological Bulletin*, vol 113, pp 129-39.

Ross, F. and Berzins, J. (1974) 'Personality characteristics of female narcotic addicts on MMPI', *Psychological Reports*, vol 35, no 2, pp 779-84.

Rowe, T. (2006) *Federal narcotics laws and the war on drugs: Money down a rathole*, Binghamton, NY: Howarth Press Inc.

Ruben, S. and Siney, C. (eds) (1995) 'Royal College of Midwives "women and drug use"', *The pregnant drug addict*, Hale: Cheshire Books for Midwives Press, pp 9-14.

Ruben, S. and Siney, C. (eds) (1999) 'Women and drug use', in *Pregnancy and drug misuse* (2nd edn), Hale: Books for Midwives, pp 35-42.

Rubington, E. (1967) 'Drug addiction as a deviant career', *The International Journal of the Addictions*, vol 2, no 1, pp 3-20.

Rusche, G. and Kirchheimer, O. (1939) *Punishment and social structure*, New York: Columbia University Press.

Russell, D. (1975) *The politics of rape*, New York: Stein and Day.

Russell, D. (1982) *Rape in marriage*, New York: Macmillan.

Russell, D. (1983) 'The incidence and prevalence of intrafamilial and extra familial sexual abuse of Female children', *Child Abuse and Neglect: The International Journal*, vol 7, no 2, pp 133-46.

Russell, D. (1984) *Sexual exploitation*, London: Sage Publications.

Russell D. (1986) *The secret trauma*, London: Free Press.

Russell, S. and Wilsnack, S. (1991) 'Adult survivors of child sexual abuse: substance abuse and other consequences', in P. Roth (ed) *Alcohol and drugs are women's issues, Volume 1: A review of the issues*, Metuchen, NJ: Women's Action Alliance and The Scarecrow Press Inc, pp 61-70.

Sabol, W. and West, H. (2008) *Prisoners in 2007*, Office of Justice Programs – Bureau of Justice Programs.

SAMHSA (Substance Abuse and Mental Health Services Administration)/CSAT (Centre for Substance Abuse Treatment) (2009) *Substance abuse treatment: Addressing the specific needs of women*, Treatment Improvement Protocol (TIP) Series No. 51, Centre for Substance Abuse Treatment, US.

SAMHSA (Substance Abuse and Mental Health Services Administration) (2012) *SAMHSA's Working Definition of Recovery*, Rockville, MD: SAMHSA.

Sanchez, R. (1990) 'Addicts' children: a new challenge to schools', *Washington Post*, 14 November.

Sargent, M. (1992) *Women, drugs and policy in Sydney, London and Amsterdam*, Aldershot: Avebury.

SCCCJ (Scottish Consortium for Crime and Criminal Justice) (2002) *Making sense of drugs and crime: Drugs, crime and penal policy*, Edinburgh: SCCCJ.

Schilling, R., El-Bassel, N., Schinke, S., Nichols, S., Botvin, G. and Orlandi, M. (1991) 'Sexual behaviour, attitudes towards safer sex, and gender among a cohort of 244 recovering IV drug users', *International Journal of Addiction*, vol 26, pp 865-83.

Schirmer, S., Nellis, A. and Mauer, M. (2009) *Incarcerated parents and their children: Trends 1991-2007*, Washington, DC: The Sentencing Project.

Schroedel, J. and Fiber, P. (2013) 'Punitive versus public health orientated responses to drug use by pregnant women', *Yale Journal of Health Policy, Law and Ethics*, vol 1, issue 1.

Schutz, A. (1962) *Collected Papers 1: The problem of social reality*, The Hague: Martinos Nihoff.

Schwartz, B. (1976) 'The female addict', in A. Bauman et al (eds) *Women in treatment: Issues and approaches*, Arlington, VA: National Drug Abuse Centre for Training and Resource Development, pp 81-95.

Scott, P. (2003) *Drugs, oil and war: The United States in Afghanistan, Colombia and Indochina*, Lanham, MD: Rowman & Littlefield Publishers.

Scott, P. (2010) *American war machine: Deep politics, the CIA global drug connection, and the road to Afghanistan*, War and Peace Library, Lanham, MD: Rowman & Littlefield Publishers.

Scottish Drugs Forum (1994) *Scottish Drugs Forum Policy Statement: Women and drug use*, Glasgow: Scottish Drugs Forum.

Scottish Executive (2002) *A better way: The report of the Ministerial Group on women's offending*, Edinburgh: Scottish Executive.

Scully, D. (1990) *Understanding sexual violence*, London: HarperCollins Academic.

Seddon, T. (2007a) 'Drugs and freedom', *Addiction Research and Theory*, vol 15, no 4, pp 333-42.

Seddon, T. (2007b) 'Coerced drug treatment in the criminal justice system: conceptual, ethical and criminological issues', *Criminology and Criminal Justice*, vol 7, no 3, pp 269-86.

Seddon, T. (2008a) 'Risk, security and the criminalization of British drug policy', *British Journal of Criminology*, vol 48, pp 818-34.

Seddon, T. (2008b) 'Women, harm reduction and history: gender perspectives on the emergence of the "British system" of drug control', *International Journal of Drug Policy*, vol 19, pp 99-105.

Seddon, T. (2010) *A history of drugs: Drugs and freedom in the liberal age*, Abingdon: Routledge.

Seiler, W. (2008) *The war on drugs and the shaping of hemispheric policy: United States hegemonial politics, drug trade and social forces in Colombia and Mexico*, Saabrurcken: VDM-Verl-Dr Muller.

Selltiz, C., Jahoda, M., Deutsch, M. and Cook, S. (1965) *Research methods in social relations*, London: Methuen.

SEU (Social Exclusion Unit) (2003) *Tackling social exclusion: Achievements, lessons learned and the way forward*, London: Office of the Deputy Prime Minister.

SEU (2004) *About us, Contacts*, SEU leaflet, London: SEU.

Sheehan, R., McIvor, G. and Trotter, C. (2007) *What works with women offenders*, Cullompton: Willan Publishing.

Shiner, M. (2009) *Drug use and social change: The distortion of history*, Basingstoke: Palgrave Macmillan.

Shiner, M. and Newburn, T. (1997) 'Definitely, maybe not: the normalisation of recreational drug use amongst young people', *Sociology*, vol 31, no 3, pp 511-29.

Shiner, M and Newburn, T. (1999) 'Taking tea with Noel: drugs discourse for the 1990s', in N. South (ed) *Drugs: Cultures, controls and everyday life*, London: Sage Publications, pp 139-59.

Shover, N. and Norland, S. (1978) 'Sex roles and criminality: science or conventional wisdom?', *Sex Roles*, vol 4, no 1, pp 111-25.

Siegal, H., Carlson, R., Falck, R., Forney, M., Wang, J. and Li, L. (1992) 'High risk behaviors for transmission of syphilis and human immunodeficiency virus among crack-cocaine-using women: a case study from the Midwest', *Sexually Transmitted Diseases*, vol 19, no 5, pp 266-71.

Siegal, L. (1990) 'The criminalization of pregnant and child rearing drug users', *Drug Law Report*, vol 2, no 15, pp 169-76.

Simpson, M. and McNulty, J. (2008) 'Different needs: women's drug use and treatment in the UK', *International Journal of Drug Policy*, April, vol 19, pp 169-75.

Simon, R. (1975) *Women and crime*, Lanham, MD: Lexington Books.

Siney, C. (ed) (1995) *The pregnant drug addict*, Oxford: Books for Midwives.

Singer, L., Salvator, A. and Kliegman, R. (2002a) 'Effects of cocaine/polydrug exposure and maternal psychological distress on infant birth outcomes', *Neurotoxicology and Teratology*, March–April, vol 24, no 2, pp 127–35.

Singer, L., Arendt, R., Minnes, S., Farkas, K., Salvator, A., Kirchner, H.L. et al (2002b) 'Cognitive and motor outcomes of cocaine-exposed infants', *Journal of the American Medical Association*, vol 287, pp 1952–60.

Singer, M., Petchers, M. and Hussey, K. (1989) 'The relationship between sexual abuse and psychiatrically hospitalised adolescents', *Child Abuse and Neglect*, vol 13, pp 319–25.

Sjoberg, G. and Nett, R. (1968) *A methodology for social research*, London: Harper & Row.

Sloan, A. and Murphy, D. (1988) 'Drug treatment during pregnancy', *Mersey Drugs Journal*, vol 2, no 3, pp 15–16.

Smart, B. (1983) 'On discipline and social regulation: Foucault's genealogical analysis', in D. Garland and P. Young (eds) *The power to punish*, London: Heinemann/Humanities Press, pp 62–83.

Smart, B. (2002) *Michel Foucault* (Revised edn), London: Routledge.

Smart, C. (1976) *Women, crime and criminology: A feminist critique*, London: Routledge & Kegan Paul.

Smart, C. (1977) 'Reply to Paul Rock', *British Journal of Criminology*, vol 17, pp 397–9.

Smart, C. (1979) 'The new female criminal: reality or myth?' *British Journal of Criminology*, vol 19, pp 50–9.

SMART Recovery (2010) 'Response to the Drug Strategy Consultation 2010 from SMART Recovery UK' (http://cdn.smartrecovery.org.uk/doc/SMART_Recovery_response_to_UK_Drug_Strategy.pdf).

Smith, C. (1997) 'Illegal drug use in women's prisons in England', *Connections: the Newsletter of the European Network of Drug and HIV*, April, vol 4, pp 1–2.

Smith, L. (2011) 'Should women who take drugs in pregnancy face murder charges?', *My Daily*, 29 June (*www.mydaily.co.uk/2011/06/29/should-women-who-take-drugs-in-pregnancy-face-murder-charges/*).

Smith, P. (2007) 'The conviction that keeps on hurting – Drug offenders and federal benefits', Drug War Chronicle, 4 February (http://stopthedrugwar.org/chronicle/2007/feb/04/feature_conviction_keeps_hurting).

Smithberg, N. and Westermeyer, J. (1985) 'White dragon pearl syndrome: a pattern of female drug use', *American Journal of Drug and Alcohol Abuse*, vol 11, pp 109-11.

Snyder, H., Finnegan, T., Stahl, A. and Poole, R. (1999) *Easy access to juvenile court statistics*, Pittsburgh, PA: National Centre for Juvenile Justice.

Spooner, C., Hall, W. and Mattick, R. (2001) 'An overview of diversion strategies for Australian drug-related offenders', *Drug and Alcohol Review*, vol 20, pp 281-94.

SSAC (Social Security Advisory Committee) (2010) *Report of the Social Security Advisory Committee made under Section 174(2) of the Social Security Administration Act 1992 on the Social Security (Welfare Reform Drug Recovery Pilots) Regulations 2010* (www.ssac.org.uk/pdf/SSAC-drugs-pilot-report.pdf).

SSAC (2013) *Universal Credit and conditionality*, Social Security Advisory Committee Occasional Paper No 9, London: SSAC.

Stanley, L. and Wise, S. (1993) *Breaking out again: Feminist ontology and epistemology*, London: Routledge.

Staples, R. (1990) 'Substance abuse and the black family crisis: an overview', *Western Journal of Black Studies*, vol 14, no 4, pp 196-204.

Statistics Canada (2000) *Women in Canada 2000: A gender-based statistical report*, Ottawa, ON: Ministry of Industry.

Statzer, D.E. and Wardell, J.N. (1966) 'Heroin addiction during pregnancy', *American Journal of Obstetrics and Gynaecology*, vol 94, pp 253-7.

Steffensmeier, D. (1980) 'Sex differences in patterns of adult crime, 1965-77: a review and assessment', *Social Forces*, vol 58, pp 1080-108.

Steffensmeier, D. (1983) 'Organisation, properties and sex-segregation in the underworld: building a sociological theory of sex differences in crime', *Social Forces*, vol 58, pp 1010-60.

Stein, S. (1985) *International diplomacy, state administrators and narcotics control: The origins of a social problem*, Aldershot: Gower.

Stella Project (2004) *Domestic violence, drugs and alcohol: Good practice guidelines*, written by Michelle Newcomb, London: Greater London Domestic Violence Project.

Stengal, C. and Fleetwood, J. (2014) *Developing drug policy: gender matters*, Swansea University: Global Drug Policy Observatory. (www.swansea.ac.uk/gdpo/files/GDPO%20Situation%20Analysis%20Gender%20digital.pdf).

Stensen, K. (1999) 'Crime control, governmentality and sovereignty', in R. Smandych (ed) *Governable places: Readings in governmentality and crime control*, Aldershot: Dartmouth, pp 45-73.

Stephenson, F. (1989) *A discussion of women's experience of illicit and prescribed drug use and its relationship to the socio-economic position of women in Britain*, London: Drug Concern (Barnet).

Sterk, C. (1999) *Fast lives: Women who use crack cocaine*, Philadelphia, PA: Temple University Press.

Sterk, C. and Elifson, K. (1990) 'Drug-related violence and street prostitution', in M. de la Rosa, E. Lambert and B. Grooper (eds) *Drugs and violence: Causes, correlates, and consequences*, NIDA Research Monograph 103, pp 208-21.

Stevens, A., Bertolini, C., Heckmann, W., Kerschl, V., Oeuvray, K., van Ooyen, M., Steffan, E. and Uchtenhagen, A. (2005) 'Quasi-compulsory treatment of drug dependent offenders: an international literature review', *Substance Use and Misuse*, vol 40, pp 269-83.

Stevens, S., Tortu, S. and Coyle, S. (eds) (1998) *Women's drug use and HIV infection*, London: Haworth Medical Press.

Stevenson, B. (2011) 'Drug policy, criminal justice and mass imprisonment', Global Commission on Drug Policies (www.globalcommissionondrugs.org/wp-content/themes/gcdp_v1/pdf/Global_Com_Bryan_Stevenson.pdf).

Stewart, T. (1987) *The heroin users*, London: Pandora.

Stimson, G. (1995) 'AIDS and injecting drug use in the United Kingdom, 1987-1993: the policy response and the prevention of the epidemic', *Social Science & Medicine*, vol 41, no 5, pp 699-716.

Stimson, G. (2000) 'Blair declares war' or 'The unhealthy state of British drugs policy', Text of a speech delivered by Professor Gerry Stimson at the Methadone Alliance Conference, Methadone and Beyond: Expanding and Exploring Drug Treatment Options, 22 March, London.

Stone, M., Salerna, L. and Green, M. (1971) 'Narcotic addiction in pregnancy', *American Journal of Obstetrics and Gynaecology*, vol 109, p 716.

Strang, J. and Members of the Recovery-oriented Drug Treatment Expert Group (2012) *Medications in recovery: Re-orienting drug dependence treatment*, London: National Treatment Agency.

Strang, J., Metrebian, N., Lintzeris, N. Potts, L., Carnwath, T., Mayet, S., Williams, H., Zador, H., Evers, R., Groshkova, T., Charles, V., Martin, A. and Forzisi, L. (2010) 'Supervised injectable heroin or injectable methadone versus optimised oral methadone as treatment for chronic heroin addicts in England after persistent failure in orthodox treatment (RIOTT): a randomised trial', *The Lancet*, 29 May, vol 375, issue 9729, pp 1885-95.

Strategy Unit Drug Report (2003) *Understanding the issues*, Strategy Unit.

Straus, M., Gelles, R. and Steinmetz, S. (1980) *Behind closed doors: Violence in the American family*, New York: Doubleday/Anchor.

Students for Sensible Drug Policy (2014) *Be sensible: Stop the war on higher education: Brief history of the aid elimination penalty* (http://ssdp.org/campaigns/the-higher-education-act/).

Su, S., Pach, A., Hoffman, A., Pierce, T.G., Ingels, J., Unfred, C. and Gray, F. (1996) 'Drug injector risk networks and HIV transmission: a prospective study', Unpublished report to NIDA.

Sudbury, J. (ed) (2005a) *Global lockdown: Race, gender and the prison-industrial complex*, New York: Routledge.

Sudbury, J. (2005b) 'Mules, yardies and other folk devils: mapping cross-border imprisonment in Britain', in J. Sudbury (ed) *Global lockdown: Race, gender and the prison-industrial complex*, London: Routledge, p 167.

Suffet, F. and Brotman, R. (1976) 'Female drug use: some observations', *The International Journal of the Addictions*, vol 11, pp 19-23.

Sullivan, R. and Hagen, E. (2002) 'Psychotropic substance-seeking: evolutionary pathology or adaptation?', *Addiction*, vol 97, pp 389-400.

Surratt, H., Inciardi, S., Kurtz, P. and Kiley, M. (2004) 'Sex work and drug use in a subculture of violence', *Crime and Delinquency*, vol 50, p 43.

Sutter, A. (1966) 'The world of the righteous dope fiend', *Issues in Criminology*, vol 2, no 2, pp 177-222.

Symonds, A. (1998) 'Social construction of the concept of "community"', in A. Symonds and A. Kelly (eds) *The social construction of community care*, London: Macmillan.

Szalavitz, M. (1999) 'War on drugs, war on women', *On the Issues Magazine*, Winter (http://ontheissuesmagazine.com/1999winter/w99_Szalavitz.php).

Szasz, T. (1970) *The manufacture of madness*, New York: Harper & Row.

Tardiff, K., Marzuk, P., Leon, A., Hirsch, C., Portela, L. and Hartwell, N. (1997) 'HIV infection among victims of accidental fatal drug overdoses in New York City', *Addiction*, vol 92, no 8, pp 1017-22.

Task Force to Review Services for Drug Misusers (1986) *Report of an Independent Survey of Drug Treatment Services in England*, London: Department of Health.

Taylor, A. (1993) *Women drug users: An ethnography of a female injecting community*, Oxford: Clarendon Press.

Taylor, A., Frischer, M., McKeganey, N., Goldberg, D., Green, S. and Platt, S. (1993) 'HIV risk behaviours among female prostitute drug injectors in Glasgow', *Addiction*, vol 88, pp 1561-4.

Taylor, C. (1993) *Girls, gangs, women and drugs*, East Lansing, MI: Michigan State University Press.

Taylor, D. (1998) 'Children or crack: which would you choose?', *The Guardian*, 3 December, p 6.

Taylor-Gooby, P. (2001) 'Risk, contingency and the third way: evidence from the BHPS and qualitative studies', *Social Policy & Administration*, June, vol 35, issue 2, pp 195-211.

Taylor, J., Fulop, N. and Green, J. (1999) 'Drink, illicit drugs and unsafe sex in women', *Addiction*, vol 94, no 8, pp 1209-18.

Taylor S.J. and Bogdan, R. (1984) *Introduction to qualitative research methods* (2nd edn), New York: John Wiley & Sons.

Teets, J.M. (1995) 'Childhood sexual trauma of chemically dependent women', *Journal of Psychoactive Drugs*, vol 27, no 3, pp 231-8.

Thom, B. and Edmondson, K. (1989) 'Women, family and drugs: women talking', Report of a workshop, London, 20-22 June, London: Institute of Psychiatry, Addiction Research Unit.

Thoma, R. (2005) 'A critical look at the foster care system: how widespread a problem?', *Lifting the veil: Examining the child welfare, foster care and juvenile justice systems* (http://liftingtheveil.org/foster04.htm).

Thorpe, D. (1994) *Evaluating child protection*, Buckingham: Open University Press.

Timms, P. (2006) 'Antidepressants', The Royal College of Psychiatrists Mental Health Information Leaflet (www.rcpsych.ac.uk).

Tippell, S., Aston, F., Hunter, A. and Painter J. (1990) *Cocaine use: The US experience and the implications for drug services in Britain*, London: Community Drug Project.

Tombs, J. (2004) *A unique punishment: Sentencing and the prison population in Scotland*, Edinburgh: Scottish Consortium on Crime and Criminal Justice.

Tonry, M. (1995) *Malign neglect: Race, crime and punishment in America*, Oxford: Oxford University Press.

Transform (2006) *After the war on drugs: Options for control*, Bristol: Transform (www.tdpf.org.uk/resources/publications/after-war-drugs-options-control).

Turnipseed, T. (2000) 'From Columbia to Columbia: The war on drugs is a war on poor and black people', CommonDreams, Thursday 31 August (www.commondreams.org/views/2000/08/31/colombia-columbia-war-drugs-war-poor-and-black-people).

Tyler, J. (2010) 'The drug war: A war on women and their families' (www.bluelight.ru/vb/showthread.php?t=498406)

UKDPC (UK Drug Policy Commission) (2008a) *Working towards recovery: Getting problem drug users (back) into employment*, London: UKDPC.

UKDPC (2008b) *The UK drug classification system: Issues and challenges, Written Evidence to the Advisory Council on the Misuse of Drugs as part of its review of the classification of MDMA ('ecstasy')*, London: UKDPC.

UKDPC (2010) *Submission to the 2010 Drug Strategy Commission*, London: UKDPC.

UN (United Nations) (1976) *Economic crises and crime*, New York: UN Social Defence Research Institute.

UN (2013) *The International Drug Control Conventions: Schedules of the Single Convention on Narcotic Drugs of 1961 as amended by the 1972 Protocol, as at 25 September 2013*, United Nations, New York. (www.unodc.org/unodc/en/treaties/single-convention.html)

Undercurrents (1976-77) 'Drugs and women', December-January, vol 19, pp 34-5.

Unell, I. (1987) 'Drugs and deprivation', *Druglink*, November/December, pp 14-15.

UNODC (United Nations Office on Drugs and Crime) (2004) *Substance abuse treatment and care for women: Case studies and lessons learned*, Hemdon, VA: United Nations Publications.

UNODC (2008) *A century of international drug control*, Hemdon, VA: United Nations Publications.

Valverde, M. (1997) 'Slavery from within: the invention of alcoholism and the question of free will', *Social History*, vol 22, no 3, pp 251-68.

Valverde, M. (1998) *Diseases of the will: Alcohol and the dilemmas of freedom*, Cambridge: Cambridge University Press.

Vandor, M., Juliana, P. and Leone, R. (1991) 'Women and illegal drugs', in P. Roth (ed) *Alcohol and drugs are women's issues, Volume 1: A review of the issues*, Metuchen, NJ: Women's Action Alliance and The Scarecrow Press Inc, pp 155-60.

Void, J. (2014) 'The benefit sanction debt trap: is this Iain Duncan Smith's nastiest move so far?', *The Void*, 14 February (http://johnnyvoid.wordpress.com/2014/02/13/the-benefit-sanction-debt-trap-is-this-iain-duncan-smiths-nastiest-move-so-far/).

Volpicelli, J., Markman, I., Monterosso, J., Filing, J. and O'Brien, C. (2000) 'Psychosocially enhanced treatment for cocaine-dependent mothers: evidence of efficacy', *Journal of Substance Abuse Treatment*, vol 18, pp 41-9.

Wacquant, L. (2001) 'Deadly symbiosis: when ghetto and prison meet and mesh', *Punishment & Society*, vol 3, no 1, pp 95-133.

Wacquant, L. (2009) *Punishing the poor: The neoliberal government of social insecurity*, Politics, History and Culture series, Durham, NC: Duke University Press.

Wacquant, L. (2010) 'Crafting the neoliberal state: workfare, prisonfare, and social insecurity', *Sociological Forum*, June, vol 25, no 2, pp 197-220a.

Wald, M.S. (1975) *Child development and public policy: Juvenile justice*, Transcription of speech presented to the Society for Research in Child Development Panel Symposium, Denver, CO: ERIC Document, ED111493.

Wald, M.S. (1976) 'State intervention on behalf of "neglected" children: standards for removal of children from their homes, monitoring the status of children in foster care, and termination of parental rights', *Stanford Law Review*, vol 28, no 4, pp 623-706.

Waldby, C. (1988) *Mothering and addiction: Women with children in methadone programs*, National Campaign Against Drug Abuse, Canberra: Australian Government Publishing Service.

Waldorf, D. (1970) 'Life without heroin: some social adjustments during long-term periods of voluntary abstention', *Social Problems*, vol 18, pp 228-43.

Waldorf, D. (1973) *Careers in dope*, Englewood Cliffs, NJ: Prentice Hall.

Wallach, R.C., Jerez, E. and Blinick, G. (1969) 'Pregnancy and menstrual function in narcotics addicts treated with methadone: the methadone maintenance treatment program', *American Journal of Obstetrics and Gynaecology*, vol 105, no 8, pp 226-9.

Waterston, A. (1993) *Street addicts in the political economy*, Philadelphia, PA: Temple University Press.

Waterson, J. and Ettorre, B. (1989) 'Providing services for women with difficulties with alcohol or other drugs: the current UK situation as seen by women practitioners, researchers and policy makers in the field', *Drug and Alcohol Dependence*, vol 24, no 2, pp 119-25.

Waterson, J., Ettorre, B., Griffiths, R. and Kent, R. (eds) (1988) 'Women's problems with alcohol and other drugs: improving our response', Proceedings of a conference organised by the Alcohol Interventions Training Unit, University of Kent at Canterbury with the Addiction Research Unit, Institute of Psychiatry, London, 5 July, Eliot College University of Kent, Drugs Alcohol Women Nationally.

Wayment, H.A., Newcomb, M.D. and Hanneman, V.L. (1993) 'Female and male intravenous drug users not-in-treatment: are they at differential risk for AIDS?', *Sex Roles*, vol 28, nos 1 and 2, pp 111-25.

Weaver, S. (2007) '"Make it more welcome": best practice child welfare work with substance-using mothers', in S. Boyd and L. Marcellus (eds) *With child: Substance use during pregnancy*, Halifax, NS: Fernwood Press, pp 76-89.

Webster, C. and Doob, A. (2007) 'Punitive trends and stable imprisonment rates in Canada', in M.H. Tonry (ed) *Crime and justice: A review of research*, vol 36, Chicago, IL: University of Chicago Press, pp 297-370.

Wechsberg, W.M., Dennis, M.L. and Ying, Z. (1995) 'Women and men infectors: differences and trends in their drug use patterns and HIV risk', Presented at the meeting of the American Public Health Association, San Diego, November.

Wedderburn, D. (2000) *Justice for women: The need for reform*, London: Prison Reform Trust.

Weissman, G., Melchior, L., Huba, G. and Smereck, G. (1995) 'Women living with drug abuse and HIV disease: drug abuse treatment access and secondary prevention issues', *Journal of Psychoactive Drugs*, vol 27, pp 401-11.

Welle, D., Falkin, G.P. and Jainhill, N. (1998) 'Current approaches to drug treatment for women offenders – Project Worth', *Journal of Substance Abuse Treatment*, vol 15, no 2, pp 151-63.

Wellisch, D., Gay, G. and McEntee, R. (1970) 'The easy rider syndrome: a pattern of hetero-and homosexual relationships in a heroin addict population', *Family Process*, vol 9, no 4, pp 425-30.

West, H. and Sabol, W. (2009) *Prison inmates at midyear 2008 – Statistical tables*, Bureau of Justice Statistics, March, p 11.

Western, B. (2010) 'The war on drugs is a war on poor people', *The Nation*, 16 December (www.alternet.org/drugs/149215/the_war_on_drugs_is_a_war_on_poor_people?page=1)

White, R. and Habibis, D. (2005) *Crime and society*, Oxford: Oxford University Press.

White, W. (2000) 'Toward a new recovery advocacy movement', Presented at Recovery Community Support Program Conference 'Working Together for Recovery', 3-5 April, Arlington, Virginia (www.facesandvoicesofrecovery.org).

White, W. (2007) 'Addiction recovery: its definition and conceptual boundaries', *Journal of Substance Abuse Treatment*, vol 33, pp 229-41.

Whitehead, T. (1978-79) 'Drugs in a women's prison', *PROP*, vol 2, no 6, pp 11-12.

WHO (World Health Organization) (2000) *The World Health Report 2000: Health systems: Improving performance*, Geneva: WHO Press.

WHO (2009) 'Women's health', Fact sheet No 334, November (www.who.int/mediacentre/factsheets/fs334/en/).

WHO (2010) 'Why tobacco is a public health priority', Tobacco Free Initiative (www.who.int/tobacco/health_priority/en/).

WHO, UNODC (United Nations Office on Drugs and Crime) and UNAIDS (United Nations Programme and HIV/AIDS) (2004) Substitution maintenance therapy in the management of opioid dependence and HIV/AIDS prevention: WHO/UNODC/UNAIDS Position Paper, WHO Press.

WHO, UNODC and UNAIDS (2009) *Technical guide for countries to set targets for universal access to HIV prevention, treatment and care*, Geneva and Vienna: WHO, UNODC and UNAIDS.

Wilks-Wiffen, S. (2011) *Voice of a child*, London: Howard League for Penal Reform.

Williams, T. (1989) *The cocaine kids*, Reading, MA: Addison Wesley.

Willis, K. and Rushforth, C. (2003) *The female criminal: An overview of women's drug use and offending behaviour*, Griffith, ACT: Trends and Issues in Crime and Criminal Justice, Australian Institute of Criminology.

Willis, M. and Makkai, T. (2008) *Ex-prisoners and homelessness: Some key issues*, Parity, October, Australian Institute of Criminology.

Wilner, J. (2015) *Kilmon vs State: Court of Appeal of Maryland*, no 91, Sept. Term, 2005. Findlaw, Caselaw, Maryland Court of Appeals (http://caselaw.findlaw.com/md-court-of-appeals/1380705.html).

Wilson, C. (2004) *Children who die or are murdered in foster care*, Equal Justice Foundation (www.ejfi.org/family/family-122.htm).

Wilson, G., McCreary, K., Kean, J. and Baxter, J. (1979) 'The development of pre-school children of heroin addicted mothers: a controlled study', *Paediatrics*, vol 63, pp 135-41.

Wilson, N. (1993) 'Stealing and dealing: the drug war and gendered criminal opportunity', in C. Culliver (ed) *Female criminality: The state of the art*, New York: Garland Publishing, pp 169-94.

Wincup, E. (2000) 'Surviving through substance use: the role of substances in the lives of women who appear before the courts', *Sociological Research Online*, vol 4, no 4 (www.socresonline.org.uk/4/4/wincup.html).

Wintour, P. (2002) 'MPs back plans for radical new drug laws', *The Guardian, Society*, 2 April.

Wolcott, H.F. (1995) *The art of fieldwork*, Walnut Creek, CA: Altamira Press.

Wolfe, T. (1999) *Counting the cost: The social and financial consequences of women's imprisonment*, Report prepared for the Wedderburn Committee on Women's Imprisonment, London: Prison Reform Trust.

Wolfson, D. and Murray, J. (1986) *Women's personal accounts of drug and alcohol problems*, London: Drugs Alcohol Women Nationally.

Women 2000 (1987) 'Women and drug abuse', p 2, UN Centre for Social Development and Humanitarian Affairs (www.popline.org/node/382213).

Woodhouse, L.D. (1992) 'Women with Jagged Edges: Voices from a Culture of Substance Abuse', *Qualitative Health Research*, vol 2, no 3, pp 262-81.

Worrall, A. (1990) *Offending women: Female lawbreakers and the criminal justice system*, London and New York: Routledge.

Worrall, A. (2001) 'Girls at risk? Reflections on changing attitudes to young women's offending', *Probation Journal*, vol 48, p 86.

Worth, D. (1989) 'Sexual decision-making and AIDS: why condom promotion among vulnerable women is likely to fail', *Studies in Family Planning*, vol 20, no 6, pp 297-307.

WPA (Women's Prison Association) (2009) 'Quick facts: Women and criminal justice – 2009', New York: WPA (www.wpaonline.org/wpaassets/quick_facts_Women_and_CJ_Sept09.PDF).

WPRC (Women Prisoners Resource Centre) (1985) 'Women, drugs and alcohol', After-care information pack presented at WPRC Seminar, 29 November, London: WPRC.

Young, J. (2007) *The vertigo of late modernity*, London: Sage Publications.

Zeese, K. (2001) 'Are we addicted to drug war money?', Common Sense for Drug Policy (www.csdp.org/ads/addicttowar.htm).

Zeese, K. and Lewin, P. (1999) *The Effective National Drug Control Strategy*, Common Sense for Drug Policy (www.csdp.org/edcs/edcs.htm).

Zelson, C. (1973) 'Infant of the addicted mother', *New England Journal of Medicine*, vol 288, p 26.

Zola, I. (1972) 'Medicine as an institution of social control', in P. Conrad (ed) *The sociology of health and illness: Critical perspectives*, New York: Worth, pp 404-14.

Zola, I. (1983) *Socio-medical inquiries*, Philadelphia, PA: Temple University Press.

Zuspan, F., Gumpel, J., Mejia-Zelaya, A. et al (1975) 'Fetal stress from methadone withdrawal', *American Journal of Obstetrics and Gynaecology*, vol 2, pp 43-8.

Index

A

abstinence
  as choice 270
  and methadone maintenance 101, 102, 259
  mothers 131
  as policy focus 100, 101, 105, 257
  as recovery 105, 110, 115, 259
  welfare discourse 135, 238
abuse, history of 68, 163, 210
accountability 131
ACMD *see* Advisory Council on the Misuse of Drugs
'addiction', concept of 94–5, 148
'addictive personality' 95
Adler, F. 34, 51
adoption 80
Adoption and Safe Families Act (UK) 80
Advisory Council on the Misuse of Drugs (ACMD) (UK) 99, 129
age, of first exposure to drugs 209
agency
  female crime 31, 33, 34
  Foucault and 4, 138, 201
  and identity construction 142
  safe sex and 30
  and victimhood 27, 234, 271
  see also rational choice model
AIDS, drugs, and prostitution (Plant) 29
AIDS *see* HIV/AIDS
alcohol
  benefit sanctions 126
  as coping mechanism 79, 164
  dependency 155, 190
  effect of in pregnancy 20, 83
  as harmful 49
  history of sexual abuse 26
  medicalisation of 92
  parental 84, 128, 163, 169, 209
  poverty and unemployment 119, 125
  use of to control women 86
Alexander, B.K. 63, 65
Ambrose, Rona 69
amphetamines 156, 163, 167
Anderson, E. 32
Anderson, T. 142
Andreas, P. 46, 47
Anslinger, Harry 44, 46
anti-depressants 96, 204, 205, 206
Anti-Drug Abuse Acts (US) 71
anxiety 6, 24, 26, 96, 165, 174
appearance 217
'at-risk' register 85, 112, 130
Australia 54, 70, 97

B

Baird, John 127
Barry, A., Osborne, T. and Rose, N. 147
Baskin, D., Sommers, I. and Fagan, J. 36
Bauman, Z. 53
Bean, P. 111
begging 127, 217, 220, 221
Belenko, S. 112
benefit sanctions 126, 127, 135
bereavement 153, 163, 170, 171, 230, 231
biopower 143
black population
  higher education 124
  imprisonment 39, 78, 149
black women
  effect of war on drugs 51
  HIV/AIDS 100
  imprisonment 36, 39, 68, 70, 72
  medicalisation 94
  prosecution prenatal drug use 82–3
  welfare dependency 132
Blair, Tony 55
blame 53–4, 63, 109, 119, 120, 133
blame, self- 174, 184, 196–200, 215
bonding, maternal 22
boredom 199
Bourgois, P. 34, 35
Bourne, Peter 103
Boyd, S. 37, 39, 45, 48, 58, 79, 80, 112, 113, 132
Braithwaite, J. 53
'British system' 47, 48
Brook, H. and Stringer, R. 93
Brooks, C., Zuckerman, B., Bamforth, A., Cole, J. and Kaplan-Sanoff, M. 21
Buchanan, J. and Young, L. 130
Bush-Baskette, S. 39, 73, 76

C

CAAAD (Community Action Around Alcohol and Drugs) 85
CAB *see* Citizens' Advice Bureau
Cameron, David 55
Canada
  abstinence policy 112
  child custody 112, 190
  community treatment 113
  cuts to welfare state 55, 56
  disease model and recovery 105
  drug strategy 8, 66, 67–70
  drug testing 131
  identity 106
  imprisonment 70, 71, 72, 78, 80
  methadone maintenance 101
  National Anti-Drug Strategy 129
  neoliberalism 53
  pregnancy 19
  public health approach 48
  racism 77
  social work education 133
  stricter enforcement 58
  treatment and trauma 108
  welfarisation 127, 128, 129
Canada Health and Social Transfer 56
Canadian Medical Association 127
cannabis *see* marijuana
capitalism 53, 94, 117, 144
'career' 37
Carr, J.N. 21, 22
Centre for Addiction and Mental Health, The (Canada) 127
characteristics, ascription of 7, 139–42
Chasnoff, Ira 19
Chein, I., Gerard, D., Lee, R. and Rosenfield, E. 23
chemical addiction 181–4, 185
Chigwada-Bailey, R. 75
childbirth 84, 85
childcare 110, 122
children
  adoption 80
  'at-risk' 85, 112, 130
  carers and poverty 73
  enforced drug taking 160
  foster care 78, 79, 128, 206
  illicit drugs and harm 66, 67–9, 129
  loss of custody 19, 22, 23, 110, 112, 133, 134, 240–5
  loss of maternal contact 80
  maternal imprisonment 77, 78–81, 235, 236, 237
  as maternal responsibility 132, 133
  neglect 132
  physical abuse 133, 166–7
  psychological and physical danger of rehoming 78
  risk discourse 128–34, 239
  separation from siblings 78
  sexual abuse 26, 27, 163, 164–5, 167
  strict upbringing 169, 170
  of 'undeserving poor' 119
  welfarisation 190–5
Christianity 39, 44
Citizens' Advice Bureau (CAB) (UK) 127
Clancey, G. and Howard, J. 114
classical paradigm 39
Clinton, Bill 55
cocaine
  'dangerous classes' 44
  effect of in pregnancy 19, 20
  fears of interracial sexuality 45
  history of use of 43
  as not prescribable in UK 48
  in pregnancy 19
cognitive behavioural therapy 149
Cohen, S. 117, 144
Cold War 44
Collins, W. 95
communism 44
communities 66, 67–9, 70
Community Action Around Alcohol and Drugs *see* CAAAD
comparative approach 8, 9
condom provision 259, 260
confidence, lack of 156, 168, 198, 247
conformity 153
Conrad, P. 62
Conrad, P. and Schneider, W. 44
consent, informed 110
coping mechanism
  prescribed drugs 62, 96
  as self-medication 25–6, 27, 87, 108, 162, 163–74, 204–7, 210
  short term 152–4
counselling 197, 260
Covington, J. 32, 33
crack cocaine
  and acquisitive crime 186–7, 188
  addictiveness 172–3
  blame for crime 184
  as coping mechanism 166
  effect on friendships 178
  female involvement 34, 35, 36, 37, 73
  and HIV/AIDS 27–30, 100
  imprisonment 76
  interview group 155, 157–8, 235, 236, 249
  mandatory sentencing 47
  marginalisation and 39
  motherhood 21

in pregnancy 19
and prostitution 32
use and employment 125
'vicious cycle causation' model 26
violence 227
weight loss 163
welfare benefits 55
'crack babies' 19, 20, 81, 82
crime
  and employment 250
  to fund habit 174, 183, 184, 185–90, 215
  organized 50
  protection from 69
  rational choice 223–4, 225
  reduction and methadone maintenance 102
  strategy to control 66
  as way out of poverty 213, 222, 274
  women as victims 225–31
criminal justice system
  effect on women's lives 235–7, 238, 274
  gendered 87, 88, 113, 233
  and medicalisation 114
  punishment 61, 62, 185–90, 231–3, 270, 271
  punitive regulation 46–51
  self-blame 222
  sentencing 47–8, 67, 68, 71, 72, 74, 75, 76, 80, 82, 150, 189, 231–2, 233
  treatment orders 66
  women as both criminals and victims 113
criminalisation 31, 32–6, 37
  and class 48
  gender roles 32, 33, 34–6
  health problems 50
  history of origins around drug use 44
  and medicalisation 114
  as permanent 62
  stigmatization 107, 180
  US 47

D

'danger' 49, 58, 67, 69, 96, 93
Davis, A. 72
Drug Enforcement Agency see DEA
'deadly symbiosis' 64, 91
Dean, M. 4
decriminalisation 50
'delinquent' 143
Denmark 97
Densen-Gerber, J., Weiner, J. and Hochstedler, R. 22
Department of Housing and Urban Development (HUD) (US) 122
Department of Justice (US) 79

dependency cultures 56
depression 24, 26, 163, 165, 204
deregulation 53
detox, solo 259
deviancy 7, 160, 270
Dilner, L. 96
discipline 253–6
disease model 91, 92–116, 270
  coercive treatment 110–13
  harm minimisation 97–8, 99
  internalization of 180, 183
  irresponsibility 62, 97
  pathological behaviour 148, 155
  social control 93, 94–6, 101–4
  and stigma 107, 115
disinhibition 30
dislocation 65
domesticity 35
D'Orban, P. 24
drug courts 111, 112, 113
drug dealing 185, 223–4
Drug Enforcement Agency (DEA) (US) 77
drug policy discourse 65–6, 272, 273
'drug scene' 160, 162, 174, 180, 208, 213–15
Drug Strategy (UK)
  benefit sanctions 55
  and blame 119
  focus on abstinence 101, 105
  targeting of mothers 129
  welfare sanctions 124, 125–6
  and young people 68, 69
drug testing 131
drug trafficking 47, 73, 74, 75, 77
Drug Treatment and Testing Orders (DTTOs) (UK) 111

E

ecstasy 38, 156, 160
educational attainment 73, 124, 210–11, 212
Ehrlich, J. 85
'emancipation' thesis 34–6
embarrassment 176, 177
employment 73, 104, 212, 213
empowerment 37–9
ethnic minority population
  higher education 124
  imprisonment 68, 70, 72
  and war on drugs 45
  welfare dependency 132
Ettorre, E. 38, 39, 58, 140, 141
expertise 5–6, 15–16
  faith in 196
  medical 62, 94, 96, 140, 163
  and own views 132, 241
  and politics 49

and rational choice 146, 147, 207
social work 241
technologies of the self 138, 139

F

Fagan, J. 36
families, protection of 68–9, 70
family backgrounds 23, 169–70, 209–10
family courts 131
fathers 79, 84, 128, 133
Federal Bureau of Narcotics (FBN) 46
feminist approach 7, 8, 23, 25, 26, 37–40, 41
Fernandez, H. and Libby, T.A. 102
flashbacks 164, 165
food insecurity 127
food stamps 122
Foucauldian framework 40
Foucault, Michel
  and control through welfarisation 117
  expertise 5
  freedom 52
  governmentality 2–4, 15, 61
  normalisation 142, 143–5, 243
  resistance 201
  responsibilisation 145
  technologies of power 6, 61, 139–40
  technologies of the self 7, 137, 138
Fraser, A. 18, 19
fraud 120, 220, 236, 253
freedom, individual 3, 4, 61, 145–6, 148
friendships 178, 179, 180

G

Garland, D. 94, 95, 120, 130, 132, 149
gatekeeping 36
gender
  constructions of 57, 58–9
  criminal justice system 86, 87, 88, 233
  and identity 140, 141
  norms 143
  roles 17, 25, 33, 38, 118
Gordon, D. 54, 72
governmentality approach 2–5, 15, 61, 138
GPs (general practitioners) 254, 259
Green, D. 118
guilt 188–9, 190–5
Guy, P. 45

H

Hacking, I. 139
Hannah-Moffat, K. 58, 149
harm minimisation 97–8, 99
  as control 101–4

and HIV/AIDS 92, 99–101
interventions 98
and risk 114, 147, 148
towards recovery 260
Harris, Mike 56, 127
Harris, N. 126
Hay, G. and Bauld, L. 125
Health Canada 69
health problems, drug-related 50, 174
hemp 45
Henderson, S. 31, 38
hepatitis 50, 98, 100
heroin
  addictiveness 172–3, 181, 182
  'career' 37
  compulsory treatments 111
  as coping mechanism 153, 162, 164, 167–9, 171, 195, 198, 204–6
  effect on friendships 178
  experimentation 155, 157–60
  family relationships 176
  interview group 235–6, 243, 244, 249, 261
  marginalisation and 39
  in media 96
  methadone maintenance 101–4, 115
  as not prescribable UK 48
  in pregnancy 18, 19, 20, 239
  use and employment 125
  violence 227
  welfare benefits 55
  working class 250
Hidden harm (ACMD) 129
higher education 123, 124
Higher Education Act (US) 123
'hippy scene' 161, 214
Hispanic population 78, 100
HIV/AIDS 27–31
  criminalisation of drug users and 50
  demonisation of female drug users 27, 270
  harm minimisation 97, 98, 99–101, 114
  and intravenous drug use 28, 29
  power relationships 28
housing 73, 122, 123, 243, 244, 245, 260
Housing Opportunity Program Extension Act (US) 122
HUD *see* Department of Housing and Urban Development
human rights 50
Human Rights Watch 79
Hunt, N. and Stevens, A. 113
Husak, D. 50, 51

I

identities 137–42
  positive 115
  and prohibition 67
  rational 208
  and recovery 106–7
  and risk discourse 120
  'technologies of the self' 7
IDPC *see* International Drug Policy Consortium
illicit drugs, construction as 49, 66
imprisonment
  as deterrent 67, 233
  detox/counselling 262–3, 264
  effect on future 235
  and further marginalisation 73, 250
  increase in 46, 51, 70–2
  interview group 231–3
  mothers 68, 75, 77–81
  and normalisation 143, 144
  shoplifting 189
impurities 50
incest 26
Inciardi, J., Lockwood, D. and Pottieger, A. 29, 30
independence 153, 154
individuals and harm 66, 67
informed choice 97, 98
inner cities 36
international borders 67, 69
International Drug Policy Consortium (IDPC) 50
interventionism, state 52, 53
isolation 174, 175–6, 179–80, 252

J

Japan 70
Jobcentres 127
Johnson, T. 5
'junkie-whore' 29
Justice Policy Institute (US) 72

K

Kilmon vs State 83
Kilty, J. 106, 107, 181
Kullar, S. 133

L

Latino population 83
legal representation, access to 75
Longshore, D., Prendergast, M.L. and Farabee, D. 111
Luck, P.A., Elifson, K.W. and Sterk, C.E. 125
Lupton, D. 141, 142

M

Maher, L. 34, 39, 73, 101, 229, 234
Maher, L. and Daly, K. 36
Malloch, M. 38, 39, 88, 109
mandatory sentencing 47
marginalisation 246–50
  and drug dependency 148, 149
  drug-related health problems 50
  effect of welfare cuts 55
  and identity 107
  and low priority 113
  and war on drugs 74
marijuana (cannabis)
  effect of in pregnancy 20
  first experiences 156, 164
  harmfulness 49
  history of use of 43, 44
  most arrests for 46
Marxism 94
McIntosh, J. and McKeganey, N. 106
McKnight, Regina 82
medical profession, and women 6
Medical Reform Group of Ontario 127
medicalisation 91–116
  coercive treatment 110–13
  harm minimisation 97–8, 99
  history of 94
  HIV/AIDS 99–101
  medical-moral-legal hybrid 62–5, 120
  methadone maintenance 101–4
  as patriarchal 94, 114
  as social control 6, 91, 93, 94–6
  technology of power 61
men
  drug use 8, 17, 24, 37, 38
  fathers 79, 84, 128, 133
  sexuality 31
  social construction of 8
  traditional role 31
mental health issues 109
'Methadone: An American way of dealing' (film) 103
methadone maintenance 101–4
  and employment 125
  failure to meet needs of women 104
  interview group 191, 193, 196, 255–9
  non-compliance punished 104
  in pregnancy 18
  social control 115
middle class population 73, 87, 249, 252, 253
Miller, E. 32
misery 172–4, 184
Misguided justice (Bush-Baskette) 39

Misuse of Drugs Act 49
moderated consumption 105
moral standards 27–8, 94, 215–17, 254, 270
motherhood 238–45
  assessment of 129
  bonding 22
  imprisonment 68, 75, 77–81
  multiple problems 193
  normalisation 238
  recovery 106
  research context 17, 21–3
  separation from children 194, 195
  'unfit' 6, 19, 21, 23, 37, 58, 80, 83–4, 89, 94, 110, 128–35, 190–5, 266
  welfarisation 128–34
  Western views of 39
Mothers and illicit drugs (Boyd) 37
Murphy, J. 64
Murray, Charles 118

N

NA (Narcotics Anonymous) 197, 259
narcotics 43
National Anti-Drug Strategy (Canada) 69, 129
National Drug Control Strategy (US) 69, 93, 121, 128
National Institute on Drug Abuse *see* NIDA
National Treatment Agency (NTA) 6
Navarro, V. 94
needle exchange programmes 100, 259, 260
negative addiction 65
neglect 256–61
Nelson-Zlupko, L., Dore, M.M., Kauffman, E. and Kaltenbach, K. 107, 108
neoliberalism 52–9
  and addiction 65
  class and punishment 54
  and consumption/production 53
  and criminal justice system 46, 48, 54
  and deviance 141, 142
  and freedom 52, 53–4, 55
  risk management 120
  and stigmatisation 115
  underclass 147, 148
  welfare policy 55–9, 118–19
Netherlands 97
New Zealand 70
NIDA (National Institute on Drug Abuse) 19, 20
Nixon, Richard 47, 102
non-state agencies 3

normalisation 7, 125, 130, 142, 143–4, 207, 238
'normality' 246–8, 250, 251, 273, 275
Norwich Union Healthcare 96
NTA *see* National Treatment Agency

O

Office of National Drug Control Policy (ONDCP) (US) 19
O'Malley, P. 54, 95, 97, 146, 147, 149
O'Malley, P. and Valverde, M. 95
Ontario Human Rights Code 127
opiates 29, 44
opium dens 45
'othering' 140
overdose, intentional 163, 164

P

Pagliaro, A.M. and Pagliaro, L.A. 21, 22
pain management 95
panic attacks 165
Paone, D. and Alperen, J. 84, 85
Parton, N. 130
pathology, discourse of *see* disease model
Patton, C. 31
Personal Responsibility and Work Opportunity Reconciliation Act (PRWORA) (USA) 55, 56, 122
Pettiway, L.E. 32
PHDEP *see* Public Housing Drug Elimination Program
Phoenix, J. 29
physical abuse 166–7, 168
Pierson, J. 250, 251, 252
pimps 229, 230
Plant, A. 29, 30
pleasure 38, 95, 155, 156–8, 162
police 226, 228, 240
police profiling 73
Political Research Associates 87
Pollack, S. 57
Poor Law (UK) 118
Portugal 97
possession 46
post-modern paradigm 39, 40
post-natal depression 206, 235
poverty 72–5
  background 209
  caused by drug use 125
  childhood 213–14
  as choice 118, 119
  deserving/undeserving 234
  effect of prohibition 46
  effect of medicalisation 94
  HIV/AIDS 100
  leading to female drug use 68

imprisonment 70
  prior to drug use 208, 221
  victimhood 234, 237, 238
  war on drugs as attack on poor 45
pregnancy
  compulsory treatment 112
  control of 20, 94, 239
  criminalisation of 20, 81–6, 100, 114, 190
  effects of illicit drugs 19, 20, 81
  foetal homicide legislation 82
  foetal responsibility 18, 19, 84
  research context 17, 18–20
  scientific evidence 20
  social problems 109–10
  termination of 85, 86
  unplanned 19
prescription drugs
  and class 87
  dangers of 49, 96, 204, 205
  dependency 62
  gendered use 24
  over-prescription 96
  in pregnancy 19
prohibition 67–90, 270, 271
  black and ethnic minority women 75, 76–7
  and control of threatening populations 45
  criminalisation of pregnancy 81–6
  criminals as victims 86–8
  failure to reduce drug use 49
  female imprisonment 70–2
  female sexuality 45
  global 46, 48, 49
  history of 43–6
  and immigrants 45
  international 44
  and national security 47
  neoliberalism 52–9
  origins of 119, 120
  and power 6
  protection 49, 68–9, 70, 77, 78–81
  and public health 92–3
  punitive regulation 46–51
  sentencing 74
  technology of power 61, 62
  underclass 72–7
  and women 45–6
prostitution *see* sex work
'psy' sciences 5, 6, 21, 94, 147
psychoactive drugs 29, 43–4
psychologicalisation 109
public health discourse 270
  Canada 48
  children of drug users 22
  female sexual behaviour 28–31, 114
  and identity 106–7

  medicalisation 91–3
  UK 47
  see also harm minimisation
Public Housing Drug Elimination Program (PHDEP) (US) 123
Putting full recovery first (UK Home Office) 105

R

racism 44, 45, 74, 76, 77
rape 26, 164, 165–6, 175, 228–9
rational choice model
  as active 32, 34, 37–41, 148
  and 'expertise' 146
  and marginalisation 208, 213, 222, 265, 274
  medicalisation 181
  neoliberalism 54
  and pleasure 162, 180, 205
  responsibilisation 98
  self-identity 12
'rave scene' 160, 162
recidivism 70, 120, 214
recovery 104, 105–7, 195–200
  and abstinence 115
  and class 249
  failure 109, 116, 246, 271
  therapy 148, 149
  as UK focus 124
  US policy 121
  welfarisation 63
recreational users 124, 155, 158, 160
rehabilitation centres 110
Reith, G. 4, 53, 54, 98, 140, 146, 148
relationships, abusive/coercive 112
relationships, romantic 179–81, 199, 200, 219–21, 222
reproductive healthcare 6
research methods 277–8
resistance 4, 39, 40, 138, 141, 142
responsibilisation 7, 144, 145–50
  and coercive policy 116
  harm minimisation 97–8, 99
  social problems 129
  victimhood 234, 237
  and welfarisation 63, 64, 119, 125
responsibility, individual 55, 57, 63, 273
risk discourse 55–9, 91, 97–8, 99, 120, 130–4
risk identity 141, 142
risk management 146–7
Rolleston Committee 48
Rose, N. 4, 5, 6, 61, 145, 146, 147–9, 184, 189, 237
Rosenbaum, M. 37, 40, 103, 104, 160, 212, 213, 250, 252
Russell, S. and Wilsnack, S. 26

S

safer sex 28–31, 99
SAMHSA *see* Substance Abuse and Mental Health Services Administration
'scientific' knowledge 16, 19, 20, 40, 49, 115, 138
Scottish Consortium for Crime and Criminal Justice (SCCCJ) 92, 93
secrecy 175, 176, 177, 180
Seddon, T. 48, 53, 119, 120, 145
self-esteem, low 25, 26, 27, 153, 154, 163, 198
self-governance 3
self-harm 163
self-improvement 146, 149
self-punishment 154, 189
self-regulation 2, 4, 5
sex work
  association with drug use 28, 58
  drug dealer as pimp 32
  as exit from poverty 213, 224, 274
  to fund habit 174, 215, 219, 220, 221
  HIV/AIDS 29–31
  increase in 36
  independence 33
  interview group 232, 233, 236, 237
  loss of control 183
  rejection of 217
  as temporary 217
  violence 87, 194, 228–30
Sexed work (Maher) 39
sexual activity, interracial 45
sexual harassment 107
'sexual maladjustment' 25
sexuality, female 31, 45, 114
shoplifting 167, 185, 186, 189, 219, 231–2, 237
Simon, R. 51
Siney, C. 19
single parent households 73, 78, 123, 127
SMART Recovery 105
Smith, P. 121
'snowballs' (heroin and crack cocaine) 157, 158
social connection 158, 159–62
social institutions 24
social networks and support 250, 251–3
social order, threatened 44
social services 75, 243–4, 274
social workers
  attitude 238
  and control 130–1
  training 133–4, 240–1, 243
soliciting 185, 186t, 232

speed *see* amphetamines
Stanford University 78
stereotypes 29, 37, 51, 107, 120, 127, 133
Sterk, C. 107
Stevens, A., Bertolini, C., Heckmann, W., Kerschl, V., Oeuvray, K., van Ooyen, M., Steffan, E. and Uchtenhagen, A. 112
stigmatisation 107
stopping use 196, 197
'street scene' 161
street-level users and dealers 73
Substance Abuse and Mental Health Services Administration (SAMHSA) (US) 105
Substance use among women (Pagliaro and Pagliaro) 21
substitute prescribing *see* methadone maintenance
suicide 127, 163, 164, 165, 175, 242, 263
surveillance 5, 6, 62, 64, 80, 117, 131
Sutherland, Victoria 122

T

Taylor, A. 35, 37, 213, 215, 224, 225
technologies of power 6–7, 61, 138, 139–40
technologies of the self 7, 137–8, 139, 145
Temporary Assistance for Needy Families (TANF) (US) 55
Thatcher, Margaret 55
Thorpe, D. 130, 131
tobacco 20, 49, 104
tranquilizers 96
trauma *see* coping mechanism
treatment
  community-based 79
  coercive 110–13
  compulsory 110–11
  as condition of state benefits 55, 125
  funding for 48
  gender-specific 107, 108–9, 112, 113, 115
  mandatory 83
  quasi-compulsory 110–11, 112
  registry as deterrent 50
  as strategy to control crime 66
truanting 210–11
Tyler, J. 79

U

UK (United Kingdom)
  child custody 112, 190
  coercive treatment 111
  cost of benefit claimants 125

cuts to welfare state 55, 56
drug strategy 8, 66, 67–70
fears of interracial sexuality 45
harm minimisation 97
HIV/AIDS 28, 31, 99–101, 114
imprisonment 70–1, 72, 78, 79
methadone maintenance 101, 102, 103
mothers 128, 129
neoliberalism 53, 54
pregnancy 18, 19
public health approach 47
racism 76, 77
sentencing for importation 74
stricter enforcement 58
welfarisation 124, 125–7
UN (United Nations) 46, 48, 50, 85
underclass 118
'undeserving poor' 62, 118–120, 234
unemployment 73, 125–6
United Nations Office on Drugs and Crime (UNODC) 100
United Nations Programme on HIV/AIDS (UNAIDS) 100
United Nations Single Convention 8
upper-class population 44, 73, 87
US (United States)
  coercive treatment 111
  community treatment 113
  criminalisation of pregnancy 19, 20, 85, 110, 112, 190
  cuts to welfare state 55, 56
  denial of social services 121–4
  disease model and recovery 105
  drug strategy 66, 67–70
  effect of legislation on marginalised 122
  female involvement with crack 34, 35
  foetal protection policies 81, 82–3
  funding for treatment 48
  global leader in prohibition 46–47
  HIV/AIDS 27, 28, 100, 114–15
  imprisonment 70–1, 72, 75, 76, 78, 79, 80
  influence 49
  lack of treatment for mothers 128
  mandatory minimum sentences 74
  methadone maintenance 101
  neoliberalism 53, 54
  origins of attitude towards drugs 44
  stricter enforcement 8, 53, 58
  treatment and trauma 108
  'undeserving poor' 119
  women as dealers 73

V

Valverde, M. 95
verbal abuse 168
'vicious cycle causation' model 26

victimhood 39, 87, 232, 233–4, 235
victimisation 88, 144, 231, 243, 266, 272, 274
violence, gender-based
  in 'drug world' 174, 226–30
  and housing 193
  inflexibility of system and 115
  lack of punishment 86
  leading to female drug use 68
  and methadone maintenance 115
  prior to drug use 221
  and safe sex 30
  self-blame 175, 176
  sexual 87
  unreported 85
  women's-only services 41, 108
Visions of social control (Cohen) 144
voluntary treatment 48, 112, 113

W

Wacquant, L. 64, 91
'war on drugs' 2, 47, 49–51, 54, 74
Weaver, S. 133
weight loss 163
Welfare Reform Act (US) 122
welfare to work 122
welfarisation 62, 64, 117–36, 271
  assessment 120
  Canada 128
  drug-using mothers 128–34
  effect of cuts 46, 53, 55, 127, 128
  effect on women and children 120
  gendered 260
  and marginalisation 124, 125
  and motherhood 190
  punitive regulation 125
  social control 6, 61, 117, 119, 144
  surveillance 117
  testing as condition 127
  UK 125–7
  'unfit mothers' 238
  US denial of 121–4
Welle, D., Falkin, G.P. and Jainhill, N. 112
White, W. 106
Whitner, Cornelia 82
WHO *see* World Health Organization
will, lack of, construction of 91, 95, 96, 99, 100, 109
Wilner, J. 83, 84
Wilson, N. 35, 36
witch-hunts 45
withdrawal symptoms 172, 198
women
  'abnormal' 19, 21, 25, 141, 200, 271
  construction as 'difficult' 107
  control of bodies 94
  and crime 51

effect of war on drugs 50
  imputed immorality 56, 58
  introduction to drugs 86
  passivity and dependency 31, 32–3
  positive functions of drugs 24
  poverty and self-medication 43
  psychopathological and emotionally disturbed 23–7
  punishment and stereotypes 51
  role models 36
  sexual health 94
  as targets of pharmaceuticals 96
  as victims of crime 225–31
  as victims of men 31, 32–3
Women and crack cocaine (Inciardi et al) 29, 30
Women on heroin (Rosenbaum) 37, 103
Women 2000 24
Woodhouse, L.D. 21
workfare 56
working class population
  disease model 62, 95
  interviewees 209, 210, 248–53
  male heroin use 48
  parenting 170
  policing and punishment 54
World Health Organization (WHO) 100
Worrall, A. 3

Y

young people, protection of 68–9, 70

Z

Zola, I. 92